Uncle Sam in Barbary

An ADST-DACOR Diplomats and Diplomacy Book

Florida A&M University, Tallahassee
Florida Atlantic University, Boca Raton
Florida Gulf Coast University, Ft. Myers
Florida International University, Miami
Florida State University, Tallahassee
New College of Florida, Sarasota
University of Central Florida, Orlando
University of Florida, Gainesville
University of North Florida, Jacksonville
University of South Florida, Tampa
University of West Florida, Pensacola

Uncle Sam in Barbary

A Diplomatic History

Richard B. Parker

An ADST-DACOR Diplomats and Diplomacy Book

University Press of Florida
Gainesville Tallahassee Tampa Boca Raton
Pensacola Orlando Miami Jacksonville Ft. Myers Sarasota

Copyright 2004 by Richard B. Parker
Printed in the United States of America on acid-free paper
All rights reserved

First cloth edition, 2004
First paperback edition, 2008

Published in cooperation with the Association for Diplomatic
Studies and Training

Library of Congress Cataloging-in-Publication Data
Parker, Richard Bordeaux, 1923–
Uncle Sam in Barbary : a diplomatic history / Richard B. Parker.
p. cm. — (The ADST-DACOR diplomats and diplomacy series)
"An ADST-DACOR diplomats and diplomacy book."
Includes bibliographical references (p.) and index.
ISBN 978-0-8130-2696-1 (alk. paper)
ISBN 978-0-8130-3344-0 (pbk.)
1. United States—History—Tripolitan War, 1801–1805. 2. United
States—History—War with Algeria, 1815. 3. United States—
Foreign relations—Africa, North. 4. Africa, North—Foreign
relations—United States. 5. United States—Foreign relations—
1783–1815.
I. Title. II. Series
E335.P37 2004
973.4'7—dc22   2003066593

The University Press of Florida is the scholarly publishing agency
for the State University System of Florida, comprising Florida
A&M University, Florida Atlantic University, Florida Gulf Coast
University, Florida International University, Florida State
University, New College of Florida, University of Central Florida,
University of Florida, University of North Florida, University of
South Florida, and University of West Florida.

University Press of Florida
15 Northwest 15th Street
Gainesville, FL 32611-2079
http://www.upf.com

To Jeanne, who put up with it all

Contents

List of Illustrations ix
Foreword: The ADST-DACOR Diplomats and Diplomacy Series xi
Preface xiii
Map xix
Chronology xxi
List of Abbreviations xxix

1. Algiers 1
2. The Deys 24
3. First Steps 33
4. The Crisis Begins 43
5. Things Get Worse: The Mathurins, John Paul Jones, Barclay, Humphreys, and the Portuguese Truce 66
6. Negotiations at Last 87
7. Money Problems 103
8. Tripoli, Tunis, and Morocco 131
9. Relevance 158

Postscript: Return of the Natives 173
Appendixes
  1. The Procession of the Tribute 183
  2. Algerian Coinage 197
  3. Hasan Dey's Accession and Related Incidents 201
  4. The American Prisoners and Their Ships 208
  5. The De Castries Letter 217
  6. The Sailors' Petition 220
  7. Jefferson to Congress, December 30, 1790 223
  8. The Portuguese Truce 225
  9. Hasan Dey of Algiers to George III, March 27, 1794 231
  10. The Dey's Wish List 233
  11. List of Naval Stores Requested by Algiers 236
  12. Cathcart's Tunisian Truce 238
  13. Thomas Jefferson to Hamuda Bey of Tunis, June 8, 1806 239

Notes 243
Bibliography 263
Documentary Sources 271
Index 273

Illustrations

Map 1. Barbary in 1800   xix

Fig. 1. *View of Algiers from the Sea,* ca. 1800, by I. Clark   4

Fig. 2. Plan of Algiers, 1784   13

Fig. 3. Street in the Qasbah of Algiers, 1976   14

Fig. 4. Rooftops of the Qasbah, 1976   15

Fig. 5. George Washington's Instructions to Thomas Barclay   72–73

Fig. 6. *Colonel David Humphreys,* by Gilbert Stuart   75

Fig. 7. *Mattias Skjöldebrand,* by N. Lafrensen   81

Fig. 8. *Per Erik Skjöldebrand,* by P. Krafft   83

Fig. 9. *James Leander Cathcart,* by C. Coltellini   88

Fig. 10. *Joel Barlow,* by Charles Willson Peale   108

Fig. 11. Sail Plan of the *Skjoldebrand*   125

Fig. 12. *U.S. Squadron Before the City of Algiers, June 30, 1815,* by N. Jocelin   129

Fig. 13. *Commodore Preble's Squadron Engaging the Gunboats of Tripoli, August 3, 1804,* by Charles Denoon   142

Fig. 14. *Tunisian Corsair Boarding the Ship* Mercury *of Boston off Sardinia,* attributed to M. Corne   153

Foreword

The ADST-DACOR Diplomats and Diplomacy Series

For more than 225 years, extraordinary men and women have represented the United States abroad under all kinds of circumstances. What they did and how and why they did it remains little known to their compatriots. In 1995 the Association for Diplomatic Studies and Training (ADST) and the Diplomatic and Consular Officers, Retired (DACOR) created a book series to increase public knowledge and appreciation of the involvement of American diplomats in world history. The series seeks to demystify diplomacy by telling the story of those who have conducted our foreign relations, as they lived, observed, and reported them. Former ambassador and Middle East scholar Richard B. Parker's extensively researched historical account *Uncle Sam in Barbary* well serves these aims.

Written from the viewpoint of a diplomatic practitioner who served in and studied the Arab world for fifty years, this book tells the story of the young American republic's earliest encounter with Islam, beginning in 1785. Front-page news at the time, these events are poorly understood today, even by specialists. Readers will discover that America's response to the challenge presented by the corsair states of North Africa was not what many commentators today imagine. Lucidly written and abundantly instructive, the account presented here holds serious lessons about the limitations of force not backed by diplomacy, lessons of continuing relevance to U.S. foreign policy in a region again presenting a major challenge.

In Ambassador Parker's thirty-one years in the U.S. Foreign Service, he distinguished himself as an Arabic language and area specialist and represented the United States as ambassador to Algeria, Lebanon, and Morocco in the Ford and Carter administrations. He served as ADST's founding president and in 1989 received DACOR's Foreign Service Cup for service in retirement. He has taught at the University of Virginia, Lawrence University, and the Johns Hopkins School of Advanced International Studies, and edited the

Middle East Journal (1981–87). Ambassador Parker has pursued his research and writing as a fellow at the Woodrow Wilson International Center for Scholars, as the John Adams Fulbright Fellow in London, and as scholar-in-residence at the Middle East Institute. He has published six other books: *North Africa: Regional Tensions and Strategic Concerns* (Praeger, 1984), *The Politics of Miscalculation in the Middle East* (Indiana University Press, 1993), *The Six-Day War* (University Press of Florida, 1996), *The October War* (University Press of Florida, 2001), and guides to Islamic architecture in Cairo and in Morocco. In *Uncle Sam in Barbary*, Dick Parker puts new flesh on an old narrative and discloses surprising details uncovered in his research.

Kenneth L. Brown, president
Association for Diplomatic Studies and Training
Robert L. Funseth, president
Diplomatic and Consular Officers, Retired

Preface

> This subject, than which none deserves a more affectionate zeal,
> has constantly commanded my best exertions.
> George Washington to Congress, February 28, 1795

Washington was referring to America's first hostage crisis, which began in 1785 with the capture of two American ships off the coast of Portugal by corsairs from Algiers. This book is a study of that crisis and the diplomacy of its resolution. It tells a story of captives and ransoms—of seamen who spent eleven years as prisoners in Algiers and were finally rescued by a Connecticut poet. It is written from the perspective of a diplomatic practitioner and area specialist who is interested in the operational details: Who were the actors and what did they do? What went right and what went wrong and why? What do we know about the prisoners and their ships? Are there lessons to be learned? While the book is concerned primarily with Algiers, a chapter is devoted to our problems with the rest of Barbary, which are the source of today's popular myths about our North African experience.

America's problems with the rulers of North Africa extended over a period of thirty years, from 1785 to 1815. The story does not loom large in the national consciousness today, but it was a major issue in our early foreign affairs. A list of the Americans actively involved reads like a roll call of the founding fathers: George Washington, Thomas Jefferson, John Adams, Benjamin Franklin, James Madison, James Monroe, Alexander Hamilton, John Paul Jones, and a variety of lesser lights all came into the picture at one point or another. Jefferson was involved with North African issues off and on for more than twenty years.

This episode was America's first challenge from the Muslim world, a challenge it had difficulty meeting. Although a number of commentators since September 11 have cited America's experiences with the "Barbary pirates" as an example of how it must deal with terrorists today, the details of what happened and the nature of the American response two centuries ago are poorly understood by the writers and their readers (or listeners) today. Some will remember vaguely that we fought a battle on the shores of Tripoli, and we must have won or the Marines would not sing about it. None will know anything about the Algiers hostage crisis and how it was resolved, or be aware of the importance of these incidents in the early history of the United States. Nor is there much knowledge, even among area specialists, of the strange set of rules by which the game was played in the Mediterranean two hundred years ago. There is even uncertainty, in the minds of most Americans, about where "Barbary" was.[1]

While this ignorance of history may not seem catastrophic, the misunderstandings of decision makers about what they see as precedents that have been sanctified by time and experience can have fateful consequences for Americans today. Basing a response to today's terrorism on an imagined response to the Barbary corsairs two centuries ago does not make a great deal of sense.

In the first place, the corsairs were not terrorists as we understand that term today. They were not involved in random killings for political ends. They were interested in booty and ransom money, and there was nothing clandestine about their activities. Their businesslike approach stands in stark contrast to the fanaticism of al-Qa'ida. They were not, as Serge Schmemann in the January 27, 2002, *New York Times* described them, "international criminals outside the rules of law." They were operating openly under the instructions of recognized governments and following a formal set of rules that the European powers, and eventually the United States, accepted and honored.

These rules arose from the intermittent hostilities between North Africa and southern Europe that began with the Muslim invasion of Spain in 711 and had stabilized into a corsair war by the late sixteenth century. The Barbary corsairs were not much different in their tactics and rapaciousness from their contemporaries in Europe. The attacks on North African communities and commerce by European corsairs such as the Knights of St. John of Malta and the Tuscan Knights of San Stefano were of a kind with the raids on European communities and commerce emanating from Barbary. The most important difference in American eyes was that the North Africans enslaved captured Christians, while the Europeans did not. They found the concept of white Americans being enslaved outrageous, even though they were engaged in the slave trade themselves. For their part, the Spanish, French, and Italians reciprocated in kind and enslaved Muslims whenever they captured them.

In the second place, in spite of the popularity of the expression "Millions for defense, not one cent for tribute," the United States had to buy its way to peace with all the Barbary powers except Morocco. It spent close to a million dollars in 1796 for a peace treaty with Algiers and the ransom of captive seamen, and under that treaty it paid Algiers an annual tribute of $24,000 until 1812. Peace with Tunis cost $107,000, and our first peace treaty with Tripoli in 1796 cost $53,000. We paid Tripoli another $60,000 in 1805 to ransom some three hundred prisoners. This followed a protracted effort at naval blockade and bombardment of the town of Tripoli, and the capture of Derna, a provincial capital that was the "Tripoli" of the Marine hymn. These actions contributed to Tripolitanian willingness to settle for less than originally demanded, but did not suffice by themselves to bring about a peace.

It was diplomacy, not force, that eventually resolved our major crises with the Barbary states. Naval force *was* instrumental in imposing a new peace treaty on Algiers in 1815, but that peace was kept intact through diplomacy. There are lessons to be learned from the Barbary experience, but they are not what the commentators seem to think. They are lessons about the utility of force as an adjunct of diplomacy, not as a substitute for it.

On the other hand, the most important single effect of the problems with the North African states was the creation of the American navy. The Americans had hoped to rely on diplomacy and their neutral status as commercial traders to save them the need to pay for a navy, but eventually decided from their experience with Algiers that they must have one if they wanted to trade with the Mediterranean.

Thanks to the protection afforded by British treaties with the North African states, that trade had been very important to the economy of the colonies. Jefferson reported to Congress in 1790 that before the Revolution one-sixth of the wheat and flour and one-fourth of the dried and pickled fish exported by the colonies went to the Mediterranean, and that eighty to one hundred ships manned by about 1,200 seamen were involved in the trade. The value of exports to southern Europe and Africa in 1770 has been estimated at about $3.5 million, while imports from there were valued at $1 million. Most of these commodities were carried in American bottoms.

Trade with the Mediterranean had been suspended during the hostilities with Britain, but once peace was signed in 1783 the Americans hoped to resume it. Unfortunately, they no longer enjoyed the protection of British treaties, and all the North African states routinely considered themselves at war with states that did not have a treaty relationship with them. Although the Americans were eventually able to resolve their problem with Algiers diplomatically, they soon felt the need for naval help with Tripoli, and the U.S. Navy has been patrolling Mediterranean waters off and on ever since. Today's Sixth Fleet is a direct descendant of the first American man-of-war to enter the Mediterranean, the frigate *George Washington* under Captain William Bainbridge in 1800.

When the crisis began, in 1785, the thirteen original states were governing themselves under the Articles of Confederation, a famously dysfunctional arrangement under which the federal government had no power of taxation or regulation of trade. Although the Americans had great promise, they were weak and poor. They had no navy, and their army numbered only seven hundred men. They had little international experience, and none outside Europe. The Ottoman sultan in Constantinople was not even aware of their existence. They had admirers abroad, but no government prepared to intercede for them seriously with the Barbary powers. This is the story of how they coped on their own. It is a story of perseverance through frustration and problems of communication that would be unthinkable today.

The problems with Algiers have been well described from an American point of view by various writers and historians over the years. In 1847 Charles Sumner of Massachusetts claimed to be the first "to combine in a connected essay the scattered materials with regard to it."[2] The bibliography contains an annotated list of other works. They tend to be Americocentric. I have sought to describe more fully than usual the local context in which the events occurred and to explore questions of procedure and tactics that interest a practitioner. While the basic story would be worth retelling even if there were nothing new to add, I have found some new meat to put on the barebones narrative of our first effort at negotiations with Algiers, have documented the unhelpful roles of the British and the French, and have assembled in one place the scattered information on the identities and fates of the American captives at Algiers. I have also sought to give a fuller picture than is usually presented of what happened diplomatically with Tripoli and Tunis, an aspect of the story that is normally dwarfed by the naval details.

There is copious documentation of these events in the *American State Papers* for the period, in the splendid *The Emerging Nation: A Documentary History of the Foreign Relations of the United States Under the Articles of Confederation, 1780–1789,* edited by Mary A. Giunta and published by the National Historical Publications and Records Commission in 1996, in the holdings of the U.S. National Archives, and in the admirable six-volume *Naval Documents Related to the United States Wars with the Barbary Powers,* published by the U.S. Navy's Office of Naval Records and Library in 1939, which has become a primary source for writers working in the question.

All of the "scattered materials" that Sumner mentioned have yet to be brought together fully. Indeed, the task of assembling all of the material available in documents and publications is overwhelming, and the constraints of time have made me forgo many tempting detours into details. The result here is a collection of essentials culled from the documents. It is incomplete. There are still points that need to be clarified and questions to be answered.

Describing the scene of action also poses problems. The history of Algeria in this period is not well chronicled. The local population, the Arabs and

Berbers, left few descriptions of their world, and we know very little about their societies. Contemporary descriptions of the country can be found in books listed in the bibliography, but they rely largely on the observations of outsiders—travelers, captives, and consuls—most of whom had limited contact with the local population and limited knowledge of the Arabic, Turkish, and Berber languages, although they may have had some command of the local lingua franca. With no contemporary censuses and few government records, the economic and social data used by writers to date have largely been taken from the estimates of these foreigners and from consular records. Recent research in the archives is shedding some light, and we are now beginning to have more reliable contemporary data about the size of the population and the true state of the economy, but the information is still quite fragmentary. Reconstructing the past from these fragments is an archeological task, the results of which are not fully satisfactory. Too much must be left to imagination and interpretation.

As primary sources for details of the events involving the American prisoners and negotiators in Algiers I have relied largely on their writings and on the consular correspondence found in the British, French, and American archives. These events are well described in detail in H. G. Barnby's *The Prisoners of Algiers,* which draws on both American and British archives. I have leaned heavily on that book as well as on the memoirs of James Leander Cathcart, one of the American prisoners, who rose to be the ruler's chief Christian secretary, and on the writings of Joel Barlow, who secured the prisoners' release in 1796. For Algerian insight I have used mainly the memoirs of Ahmad Sharif al-Zahhar (1781–1872), the naqib al-ashraf, or leader of the prophet Muhammad's descendants, in Algiers. This is the only "contemporary" Arabic text I have found. Some of its accounts must have been based on hearsay or oral tradition, because they were written well after the events described, but it is the nearest thing to an indigenous chronicle for the period. Today's Algerian national archives have so far yielded nothing relevant to the diplomatic story.

These sources have been supplemented by standard works on Algeria listed in the bibliography. Two works are particularly useful—*Sketches of Algiers,* by William Shaler, who was the American consul in Algiers from 1815 to 1828, and *Tunis et Alger au XVIIIe siècle,* written in the period of 1780–1790 by Jean-Michel Venture de Paradis, a French consular official.

I have quoted liberally from original sources in the belief that contemporary accounts are more evocative of the period than summaries or paraphrases written two centuries later. I have restricted the documents in the appendixes to those unlikely to be found in a university library today.

Finally, I have had a good deal of help with this work from a variety of people, including: Martha Smart of the Connecticut Historical Society, Mary M. Thacher of the Stonington Historical Society, Alice D. Sheriff of the New London County Historical Society, Greg Laing of the Haverhill Public Library, Carolyn Singer of the Haverhill Historical Society, Martha Oaks of the Sargent House Museum in Gloucester, Ellen Nelson of the Cape Ann Historical Association, Bertram Lippincott of the Newport (R.I.) Historical Society, Philippe Henrat of the Archives Nationales in Paris, Bruno Ricard of the Centre des Archives Diplomatiques in Nantes, Daniel Panzac and André Raymond of IREMAM at Aix-en-Provence, H. E. Francesco Mezzalama, a cherished former ambassadorial colleague, Salvatore Bono of the Société Internationale des Historiens de la Mediterranée, Mary Jane Deeb of the Library of Congress, Moussa Saker of Oxford, Richard Arndt, Lutfi Ben Rejeb of Tunis, Nicholas Scheetz of the Lauinger Library at Georgetown University, Milton Gustafson of the National Archives, L. Carl Brown and Erika Gilson of Princeton, Amy Gorelick, Judy Goffman, and Ann Marlowe, the eagle-eyed copyeditor, of the University Press of Florida, Margery Thompson of the Association for Diplomatic Studies and Training, Francis De Tarr, Karin Hård af Segerstad of Stockholm, and others.

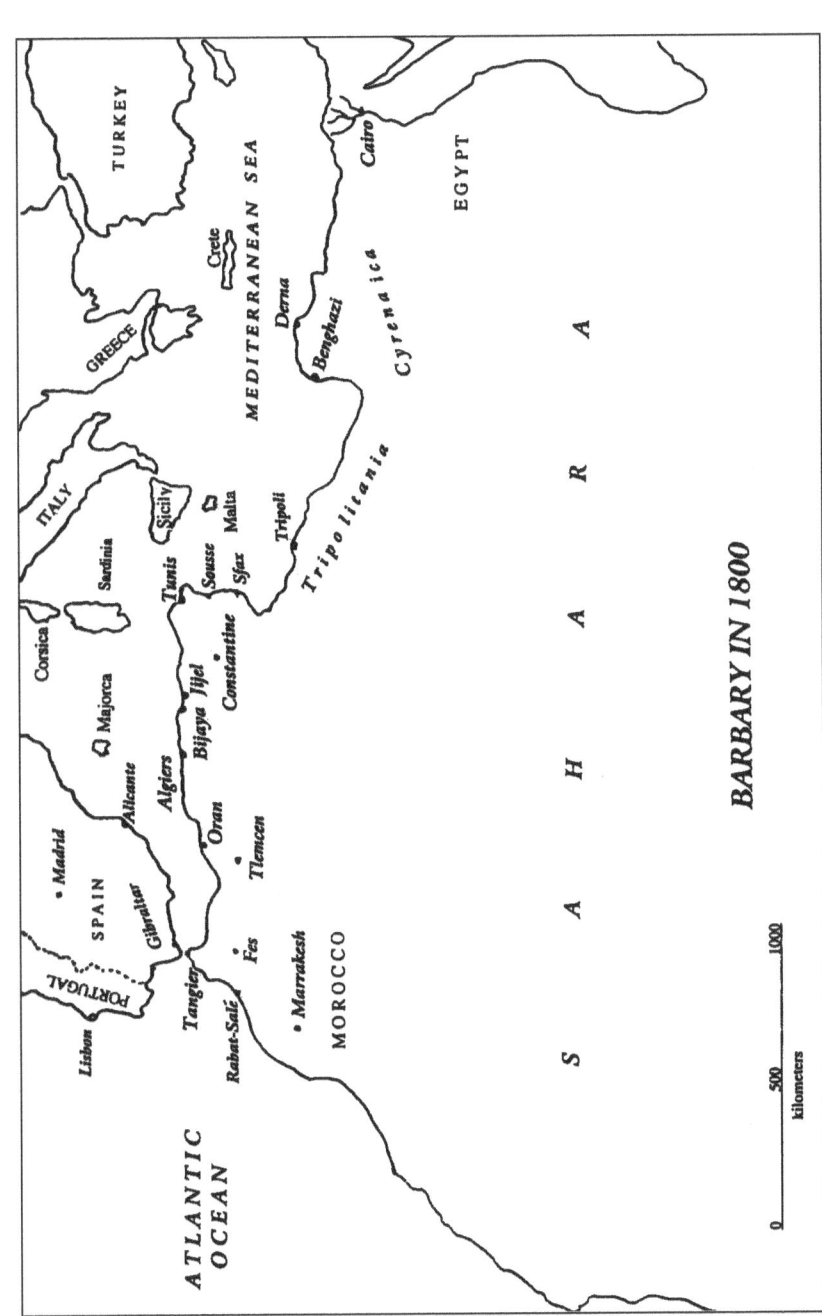

Map 1. Barbary in 1800. Designed by author.

Chronology

1492 Spanish complete Reconquest with capture of Granada.

1505 Spanish take Mers al-Kabir in Algeria.

1508 Spanish take Peñón de Vélez, island off Morocco.

1509 Spanish take Oran in Algeria.

1510 Spanish take Bijaya (Bougie) in Algeria, and Tripoli.

1511 Spanish occupy islands in Algiers harbor.

1514 Turkish corsair 'Aruj is master of Jijel, east of Bijaya.

1516 'Aruj takes Algiers.

1518 Spanish kill 'Aruj in battle near Tlemcen. He is succeeded by his brother Khayr al-Din (Barbarossa).

1519 Khayr al-Din offers submission to Ottoman sultan and asks for military help against Spaniards. Ottomans respond positively, but not before local opponents force Khayr al-Din to evacuate Algiers. He moves back to Jijel and takes up privateering on a large scale.

1522 Ottomans expel Knights of St. John from Rhodes.

1525 Khayr al-Din reconquers Algiers.

1529 Ottomans begin first siege of Vienna.

Khayr al-Din expels Spaniards from their fortress in Algiers harbor. Algiers becomes important naval base and Khayr al-Din's capital.

1533 Khayr al-Din places Hasan Agha, a military commander, in charge of Algiers when he leaves for Istanbul.

1534 Khayr al-Din is appointed admiral of the Turkish fleet in February, occupies Tunis in August.

1535 Spanish take Tunis, cede Tripoli to the Knights of St. John.

1536 Francis I of France concludes treaty with Ottoman sultan. Secret clauses provide for cooperation of France and Ottoman Empire against Spain.

1538 Charles I of Spain (Charles V of the Holy Roman Empire) offers to recognize Khayr al-Din as king of region from Algiers to Tripoli under Spanish suzerainty. Khayr al-Din evidently considers offer seriously.

1541 Spanish fail in attempt to take Algiers.

1544 Treaty of Crépy-en-Laonnais between Spain and France means end of French-Ottoman alliance. Khayr al-Din retires. His son Hassan becomes first governor, or *beylerbey*, of Algiers appointed by Ottoman government.

1551 Ottomans take Tripoli. Knights leave for Malta.

1565 Ottomans besiege Malta (unsuccessfully).

1571 October 7, Battle of Lepanto—Holy League fleet, commanded by Don Juan of Austria, defeats Ottoman navy under Ochiali Pasha, ending threat of Ottoman naval domination of Mediterranean.

1574 Ottomans retake Tunis.

1580 Spanish-Ottoman truce. Ottomans can look beyond war with Spain as justification for their presence in Maghrib.

1587 Ottomans install provincial administration in Algiers.

1601 Spanish bombard Algiers.

1617 French bombard Algiers.

1620 English bombard Algiers.

1627 Corsairs from Algiers capture 302 men, women, and children from Iceland.

1631 Algerines take 129 men, women, and children from Baltimore, near Cork, Ireland.

1659 Janissaries of the *ojak*, or garrison, assume control in Algiers.

1683 Ottomans begin second siege of Vienna, high-water mark of Ottoman expansion in Europe.

1708 Ottomans take Oran from Spanish.

1705 Husayn bin Ali, military officer, takes power in Tunis as bey, founds Husaynid dynasty that will be on throne until 1957.

1711	Ahmad Qaramanli, commander of Tripolitanian cavalry, assumes power in Tripoli, founds Qaramanli dynasty that will rule until 1835.
1732	Spanish retake Oran.
1766	April 8, Muhammad bin Uthman becomes dey of Algiers.
1775	Second Spanish attempt to take Algiers fails.
1776	July 18, Continental Congress discusses requesting French protection against Barbary corsairs.
1777	November 15, Congress adopts Articles of Confederation.
	December 20, Moroccan sultan extends most favored nation status to American shipping in Moroccan ports.
1781	March 1, Maryland ratifies Articles of Confederation and they go into effect.
	October 19, General Cornwallis surrenders at Yorktown.
1783	August 1–10, Spanish make third unsuccessful attack on Algiers.
	September 3, with signing of Treaty of Paris, Britain recognizes American independence.
1784	December 21, John Jay assumes post of secretary of foreign affairs.
1785	Spain and Algiers conclude truce sometime prior to July 14. Algiers declares war on United States soon thereafter.
	July 25, Algerine corsairs capture *Maria* of Boston.
	August 1, Algerines capture *Dauphin* or *Dolphin* of Philadelphia.
1786	March 25, John Lamb arrives in Algiers accompanied by Paul R. Randall.
	March 30, Randall departs for Spain.
	April 20, Lamb departs Algiers for Alicante.
	June 23, Thomas Barclay concludes treaty of friendship with Morocco.
1787	Constitutional Convention is held in Philadelphia.
1788	June 21, U.S. Constitution is ratified.

1789   April 30, George Washington becomes first president of United States.

July 14, French mob storms Bastille.

1790   March 22, Thomas Jefferson becomes first secretary of state.

1791   May 13, David Humphreys presents credentials as minister resident to Portugal.

July 12, Muhammad bin Uthman dies. Hasan Pasha becomes dey of Algiers.

1792   Spanish finally cede Oran to Algiers.

1793   September 12, truce between Portugal and Algiers goes into effect, permitting Algerine corsairs to enter Atlantic.

October–November, Algerine corsairs take eleven American merchant vessels with 108 men.

1794   January 2, Edmund Randolph succeeds Jefferson as secretary of state.

April, James Leander Cathcart becomes chief Christian secretary of dey of Algiers.

November 19, "Jay's treaty" with Britain is signed, alienating French.

1795   September 2, Joseph Donaldson Jr. arrives in Algiers.

September 5, Donaldson and dey agree on peace terms.

December 10, Timothy Pickering becomes secretary of state.

1796   March 4, Joel Barlow arrives in Algiers.

July 13, American prisoners depart Algiers on *Fortune*.

November 4, Richard O'Brien negotiates peace treaty with Tripoli.

1797   February 9, sixty-five of American captives from Algiers reach Philadelphia on Swedish bark *Jupiter*.

March 4, John Adams becomes president, Jefferson vice president.

August 1, Joseph Famin, French merchant, negotiates peace with Tunis.

1798   January, O'Brien arrives in Algiers to assume post of American consul general.

Hasan Dey dies and is succeeded by nephew Mustafa.

En route to Egypt, Napoleon takes Malta.

1798– United States and France fight undeclared Quasi-War involving
1801 privateering and combat between naval vessels.

1799 January, William Eaton arrives in Tunis as first American consul.

April, Cathcart arrives in Tripoli as first American consul.

1800 May 13, John Marshall becomes secretary of state.

September, frigate *George Washington* under Captain William Bainbridge, first U.S. Navy warship to enter Mediterranean, calls at Algiers and is forced to take dey's tribute to Constantinople.

British take Malta from French.

1801 February 17, presidential election tie in House of Representatives is broken in Jefferson's favor.

March 4, Jefferson becomes president, Aaron Burr vice president.

March 5, James Madison becomes secretary of state.

May 14, Tripoli declares war on United States. Cathcart and family soon leave for Livorno.

July 24, American squadron of three frigates and a schooner under Captain Richard Dale imposes blockade on Tripoli. Yusuf Qaramanli, pasha of Tripoli, offers to negotiate peace. Dale, claiming authority only to negotiate truce, sails away after three weeks of blockade.

July 31, schooner USS *Enterprise* under Lieutenant Andrew Sterett captures Tripolitanian polacca *Tripoli* in fierce battle, first American victory of Barbary Wars.

1802 May 25, Captain Richard V. Morris arrives at Gibraltar as new commodore of Mediterranean squadron.

June 22, Moulay Slimane, sultan of Morocco, declares war when Americans refuse to let Tripolitanian ship *Meshuda* leave Gibraltar with cargo of Moroccan wheat for Tripoli.

August, United States offers Morocco one hundred gun carriages. Peace is restored.

October 12, Commodore Morris authorizes consuls to issue passports permitting *Meshuda* to leave Gibraltar under Moroccan flag.

1803   March 1, bey of Tunis orders William Eaton to leave Tunis over financial mess. Dr. George Davis of U.S. schooner *Enterprise* succeeds Eaton as consul.

May 12, frigate *John Adams* under Captain John Rodgers captures *Meshuda* preparing to run blockade into Tripoli with load of military and naval supplies. Infuriated, Moulay Slimane orders Moroccan naval vessels to seize American ships.

May 29, after inconclusive engagement with Tripolitanian gunboats, Morris begins direct negotiations with Tripoli, but there is no meeting of minds.

August 26, U.S. frigate *Philadelphia* under Bainbridge captures Moroccan cruiser *Mirboka* under Captain Ibrahim Loubaris with American brig *Celia,* captured by Loubaris on August 17.

September 12, Captain Edward Preble, new commodore, arrives at Gibraltar on *Constitution.*

October 4–6, combined squadron of four American frigates calls at Tangier in display of strength. Moulay Slimane reaffirms treaty of 1786. Peace prevails.

October 31, *Philadelphia* runs aground off Tripoli. Bainbridge and 306 men are made prisoners.

November, Tobias Lear succeeds O'Brien as consul general in Algiers.

1804   February 16, Stephen Decatur and men of ketch *Intrepid* destroy *Philadelphia* in Tripoli harbor.

March 26, Preble in *Constitution* calls at Tripoli, opens negotiations through French consul Beaussier.

March 28, Sudden gale forces Preble to leave.

June 12–13, Preble returns, sends O'Brien ashore to reopen negotiations with offer of $40,000 to ransom prisoners from *Philadelphia,* $10,000 for bakhsheesh to senior officials, and a prospective $10,000 present from the first consul to be appointed. Offer is rejected out of hand.

August 3, Americans attack Tripoli fortifications with one frigate, three schooners, three brigs, six Neapolitan gunboats, and two bomb vessels. Hand-to-hand fighting among gunboats of Tripolitanian fleet is fierce.

August 4, Preble informs Beaussier that June 13 offer stands, but only until arrival of expected reinforcements. Yusuf Pasha says he is still interested in peace but not on such dishonorable conditions.

August 7, Preble attacks again, mostly targeting shore batteries. Tripolitanian counterfire kills fourteen Americans. *John Adams* brings word that Captain Samuel Barron, arriving with four frigates, is to replace Preble.

August 10, Preble sends O'Brien ashore to offer $80,000 in ransom and a $10,000 consular present. Beaussier suggests Tripolitanians might settle for $150,000. Preble ups ante to $120,000.

August 24 and 27, Americans bombard Tripoli by night.

August 30, Beaussier reports that Yusuf, unimpressed, demands $400,000 plus presents.

September 1, Beaussier thinks Yusuf might settle for $300,000.

September 3, Preble bombards again. Tripolitanian position shows no sign of softening.

September 4, *Intrepid,* sent into harbor as fire boat, blows up prematurely, killing thirteen Americans on board. This is last use of force against Tripoli by Preble.

September 10, Preble's successor Barron arrives on frigate *President*.

1805 April 25, Eaton and army of four hundred men and eight marines, supported by schooner *Nautilus,* brig *Argus,* and sloop *Hornet,* take town of Derna in what is now eastern Libya. Next stop Tripoli, aiming to restore Ahmad Qaramanli, elder brother of Yusuf, to rightful throne.

May 22, Rodgers replaces ailing Barron as commodore.

June 4, Lear and Rodgers reach agreement on peace treaty with Yusuf Pasha. Price is $60,000 and no annual tribute. Eaton and Ahmad are left high and dry.

June 12, Eaton, Ahmad, and various others are evacuated from Derna on *Constellation*. This marks end of America's first attempt at regime change.

That summer in Algiers, Mustafa Dey is murdered, succeeded by Ahmad Khoja.

August 1, U.S. squadron sails into Tunis harbor. In ultimatum, Rodgers tells ruler, Hamuda Bey, to choose between peace and war. Hamuda appoints ambassador to go to Washington and settle differences arising from American seizure of Tunisian ships.

1806 June 28, Jefferson writes to Hamuda Bey apologizing for Rodgers's behavior.

1807 U.S. squadron withdraws from Mediterranean.

1808 November, Ahmad Khoja is murdered and succeeded as dey by Ali Pasha, who lasts four months.

1809 March, Haj Ali succeeds Ali Pasha as dey.

March 4, James Madison becomes president, Robert Smith secretary of state.

1811 April 2, James Monroe becomes secretary of state.

1812 June 12, United States declares war on Britain.

July, Haj Ali declares war on United States. Lear and family return home.

1815 March 2, Senate ratifies Treaty of Ghent, ending War of 1812.

June, U.S. Navy returns to Mediterranean with two squadrons, one under Bainbridge, one under Decatur.

June 17, Decatur's squadron defeats Rais Hamidou, leading Algerine corsair captain, in three-hour battle. Decatur and William Shaler proceed to Algiers and dictate terms of peace.

Abbreviations

AE	Affaires Etrangères (French foreign ministry files, Archives Nationales, Paris)
ASP	*American State Papers: Foreign Relations*
EN	*The Emerging Nation,* ed. Mary A. Giunta
FO	Foreign Office (Britain)
JCC	*Journals of the Continental Congress*
LDC	*Letters of Delegates to Congress, 1774–1789,* ed. Paul H. Smith
LMCC	*Letters of Members of the Continental Congress,* ed. Edmund C. Burnett
LTDH	*Life and Times of David Humphreys,* by Frank Landon Humphreys
NA	National Archives (U.S.)
NavDocs	*Naval Documents Related to the United States Wars with the Barbary Powers,* comp. Office of Naval Records and Library
PRO	Public Record Office (Britain)
PTJ	*Papers of Thomas Jefferson,* ed. Julian P. Boyd

Algiers

Most of our story takes place in Algiers, the seat of a pirate republic governed by a junta of Ottoman soldiers and corsair captains who preyed on Mediterranean shipping more or less at will. Various efforts by European states to put them down had been unsuccessful, and they cherished illusions of invulnerability until they were overcome by the French in 1830. Their regime was called a regency because it was part of the Ottoman domain and was governed in the name of the sultan in Istanbul.

There were similar regencies in Tunis and Tripoli, but Morocco was not part of the Ottoman Empire. All four of these states were lumped together by the Europeans under the general term "Barbary." To the Arabs this region was, and still is, the Maghrib, or Occident, where the sun sets, as opposed to the Orient, or Mashriq, where it rises.

Although they did not look much like modern nation-states, the regencies had governments that were able to control their territories effectively and to observe their international obligations (if arbitrarily at times). They had identifiable bodies of subjects who recognized their authority, even though some of them may have been in a state of dissidence or revolt much of the time. They thus met the criteria traditionally applied by the United States in determining whether recognition of a state or government is appropriate.

Sovereign states dealt with these governments regularly and maintained representatives in their capitals. Algiers had the usual offices and officers of government common to Muslim societies of that period—courts and judges, mosques and Qur'anic schools, police and market inspectors, and municipal facilities such as aqueducts, fountains, and baths. Order was maintained. Merchants and artisans were able to trade and sell their products and keep the proceeds. Financial records were kept and, at least among the civilian population, the accumulation of wealth and its transfer to descendants was possible. Private property was respected, judging by contemporary accounts and the transactions and bequests recorded in the archives.

For a government of the period, the regency of Algiers was not all that bad. Western observers before the French occupation of 1830 were nevertheless critical of what they saw as its barbarity, and this is understandable when one considers the scope of corsair activities emanating from Algiers and the harsh treatment meted out to captives and to foreign representatives from time to time. French consuls in particular were subject to being put in chains and sent off to join the slaves in their barracks in the lower town, and on two occasions, in 1683 and 1688, during bombardment of the town by French warships, French consuls were executed by being blown from the mouths of cannons, while the British consul was cut to pieces in front of the ruler's palace in 1673 or 1674. The British and French seem to have taken this with remarkable forbearance, but it certainly affected their view of the state of civilization in Algiers. Their attitude was widely, perhaps universally, shared in western Europe and North America in the eighteenth century. (For a scholarly account of eighteenth-century European attitudes toward North Africa and particularly Algiers, see *Barbary and Enlightenment*, by Ann Thomson.)

Here, for instance, are comments of French consul André Alexandre Le Maire, writing in 1757 in a memorandum of advice to his successor:

> It will suffice to say that an extreme ignorance, a grossness without equal, and an inconsistency which disconcerts the most measured approaches are today the foundation on which the government rests. The dey is an imbecile who has outbursts of puerility like a child and who reflects on nothing, before or after giving his orders. He has removed from his entourage all those who had any common sense at all and has chosen for his ministers people who resemble himself....
>
> The Turkish dragoman [*turjman,* or interpreter], who serves the consul and the French community, is an inescapable calamity. The dey alone appoints him, and the consul almost never has enough influence to change him when he is unhappy with him, because he is less an officer given to serve him than a spy who reports his actions and everything that happens at the consulate. The best tactic is to indulge him and get him to give good reports and conceal from him everything that might give offense to the regency. The Algerines are excessively suspicious. A word, an inconsequential visit, a walk in a place that is not much frequented, will often excite violent suspicions, above all when it is a matter involving consuls. If one writes much they claim that one is delving into their secrets, and that one is plotting against the tranquility of the state. One should therefore conceal ones self from the dragoman and do before him only those things that are not subject to a malicious interpretation.

A similar appraisal was made by Admiral Joseph de Bauffremont, who was charged with representing France in the Levantine trading ports and led a squadron of four warships on a protocol visit to Algiers in 1766. He commented in his journal, after describing his ceremonial call on the dey:

> I won't dilate on Algiers or its government, the most baroque and ridiculous that ever existed. . . . These people could be happy if they wished. Nature has given them a beautiful, large country where everything would grow in abundance if these miserable people knew how to exploit it. But they abandon the land so fertile to scour the sea in search of slaves. Their dey . . . never dares leave his palace for fear of being assassinated. . . . The people of the country have surrendered it to sixteen thousand Levantines [i.e., the janissaries] . . . who treat them like slaves. . . . One is ashamed to be human when one sees others govern themselves with such stupidity.[1]

There was fabrication, exaggeration, and ignorance, not to mention ingrained stereotyping, in the contemporary accounts of life in Algiers written by foreigners, including those above. In modern times various authors, and notably Godfrey Fisher in *Barbary Legend,* have sought to put things into a more balanced perspective and to paint a more favorable picture of the regency, but without question the regime could be arbitrary and sometimes cruel by today's standards in its treatment of its own members as well as the local population and foreigners it happened to capture. Whatever judgment we pass on the nature of the regime, it is evident from contemporary accounts that foreigners dealing with it had their work cut out for them. But deal with it they must if they aspired to have their merchant vessels operating in the Mediterranean. The Barbary regencies had become one of the facts of life in the maritime traffic of the era. As Daniel Panzac remarks in *Les Corsaires barbaresques* (p. 35): "At the end of the 18th century the Barbary regencies had survived two centuries of pressure, of blockades and bombardments by the much more powerful European states. Better yet, they had known how to exploit the threat of capture to obtain regular presents and payments greater than an uncertain booty. They had succeeded in imposing on them [the Europeans] a diplomatic recognition, first de facto and then de jure, in total independence from the Ottoman empire."[2]

The Setting

At the beginning of the sixteenth century, Algiers was merely one of a number of towns, and not the most important of them, along the North African littoral between Morocco and Tunisia. Writing in that era, Leo the African estimated its population at 4,000 *feux* (hearths or households), as opposed to 8,000 in Bijaya or Bougie, two hundred kilometers to the east, and 13,000 in

Fig. 1. *View of Algiers from the Sea,* ca. 1800. Engraving by I. Clark after a drawing by Henry Parke, published in *Narrative of a Residence in Algiers*, by Filippo Pananti, 1818. Courtesy of the Naval Historical Center, Washington, D.C.

Tlemcen, five hundred kilometers to the west. It had never been a cultural center, and its inhabitants were not noted for their learning or arts.

Leo describes the town as having splendid walls, beautiful houses, well-organized markets in which each profession had its own emplacement, a good number of hostelries and bakeries, a superb mosque, and a very beautiful esplanade on top of the city wall along the seafront. He mentions its being surrounded by gardens and orchards, and this aspect of the site still surprises today's visitor who arrives with a preconceived image of a desert setting out of *Beau Geste*.

The town takes its Arabic name, al-Jaza'ir (the Islands), from a group of rocky islets that provided a sheltered anchorage in a wide bay. This name was subsequently given to the entire stretch of country we know as Algeria, a name coined during the French occupation that began in 1830. Its fate was changed forever by the success of the Spanish reconquest and the expulsion of Moors and Jews from Spain after the fall of Granada in 1492, and by the subsequent Spanish effort to take control over all of the North African coast from Tangier to Tripoli.

Muslim and Jewish expellees from Spain settled in Algiers, among other places, bringing new skills and culture and a desire for revenge against the

Spanish. The desire for vengeance was reinforced by the need for self-preservation as the Spaniards progressively occupied towns and harbors along the coast, and the resulting struggle, or jihad, an important aspect of which was piracy or privateering, was carried out on land and sea for the better part of three centuries.

The Spaniards made no attempt to occupy the North African hinterland, which to the east of Morocco was controlled by an assortment of Arab and Berber tribal leaders and remnants of earlier kingdoms, but concentrated on occupying strategic towns such as Oran, or coastal islets from which they could control harbors. At Algiers they occupied the rocks in the harbor in 1510 and immediately began constructing on them a small fortress, from which they effectively controlled shipping from the town. In response, the inhabitants of Algiers invoked the aid of 'Aruj, a famous Ottoman corsair who was operating in North African waters as the Turks began contesting control of the western Mediterranean with Spain. 'Aruj and his brother Khayr al-Din, better known as Barbarossa, between them evicted the Spanish from Algiers in 1529 and, with the aid of troops supplied by the Sultan, eventually incorporated into the Ottoman Empire the province that came to be called Algeria.

Ottoman control over Algeria was never very tight, and by the time of our story the regency was only nominally subject to Istanbul. The sultan had stopped sending pashas or governors to Algiers in 1659, and the power of government had been taken by the *ojak* (*ocak*, hearth in Turkish, originally meaning a military mess unit, especially in the janissary corps), the body of Ottoman troops who garrisoned the regency and who chose one of their number to serve as the dey or ruler. The deys relied on the Ottoman sultan for formal investiture when they assumed office and for permission to recruit a continuing supply of Anatolian, or Levantine, soldiers through whom they controlled the country.[3] They paid tribute, and they supplied ships for Ottoman naval expeditions, but they enjoyed a high degree of autonomy, not to say independence, in both foreign and domestic affairs.

The Corsairs

For the Algerines, as the people of Algiers were called by westerners two hundred years ago, piracy or privateering against the Christian powers was both a patriotic-religious obligation and an important, if highly variable, source of revenue. The Algerine fleet was under government direction, although some of its vessels were owned by private individuals or syndicates.[4] Its captains or *ru'asa'* (singular *ra'is*) were sent out with orders as to which ships they could attack and which they should respect, and their booty was shared with the ruler. Westerners have almost universally called them pirates, but the term "corsairs" is more accurate. Although the two words originally meant the same thing, through usage corsair has come to mean a privateer. Those from Algiers were operating within the limits of then current international practice, much like their contemporaries in America, Britain, France, Holland, Italy, and Malta, among other places. (French privateers, for instance, captured 10,871 merchant ships between 1793 and 1815, according to the article on "la course" (vol. 13, 178) in *La Grande Encyclopédie*, (H. Lamiraut, Paris, 1886–1902)and American claims against France arising from such activities were finally settled in 1915 for $12,149,306.10, according to Samuel Flagg Bemis's *Diplomatic History of the United States*.)

The distinction between piracy and privateering was that privateers were authorized by governments to raid enemy shipping, while pirates were not and were as likely to prey on their own shipping as on that of foreigners. Documentation was an important part of the game, and in western practice privateers were given "letters of marque and reprisal," commissions authorizing them to capture enemy vessels and to profit from the proceeds. Piracy and privateering were both embraced enthusiastically by the early Americans, and the world's last recognized privateers were those who were issued letters of marque by the Confederate government during the American Civil War and who did great damage to Union shipping.

Privateering was recognized as legal until it was abolished by the Declaration of Paris in 1856. It was an inexpensive way for states to harass their opponents, but the hope of gain often led privateers to be less than scrupulous about identifying other craft as enemy and in their treatment of captured crews and passengers. A veneer of legality was maintained by the establishment of prize courts in which judgement was rendered as to whether a given vessel was "good prize"—a legitimate prey of the privateer who had captured it. There was a considerable body of maritime law and tradition governing the decisions of such courts, and consular annals from the sixteenth to the nineteenth century are full of accounts of ships being captured, rightly or wrongly, of disputes over origins and nationalities, and of negotiations over the disposition of their crews and contents. In terms of privateer practice—general duplicity (flying false flags and feigning friendship toward the prey), mistreatment of captives, and lack of consideration for the victims—the Barbary corsairs appear to have been no worse than their European colleagues, and in some cases may have been more humane. Their victims were, after all, valuable property that could be sold in slave markets or held for ransom. Illness or weakness lessened their value, and death meant a clear loss.

The Rules of the Game

As noted in the preface, the Barbary states took the position that in the absence of a peace treaty between themselves and another state, or in the event of what they saw as a breach of such a treaty, they were free to be at war with that state, and its ships, citizens, and goods were legitimate prey and booty. By the eighteenth century, certain formalities about declaring war were observed in cases where there had been a peace treaty in effect. The Algerines, for instance, would notify the new enemy's consul (if one was present) and send him away, with a grace period before attacks on his nation's shipping were to begin.[5] When peace was restored, the Algerines raised the other state's flag at the admiralty. (The flying of the flag and the firing of salutes had considerably more symbolic and practical importance throughout the Ottoman provinces than they do today. The Tunisians and Tripolitanians, for instance, declared war by cutting down the flagpole of the offending power's consulate. I have come across no mention of this practice in Algiers, but the flying of the enemy's flag beneath the bowsprit of corsair vessels going out on cruise was regarded as a declaration of war, according to Shaler. The same practice was followed in seventeenth-century Tripoli, according to Thomas Baker.)

These procedures were acquiesced in by the states trading with the Mediterranean, and there was a remarkable symbiosis between the corsairs and the foreign consuls, the latter being among the buyers of captured ships and cargo brought into Barbary ports. Traffic in such purloined goods was a valued perquisite, and the consuls, who usually were paid very little by their governments, often supported themselves in part through trade. The Swedish consul, for instance, bought one of the American prizes in 1794. Joel Barlow bought two prizes while in Algiers as consul, and James Cathcart, a captive, bought one that he sailed to the United States.

There was also a remarkable routinization of the process by which the consuls, including Americans, issued passports to Barbary corsairs going out on cruise. The passports, often elaborately printed, protected the vessel from seizure by naval units of the issuing consul's state and often entitled it to the use of port facilities of the consul's state on a reciprocal basis. Both the Americans and the British issued passports with scalloped upper edges which were matched against similarly scalloped templates held by the vessels of their navies. The patterns were changed from year to year to combat counterfeiting.

Because the revenue that accrued from corsair actions was important, the North Africans were not anxious to conclude peace treaties, which would decrease the number of ships they could attack, and they usually exacted a price for doing so. The presents and annual tribute they demanded were more reliable than privateering and often quite substantial—Venture de Paradis in *Tunis et Alger* (237) gives figures showing that the states of Holland, Denmark, Venice, and Sweden among them paid about $250,000 in goods and cash each year to maintain peace with Algiers. This was about one-third the amount he estimated was raised by local taxation and fees. Still, it might not offset fully the revenue, real or imaginary, the corsairs would forgo as a result of peace.

The only two states with which the regency maintained a lasting peace were Britain and France, whose navies by the eighteenth century were too much for them. According to Venture de Paradis, in the late eighteenth century France continued to pay an annual tribute, but he does not give a figure. The British did not do so, but gave substantial presents when changing consuls and when there was a change of monarch at home.

Spain was in a more or less continual state of war with Algiers until 1785, and made three unsuccessful attempts to take the city. Its failure to do so, largely by virtue of what the Algerines saw as divine intervention, earned the city the epithet *mahrusa* or "well-guarded," and fostered an unjustified belief that it was impregnable.[6] When the Spanish finally concluded a truce with Algiers in 1785, they were alleged to have agreed to pay a total of $3 million (about $45 million today), half of which was for the ransom of their captives.

The most notorious of the corsairs were those of Algiers and of Salé (Sla), Morocco, popularly known as the Sallee, or Sally, Rovers. Both were a serious nuisance, raiding as far away as England, Ireland, and Iceland, disrupting shipping from the west of England, ambushing fisherman coming back to England from Newfoundland, and sometimes raiding coastal communities in search of slaves and booty. While attacks on coastal communities were less frequent in the northern regions than in the Mediterranean, there were some remarkably bold exploits in the colder regions. In 1627 the Algerines captured 302 men, women, and children from Iceland, and in 1631 they took 89 women and children and 20 men from the Irish village of Baltimore, near Cork. The Baltimore raid was led by a Dutch renegade from Haarlem named Jan Jansen, known as Murad Rais, who operated for a time out of Salé but eventually settled down as a member of the corsair corporation in Algiers. Remarkably, of the Baltimore captives, only one is recorded as having been ransomed and returned home. We have no data on the contribution these captives made to the Algerian gene pool.[7]

In the Mediterranean, corsair descent on coastal communities was most common in Spain, France, and Italy, and coastal areas from Gibraltar to the Adriatic are dotted with reminders of such raids, in the form of defensive towers and fortifications and of place-names that somehow record the threat. As late as 1798 the Tunisians took 900 captives, the majority of whom were women and children, from the village of Carloforte on the island of San Pietro off southwestern Sardinia.[8]

An indication of the scale of corsair operations affecting just one European country in the seventeenth century is given by the figures compiled by David Delison Hebb in *Piracy and the English Government, 1616–1642*. He notes that English residents in Algiers recorded 164 English ships and 2,828 persons taken captive and brought into Algiers in the thirteen years from 1627 to 1640. These figures do not include those taken by corsairs from other Barbary ports such as Salé and Tunis, or by ships from Algiers that sold their cargoes elsewhere. Hebb calculates from contemporary records that some 400 English ships and 8,000 persons were captured throughout Barbary in the period 1626–42. He puts the direct cost to England at £1,000,000–1,300,000. This does not include the costs of disrupted trade and the social costs of wage earners and household providers lost. When the Algerines took the *Rebecca* of London with a cargo of £260,000 in silver in 1640, the news of her capture caused the pound sterling to slump as bankers, especially the Dutch, withdrew funds, fearing more losses in the future.

In the early seventeenth century, estimates of the number of Christian captives in Algiers ranged as high as 35,000 in a population of 100,000 to 130,000. These figures, and the population figures in particular, look inflated. The town of Algiers was not big enough to hold that many people. By the time of our story, in any event, the period of corsair glory was over, thanks in part to the improved naval strength of the west European states. The number of prisoners had shrunk to perhaps 3,000 in 1785 and to only 700 in 1791. Two-thirds of these were deserters from the Spanish garrison at Oran and therefore unredeemable, according to the American captives.[9] The number was up to 1,342 in 1799 and to 1,500 at one point in 1802, according to reports from the American consul.

Capture and enslavement was not a one-way street. From the sixteenth to the eighteenth century, European corsairs were regularly raiding the coast of North Africa and capturing Muslim shipping on the high seas. There are no reliable statistics on the total number of Muslim slaves in Europe, but recent archival research indicates that there were more than modern Europeans have realized. They were particularly valued as galley slaves. Thus, Daniel Panzac in *Les corsaires barbaresques* writes that at the end of the seventeenth century almost a quarter of Louis XIV's 12,000 galley oarsmen came from the Ottoman empire, and that in the eighteenth century it was Spain and Malta (still ruled by the crusader-descended order of the Knights of St. John) in particular where one found North Africans as captives. The Moroccan sultan, Sidi Muhammad bin Abdallah, ransomed 600 slaves (only 57 of whom were Moroccan) at $450 a head from Malta in 1789, and Napoleon reportedly liberated another 2,000 Muslim prisoners when he took Malta in 1798.

Salvatore Bono's *Schiavi musulmani nell'Italia moderna* is a very detailed study of Italian practices in this regard. He documents the presence of slave markets in Naples, Civitavecchia, Livorno, and Genoa and demonstrates that the buying, selling, and employment of slaves occurred throughout the peninsula. The number declined as the great galleys were replaced by sailing vessels in the eighteenth century, but he estimates that in the sixteenth and seventeenth centuries there were as many as 40,000 to 50,000 Muslim slaves in Italy at any one time—some rowing in the galleys, some working on construction projects and in various trades, and some employed as domestic servants. An annual attrition rate of 2,000–2,500 would require capturing or buying a total of 200,000 to 250,000 per century to maintain such a slave labor force. Some idea of their number in the galleys is given by these figures:

Tuscan galleys, 1685	647 Muslims
Pontifical galleys, 1726	475 Muslims
Naples, 1740	352 Muslims
Livorno galleys, 1749	250 Muslims (201 from North Africa)

Seamen and other nationals of enemy states that were captured by both European and North African corsairs were likely to be sold to local owners or retained by the government as slaves if they were of the wrong religion. They could eventually be ransomed if they were fortunate, and there were established procedures by which this was done. There was some ransoming of Muslim captives in Europe, but it was less common than the ransoming of Christians in Barbary, and there was no Muslim equivalent of the European religious orders devoted to the redemption of Christian prisoners.

Ordinary seamen who were captives in Algiers were likely to be put to work in the quarries and building the breakwater, which seems to have been a never-ending task. Those with useful skills might be employed in their trade. Some managed to accumulate capital and were allowed to operate taverns or wineshops which sold to local people as well as to other captives. Those who elected to convert to Islam might be employed as corsairs. Ship's officers were not normally forced to work and were not confined, provided they paid a nominal monthly fee—for which they were labeled *pagar luna*, to pay (by) month—but judging from the accounts of American prisoners, they were on parole not to escape. According to the French consul in 1785, some consul would have to go surety for them, and if they escaped or died "outside the hospital" he would be held financially responsible for the loss of potential ransom.

Some of the captives, because of professional competence or personality, rose to positions of influence, although still considered prisoners and not free to leave. Younger crew members might become servants in the dey's house, one of the routes to positions of influence.

There seems to be no reliable account of what happened to women prisoners, of whom there were an indeterminate number. Shaler says (*Sketches*, 76) that women prisoners were "always treated with the respect due their sex," but cites no examples. The lurid claims of Maria Martin—to have been the wife of a British ship's captain, to have been wrecked on the coast of Algeria, and to have spent three years in a dungeon on bread and water because she rejected the advances of her "Turkish" captor—appear to be a hoax. Here is a subject for more research.

The ordinary captives were housed in barracks called bagnios, or baths (*banyolar* in Turkish), from the Italian *bagno,* which today means prison as well as bath. From the descriptions it is clear that the buildings in question had nothing to do with bathing, Turkish or otherwise.[10] There were three bagnios in use at the time we are discussing, all of them located in the lower town near the harbor, a district referred to by the French as *la marine*. The description by William Spencer makes them sound almost commodious: "The banyolar (barracks) assigned to Christian prisoners, far from being the dark holes which gave rise to European legends of slave mistreatment, were comparable in amenities to the quarters of the ocak. Thus the Grand Banyo, wherein captives belonging to the state itself were housed, was a large building, seventy by forty feet, divided into small rooms, with a cistern in the middle. Below, at ground level, was an oratory where mass was said regularly for Catholic prisoners" (*Algiers in the Age of the Corsairs*, 33).

This may be a relatively accurate portrayal of the physical framework (although Cathcart says this bagnio was 140 by 60 feet), but it says nothing about the deplorable sanitation and abuse that was the prisoners' lot by all accounts. Nevertheless, their living conditions were probably no worse, and perhaps better, than those of Muslim prisoners held by the Europeans and condemned to work as oarsmen in the galleys. Nor do the conditions under which they were transported and held sound nearly as bad as those inflicted on African slaves being brought to America. But they were fed poorly, often worked cruelly, and crowded into unhealthy proximity to each other. When the plague raged in Algiers, as it did frequently, it was the prisoners in the bagnios who were at the greatest risk.

The Town

When our story begins, in 1785, Algiers was a walled town of perhaps 50,000 inhabitants.[11] There were numerous country houses belonging to corsair captains and other wealthy people outside the walls, some of which remain to this day, but there were no real suburbs. The population lived largely within the confines of the present qasbah, which is laid out in a walled trapezoid, with a circuit of a mile and a half, on the slope of a hill running down to the sea and crowded with masonry structures (Shaler estimated their number at 8,000 to 10,000). The administrative center was in the lower town, near the harbor. The various government offices and the dey's palace were there, near the admiralty, which controlled the port and the activities of the fleet. (The French razed much of this lower district after their occupation in 1830. A few of the public buildings—houses, palaces, mosques—remain, but there is no trace of the bagnios or the dey's palace.) The buildings in the qasbah were largely residences, two- or three-story, flat-roofed buildings of soft brick and stone, plastered and whitewashed and built around open courtyards. The streets were narrow passages through which donkeys and mules could be driven, but there was no wheeled traffic until the coming of the French, who cut a wide street through from east to west in the lower town in addition to demolishing many structures. There is still no wheeled traffic in the upper qasbah today.

The population of Algiers was cosmopolitan and polyglot. The official language of communication with Constantinople and non-Arab governments was Turkish, while court records and other local transactions were in Arabic, and servants and laborers were likely to speak a Berber dialect. The language of discourse and commerce between speakers of different languages at all levels was the widely used local lingua franca, or "language of the Franks." This was a pidgin spoken throughout the Mediterranean from about 1300 until about 1900, when it died out. There is disagreement as to its origins, but the variety used in the eastern Mediterranean was based predominantly on Italian, with an admixture of Arabic, Greek, Turkish, and other languages, including Spanish, while that in the West was based more on Spanish, with similar loan words from other languages, particularly Italian. Algiers was the approximate eastern limit of the Spanish-based variety. Its most striking feature everywhere was that verbs were used only in the infinitive, with different modifiers for the different tenses and an object form of the personal pronoun as the subject. Thus "I go" is "mi andar" and "I will go" is "bisogno mi andar" (*bisogno* being Italian for the noun "need"). The object of the verb was marked by *per*—"mi hablar per ti" is "I tell you."[12]

The first American prisoners said they found Spanish to be their only means of communication initially. Their command of that language probably

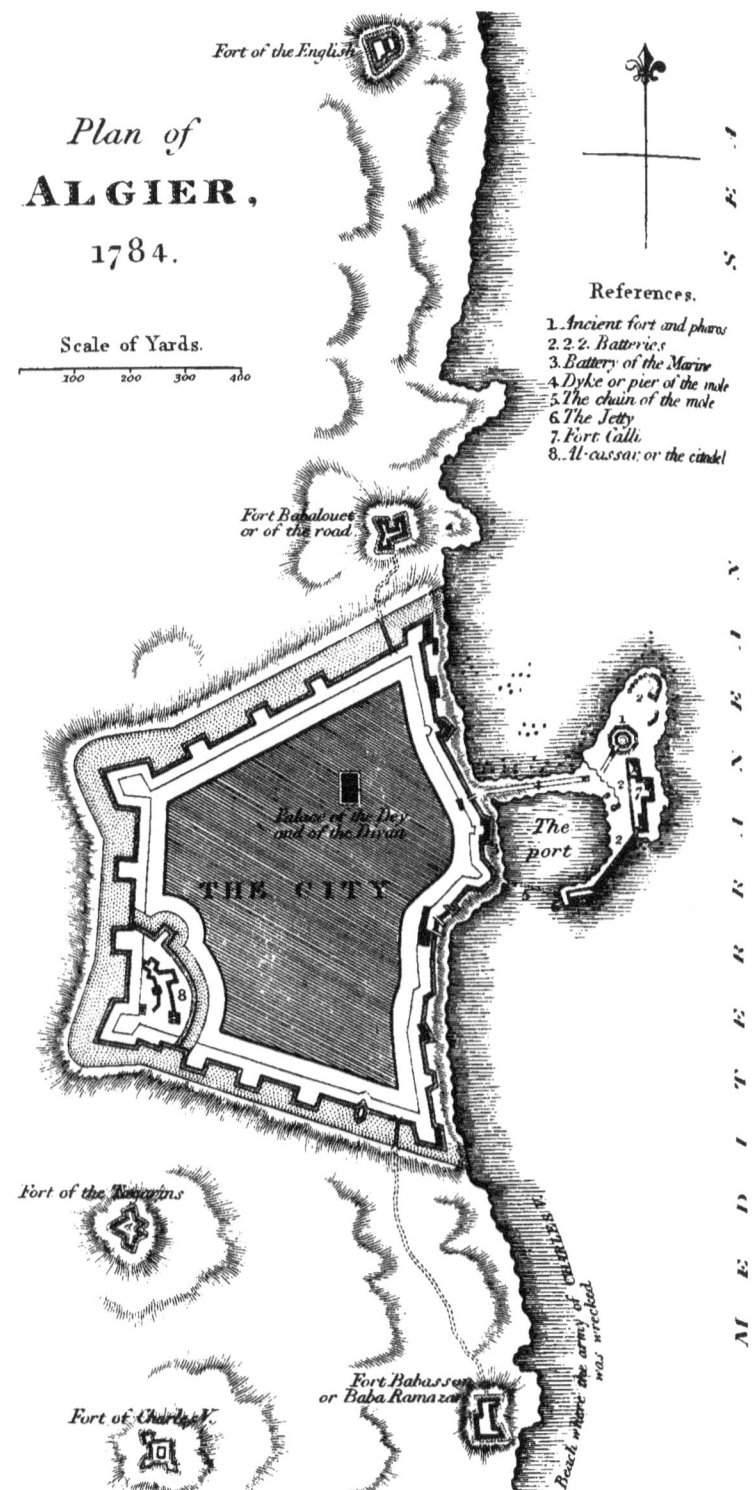

Fig. 2. Plan of Algiers, 1784. Photograph from the *London Chronicle*. Courtesy of the Naval Historical Center, Washington, D.C.

Fig. 3. Street in the Qasbah of Algiers, 1976. Photograph by author.

was not good enough for them to realize they were speaking a pidgin. This brings to mind the nineteenth-century jest that French colonists speaking lingua franca in Algeria thought they were speaking Arabic, while the Algerians who responded in it thought they were speaking French. The variety of languages spoken perhaps explains in part why the Department of State's first language trainee was sent to Algiers in 1825 to learn Turkish, Arabic, and Berber. (He succeeded in learning only the first, by going later to Istanbul.)

Social Structure

It is important to remember that Algiers was dominated by a foreign minority—the largely Turkish janissaries who formed the ojak. These professional soldiers were a far cry from the elite corps of the early Ottoman army that was made up of forcibly conscripted Christians from the European provinces who were converted to Islam as young boys or men. By the eighteenth cen-

Fig. 4. Rooftops of the Qasbah, 1976. Photograph by author.

tury the corps was a largely native Muslim career force, often involved in local commerce and trade on the side. Venture de Paradis estimated the total number of janissaries in the country at 8,000, of whom 3,000 were in Algiers, but Ahmad Tawfiq al-Madani cites a detailed register of the period that puts the total number for all Algeria except Algiers at 3,861.[13]

The recruits did not bring wives with them, and there was no substantial importation of Turkish women. Although intermarriage was discouraged, some of the Turks married local women by whom they had children who were called *kul-oghli* (usually written kouloughli), or "children of the slave," i.e., of their janissary father, who was considered a slave of the Ottoman sultan. Excluded from the highest offices of the land, which were reserved for members of the ojak and the corsair captains, the kouloughlis nevertheless formed an important and influential element in Algerian society, serving in the militia, occasionally rising to senior positions, proud of their Turkishness and looking down on those without it. They were normally unable to inherit their fathers' powers, however, and, contrary to what happened in Tunis and

Tripoli, no local dynasties arose during the three hundred years of Ottoman rule. The number of kouloughlis in the late eighteenth century is put at 6,000 by Ali Abd al-Qadr Halimi in *Madinat al-Jaza'ir*. (The American consul gave the same figure in a report of May 20, 1802.)

The corsairs formed what was called a *ta'ifa,* or faction, usually translated as "corporation." Their captains participated in the grand divan, or council of state, along with senior members of the ojak and local dignitaries such as judges and the ulama, or learned ones. This body was moribund by the time of our story, although a smaller divan of the dey and his ministers continued to function, or at least to be invoked as the final authority. Foreign representatives dealing with the ojak in the nineteenth century record occasions on which it was used as a device for justifying a decision likely to be unpopular with one party or another.[14]

Throughout North Africa the corsair captains and their crews at one time had among their members a large number of renegades—European Christians who enjoyed privateering and who converted to Islam. By the late eighteenth century, however, their number had been greatly reduced, as had the corsair trade in general. There were an estimated seventy "cruisers" or corsair sailing vessels operating out of Algiers in 1634, but in the late eighteenth century there were only ten or twelve, according to a variety of reports by foreign visitors. (In 1802 the American consul put the number at fifteen.)

The local population, Arab and Berber, was next to the bottom of the social structure.[15] There is a good deal of confusion about the use of the word "Moor" to describe them. The Berbers, the indigenous inhabitants of the region, were known to the Romans as the Mauri, whence the name Moro or Moor, often applied indiscriminately to all North African Muslims by Europeans. The more common usage in the eighteenth century reserved this term for city dwellers, and often for immigrants from Spain, as opposed to the Arabs of the countryside and the Kabyles, or Berbers. It is used here only when quoting someone.

We have no census figures to tell us what percentage of the population of Algiers was Berber or Arab, but Qadr Halimi estimates the "internal migrants"—people coming from elsewhere in Algeria to work and live full or part time in Algiers—at about 6,500, of whom 4,000 were Berbers and 2,500 were Arab. The migrant was called *barrani,* "outsider," as distinguished from the *baladi* or townsman. Some of the barranis lived, or squatted, outside the main gates, while others lived in the lower town. In time-honored fashion, they specialized in certain trades according to their locality of origin. Thus, men from Jijel specialized in baking and men from Biskra, on the desert's edge south of the Aures Mountains, specialized in the porterage trade to the extent that *biskri,* or man from Biskra, came to mean "porter."

The baladis lived close to but separately from the ojak, inhabiting the upper part of the town while the janissaries lived in barracks or private housing in the lower town, where the government officials, foreigners, and Jews also lived and where the principal suqs or markets were located. Although the Jews predominated in their quarter, there were Muslims living among them.

The local dignitaries such as the qadis, or religious judges, and the naqib al-ashraf, or deputy of the Prophet's descendants, participated in the ceremonies of state but had no authority over the members of the ojak. Judgement and punishment of the janissaries and slaves was meted out only by the officers of the ojak, and was likely to be summary and swift. In criminal matters there appears to have been little recourse to legal processes and institutions, although there were qadis of the relatively liberal hanafi school of jurisprudence to deal with civil matters involving the Turks, while there were qadis of the stricter maliki school for the local population.

At the bottom of the structure were the largely Christian prisoners captured by the corsairs and the black slaves from the Sudan and elsewhere south of the Sahara. Judging by the comments of a variety of visitors, in the late eighteenth century there probably were not more than 2,000 of the latter, a majority of whom were women in domestic service.

Although they were herded into the bagnios at night and sent out in working parties during the day, the Christian prisoners owned by the government had some freedom of movement on feast and other nonwork days and were not confined at all times. Those who had been purchased by private owners on arrival and were employed in a trade were free to move about according to the requirements of their job during the day. Those accounts we have describe their contacts with the authorities and taskmasters but say very little about their relations with the local population.

In an analogous position, certainly better off than the prisoners and much of the Arab and Berber community in material terms, and free to move about and practice any lawful trade, but oppressed and humiliated in various other ways, including limitations on what they could wear and where they could live, were a community of perhaps 5,000 Jews. With their own "king" or chief, and their own laws of personal status as *dhimmis* or members of a protected minority, they ran the mint and were the gold- and silversmiths. They performed important banking and mercantile functions, thanks to their family and commercial ties with Jews in places like Livorno and Marseille. They enjoyed monopolies in the export of grain and other products that gave them considerable wealth, and they were the exclusive brokers for the sale of booty from captured ships. Shaler said they were the only class of Algerine society possessing any accurate knowledge of foreign affairs. They were the bankers and confidants of the deys Hasan (1791–1798) and Mustafa (1798–1805) and were instrumental in the negotiations and financial operations that eventually resulted in the ransom of the American prisoners in Algiers.[16]

The essential precariousness of their position was revealed in 1805, when a janissary shot and killed the head of the community, Nafthali Bushnaq [Bu Jnah]. This was followed later in the day by a general attack on the Jewish quarter in which some two hundred men were murdered and shops and homes were looted. According to al-Zahhar, the culprits were crucified at the rate of ten per day until all of them were punished, but the dey himself, Mustafa Pasha, who was considered unduly partial to the Jews, was subsequently murdered when he tried to flee. In spite of this gory catastrophe, a member of the community was still prominent enough to be the Tuscan consul in 1826, and another was an adviser to the first French military governor in 1830.

Government

Details about the structure and functions of the regency government or *beylik* are sparse, and the various accounts often conflict. At the top of the power structure was the dey (*dayi*), who was a janissary from the ojak. Dayi, literally "maternal uncle," was a Turkish military term for a unit commander. Shaler reports that use of this term was largely restricted to Europeans. The local population normally referred to him as pasha. Al-Zahhar calls him amir (commander or prince), malik (king or sovereign), and pasha interchangeably. Any janissary—except those from Bosnia and Crete, according to Shaler—could become dey. In theory he was chosen by his comrades and there was no fixed or hereditary succession, but by the late eighteenth century the *khaznaji*, described below, had come to be considered the leading candidate to succeed to the position. (This did not continue to be the case in the nineteenth century.) The dey's authority was considerable, as long as he lasted, but he could be replaced at any time with no notice by his former comrades in arms. Half of the twenty-eight deys who ruled from 1671 to 1830 were murdered by their companions in arms while in office. The period we are discussing, however, was one of stability and was marked by the extraordinarily long reign of Muhammad ibn Uthman (1766–1791) and the reasonably long reign of his successor Hasan (1791–1797). Both died in bed of natural causes.

The dey had five ministers who were drawn from the ojak. Usually called "the Powers" by foreigners, they were, in order of seniority:

> *The khaznaji or treasurer.* Traditionally the heir apparent, he did not automatically succeed the dey. Not to be confused with a khazine-

dar, also meaning treasurer, of which each minister appears to have had one for his household.

The agha of the Arabs, or of the 'askar [soldiers]. The governor of the district around Algiers and commander of the various elements that made up the land forces.

The khojat al-khayl (or khawl). Literally, the clerk of the horses (or chattels). Actually the receiver of tribute, i.e., the tax revenues presented by the provincial governors or beys at specified intervals.

The vekil kharj (wakil al-kharj bi bab al-jihad). Literally, the quartermaster at the Gate of Jihad, the admiralty gate leading to the harbor. This officer was in charge of maritime affairs and functioned as foreign minister. He will appear frequently in this narrative. His title was consistently mangled by foreigners.[17]

The bayt al-malji (wakil bayt mal al-muslimin). The keeper of forfeited and unclaimed property, including estates of people who died without leaving heirs.

There are no detailed descriptions of the structure of the ministries or departments over which these officials presided, but there was a hierarchy of clerks, both Turkish and Arab, with scribes and ushers who did the actual work of government, recording transactions and judgements and writing correspondence. There was a regular order of succession to these clerical and disciplinary positions, which were prized for their revenue potential from *'awa'id,* the "customary" payments or tips for services real or imagined.

Al-Zahhar gives a few details regarding the costumes of some of the functionaries. The "green" ushers, for instance, who were sergeants at arms or bailiffs, wore green cloaks and red shoes heavily shod with iron, allegedly to make noise so culprits who were members of the ojak could hear them coming and flee. We can assume that other officials had their own special costumes to identify their rank and position, as they did in Turkey, but we do not have a great deal in the way of illustrations to show what official dress was. Period works are full of sketches and portraits showing Ottoman dress in Turkey, however. Headdress in particular was a place where the Turkish penchant for fantasy mixed with tradition ruled, rather like the British and their bearskins. The janissaries, for instance, wore a spoon in their headdress, which featured a draped cloth that looks like it might have represented a napkin, although one explanation is that it represented the sleeve of their patron saint, Haji Bektash.[18]

The military establishment in Algiers controlled the city and an area around it called Dar al-Sultan that included the Metidja, the rich plain to the south of the city. The rest of the country was under the authority of three beys or princes (not to be confused with dey) whose seats of governance were

Constantine in the east, Tlemcen or Mascara, and later Oran, in the west, and Titteri or Medea in the center. The beys, who were by and large appointed from the ranks of the ojak and who served at the pleasure of the dey, paid taxes and a substantial triennial tribute to the dey. Modest garrisons from Algiers were maintained on their territory, but they had their own staffs and military commanders who controlled their own military forces, and they had a good deal of independence as far as governing their territories was concerned. The majority of their forces were local and tribal levies.

The Economy

It has been common for writers to attribute the prosperity of Algiers to the corsairs, who were the state's principal source of revenue. This may have been the case in the seventeenth century, but was not by the late eighteenth. In the first place, such details as we have about the captured ships indicate that the value of the cargoes seized in this period was not that great. The vessels in question were not East Indiamen or Spanish galleons loaded with spices or gold and silver, but small merchant ships carrying agricultural products and basic manufactured items. For instance, the *Polly*, a brigantine from Newburyport, Massachusetts, captured in 1793, was a vessel of 145 tons, 70 feet long and 22 wide, according to the *Newburyport Ship Registers 1789–1820*. She was loaded with flour. A useful cargo, but not fabulous. The *Dauphin*, captured in 1785, had a cargo of salt. Other ships captured, of various nationalities, sound like they are of similar dimensions with similar homely cargoes.

Thanks to the Algerine *Registre des prises maritimes* translated by Albert Devoulx, which is discussed briefly in appendix 4, we can get some idea of the magnitude of the profits from corsair activities. The figures for the period 1787–94 show that the cargoes of fifty-four prizes taken into Algiers brought in an estimated $805,523, or about $100,000 a year. These figures are incomplete and apparently do not include cargoes sold at European or North African ports other than Algiers. It would conceivably be possible, through examination of records in various European ports, to determine what the values of those missing cargoes were. But judging by the fact that only half the American ships captured by the Algerines in 1793 can be identified in the *Registre*, it may be reasonable to assume that half the cargoes were sold abroad, where, depending on the cargo, prices would perhaps have been higher. We could then assume an income of $200,000 a year, or about four-fifths of the annual tribute paid by Sweden, Holland, Denmark, and Venice mentioned by Venture de Paradis. This would be a useful sum, but not very important compared to other sources of income.

Secondly, Algeria had considerable agricultural potential. A government more solicitous about the welfare of the local population could have greatly increased its revenue from the countryside. The thought seems not to have occurred to the soldiers of the ojak, and most of the rural population—90 percent of the estimated 3,000,000 total—lived on the edge of subsistence. Even so, Algeria had substantial exports of agricultural commodities, notably hard wheat, barley, wool, hides and skins, beeswax, and cochineal. It was an important source of wheat for the French, particularly in the Napoleonic period, and a good deal of money was made from that trade. In addition, substantial revenues were raised through taxes and levies on the people in the three beyliks or governorates—taxes and commodities that were transferred to Algiers in the form of the periodic tribute payments mentioned earlier. Venture de Paradis in *Tunis et Alger* (242–47) lists the annual revenue in cash and kind from such payments and from various fees and levies of a more municipal variety. According to my calculations, these total just under 900,000 piastres or $900,000. Balanced against that was a triennial tribute payment to Istanbul estimated by Shaler at $500,000.

Modern research makes it clear that while the economy of Algiers depended to some extent on the demand created by corsair revenues, the townspeople lived on domestic, and some foreign, commerce and light industry—textiles and handwork specialties common to Arab towns of the era. Much of the production was for local consumption, but Algiers was famous for its silk belts and its haiks, long woolen outer garments, which it exported to other towns in North Africa and the Near East. Tal Shuval found a total of 105 artisanal trades or professions recorded in contemporary documents, indicating a division of specialities that was pushed to extremes. For instance, ten different types of leatherworking specialities are listed in the records.

Various estimates of commercial exchanges show a negative balance. Shaler put imports for 1822 at $1,200,000 and exports at $273,000. He concluded that the deficit was made up from the "capitals of this city. . . . Algiers having enjoyed during three centuries the profitable privilege of pillaging the commercial world . . .[there is] a great accumulation of metallic wealth in this city." (A popular guessing game seems to have been estimating how much gold and silver was in the treasury. Shaler (176) wrote in 1826 that it had been "rated" as high as $50 million, while Richard O'Brien put it at $65 million in 1802 (NavDocs 2:198), but according to Gustave Gautherot, the French found only 48,684,582 francs' worth, equivalent to about $10 million, when they occupied Algiers in 1830.[19])

What trade existed was more with Europe than with the rest of North Africa—a situation that applies today—and it is thanks largely to the statistics of the Marseille chamber of commerce and the records of the French consulate that we know what little we do about volume and value. A detailed, Braudelian study of the Algerian economy, based on contemporary documents, remains to be completed, but it has already been begun by researchers such as Shuval, Daniel Panzac, and Mohamed Amine.[20]

Inside the Ojak

In appendix 1 is an extract from Ahmad al-Zahhar's memoirs describing the tribute ceremonies of 1785. It gives some idea of the importance of tradition[21] and of bakhsheesh or tips in the ojak. The ojak was a rigorously egalitarian association, the members of which received a simple soldier's pay and rations and had to depend on commercial activity, bribes, presents, and extortion for wealth. The dey and members of his cabinet enjoyed a number of perquisites, but their living conditions were far from the decadent luxury that Europeans imagined, and while they could all hope to rise to the top, they could also be thrown out before breakfast once they got there. The dey's palace was rather modest by the norms of that period—a four-story building around a courtyard with a garden. The garden has been called vast, but Cathcart, in a detailed description that begins on page 93 of *The Captives*, estimated the total area of the palace complex at one acre. It was in the midst of a busy town, and there was no great space for gardens. Its name, Dar al-Jnina (Junaina), is a diminutive meaning House of the *Little* Garden. It was destroyed by the French in 1856. An idea of what its central portion would have been like can be had by visiting Dar Aziza Bint al-Bey, (House of Aziza, Daughter of the Bey), a pleasant structure built around a courtyard that adjoined the rear of the dey's palace.

The dey was up every morning before dawn to meet his ministers at the front door. He could visit his wife and family only two nights a week, and otherwise was locked in at night with the palace servants. Assassination was a constant possibility,[22] and he kept the keys to the front door and the treasury himself.

Each minister had his residence and office, referred to by al-Zahhar as a *hanut* or shop, near the dey's palace, and there seems to have been little pomp or circumstance connected with government operations. The furnishings of offices were minimal, and access to the dey and other officials by petitioners and visitors appears to have been informal, with access to the dey by foreigners relatively easy, judging by the anecdotal evidence. Thus, the Swedish consul's younger brother, who was not an official, got in to see him immediately to talk about ransoming the American prisoners in 1793.

In brief, while Algiers had what would be considered a rudimentary form of government by today's standards, it functioned well enough during the period we are discussing. The Algerine corsairs were not a group of pirates hiding in a distant cove with no civil authority over them. They were agents of an established government that was recognized by the international community, and they were operating within the then current rules of international law regarding privateers and naval vessels. They took those rules seriously, although they could apply them capriciously, as when they declared war on the Americans, who had done nothing to Algiers. While ousting the Spanish from their territory was a long-term political objective, the object of their operations against foreign shipping was generally money, not politics.

The next chapter discusses the two deys of our story in greater detail.

2

The Deys

Western historians tell us little about the personality and character of the various deys. They remain abstractions, often not even named. Reading the histories, one has the feeling that it does not matter who is dey, they are all of the same mold and all but impossible for westerners to deal with—calling to mind modern stereotypes about Muslim leaders. But the personalities of the two deys with whom the Americans were most concerned, Muhammad Pasha (1766–1791) and Hasan (1791–1797), were quite different, and this affected the course of negotiations in important ways. One was interested only in the bottom line. The other was more open to personal considerations.

We have details about them from various sources, some of whom are more reliable than others. The following accounts differ, but there is a certain consistency about them.

Muhammad Pasha bin Uthman, also known as al-Mujahid and Muhammad Baba (1766–1791)

According to al-Zahhar's *Mudhakirat* (23–70):

> When Ali Pasha, who was known as Bu Sba'—He of the Finger, because he had lost one—sickened, he summoned his ministers . . . and charged them to be loyal to Muhammad Pasha and to take care of his children. He left [behind him] Haj Muhammad and his sister and her mother, who was his first wife, an infidel from Istanbul. Ali Pasha died on Sunday, the twenty-first of Shas'ban 1179 [April 8, 1766].
>
> The following day the government notables . . . gathered in the Dar al-Imara and Muhammad Pasha sat on the seat of power. . . . the notables swore allegiance. . . . he put on the official robe of honor. . . . the cannons fired and the cortege moved out and he went up to his quarters in the palace.
>
> He was, may God have mercy on him, an influence for justice and fairness. He knew the rule of governance and was devoted to the pure Shari'a. He loved jihad, and many wars occurred during his time. God gave him victory in all of them. . . .

His clothing was what he needed to cover his body, and his food what sufficed for his belly. Every year he sent his clothes to the tailor to be patched, and he did not throw a garment away until it could no longer be patched. It was the custom of the rulers and their ministers to wear golden yataghans during their meetings and when they went together to pray in the mosque. . . . But this emir carried a silver yataghan and would not have carried any if custom had not required him to do so.

In a few days his ministers advised him to get married. . . . So he said to them, "If I marry I will need much money, but you want me to marry, so tell me, how much does a bride cost?" They told him so and so much. He said, "That's little enough to me," and was silent.

The next day, when he was in the place of government near the treasury and the ministers were around him, he called the treasurer of his wealth who brought him a great deal of money by prearrangement and he ordered that it be put in the hands of the ministers and said to them, "Look at it. Is that enough for the bride price of the woman I marry?" And they said, "Yes." So he said to them, "Which is better, that I marry with this money or that we put it in the treasury and make jihad with it? It would help us repel the enemy." And they replied, "Your view is preferable." So he ordered the money to be put in the treasury. Days later he married another infidel from the Caucasus that Ali Pasha had left when he died. She spent one night with him and then he divorced her and said, "I married in order not to die a bachelor and be resurrected a devil."[1]

He had glorious deeds. He built a number of fortified towers for jihad. The first of these was Burj Sardina [still standing, in the old port area, and named for the picture of a sardine on one of its stones] and the other was Burj Ras 'Amar, built during the last of his wars with Spain. The people of the town went themselves to help build it, desiring to do so for the sake of God and hoping to be requited for this good deed. Our worthy forefathers, in the days of this pasha and before, desired jihad. They sailed the sea with the ships of the jihad and raided and bragged to each other of this virtuousness. This pasha was the first to build the lanjur.[2] Before that bombs used to fall on the town and destroy buildings, even destroying the Mosque of the Sayyida near the palace.

Among his good deeds was to rebuild this mosque and restore its decorations . . . and he brought water to the town and built an aqueduct and endowed it with a waqf for maintaining the channels and paying the water master and ordered that the water be distributed to the towers of Bab al-Jihad and to the mosques and barracks of the military and to the ablution basins. As for what was left over, he distributed it to the water points in the streets of the town. This water had come to the town before but the flow had been weak.

... He loved jihad, was always ready for war, and was fascinated with preparing ships for raids. In his days the number of captains at sea increased and the ships had a reputation. One of the greatest captains of this period was al-Haj Muhammad Qabtan, who was renowned at sea. The records show that during his voyages he captured a total of 24,000 prisoners.

In *Algiers in the Age of the Corsairs* (63–64), William Spencer has this to say about Muhammad Pasha:

> Certainly the most unusual elevation was that of Baba Mohammed ben-Osman, (1766–90), the longest reigning and most effective of Algerine rulers. He came from a small village in the vilayet of Karaman in southern Anatolia, where he had been recruited for the ocak, at an early age and taken to Algiers. There he married, had a son, and was subsequently, for unknown reasons, castrated. That ended his military career. Undaunted, he apprenticed himself to a shoemaker, and then opened his own shop where he made, sold, and repaired shoes for his former comrades in arms. He not only prospered but won the respect of all for his industry, humility and honesty. One day a cavus [shawush or usher] came looking for another Mohammed, also a shoemaker, who had been recommended for the then-vacant post of babi hocayi (hoca [khoja] of the gate). By mistake he called at the shop of Karaman and gave him the post. From then on Baba Mohammed's star brightened as he rose steadily through the administrative ranks to become eventually hazinedar [khaznaji?] and then dey. Yet his humility and awareness of his good fortune never deserted him. "It was written," he said of his accession to the highest post. He died in his bed, peacefully, and the succession passed without incident to his son Hassan.

If the story of Baba Muhammad's castration is true, it would explain his disinterest in marriage described above. Unfortunately, Spencer's book has no footnotes and Spencer informs me that he has destroyed his notes and no longer recalls the source for the castration allegation. I have been unable to confirm the allegation from other sources, but Admiral de Bauffremont in his journal (43), speaking of this dey, says, "They claim he has never known a woman." Evidently there were rumors about his sexuality, or lack of same.

That Hassan, Baba Muhammad's successor, was his son seems highly dubious, although Panzac in *Les Corsaires barbaresques* (245) makes the same statement. (He, too, does not recall where this observation came from and is removing it from the forthcoming English version of his book.) It does not square with the accounts of Hassan's accession by James Cathcart and Ahmad al-Zahhar given in appendix 3, nor does it accord with the following account by Venture de Paradis (*Tunis et Alger,* 195–99) of Muhammad bin Uthman's rise to power:

> Baba Muhammed ben Osman is from that part of Karamania which is opposite Rhodes and Stanche[?]. Being literate, he did not tarry, after his arrival in Algiers . . . once he had amassed the thousand *pataques chiques* [about $200] he must pay the beylik in order to become one of the clerks. After serving in that capacity for several years in camps and garrisons, he was made khoja of the naubatjis who guard the dey night and day. From this position of confidence he was made khaznaji by Baba Ali, his predecessor, whom he succeeded.
>
> Baba Muhammad is today [1788] a man of more than 80 years. He is very tall, austere [*sec*], and scrawny. He drags his left leg a little when he walks, because of a rifle ball in the knee he received at the siege of Oran. He has a hard and not very agreeable look, but his sight is good and so is his hearing. His mind is not enfeebled and he enjoys rather good health, which he owes to his moderation and diet. He never takes medicine.
>
> When he is sick he takes pure water and waits patiently the reestablishment of his health. He has never married and even in his youth he was never accused of chasing after women, or boys, the popular vice among the Turks in Algiers. He has always been chaste and continent, simple in his clothes, frugal, calm and parsimonious with blood. He has had very few people killed during his reign.
>
> In May 1785[3] he had the khaznaji strangled at the instigation of the bey of Constantine, who had denounced him [the khaznaji] as a man who wanted to dispose of his principality at his own desire and caprice. It will be good if Algiers can keep him for a long time yet.
>
> The only vice with which one can reproach him is too much economizing. He never lets any means of increasing the state treasury escape him, and he can never decide, even on the most important occasions, to let out money he has put in. This economizing caused a stir among the troops when they had obliged the Spanish to withdraw on July 8, 1775. They demanded to be recompensed as they had been at the taking of Tunis in 1754. Each soldier had received ten sequins [$20] on that occasion, and they demanded as much this time. The dey agreed, after much insisting, to let them have five—he could not agree to pay people who were defending their homes and their religion against the infidels. At the last bombardment the boats went out to fight and returned very quickly. They were asked why, and they said they had fought a piastre's

worth [$1], which was how much they had been given.

The current dey is perhaps the only Turk in Algiers whose morals are pure on the matter of boys and other forms of debauch. He does not permit any form of libertinage in his house, and the people who work for him must have an orderly conduct and fear that their actions, if they commit something immoral, will come to his ears. He has never drunk wine and has never permitted himself to smoke or take tobacco. His principal officers do well to take care not to drink or smoke. The dey has but one fault, that of avarice, not for himself but for the interests of the republic. . . .

The reign of Baba Muhammad has been very peaceful. At the beginning there were some obscure factions which he fortunately was able to dissipate. In 1768, as he was seated in the hall of the divan, a one-armed Turk concealed his yataghan and, going in to take his pay, struck him a violent blow on the head, which his turban deflected, fortunately. Sometime later nine Turks formed a plot to assassinate him and had concealed their yataghans under their cloaks, but the secret having leaked, the first among them were arrested by the clerk of the guards when they presented themselves on the pretext of receiving their pay. The others tried to escape but were seized, and all of them were strangled at the house of the agha of two moons, where executions are performed. The firmness he displayed at the time of the Spanish landing and their various bombardments gives a good idea of his courage. He forced that humiliated power to ask him for peace. That peace cost Spain a million piastres [$1 million], not counting the presents to everyone in the government and the ransom of Spanish, Sicilian, and Neapolitan slaves, which cost another million piastres. That immense sum was taken to the treasury and added to what was accumulated there already.

The dey has for emoluments the pay of a soldier, forty loaves of bread furnished by the shaykh al-balad [mayor of the town], his perquisites on the investiture of offices, and the presents he is given by the beys, the qa'ids, and the European consuls. The beylik supplies his table with the exactions in wheat, sheep, fowl, butter, rice, and fruits that come from the various districts of the kingdom. This cuisine feeds the dey and all the officers and solders who are attached to the divan and who do not leave until after the afternoon prayer.

De Paradis comments further that

the life of leading officials is hard and active and it proceeds with astonishing regularity. They never permit minor indispositions to keep them from work, and they must all be at the door of the dey's palace when it opens at sunrise and remain there or at their nearby offices until the afternoon prayer. They have Tuesday off, and their regular duties are in abeyance on Fridays, but they must spend much of the latter day going to the mosque with the dey or in attendance on him. For his part, the dey also has to get up before sunrise to meet his officers when the door is opened and they come in to kiss his hand and drink coffee. Their sleeping quarters are sparsely furnished, and the only luxury is the covering of the walls with hangings, weapons, and tiles. They have no beds but sleep on the floor or on a *strapontin,* or folding shelf. If they are married, their wives are housed separately and they can go to them only on Tuesdays and Fridays. Their pay is that of a simple soldier and they are dependent on presents, bribes, and exactions for anything beyond that. Their positions carry with them a number of perquisites that have substantial monetary value, and they are often able to amass wealth, but when they die the government takes everything in their, as opposed to their wives', possession. They are furthermore subject to elimination at short notice.

Muhammad bin Uthman, then, by universal report, was avaricious. Austere and upright, he would have been hard to impress or intimidate. He does not seem to have had weak spots that a diplomat could exploit, except his avarice. Nevertheless, it would perhaps have helped had the French told the Americans what they knew about him. They do not seem to have done so. As our narrative will show, the Americans did not have a clear idea of what they were up against.

Hasan Pasha (1791–1798)

Hasan Pasha was a very different sort of man, a complex individual. Judging by contemporary comments, he was much warmer and more passionate than his predecessor, and much more open to diplomacy. Al-Zahhar describes him as "knowledgeable, intelligent, and clever in affairs, but he was sometimes afflicted by rage, which made him do things that were uncalled for." He was not austere like Muhammad Pasha, but rather was someone who liked people and display and did not share his predecessor's parsimony in matters of clothing. Spencer (65) records the following as Joel Barlow's description of his appearance,

> his feet [were] shod with buskins bound upon his legs with diamond buttons in loops of pearl; round his waist was a broad sash glittering with jewels, to which was suspended a broad scimitar, its sheath of the

finest velvet. In his sash were stuck a poignard and a pair of pistols, said to have been a present from the late unfortunate Louis XVI; the dagger was of pure gold. Upon the Dey's head was a turban with the point erect, which is stylistically peculiar to the royal family. A large diamond crescent shone conspicuously in the front and on the back of which a socket received the quills of two large ostrich feathers.

In a long letter of October 18, 1796, to the secretary of state summing up his exertions in Algiers, Barlow has this to say about Hasan's character:

> His late generosity towards us, even if it did not call for gratitude on our part, is at least a proof of high esteem and confidence on his. And I think it will be easy for us to nourish those sentiments in his mind. . . . I have abused the bad sides of his character so much in my former letters (not a word of which am I going to retract) that it is time I should say something of his virtues. For I have long perceived that he has them, though I did not feel in a humour to say so. He is not personally avaritious, though he appears so in his dealings with foreign nations, but he deals out his money with remarkable liberality to his domestic slaves and to the poor, though often with little judgement. His attachments are as strong as his resentments, though they are both subject to an ungovernable caprice. He has a high sense of Barbarian honour. His dismissing the Dutch ships [i.e., letting them leave freely] with such scrupulous integrity at the beginning of his late war with that nation (O'Brien informs me that he related the circumstances to the president) is a trait that would have done honour to any State in Europe. Had the Romans done such a thing it would be known to every schoolboy in our day.
>
> A circumstance which took place last week deserves likewise to be mentioned. A few days after our money arrived he declared war against the Venitians, and sent out the cruisers with orders to take ships of that nationality after twenty days. It is a common practice to embargo the port for about three weeks before and after the cruisers sail. On this occasion, the embargo ceased the moment of the declaration, and five or six vessels, Venitians and others, sailed the same day. When the officers complained of this proceeding, saying that the Venitians being thus advertised, he would get no prizes, he replied that he chose they should be advertised—that it was a new war against a nation long accustomed to peace and it was dishonorable and wicked to take them by surprise.

In *Barbary Legend* (331), Godfrey Fisher reports that "Able British and French consuls liked and respected Sidi [Sir] Hassan, whose outbursts might impress distant admirals. 'Naturally gentle and kind,' still endowed after long official experience with 'mildness and patience,' he found himself, as a prominent neutral, subjected to an intolerable strain, but left a pleasing memory behind."

Fisher goes on to say that according to the British, "Sidi Hassan was a Georgian by birth who had come to Algiers as a soldier recruit when a very young man. He was quick-witted, literate and brave. He elected to follow a seafaring career and took service on one of the regency warships. His superior seamanship and gallantry were soon noticed. He was elected to the Taifa and given command of a cruiser. In 1770 he commanded a detachment of Algerine warships in the Black Sea, which fought alongside the Turkish Navy against the Russians. By 1775 he had already gained the most favourable notice of the dey Muhammad Bashaw."[4]

James Cathcart's description of his encounters with Hassan when he was the latter's chief Christian clerk gives the impression that Hassan was irascible but not without a sense of humor—someone whose anger was often bluster designed to intimidate and who had a soft spot for Cathcart's wit. Indeed, judging by Cathcart's account of his own dealings with the various ministers, all of them were a good deal more human than the writings of various consuls and travelers would have us believe. On page 314 of his *Journal* Cathcart says of Hassan's character: "a fine mild sensible man and lover of Justice has a Middling good knowledge of the Politicks of the Different Nations his Neighbours but more especially the Spaniards."

On page 25 of the Library of Congress manuscript of *The Captives*, however, Cathcart, in discussing the situation of the slaves in the palace, has something else to say about him that has been bowdlerized from the published version. It indicates that Hassan did not share his predecessor's restraint in the sexual arena:

> ... Hassan Bashaw ... was notoriously addicted to the unnatural and detestable sin of Sodomy. . . . Those [slaves] who refused to submit to his abominable embrace were menaced beaten bribed and if still proof against all his endeavors were bastinadoed on some false pretense and sent to the marine with orders to place them at hard labor so indefatigable was he to satisfy his lust that he would often take these lads into favor again in order to try what effect fatigue of the body had upon the mental faculty and it was remarked that they often became temporary favorites.

On the following page of the manuscript Cathcart notes that "his cowardice was likewise a source productive of much unhappiness ever fearful of assassination the least noise would make him fly to arms and terrify his attendants."

Hassan and his ministers made repeated references to the fact that he was getting old and would not be around forever. He died of natural causes in 1798, but his age is not indicated in the accounts I have found. For all Hassan's warmth of personality, he could be quite ruthless and cruel. Al-Zahhar describes a series of events, including the strangling of the khaznaji referred to above, that led to his accession to power when Muhammad Pasha died of natural causes in 1791. Al-Zahhar's account is given in appendix 3, together with accounts by Cathcart and others of Hassan's rise to power and his quarrel with the notorious adventurer Ali Burghl. Even discounting these descriptions somewhat to provide for possible embroidering and corruption, several things stand out. One is that there are two distinct personalities to be dealt with here. One dey is much more approachable than the other. It turns out that he is in fact willing to negotiate when the time comes, as we will see later. Another is that this second dey's first reaction is likely to be gruff, and angry, but his bark is worse than his bite and a negotiator should be prepared for that and not be dismayed. He can be charmed. A third is that, despite his ruthlessness and absolute authority over the ojak, the dey's control is limited. The wakil al-kharj, and other ministers, can go counter to his orders and get away with it. In that respect, the dey is but first among equals. Although the large divan or council of state was rarely, if ever, summoned in the period we are discussing, the dey must take into account the views of his former comrades and must sell any peace agreement to them, because it will directly affect their pockets. Thus, although the dey will be the key in any negotiations, he is not a completely free agent.

While these may seem matters of marginal interest to the reader, they help explain what happened. Such biographic details are of keen interest to the intelligent negotiator, who wants to be forewarned about the personality and character of the people with whom he or she will be dealing. The record does not indicate that any of these details were known to our negotiators in Algiers before they arrived on the scene. The French could have briefed them but do not appear to have done so, and even if they had, it is not clear that it would have made much difference to our first and second negotiators, John Lamb and Joseph Donaldson Jr., both of whom sound like men of limited imagination. The third negotiator, Joel Barlow, would have understood the importance of these details about Hassan, with whom he would be dealing, and undoubtedly picked them up quickly after his arrival, but he would have been better prepared had he been briefed in advance. The tone of his correspondence indicates that he arrived in a state of ignorance.

3

First Steps

The American colonists knew that once they became independent they would no longer enjoy the protection against the Barbary corsairs that was afforded to them by British treaties with the North African states. They would become fair game, and something must be done if they were to resume their profitable Mediterranean trade. One alternative was to support a navy that would protect their shipping. This would have been an expensive operation,[1] and once the Revolution was over and their fleet was no longer needed to fight the British, the Americans opted not to have a navy. They hoped treaties and international recognition of neutral rights would protect their commerce. An indication of the priority they attached to this matter is that the Continental Congress, as early as July 18, 1776, in its deliberations on a treaty to be negotiated with the French, had discussed the inclusion of provisions committing the French to extend to American shipping the same protection they provided to their own.[2] The alternative of making their own arrangements with the Barbary states does not seem to have been considered seriously at that point. This chapter describes initial efforts by the Americans to obtain French and British protection, and first steps toward negotiating their own treaties when that failed.

Earlier Experiences

The British flag had not prevented Americans from being captured in the period before the first British-Algiers treaty of 1686. A Harvard graduate of the class of 1666, Dr. Daniel Mason, for instance, apparently died in captivity in Algiers in about 1679, having sailed as surgeon in 1678 or 1679 on a ship out of Charlestown, Massachusetts, that was taken by the Algerines. Thirteen "Virginia ships" reportedly were taken in British waters in this same period, and in 1680 the governor of Massachusetts noted: "We have already lost five or six of our vessels by Turkish pirates, and many of our inhabitants continue in a miserable condition among them."[3] Joshua Gee of Boston was perhaps one of the miserable inhabitants the governor had in mind. He was captured in 1680, taken to Algiers, and sold to a corsair captain. He became the corsair's ship's carpenter and took part in a number of engagements against British, French, and Spanish ships. He was finally ransomed by family and friends in 1687, returned to Boston, married Elizabeth Harriss, and became a shipbuilder. Their son Joshua became a well-known Protestant divine.[4]

Stories like those of Mason and Gee were the exception rather than the rule after the British treaty of peace with the Algerines negotiated in 1686, and no serious, systematic threat was posed to American commerce until after the Treaty of Paris in 1783, which signaled official British recognition of the independence of the United States. To be sure, during the Revolution the British had stopped issuing to American vessels the Mediterranean passes that identified ships and crews as British, but this did not lead to immediate capture of ships, because the war limited American shipping in European waters. It was only with peace that the Americans would be able to resume such trade, and they wanted to be ready for that day.

Precautionary Measures

The Continental Congress had sent Benjamin Franklin, Silas Deane, and Arthur Lee to Paris in 1776 as "peace commissioners" to negotiate recognition and treaties with the European powers. On September 17, 1776, the Congress instructed them to have a provision that France would protect American shipping in the Mediterranean included in the treaty of friendship they were negotiating. The French were unwilling to give the broad commitment the Americans sought, but in article 8 of the Treaty of Amity and Commerce of February 6, 1778, they agreed to use "their good offices and interposition" with the rulers of Morocco, Algiers, Tunis, and Tripoli "to provide as fully and efficaciously as possible for the benefit, convenience and safety of the said United States . . . their subjects, people and inhabitants, and their vessels and effects, against all violence, insult, attacks, or depredations on the part of the said princes and states of Barbary, or their subjects." Similar language was contained in the treaty negotiated with Holland in 1782, but the Dutch were not in a position to contribute much to the American diplomatic effort. There was no such provision in the treaty with Spain.

On August 28, 1778, the commissioners wrote to the French foreign minister, the count of Vergennes, asking that the French use their good offices as intended by the treaty to protect American shipping then in the Mediterranean. Vergennes referred this request to the minister of the navy, Gabriel de Sartine, who replied that he did not think it would be possible for the French to make the Barbary states respect the American flag, but that it would be less difficult to persuade those states to recognize the independence of the United States and to negotiate treaties with it. He thought negotiations to that end would be long and arduous, but said he would "neglect nothing to assure its success if the Congress determines to prosecute it [peace] and you consider the King pledged to forward it."[5] Vergennes, in transmitting Sartine's reply to the commissioners, said they should "be assured that the King will cheerfully do all in his power to satisfy the wishes of the United States, and promote their views with the different Barbary powers."

The commissioners responded that although they thought treaties with the Barbary states would be a good idea, they had no instruction to go beyond negotiating treaties with those European powers to which no minister had been sent by Congress. They then reported their exchanges to Congress and requested instructions. Congress referred the matter to a committee of three on February 15, 1779, and there it slumbered.

Meanwhile, the British were unwilling even to sound helpful. In negotiating with them what became the Treaty of Paris, the commissioners attempted to insert language similar to that in the French treaty, but the British, concerned about competition from American shipping, refused to put in any commercial language at all. Their attitude was reflected in the famous remarks of John Baker-Holroyd, Lord Sheffield, in a pamphlet, *Observations on the Commerce of the American States,* published in 1783:

> It is not probable that the American States will have a very free trade in the Mediterranean; it will not be the interest of any of the great maritime powers to protect them from the Barbary States. If they know their interests they will not encourage the Americans to be carriers—that the Barbary States are advantageous to the maritime powers is obvious. If they were suppressed, the little states of Italy, etc., would have much more of the carrying trade. The French never showed themselves worse politicians than in encouraging the . . . late armed neutrality. . . . The armed neutrality would be as hurtful to the great maritime powers as the Barbary Powers are useful. . . . The Americans cannot protect themselves from the latter; they cannot pretend to a navy.

On May 7, 1784, Congress, belatedly responding to the 1778 request for instructions, directed the peace commissioners, by then Benjamin Franklin, Thomas Jefferson, and John Adams, to negotiate treaties of amity and commerce with the principal states of Europe and the Mediterranean.[6] The commissioners replied that they were studying European practice, but negotiations with the Muslim states would be expensive and they would be unable to do anything until Congress gave them some money. On February 14, 1785,

Congress authorized the expenditure of $80,000 for negotiations with all four of the North African powers—Morocco, Algiers, Tunis, and Tripoli.

To follow the same practice they had pursued in Europe, one of the peace commissioners should have gone to North Africa to negotiate the treaties, but neither Adams nor Jefferson showed any interest in doing that. (Franklin went home in July 1785 and was succeeded by Jefferson as minister to France, while Adams had been sent to London as minister.) Instead, they were considering appointing Thomas Barclay, the consul general in Paris, to the job when they learned that Congress was sending out a man named John Lamb to negotiate.

The Lamb Appointment

The story of John Lamb is dealt with sketchily in the histories, and little information is given about his background and his mission, which was important as our first foreign policy failure in the Muslim world. The following is an attempt to flesh out the narrative, which is something of a morality tale.

Lamb had been recommended to John Jay, the secretary of foreign affairs of the Congress, by Samuel Huntington, former president of the Congress and later lieutenant governor of Connecticut. In a letter to Jay on January 10, 1785, Huntington said that Lamb had

> formed the design of going to the Coast of Barbary where he is well acquainted having made several voyages to those Parts before the late War, and resided considerable time in that Country. He is *desirous to obtain some Aid from Congress as a Protection* [emphasis supplied], and willing to do any national Service for us in his Power.
>
> ... a Gentleman of Fidelity and mercantile Knowledge, especially in the Marine Department, of an enterprising Genius and intrepid Spirit. He hath suffered much in the late War in the Cause of his Country. I wish him success in his proposed Plan, and take the Liberty to recommend him to your favorable Notice. . . .
>
> Whether any Negotiation between these States and the Emperor of Morocco is now in Train, I am uninformed but presume yourself must be acquainted. A free and safe Navigation to his Dominions must be very advantageous to these States, if it can be obtained on just and liberal commercial principles.[7]

An experienced bureaucrat on receiving such a letter would immediately suspect that Lamb wanted to travel in an official capacity because it would facilitate some commercial purpose he had in mind. In exchange, he would attempt to carry out diplomatic tasks for which his commercial experience might, or might not, have prepared him. The nature of his knowledge of Barbary is not spelled out, but subsequent correspondence showed that he had been involved in buying mules and horses in Tangier, not the greatest (but perhaps not the worst) qualification for engaging in diplomacy. He apparently knew nothing of Algiers, Tunis, or Tripoli. Nor had he learned any of the languages that might have been useful to him. His manners and appearance were coarse, and he was argumentative, according to the reports of the American prisoners. He hardly sounds suitable for the difficult task of negotiating with a ruler as tough as Muhammad bin Uthman of Algiers.[8]

Armed with Huntington's endorsement, Lamb petitioned the Congress on February 9, 1785:

> ... believing it to be in the Interest of the United States to form some treaty of amity and Commerce with the States of Barbary; and inferring ... that it is the desire of Congress to set on foot negociations for that purpose; Your Memorialist is induced to offer his services for conducting those negociations. Your Memorialist can offer no other inducements to this trust than his zeal for the service of the United States and his knowledge of the Country, to which he desires to be sent, acquired by an intercourse of five Years and asks no reward for his services, all he requires being to have the sanction of the United States and the necessary powers to treat.[9]

Jay endorsed Lamb's petition the following day in a report to Congress, saying that in his opinion the U.S. commercial interest required treaties with the Barbary states and that presents to the rulers would be necessary to accomplish this. He thought that naval and military stores would be the most proper peace presents, that the negotiations should be under the direction of the peace commissioners, i.e., Jefferson and Adams, and that "Mr. Lamb might probably be employed by them to the advantage as an Agent in the Business."[10]

On the next day, the above-mentioned Congressional authorization to spend up to $80,000 for treaties with the Barbary states came in response to a motion by Robert Livingston of New York, seconded by John Sitgreaves of North Carolina. In addition to the money, which they were authorized to borrow in Europe, the peace commissioners were empowered "if the situation of affairs should render it inexpedient, for either of them to proceed to the above Courts, to appoint such Persons as they may deem qualified to execute this trust. ... That the Secretary for Foreign Affairs be directed to write to the above Ministers, pressing upon them the necessity of prosecuting this important business and forwarding to them Commissions and Letters of Credence *with a blank for the name of such person as may be directed to conclude the said treaties*" [emphasis supplied].[11] There was no mention of Congress having reposed faith and confidence in Mr. Lamb, or anyone else, and whether to appoint him was, in effect, left up to the commissioners.

On March 11 Jay wrote to Adams and Jefferson a letter of general instructions regarding negotiations with the Barbary states. It closes with the following about Lamb, who is identified as the bearer of the letter:

> This gentleman was recommended by the Governor of Connecticut. ... The Testimonials he has from that State contain the only Information I possess regarding his Character—They are certainly greatly in his Favor. In this matter Congress have not thought proper to interefere, and Capt. Lamb has no Encouragement either from them or from me to expect that he will be employed, it being intended to leave you in full and uninfluenced Exercise of your Discretion in appointing the Agent in question. But as Capt. Lamb informs me that he means to go to Paris, I have concluded to commit this Letter to his Care, because I am persuaded that he will be as faithful a Bearer of it as any other Person.[12]

While the above may be read as a commendable exercise in delegation of authority to the people in the field, the language immediately raises suspicions that someone had doubts about Lamb's suitability—Jay had no firsthand information about his character and does not promise him anything except a letter of introduction. A first explanation could be that in order to avoid offending the Connecticut delegation he passed the buck for rejecting him to Jefferson and Adams, who, judging by their correspondence, were uncertain what to make of the affair.

The matter is more complicated than that, however. The explanatory note with the Huntington letter in the collection of documents in *The Emerging Nation* says that Lamb had the support of Alexander Hamilton and Jay as well as prominent men from Connecticut and that this support "was linked to political and financial machinations involving the two remaining ships of the Continental Navy."[13] A fuller explanation can be found in a long editorial note in Thomas Jefferson's *Papers* (18:369–445). To summarize, the note claims that Lamb's supporters planned "to take the 32–gun Continental frigate *Alliance,* the only ship of the revolutionary navy that had not yet been sold—and present her to the emperor of Morocco. . . . The negotiation was to be conducted by Lamb as agent, sent directly from the United States." The editorial note cites "persuasive documentary evidence" that Lamb's petition was drafted by Alexander Hamilton (its language is too elegant to have been Lamb's) and speculates that the sponsors of the scheme may have hoped to purchase the vessel with depreciated securities and then sell it back to the government for hard cash from the fund authorized for the Barbary treaties.

A similar scheme also had the support, with a different recipient in mind, of Benjamin Franklin, who forwarded to Jay a January 5, 1786, letter from Charles Biddle of Philadelphia arguing that "nothing the United States could possibly employ in treating with Algiers would be so effective as the gift of the *Alliance* laden with naval stores. Such a present... would be worth more to the pirates than five times her value in specie and payment could be made in public paper which would make the Purchase easy to Congress and be of an advantage to this State [Pennsylvania]."[14]

In retrospect, Biddle's proposal might have worked. The *Alliance* was a renowned fast sailer and would have been a handsome present to the Algerines. Had Lamb gone directly to Algiers from the United States in the *Alliance,* assuming she could be refitted and loaded quickly, he could have arrived before any Americans were captured—which, as he commented ruefully in a letter to William Samuel Johnson on May 20, 1786, would have made his job much easier. Whether Lamb would have been capable of parlaying this present into a treaty is moot, but it might have been worth trying. Alternatively, it was suggested at the time, the vessel could have been the nucleus of a multinational naval effort to suppress piracy in the Mediterranean, but that too did not get approved by Congress, and the *Alliance* was sold to some Americans for $26,000 and eventually ended up in the East India trade.

Even allowing for the problems of transatlantic travel in those days, Lamb took an extraordinary amount of time to reach Paris, arriving there on September 18.[15] Jefferson noted in a letter to Adams on September 19 that Lamb brought "new full Power to us from Congress to appoint persons to negotiate with the Barbary States but we are to sign the treaties. Lamb has not even a recommendation from them to us but it seems clear that he would be approved by them."[16]

In a subsequent, and fuller, letter to Adams on September 24, Jefferson speculates that perhaps Congress had not seen fit to give Lamb an appointment out of a desire not to interfere with measures being taken by the two of them. They, impatient with the protracted delay in Lamb's arrival, had already settled on sending Barclay to Morocco and then to Algiers to negotiate, and had drawn up letters of credence for him. Jefferson proposed that instead they send Barclay to Morocco and Lamb to Algiers, where the problem had become acute with the capture of two American ships, of which they had first heard reports in mid-August. (Jefferson had already received a letter from one of the ships' captains.) Adams accepted this proposal and the two of them proceeded to execute documents of accreditation, while Jefferson endeavored to secure sponsorship by France and Spain. This occasioned further delay in the arrival of Barclay and Lamb at their destinations.

Meanwhile the Moroccan sultan, Moulay Muhammad bin Abdallah, was getting irritated because the United States had not negotiated a treaty with him. He had recognized the new republic de facto by a decree of December 20, 1777, that American vessels calling at Moroccan ports should be regarded as friendly and be given most-favored-nation treatment. This was some two months before French de jure recognition. There was no response from the Americans. In 1784 a Moroccan corsair captured the American ship *Betsey* and the sultan notified the Americans that he had not allowed the crew to be enslaved and had not sold the cargo but would release it and them as soon as they concluded a treaty. The vessel's release was nevertheless negotiated, with Spanish help, by the American chargé in Madrid, William Carmichael, in 1785, before a treaty was negotiated. By then the ship was reported to be not worth repairing.

Philosophical Differences

A famous difference of views between Adams and Jefferson on how to deal with the piracy problem surfaced after the *Betsey* incident. Adams thought paying tribute would be cheaper than building and maintaining a navy, and he doubted international cooperation on naval force was possible. Jefferson thought use of naval force would be as effective as paying tribute, probably cheaper, and more honorable. It would furthermore gain the respect of Europe, and that would safeguard American interests. Jefferson pursued the matter and drafted a proposal for an international naval force to suppress Mediterranean piracy. He was thinking in terms of six frigates, half of which would be on station at any one time, and claimed to have considerable support among the smaller European powers for the idea. Congress approved a motion directing Jefferson to go ahead with the project on July 27, 1787, but Jay reluctantly concluded that Congress was unlikely to provide the funds required and that the motion was "unseasonable by the present state of affairs."[17]

James Field, in *America and the Mediterranean World 1776–1882*, comments on this episode that "the efforts of Adams and Jefferson to open the Mediterranean to their country's commerce had at least demonstrated one of the abiding realities of American history. The practical men, the realists, are willing to make deals. It is the ideologues, even the peaceful ones, who will fight."

The Tripolitanian Ambassador

The Adams-Jefferson debate on this policy issue was also illuminated by a set of discussions with the Tripolitanian ambassador in London, whose name is given as Sidi Haji Abdul Rahman Adja. Adja had expressed an interest in seeing Adams, and the latter, evidently not anxious for such a meeting but wishing to observe protocol, paid a courtesy call on him at his residence on February 16, 1786, at an hour when he expected to find him out, and was surprised to find him in. He was further surprised to learn that the Tripolitanians considered themselves at war with the United States. Adja, however, had full powers to negotiate a peace treaty and was ready to do so. He suggested that Adams come back with an interpreter so they could discuss details. Adams remarked that the conversation had been carried on "with civility enough in a strange mixture of Italian Lingua Franca, broken French and worse English," but said Adja seemed to be "a man of good sense and temper."

Three days later Adja called on Adams, with an interpreter, and expanded on the utility of signing a treaty with Tripoli before it was too late, claiming that Algiers would follow suit, but that if any considerable number of vessels were to be captured (he doesn't say by whom) it would be hard to persuade the Algerines to desist from war. He commented that wars between Christians were mild, but war between Christians and Turks was horrible, and prisoners were sold into slavery. Adams told him the Barbary states could not expect much in the way of prizes from the Americans, who had just emerged from a calamitous war and were quite poor. To this Adja responded, "God forbid that I should consider America upon a footing at present in point of wealth with these nations. I know very well that she has but lately concluded a war which must have laid waste their territories, and I would rather leave to her own generosity the compliments to be made upon the occasion [i.e., how much he was to get in the way of commission] than stipulate anything precisely." Adams had reported earlier that Adja had told "a Gentleman" on February 15 that peace with Tripoli would cost the Americans $100,000 a year. Adams now commented that Adja was either a consummate politician or a benevolent and wise man.

Seeing here an opportunity to take care of the treaty with Tripoli, Adams sent his secretary, Colonel William Smith, to Paris to inform Jefferson of what had occurred and to ask him to come over to London to meet with Adja and also with the Portuguese minister, who now had authority to negotiate a treaty. Jefferson had long envisaged a trip to London, and this would be a good occasion for it.

Smith arrived in Paris on February 27 and returned to London with Jefferson on March 11. Adams and Jefferson met with Adja soon after and reported the results in a letter of March 28 to Jay. In brief, Adja said that peace would cost them 30,000 guineas plus 3,000 pounds for himself (roughly $172,500 at then current exchange rates or about $2.6 million in today's dollars.) Payment must be in cash, not in kind. Adams and Jefferson said they did not have that kind of money and would have to refer the matter to Congress for fresh instructions. In the March 28 letter to Jay reporting this conversation, they said that borrowing the money in Holland was the only possible way to proceed, and that if Congress gave them the authority to make the best deals they could with all the Barbary states, they would proceed accordingly. Jay, however, recommended to Congress on May 29, 1786, against authorizing them to borrow money in Europe because they probably would not obtain a sufficient amount—those states "to whom our war with the Barbary States is not disagreeable will be little inclined to lend us money to put an end to it"; no funds were available for paying interest on loans already outstanding; the unwillingness of the states to pay taxes was well known in Europe; and the United States should not borrow money without good prospect of being able to repay it. There the matter rested until January of 1787, when Adja was about to return to Tripoli and Adams informed him that no further instructions had been received. The full texts of the Adams letters concerning Adja are in volume 3 of *The Emerging Nation* and make interesting reading.

This first direct diplomatic exchange with the Muslim world seems to have been without sequel as far as negotiations with Tripoli were concerned. A treaty was eventually negotiated in 1797. (The details are in chapter 8.) The record does not indicate that the Tripolitanians made mention of the conversations with Adja, and there is no confirmation that he in fact had the authority to make an agreement that would be honored at home, although he showed Adams the original "in his own language," with a French translation, of his credentials giving him full power to treat with all the powers of Europe and maintained that it also gave him authority to negotiate with the United States.

4

The Crisis Begins

In the summer of 1785, well before Lamb and Barclay got under way, Algiers declared war on the United States and sent its corsairs out to look for American shipping. It was not quite as bad as the Tripolitanian ambassador had said it would be, but it was bad enough, and it greatly complicated Lamb's mission, which had been overtaken by events.

The Algerines seem to have had no very clear idea who the Americans were, other than that they had rebelled against Britain, which had a treaty relationship with Algiers. The Americans later blamed the British consul, Charles Logie, for having told the dey that with independence the Americans no longer enjoyed British protection and were fair game, but I have found no documentary evidence of that in the British records.

The Algerines did not send any official notification to the Americans, but by July 14, 1785, the French commandant at Toulon had reported that they considered themselves at war with the United States. The immediate result was the capture of two American vessels, the *Maria* of Boston and the *Dauphin* or *Dolphin* of Philadelphia, on July 25 and August 1 respectively. The *Maria* was taken about three miles off the Algarve coast of Portugal and the *Dauphin* about 180 miles off Portugal's west coast. Both were the incidental victims of a Spanish-Algerine truce negotiated earlier that summer.

In spite of the lack of British protection, American ships had been relatively safe in the Atlantic waters off Spain and Portugal because the Spaniards, long at war with Algiers, had prevented the Algerine fleet from venturing west of Gibraltar. The 1785 truce permitted the Algerine cruisers to go out into the Atlantic for the first time in years, and they were quick to take advantage of the opportunity. A total of three captains (one was a passenger on the *Dauphin*) and eighteen mates and men were taken prisoner on the two ships. The *Dauphin*, which was leaking, was taken to Cádiz and sold there. The fate of the *Maria* is not given in the correspondence. The crews were transferred to Algerine ships, taken to Algiers, and sold into slavery. Half of the men and one of the captains died in captivity, and most of those who survived did not see home again for eleven years. Two of the captives, Richard O'Brien, captain of the *Dauphin,* and James Leander Cathcart of the *Maria,* emerge as principal figures in the correspondence that is our basis for understanding how this drama unfolded. O'Brien in particular became the spokesman for the captives and corresponded on their behalf with Jefferson, Adams, and Washington, among others. We shall hear a good deal of him, and of Cathcart, who rose to prominence in the local power structure and left both a journal and memoirs as well as a portrait of himself. (A list of these and other captives and their fates is in appendix 4.)

O'Brien wrote to Jefferson on August 24, 1785, "our sufferings are beyond our expressing, or your conception." Cathcart described their condition in much more detail. After recounting the capture of the *Maria,* whose crew had been stripped of their clothing and possessions and been put on very meager rations, he described their arrival in Algiers:

> We arrived In Algiers on the eve of the feast of Ramadan and being private property [i.e., captured by a privately owned vessel] were conducted to the owner of the Cruiser's house, having been first entirely stripped of the remnant of our clothes which remained, and I was furnished in lieu thereof with the remains of an old dirty shirt, and brown cloth trousers which formerly belonged to a Portuguese fisherman, and were swarming with myriads of vermin, which, with the crown of an old hat, composed the whole of my wardrobe. . . . we were first carried to the Kieuchk [kiosk] or Admiralty office and permitted to regale ourselves with as much good water as we pleased, which flowed from a neat marble fountain and was as clear as crystal. . . . I shall remember the Fountain of the Kiosk of the Marine of Algiers, to the latest hour of my existence.
>
> We were marched from the Kieuchk through the principal streets and market place of Algiers and to several of the Grandee's houses followed by a mob who had gathered to view Americans, we being the first they had ever beheld, and, at last, arrived at our owner's house, having received no refreshment but water since the evening before. Here we remained but a few minutes, when we were visited by Christian slaves of all denominations, they not being at work in consequence of the festival, and those who could afford it brought us the fruits of the season, wine, bread, and everything that was cooked or could be eaten without cooking. At our owner's house we were all put into an empty room, on the ground floor, where we all sat or laid on the bare bricks. In the center of the area was placed a large cauldron in which clothes had lately been boiled, filled with water, and a quantity of coarse flesh, which we supposed to be ordinary beef, but afterwards was informed was camel's flesh, which prevented us from tasting it. This enraged our

master considerably and he declared he never would put himself to so much expense again to accommodate Christian slaves. . . .

Thus forlorn, without food or raiment, anticipating the horrors of a miserable captivity, we stretched ourselves on the bare bricks where we remained all night, tormented with vermin and mosquitoes, and at daylight were driven down to the marine to unbend [take down] the sails and do other necessary work of the Cruisers that had captured us. . . .

The next day we were taken in a kind of procession, to several of the Grandee's houses whom we had not visited on our arrival and who were curious to see Americans, having supposed us to be the aborigines of the country, of which some of them had an imperfect idea from viewing figures which ornament charts of that continent, and were much surprised to see us so fair, as they expressed themselves, so much like Englishmen. Ultimately we were taken to the British Consul's house who had ordered us some refreshments and passed his word to our Master that he would be answerable for our conduct while in his house. . . . But even here we were made sensible of our situation and exposed to new species of indignities which we did not expect and therefore felt in a superlative degree.

We remained here two days and on the third, in the morning, were marched to the Bedistan or Slave Market where we remained from daylight until half past three o'clock without any refreshments, and were treated thus for three days successively. . . . on the afternoon of the third we were taken into the Dey's palace and paraded before his Excellency when, of our crew, he took five, only leaving Capt. Stephens . . . for the service of the palace. . . . We were now taken to the hot bath by the other Christian slaves and cleansed from the filth of the Cruiser, our old rags were changed for a large shirt with open sleeves and a large pair of cotton trousers, a pair of shoes and a red cap, all made in Turkish fashion, in which no doubt, we made a curious appearance. We were allowed to remain together that night and fared sumptuously in comparison to what we had some time before, and, being clean, slept for several hours as sound as any people could do in our situation. In the morning we awakened much refreshed, and were stationed at our respective duties; two were retained as upper servants, one was sent to the kitchen and myself and another were doomed to labor in the palace garden, where we had not a great deal to do, there being fourteen of us, and, the taking care of two lions, two tigers and two antelopes excepted, the work might very well have been done by four.[1]

Cathcart, who sounds compulsively impertinent, had a difficult time with the head gardener and was finally consigned to the bagnios, where he had a much more difficult time, before gradually working his way up to become the dey's chief Christian secretary, but we shall deal with that later. The point for now is that Cathcart and his shipmates were very lucky to be assigned to the palace instead of having to work in the quarries, as much of the crew of the *Dauphin* had to do when they arrived.

The ships' officers were also treated relatively liberally. They were required to wear an iron bracelet on one ankle as a sign of their status, but they were not confined and were allowed to move around the town rather freely as parolees. Captain O'Brien describes their condition a year after his capture:

> We are treated with the greatest civility by all the French and Spaniards here. An account of how we are situated and where
> 4 of us in the house of Monsr. Ford [a British merchant]
> 7 in the Dey's palace [of whom five were from the *Maria*]
> 9 in the marine
> 1 at the Swedish Consuls—[2]

The four in Mr. Ford's house would have been Captains O'Brien of the *Dauphin,* Stephens of the *Maria,* and Coffin, who was a passenger on the *Dauphin,* plus one of the two first mates. The other mate evidently was with the Swedish consul. The seven at the dey's palace were younger members of the crews who were made servants and were relatively well fed and housed.[3] The nine in the marine were at hard labor on bread and olives, and living in considerable squalor. While the five officers lodged separately were in reasonable comfort, Cathcart claims that initially they were placed as servants in British consul Logie's house, a condition he found shameful:

> Captain O'Brien, Stephens and Coffin . . . were immediately taken to the British Consul's house to serve as domestics where they remained suffering every indignity that inhumanity could devise to render their situation humiliating in the extreme until the arrival of the Count de Expilly [the Spanish representative] who by orders of Mr. Carmichael, Charge des Affaires at Madrid, took them under his protection and hired a house where they lived very comfortably for a time upon the supplies furnished them by Mr. Carmichael and their friends in the palace. The Mates were also taken out of the Marine and placed with the Captains, but the Mariners were left at hard labor [and] were only allowed three masoons a day to clothe and maintain them which is equal to 7½ cents.[4] (O'Brien does not mention in his correspondence the humiliating circumstances described by Cathcart.)

Lamb and Barclay

Lamb spent perhaps six weeks in Paris—his date of departure is not given, but he arrived in Madrid on December 29–while Jefferson and Adams completed administrative arrangements. In addition to preparing letters of credence for both him and Barclay, they established special financial procedures for Lamb, who was not authorized to draw (write checks) directly on a bank but would be required to draw on Adams, who would be able to monitor what he was doing. Paul R. Randall, an American from New York then in London whom Barclay had recommended for his "integrity and capacity," was chosen to accompany Lamb and keep an eye on him. Lamb's letters drawing on Adams were to be written by Randall, who had left a writing sample with Adams. This would place some control on Lamb's spending.

Barclay was authorized to draw $20,000 and Lamb $40,000, since he was also supposed to negotiate a treaty with Tunis. If all went well, there would be $20,000 left for Tripoli. Lamb was also given a letter dated October 11 authorizing him to negotiate the release of the prisoners from the *Dauphin* and the *Maria*. In it Jefferson and Adams explained that, although they had no instructions to do so, they presumed that it would be the will of Congress that the prisoners be redeemed and they "trust to their [the Congress's] goodness and the purity of our own motives for our justification." The letter concluded that they did not expect Lamb to redeem the captives for less than $100 per head "and we should be fearful to go beyond the double of that sum, however we trust much in your discretion & good management for obtaining them on terms still better than these if possible."[5] This language could be read as leaving the door open to Lamb to go beyond $200 per man.

On the same day, the commissioners addressed a letter to the comte de Vergennes, referring to article 8 of the Treaty of Amity and Commerce and the French promise to use their good offices when the United States was ready to enter into negotiations with the Barbary powers, and informing him that Barclay and Lamb were about to set off for Morocco and Algiers. This was sent under cover of a letter from Jefferson to Vergennes dated October 12 saying that, while Barclay was leaving in a few days, "Mr. Lamb . . . waits to be the bearer of such letters as you may think necessary for manifesting the interest his Majesty will be so good as to take in these negotiations." The Jefferson letter suggested that "Letters of protection for their persons, effects, vessels & attendants during their passage to & from Africa and their stay there seem to be the first requisite; to which such others will be added for procuring favorable dispositions on the part of those powers as you shall think proper to honor them with."[6]

Vergennes's reaction is not reported in the documents, but from the French archives and Lamb's report described below it is evident that Lamb was given a sealed letter addressed to the French consul in Algiers. That letter and its coded supplement are discussed later.

Finally, Jefferson wrote on October 22 to the conde de Aranda, the Spanish minister to France, asking that the luggage of Barclay and Lamb, who were traveling via Madrid, not be searched when they crossed into Spain. He noted that Barclay was carrying "about a thousand guineas worth of watches, rings, and other things of that nature; he who goes to Algiers takes about a fourth of that value." These items were to be used as presents to functionaries in Morocco and Algiers. Aranda replied on the same day that he could give them passports to the interior of Spain but did not have the power to prevent their luggage from being inspected.[7] In the event, neither Barclay nor Lamb reported any problems with the Spanish customs.

Barclay Succeeds

Barclay's departure from Paris was delayed by his involvement in the settlement of the accounts of Beaumarchais, the playwright (*The Barber of Seville* and *The Marriage of Figaro*), arising from the latter's role as a clandestine supplier of arms to the Americans during the Revolution. He left Paris in mid-January 1786 accompanied by Lt. Col. David S. Franks,[8] traveling via Lorient and Bordeaux, where he had business to take care of, and then on to Madrid, where he arrived on March 10. He did not arrive in "Morocco" (Marrakesh) until June 21, but a treaty was agreed on two days later, reflecting the continued interest of the sultan, Moulay Muhammad, in such an agreement. Although Barclay's expenses were almost £5,000, indicating that he must have spent some $20,000 on presents, there was, remarkably, no stipulation that the United States would pay tribute. The Spanish were given credit for helping with the negotiations, but what made the sultan so anxious for peace with America has never been satisfactorily explained. It was a logical sequel to his order of December 20, 1777, that American ships in Moroccan waters be given most-favored-nation treatment, but that action has also not been satisfactorily explained. Whatever the reason, this treaty was the beginning of a friendly relationship that has persisted, with only an occasional hitch, down to the present.[9]

Lamb Fails

Jefferson also wrote on November 4 to Carmichael in Madrid, explaining Lamb's mission and saying that he and Barclay were passing by Madrid solely for the purpose of seeing Carmichael "as we are assured they will receive from you lights which may be useful to them." Jefferson noted that

Lamb's "manner and appearance are not promising, but he is a sensible man and seems to possess some talents which may be proper in a matter of bargain."[10]

Carmichael, however, wrote to Jay on December 9 saying Lamb, far from just seeking advice, had arrived with a letter from Adams and Jefferson asking him to interest the court of Spain in his favor. Carmichael said he had legitimate reasons for not writing to the foreign minister on the subject, but he was confident that the Americans could rely on the good offices of the court. Carmichael was subsequently assured by the foreign minister that the Spanish, as soon as they had finished their own negotiations for a treaty of peace that would replace the then current truce with Algiers, would hasten to help the Americans to the best of their abilities.[11]

Lamb left Madrid for Barcelona on February 1, 1786, and sailed from the latter port on March 11 in a fifty-ton brig he had purchased but which was flying a Spanish flag, perhaps in order to avoid capture as an American vessel. According to Randall, Lamb bought the brig as the most efficient way of reaching Algiers. He evidently planned to sell its unidentified cargo somewhere and thereby make money on the side. He and Randall did not arrive in Algiers until March 25, after a difficult voyage. He left on April 20, having failed either to negotiate a peace treaty or to ransom the American prisoners.

In his report to Jefferson of May 20 on his return to Madrid, Lamb said that the delay in his arrival was caused by a fruitless wait in Madrid for some "infuluence [sic] from that court." Four or five days before he left Algiers, he received from Carmichael an "open letter"—presumably meaning one that was unsealed, in contrast to the sealed letter given him by the French—from the court of Spain in favor of his mission, but the Spanish representative in Algiers, the comte d'Expilly, had already said he would not make use of such a letter if it came. Lamb commented later that Expilly had kept him in the dark as much as he could, but he seemed to share Carmichael's belief the Spaniards would help once their own negotiations were finished.

For his part, Expilly wrote to Carmichael on April 20, the day of Lamb's departure, to say that he had not trifled with Lamb but had explained to him that his "unseasonal" arrival would effect nothing because the dey had declared to him some days before that he would negotiate with no power about peace that had not previously concluded it with the Ottoman court in Constantinople. This idea was current among consuls in Algiers at the time, and Jefferson later asked Vergennes about it. Vergennes told him it would "not procure them a peace for one penny less." Vergennes, who had been ambassador in Constantinople, described the suzerainty of the sultan over Algiers as being purely nominal, saying that "the Barbary states acknowledged a sort of vassalage to the Porte, & availed themselves of that relation when anything was to be gained by it: but that whenever it subjected them to a demand from the Porte they totally disregarded it: that money was the sole agent at Algiers, except so far as fear could be induced also."[12] Lamb was told essentially the same thing by the wakil al-kharj in Algiers.

Accounts of what transpired in Algiers conflict on various details, some of which are more important than others. Randall's report of the visit, for instance, indicates that they lodged with the French consul, Jean-Baptiste de Kercy, but O'Brien says Lamb stayed with Logie. Lamb does not specify where he slept, but perhaps he stayed with de Kercy until Randall left and then moved in with Logie, with whom he could converse in English. In his May 20 report to Jefferson, Lamb said that the treatment he had received from the French consul was "Polite indeed he paid me Greate atention. Mr. Logie Likewise rec'd me as an ould friend and Declared to me that he had no orders to counter act my mission from his court, which I am sure of."

According to Randall, on March 27, at the suggestion of de Kercy and Expilly (who was also lodged with the Frenchman), the dragoman of the French consulate was sent to see the dey and request an audience for Lamb. The dey replied "That if we came on the Subject of Peace he would not see us, but if we wished to visit him & talk to him on other matters he would be glad to see us." Lamb mentions this response from the dey in a letter of March 28 to Jay that he sent with Randall. In it he estimates that ransom of the prisoners would cost upwards of $35,000.[13]

In his report to Jefferson the following day, Lamb quotes a lesser estimate of the ransom required but says that within three or four days of his arrival it became clear that the entire amount of money at his disposal would not ransom the captives and he had therefore dispatched Randall to Europe on the thirtieth of March (four days before he was received by the dey) to inform Jefferson of what had transpired. The letter he gave Randall to take to Jefferson is worth quoting in full:

Algiers 29th March 1786

This is by Mr. Randall, whom will tell to Your Excellency my situation at present; I am sure by the best information the sum will by no means answer our object, if the amount is not greatly Ogmented. It is my Duty to advise to abandon the undertaking as it will be intirely in vane to parsivear. It is lost money the expences that arise on the attemt: the last amount I can give please to let me know. I shall wate at Cahrthergina for the same. The people will cost for their redemption at least Twelve hundred heard Dollars pr. head; the number is Twenty-one. Your Excellency sees how feable we are. I have good reason to think that peace may be made with these People but it will cost a Tower

[tour] to Constantinople. Much may be Done in france if they please to forward our peace here. If we fight these people five Thirty six Gun Frigates will be the leas force and Two larg Tenders. Your Excellency hath an account of the place by Mr. Randall and I shall Indeavor to secure as much as I can. I shall leave a safety here for a future coming to this place. Have desird Mr. Randall to make all possible Dispatch.

With due respect, etc.[14]

Thus, Lamb had decided even before seeing the dey that his mission was hopeless unless he had a greatly augmented sum of money to work with. He evidently wanted Jefferson to know this as soon as possible, but this meant sending away prematurely the man who was assigned as his secretary and whose signature was needed on his drafts on Adams. Randall explained in his letter to his father mentioned below that there was a Spanish navy vessel leaving and he had left sooner than expected in order to take advantage of its departure. He was careful to obtain a certificate that he was departing at Lamb's orders. Perhaps Lamb was glad to be rid of him. Judging by his letters, Randall was overly deferential and he may have grated on Lamb's nerves. It seems that relations between them were not cordial: Randall wrote to his father that before departure he had asked Lamb what he could say to Jefferson and Adams except that the dey refused to treat of peace, but Lamb would not answer and would not give him any instructions.

Lamb had thought he was sending Randall off to Paris with his gloomy message, but on arriving back in Madrid on May 17 he found that Randall, apparently ill, had gone no further than the resort town of Aranjuez, thirty miles south of Madrid. Randall had, however, forwarded to Adams and Jefferson on May 14 copies of a long, newsy letter of April 2 to his father describing the five days he spent in Algiers with Lamb and giving many details on the state of affairs there, evidently responding to instructions from Adams and/or Jefferson to report on the economy and military capabilities. (A similar report was written by Barclay for Morocco. The full texts of these early examples of Foreign Service reporting can be seen at pages 3:139 and 3:296 of *The Emerging Nation*.) In a covering letter, Randall explained that he had been waiting for a "secure opportunity" for forwarding his report. It appears, however, that he had earlier forwarded to New York Lamb's March 28 report to Jay.

In his letter of May 20 Lamb said he met with the dey on April 3 and found that he would not discuss a peace treaty and set an exorbitant price for ransoming the captives. He saw him again on the seventh and found him of the same mind. He met him for a third time on April 17, and while the dey came down slightly, the price was still enormous. Lamb then, through distribution of presents, managed to see the wakil al-kharj, Hasan, who told him that he personally wanted to see a peace with America, that Lamb should not be put off by the price set by the dey, which was a bargaining ploy in the more important negotiations with the Spanish, and that nothing could be accomplished until those negotiations were over.[15] He advised Lamb to return to Spain and wait until the Spanish negotiations were completed, and promised to write to him at that point. (The French consul, on the other hand, thought that success of the Spanish negotiations would diminish the regency's interest in concluding a peace with America.)

The dey's final price on April 17 as reported by Lamb was:

$6000 per captain x 3	$18,000
$4000 per mate x 2	$8,000
$4000 per passenger x 2	$8,000
$1400 per seaman x 14	$19,600
	$53,600
Plus the dey's usual 11 percent	$5,896
Total	$59,496

(The two "passengers" are not identified. One was presumably Capt. Coffin. The other was perhaps Jacob Tessanier, the French "boy" on the *Dauphin*.)

Subsequent allegations raised doubts about Lamb's account. Captains O'Brien, Stephens, and Coffin wrote to Jefferson on June 8, 1786, saying that Lamb had offered $10,000 for the prisoners.[16] Then O'Brien wrote on July 12 to say that Lamb had "Actually agreed with the Dey of Algiers for the redemption of us unfortunate captives. It is near three months since mr. Lamb left Algiers and was to get the money in four months. I hope for our sakes, & the honor of his country, that he will not deviate from his word with the Dey of Algiers. We received a few lines from mr. Lamb by the Spanish Brig. Mr. Lamb says he had stated our situation to you some months ago and that he had not received any answer from you or Mr. Adams and therefore cannot tell what will be determined on our behalf."[17]

The captives subsequently wrote to Adams on February 13, 1787, that Lamb had in fact had four audiences with the dey and had offered first $10,000 and then $30,000 as ransom, and they criticized him for having given the impression that he had accepted the dey's price. Three years later, in a letter of July 12, 1790, O'Brien claimed that he understood from two Jewish merchants that Lamb had agreed to the dey's full price and promised to return with the money but never did, and that the dey's justifiable irritation delayed and complicated subsequent negotiations.[18]

Cathcart gave an even more circumstantial account. In *The Captives* (38–39) he claimed that Lamb had *five* meetings with the dey, and that on the fourth meeting the dey had knocked his share, 10 per cent [*sic*], off the price and had offered to release the captives for $48,300, a price Lamb had accepted, although he could not promise to return with the cash in less than four months (the dey's offer seems to have been that he would both reduce the amount by 10 percent and forgo his 11 percent). Lamb had then gone to the French consul's house, from which he was summoned shortly thereafter and asked by the dey if he was perfectly content with the agreement he had made, to which Lamb had responded that he would have been more content if the price were lower, but that he "ratified the agreement" and hoped that the dey would be disposed to listen to proposals for peace once the ransom was paid. The dey had replied, "Make peace with your father the King of England and then come to me and I will make peace with you." He then ordered his principal secretary to record in the books of the regency that Lamb had agreed to ransom the prisoners for $48,300 and to return in four months with the money.

On page 49 of the manuscript "A Concise Account of Negotiations" among his papers in the Library of Congress, Cathcart claims that on April 7 (or 17?) he had "waited on Mr. Lamb in the upper gallery [of the palace]. He desired me to keep up my spirits that all was settled that I might depend we would be released in less than four months and that he would bring the money himself to Algiers in order that no unnecessary delay might be made in its transportation." This account, written well after the events—it is undated but, given other dates in the manuscript, was written at least seven years after Cathcart's release from captivity in 1796—may have been embroidered, but it is clear from the record that there was tenacious belief among both the captives and the Algerines that Lamb had promised to come back with the money in four months.

Lamb gives no hint of any such agreement in his report, but his letters, such as that of March 29 to Jefferson, show that he hoped for further instructions as to how much more ransom he could pay. He even made arrangements to facilitate a return to Algiers to resume negotiations ("I shall leave a safety"—a reference to unspecified commercial goods of his that he left with the British merchant John Wolfe at Algiers), although he did not in fact go back there because his further negotiating instructions never came.

Instead, Jefferson wrote to Lamb at Alicante on June 20 saying that, judging by his comments and those of Randall and Carmichael, the sum demanded for the prisoners was "infinitely beyond our powers" and the whole matter should be referred back to Congress. He therefore asked Lamb, in his name and Adams's, to go immediately to New York to report to Congress, suggesting that he go via Paris as possibly being quicker and more expedient than trying to find a ship from Alicante to America.[19]

While Jefferson evidently felt that he and Adams had no authority to offer more, and that they were already acting beyond their authority in permitting any offer at all, his response perhaps reflected the fact that on February 24 he had received a January 19 letter from James Monroe, partly in cipher, briefly describing the *Alliance* affair and reporting that Lamb was "from his station in life & probable talents by no means worthy of such a trust." He may also have heard by mid-June that on May 2 Charles Pinckney had declared in Congress that Lamb was "not a sober Man but of a Loose character unfit for that purpose, that he was surprised that Congress appointed such a person, etc."[20]

Lamb replied on July 15, saying that he learned from Jefferson's letters that Randall (who was in Bordeaux on June 20) had not yet arrived in Paris with his full explanation of affairs in Algiers, that his health would not permit him to travel at the moment, and if that was not sufficient excuse for a delay he had no desire to continue in the job and requested that his accounts be settled in Europe as had been promised him before he left the U.S. He concluded by saying that something should be done about the unfortunate Americans in Algiers, to whom he had given more than $800 for clothing and expenses.[21]

Lamb wrote to Jefferson again on July 18 to confirm his previous letter and to repeat that he was indisposed and could not travel to the United States as requested.[22] He said his letter and Randall's had fully informed the Congress as to what had transpired and that he could add nothing by being present. He gave a fuller explanation of his "Greate Expectations of a Settlement with that Regency by next Season." He added that he was aware that various "Gentlemen" had written erroneous accounts of his conversations with the Algerines and that they knew nothing of his business. This letter was received by Jefferson on August 4. Jefferson and Adams wrote to him again on September 26 expressing regret at his indisposition but reiterating their request that he travel to the United States as soon as possible. Meanwhile they could not settle his accounts in Europe.[23]

Lamb seems not to have taken these orders very seriously. He arrived in Boston on August 5, 1787, but did not report to Jay in New York until April 10, 1788. The *Emerging Nation* volume does not contain any report to Congress of his conversation(s) with Jay or others, but a congressional resolution of September 13, 1788, authorizing the use of U.S. funds for the provision of subsistence to the captives looks to have been designed to permit, among other things, reimbursement to Lamb for the $800 he claimed to have expended on their behalf.

What Really Happened?

Who was telling the truth about what Lamb did in Algiers? Are we dealing here with a bagnio rumor that assumed the status of fact in the minds of people brooding over the affair? It seems strange that, if Lamb had reached some tentative agreement, he would not have mentioned it and made an effort to obtain authorization to pay for it. He may have been uncouth and ungrammatical, but he sounds rational—"sensible," Jefferson had said—and should have known that he would have to make a specific proposal to Jefferson if he expected to receive money to carry out a transaction.

On the other hand, Lamb's prose is elliptical, and he may have thought that he was making such a proposal in his letter of May 20. He could perhaps have taken Jefferson's language of June 20 to the effect that the Algerine demands were "so infinitely beyond our powers and the expectations of Congress, that it has become our duty to refer the whole matter back to them" as indicating that instructions one way or the other would be forthcoming, even though Jefferson's immediate instructions were for him to return home.

That Lamb was hoping for more substantive instructions is also indicated by his correspondence with William Samuel Johnson, the Connecticut Congressman. On December 24, 1785, he had written from Madrid, well before he sailed for Algiers, saying that the amount he was authorized to offer was insufficient and asking Johnson to lay the case before Congress and press for their orders "wheather I am to promis more or to act on this sum which I have at Command." Then, back in Madrid on May 20, 1786, he wrote to Johnson again, enclosing a copy of his letter of the same day to Jefferson and asked him to lay it before Mr. Jay, "as I have no further power to write to Congress."[24]

Furthermore, as we have seen, when Lamb sent Randall off to Europe, he sent with him the letter to Jay in which he said that the dey had refused to discuss peace, that ransoming the prisoners would take upwards of $35,000, and that he would await Jay's further commands.

It is also possible that Lamb left Algiers with the firm intention of making a specific proposal to Jefferson but thought better of it by the time he sat down to write to him. Or perhaps he decided to wait until he heard from the wakil al-kharj. In that regard, he gives a somewhat expanded account of his meeting with Hasan in a letter of July 18, 1786, from Alicante:

> I had commd. an Acquaintance with one of the princaple officers at Algiers, and from him I had Greate Expectations of a Settlement with that Regency by the next Season, Or at least to have the last price for Our unfortunate people, and what they would have for peace, and to

Strive for hostile proceedings to sease for one year, so that Congress might have more time to prepare, and supposd. that in case I brought to pass the above which I had every Incouragement of, it would at least be worth the Expences we have allreadi been at. these ware my reasons and these my Prospect and in consequence of the same thought best to Porseveor. and Exiboted as Soon as I possible Could to ministers and Likewise to Congress., as I well know how far Short the Apropriation was for the peace and that none could be Added to it by gentlemen Abroad; it is my Opinion that it is out of the Power of the united States to force those people to a compliance of a peace, and to have them Going on in the manner they Do it is not so well. to buy a peace will no Doubt cost a considerable Sum; but however notions of a Strong navy hath Given the preference to a purchase &c.[25]

Lamb was not wrong to expect something further from the wakil al-kharj. There was an unanswered letter of February 25, 1787, to Congress from "Sidji Assan Nickilange [Hasan the wakil al-kharj] of the Marine of Algiers" that read:

> I cannot omit writing to your Excellencies, to inform you that Mr. Lamb has been here at Algiers and having treated and spoken on certain Points respecting Peace and Captives, went away and has not returned; and to Assure you that he is a Gentleman of good Deportment, and I really like and esteem him for his good Qualities, as I have also written to Mr. Carmichael at Madrid; and I shall be well content with the said Mr. Lamb in preference to any other Person, whenever it shall be proposed to treat on any Point. And this I have the Honor to communicate to your Excellencies for your Information and Satisfaction—
> May God preserve your Excellencies many Years.
> Sidji Asan Nickillange
> [Superintendent] of the Marine of Algiers[26]

Although it is possible that the letter was stimulated by Lamb, it seems clear that Hasan was expecting to hear further from the Americans. That he received no response may help explain his angry reaction when the subject came up again in 1793, after he had become dey.

In a letter of June 1, 1792, to John Paul Jones (discussed in the next chapter), Jefferson commented on this story:

> He [Lamb] proceeded to Algiers but his mission proved fruitless. He wrote us word from thence, that the Dey asked 59,496 dollars for the twenty-one captives and that it was not probable he would abate much from that price, but he never intimated an idea of agreeing to give it. As

he has never settled the accounts of his mission, no further information has been received. It has been said that he entered into a positive stipulation with the Dey, to pay for the prisoners the price above mentioned, or something near it; and that he came away with an assurance to return with the money. We cannot believe the fact is true; and if it were, we disavow it totally, as far beyond his power. We have never disavowed it formally because it never has come to our knowledge with any degree of certainty.[27]

Whatever the truth was, the Algerines evidently believed their version was correct, and that became more important than the facts.

In setting a price that the United States would be willing to pay for the prisoners, Jefferson had sought guidance from the Mathurins, the French branch of the Trinitarian order devoted to the ransoming of Christian captives in Muslim hands. He may have been misled by their experience. They had just paid somewhat more than $200 per head to ransom three hundred French captives. Three hundred at $200 each would not have been all that much money, but twenty-one Americans at the same unit price, or $4,200, would have been a good deal less.

The going price for captives during this period varied from time to time and depending on the circumstances and the status of the prisoner, but $200 a head was obviously not enough. It might have been better if the Americans had consulted the Spanish about current prices and had not entered into negotiations if they were unable to be more realistic, but Jefferson seemed not to realize how far off the mark he was.

In Jefferson's defense, he and Adams had to work with very limited means and authority for a government that was notoriously dysfunctional and impoverished. They were authorized only to negotiate a treaty of peace, not to ransom captives, because there had been none when Congress voted the treaty money. They were being realistic by their lights. The $80,000 they were authorized to spend, reduced to $55,000 by Barclay's expenditures in Morocco, would have been sufficient to ransom the prisoners in Algiers, but it would not have bought a peace treaty, and there would have been nothing left for negotiating with Tunis and Tripoli. On the other hand, the entire $55,000 would not have sufficed to buy peace with the latter two in any event. In hindsight, spending all of it on ransom in Algiers would have saved a number of lives, and the final cost to the United States might have been less, but Jefferson and Adams could not be expected to know that.

Although Jefferson may have thought peace with all of Barbary could be bought for the $80,000 authorized, others knew from the start that it was insufficient. Lamb said so repeatedly in his letters before leaving Spain for

Algiers, and the delegates to Congress seemed to agree, judging by the comments to be found in *Letters of Delegates to Congress*[28] and by their appointment of a six-man committee on March 29, 1786, to consider the problem of Algiers. It recommended on April 5 that a way be found to borrow money "for the purpose of securing the commerce of the United States against the Depredations of the Barbary States" and that Congress "turn their earliest attention" to the creation of a navy.[29] Six years passed before sufficient peace-and-ransom money was authorized.

If it is true that Lamb went beyond his instructions and offered as much as $30,000 for ransom, or $1,500 a man, and the dey rejected the offer, that could conceivably indicate that someone was urging the dey not to bargain, perhaps telling him the Americans were rich. The captives suspected that Charles Logie, the British consul, was doing just that. But supply and demand was a more likely explanation. In his report of May 20, 1786, Lamb commented: "The price the Spaniards are giving for their people is little short of what is charged us; and they have eleven hundred men and some upwards in Algiers. It will cost Spain more than one million and one half of dollars for their slaves only. The peace of Spain, and their slaves will amount to more than three millions of dollars." The amount of cash Algiers was about to receive, and the shortage of slaves that would result from the redemption of Spanish prisoners, may have been the prime considerations affecting the dey's attitude. He was in no financial need to strike a bargain, and prisoners were an increasingly scarce commodity in the local economy. He told Lamb, according to Cathcart, that the Americans were wanted for work and were the best sailors the Algerines had. Meanwhile the Algerines had plenty of bread and olives with which to feed them, and if Lamb did not choose to pay the sum demanded, he was free to leave them.

Lamb at least had a more realistic view after going to Algiers of what it was going to cost, but he was still short of the mark. His estimate of $1,200 per head was only half right. When the affair was over some ten years later, the United States had spent a total sum for a peace treaty and ransom of the captives that averaged roughly $10,000 per man, $2,500 of which was for ransom.

Perfidious France

As noted, when Jefferson requested French support for Lamb's mission, Vergennes responded with a sealed letter that Lamb delivered to the French consul in Algiers. A copy from the French archives at Nantes of that letter, which Lamb said "was of no consequence," is in appendix 5. The document, addressed to de Kercy, refers to the French court's commitment in the treaty of 1778 to use its good offices with the Barbary regencies and says: "His Majesty therefore charges you to render to Mr. Lamb all the services which you can and which comport with the nature of their propositions and claims to the regency. I do not doubt your eagerness not to forget anything to facilitate, to the extent you can, the success of Mr. Lamb's negotiations."

In the same archival folder, however, is a cryptogram sent to de Kercy, dated October 31, 1785. Also in the folder is the plain-text original. It tells de Kercy:

> On the 23d of this month I gave Mr. Lamb, agent of the United States to the Dey of Algiers, a letter of recommendation for you. You will easily sense that there is no advantage to us in their [the Americans] procuring a tranquil navigation in the Mediterranean. You will therefore limit yourself to giving them satisfaction to the extent that you can acquit yourself outwardly of the king's promise, but you will not go further, and above all you will avoid démarches and demands effectively pronounced in a negotiation in the success of which we have no real interest."30

De Kercy's report on Lamb's mission, which was contained in his *bulletin de nouvelles* attached to his dispatch number 13 of June 23, 1786, said, "M. Lamb, the American agent, arrived in Algiers from Barcelona on 9 [sic] March, and left on 20 April for Alicante. The Dey did not want to enter into any discussion concerning peace negotiations with the Americans and he placed a very high price on ransoming those of that nation who are in slavery [here]."31

In an attachment to this dispatch, de Kercy recounted details of Lamb's ownership of the Spanish brig on which he arrived and which, according to de Kercy, Lamb's old friend Logie tried to get the Algerines to seize as enemy property. De Kercy congratulated himself on having advised Lamb to go to Spain to await the orders of Congress rather than wait in Algiers, where one could always find oneself exposed to disagreeable incidents. He was probably alluding to the possibility that Lamb's vessel could be seized and Lamb himself imprisoned as a national of a state with which Algiers was at war. De Kercy's report of this incident indicates that the vessel had been sold to Expilly and Lamb had already departed by the time Logie received word from his colleague at Barcelona that it was Lamb's property. Logie went to the wakil al-kharj anyway and told him the vessel was American property, to no effect. De Kercy commented that Logie thought he had kept his actions secret, but he was mistaken. De Kercy's account of the vessel's status is not confirmed by Lamb. In his letter of May 20 to Jefferson, Lamb said he had to buy the "packet" as the only way to travel, that he had loaded it with freight, and that although he had consigned it to Expilly on his departure, he still owned it.

De Kercy's advice may have been motivated by genuine concern for Lamb's welfare, but one cannot help wondering whether he was trying to frighten Lamb away. If that was his intent, he succeeded. It would be interesting to see if he reported anything by cipher. (I found no such message in the French archives.)

In any event, it is clear that de Kercy followed his coded instructions and did nothing to help Lamb reach an agreement with Algiers, beyond being polite and friendly and presenting Lamb's request for an audience to the dey. He seems to have done this very skillfully, and received good marks from the Americans for generosity, but Lamb noted sourly that only a letter from the French court to the regency, and not to the consul, would have had an effect. Subsequent events indicate that Jefferson and others did not realize that France had not in fact given Lamb any backing to speak of, and that they continued to harbor illusions about French desires to be helpful.

Perfidious Albion

Lamb, then, was alone, although he may not have realized it fully. In particular, he could not count on the British, who, according to the Algerines, actively sought to frustrate his efforts and those of subsequent envoys, despite Logie's claim to Lamb that he had no orders to do so. Lamb seems not to have understood the British attitude, and continued to correspond with Logie after his departure, according to the American prisoners.

O'Brien and the Algerines made much of the fact that Lamb spoke no language but English. Logie may have been the only official of any nation with whom he could speak without an interpreter. This plus the fact that Lamb knew Logie from his horse-trading visits to Tangiers could explain his staying with him when the French consul's house would have been more appropriate.

O'Brien called Charles Logie the "bosom friend" of Lamb and was deeply suspicious of Logie's intentions. Indeed, he was convinced that none of the major powers—Spain, France, or England—had an interest in seeing a successful conclusion to the American negotiations, although he expressed thanks for the "civility and attention" that had been paid to the captives by Expilly and de Kercy.[32]

Logie, whose father, George Logie, had been Swedish consul in Algiers, was a former naval lieutenant who had served as British consul general at Tangiers from 1772 to 1782. He left there under a cloud—the British were having difficult times with the Moroccans and the sultan evidently did not like him. He was appointed to Algiers as consul general in 1785 and arrived in July of that year.[33] Playfair says Logie was removed from Algiers in 1791 to make room for Charles Mace, then consul in Gibraltar. In fact, the documents in the PRO show that Logie had asked for a leave of absence for health reasons in December 1790 but did not actually leave Algiers until January 1794, when Mace finally arrived.[34]

The American documents do not say much about what sort of person Charles Logie was, although in his letter of September 13, 1786, O'Brien called him "a proper mischief maker, a good spy for the Algerines." His father, who claimed descent from the kings of Scotland, was unpopular with both the British and the French. The French consul Le Maire, whose remarks to his successor were mentioned in chapter 1, had this to say about the senior Logie:

"Mr. Logie plans to leave Algiers and that will be very good for the Europeans who live there. A nasty man by choice and by the pleasure he takes in dark deeds, he has done ill to all the foreigners and principally the French, whom he hates by educational principle, having been born Scottish. He would have sold his God and his country to the Algerines if he could have derived some benefit to his fortune and his credit."

This estimate of George Logie's character is supported by British accounts of his efforts to spoil the ground for the British consul in 1729–30.[35] It would be unfair to visit Charles Logie's father's character upon him, and there are indications here and there of a humane spirit on his part, but, as we shall see, in carrying out his orders zealously he bears a good deal of responsibility for the disaster that befell U.S. shipping later in our story.

As noted earlier, Logie was involved with the captives from the time of their arrival in Algiers. In a letter to London dated December 20, 1785, Logie mentions the existence of "12 American slaves here" and encloses "a petition from 12 British men captured by Algerians under American colours. . . . The two ships [one] from Philadelphia was captured in July 1785, the other was from Boston. All the 12 men stated their previous work and how they were forced to serve under the American colours or as passengers. They were aged between 17 years old & 25 years old. Most of them were Scots or from north Britain."

The text of this petition is in appendix 6. Note that one of the signers is James Cathcart, who makes much of his steadfast American nationality in his later writings.

It sounds from the petition as though the seamen claiming British nationality were "forced" to sail on American ships by circumstances and were not victims of press gangs. They do not in fact mention impressment but only imply it. For some, the claim of British nationality was undoubtedly genuine.

There were large numbers of foreign nationals, including British subjects, working as seamen on American vessels, even including ships of war, in this era. Captain William Bainbridge of the ill-fated *Philadelphia,* for instance, estimated in 1804 that three-fourths of the crew being held prisoner in Tripoli were British and wondered whether it might be "policy" to ask Admiral Nelson to seek their release.[36] Similarly, Captain Edward Preble of the *Constitution,* when in the process of recruiting her crew, remarked in July 1803 that of the 165 men he had on board, he did not believe he had more than twenty native-born Americans.[37]

Logie's letter raises interesting questions. If the men were British subjects, why did he not do more to obtain their release? Randall reported in his letter of April 2, 1786, that there was "a provision in the English treaty that all British subjects taken in any vessel whatever were not to be deemed a real captive," but that Logie did not think it proper to make application for the men concerned in this case. Why? What happened to their petition? Three of the men were in fact ransomed by British friends, and a fourth tried to be, but the correspondence does not indicate whether Logie was instrumental in these cases.

Logie's failure to do more may have related to the fact that, whatever the provisions of the British treaty, the Algerines seem to have distinguished between the status of passenger and that of seaman in cases where a man was of a different nationality than the vessel on which he was traveling or working. Members of the crew appear to have been considered as having taken on the nationality of the vessel, while passengers who were nationals of states with which Algiers was at peace were not enslaved and were released. At least, that is the deduction one can make from the case of Jacob or Jacques Tessanier, the young French national—his age is not given in the correspondence, but he is described by the French as an *enfant* (meaning less than 13 years old)—who was a *mousse,* or ship's boy, on the *Dauphin*. The French sought his release as a passenger, and he was so classified by the Americans, but the Algerines said he had described himself as a crewman and therefore they could not release him. He remained a prisoner and died of the plague in 1793.

We can only guess at answers to some of the other questions. We do not know for certain, and probably never will, what Logie may have said to the dey about the captives. We do not know what advice he gave Lamb. Whatever British policy was, there seem to have been good, or at least civil, relations between individual Americans and some British officials in the region. Logie, for instance, went surety for the officers of the *Maria* and *Dauphin* and paid the authorities five guineas so that they were not sent to the bagnios.

He was given credit for this apparently unrequited generosity by the Americans in London, according to Randall. Whatever the unpleasant circumstances of the domestic arrangements he may have provided to the officers, O'Brien mentions subsequent conversations with Logie, indicating that some civil contact was maintained. Also, American officials stayed at Gibraltar from time to time, where they were treated with courtesy and even kindness by the British military.

On the other hand, we have the text of Logie's account of the Lamb affair, and it does not sound very friendly to the Americans:

> On the 25th March a Mr. Lamb and Randal arrived here in a Spanish Vessel from Barcelona, as Agents from the Americans, to negotiate a Peace, and Redeem their Subjects, they had Letters of recommendation to the French and Spanish Consuls. The French Consul sent to the Dey to notify their arrival. I have great pleasure and satisfaction in conveying to your Lordship the Dey's conduct on that occasion. The Dey said, "What are they come to purchase a Peace? Tell them to carry their Money to the King of England, their King I have no War with His Subjects, I have never heard of such a Nation as Americans, if they come to redeem any of my Slaves they may come on shore but I will hear of no Treaties of Peace," they accordingly landed as Agents to redeem slaves.[38]

The Verdict on Lamb

O'Brien's letter to Jefferson of June 8, 1786, was not reproduced in the American State Papers series, perhaps because of his remarks about Lamb.[39] O'Brien's meaning is not always clear, but his letter, signed also by Captains Stephens and Zachaeus Coffin, reports that:

(1) They were surprised that between November 4, 1785, when Jefferson issued instructions to Lamb to redeem the captives, and March 20, 1786, when he finally arrived in Algiers,

> he did not get our redemption ascertained by some person in Algiers . . . not informing himself of the method generally used towards the redemption of captives, but on the contrary comes to Algiers and gives out that he came to redeem the Americans. . . . It was immediately signified to the Dey that Mr. Lamb had brought money for that purport, it became such town talk that the Dey hardly knew what sum to ask. After a few days the Dey asks what sum Mr. Lamb would give. Mr. Lamb signified he would give ten thousand dollars. The Dey then said

50,000. I think the demand was very a propos to the offer of Mr. Lamb. Mr. Lamb tried to get the Dey to lower his price, but the Dey determined not to lower his price anything worth mentioning.

(2) Lamb in any event had no money with him with which to redeem the captives. All he had was authorization to draw up to £3,300 on the legation in Paris for use in providing the customary presents to officials on the occasion of a peace treaty. (In his subsequent letter of September 13, 1786, O'Brien said that Lamb had only $6,000 with him. Adams wrote to Jefferson on January 25, 1787, that Lamb had drawn on him for £3,212, which would be about $12,000. De Kercy reported that he had 8,000 *piastres fortes*, which would be about $8,000.)

(3) Lamb had behaved in an ungentlemanly fashion. His "unguarded expressions, his hints, threats, etc. despising the French and Spaniards, signifying their defeat and in fact everything that he could possibly utter in the most vulgar language that it was with pain we see him so unworthy of his commission and the cloth he wore." Later in the letter O'Brien expressed surprise that Lamb did not pay Logie the five guineas the latter had advanced to keep the ships' officers out of the marine.[40]

The least we can say is that Lamb does not seem to have been a very good choice for the job. That the United States did not send someone who understood French or Spanish was unfortunate. On the other hand, the cards were stacked against him. He had signed on to negotiate a treaty of peace, expecting to start with Morocco, before any prisoners were taken. He had expected to have a handsome present, the *Alliance,* to offer as an inducement. Instead, he was sent to Algiers without it and with the scene much complicated by the presence of American captives. He was authorized to offer a sum for their release that was ridiculous, while the dey was unwilling to talk about peace, only about ransom. With no telephone or telegraph to give him contact with his superiors, Lamb was totally on his own, with instructions that gave him no leeway, from people who had not understood the circumstances in which he would be operating. The fact that Hasan, the wakil al-kharj, spoke well of him in his letter of February 27, 1787, is an indication that, for all his unsuitability, he had made the right connection with the right man and had been accepted as an emissary. It is unfortunate that no attempt was made to follow up on that invitation.

The fatal flaw in the American approach at this point was an unwillingness as well as an inability to pay what was needed. Jefferson, as secretary of state, in a letter to Congress of December 28, 1790, explained that since he and Adams had been acting without authority from Congress, they "thought themselves bound to offer a price so moderate as not to be disapproved." They therefore restricted Lamb to two hundred dollars a man. Jefferson later wrote in his letter to John Paul Jones of June 1, 1792, discussed in chapter 5, that this was not out of concern for the money but out of a desire not to give the Algerines exaggerated ideas about how much the Americans would pay and thereby expose other American shipping to attack.

Had the Americans paid the ransom without an accompanying treaty of peace, there was no assurance that there would not be further captives. Indeed, as long as there was no naval sanction to protect American merchant shipping, a continuation of the state of war might have seemed even more attractive to the Algerines. Immediately, however, some lives would have been saved.

Lamb's failure sounds like a classic illustration of the dangers of ignorance. Jefferson and Adams had no experience with the Barbary powers and very little knowledge of the situation in the region. Lamb did not appear to know much more than they did. His Moroccan trading experience did not stand him in very good stead. In fairness to him, the limitations on what he could offer were crippling, and it is not clear that anyone else could have done better under those conditions. As Adams commented in a letter of January 25, 1787, to Jefferson, "If Congress had Sent the Ablest Member of their own body, at Such a Time and under such pecuniary Limitations he would have done no better."[41]

5

Things Get Worse

The Mathurins, John Paul Jones, Barclay, Humphreys, and the Portuguese Truce

With the Lamb fiasco, and word that the plague was raging in Algiers, attention shifted from peace to ransoming the prisoners. Peace remained a goal, but was not attempted seriously until 1793. Meanwhile, the United States passed from congressional government under the Articles of Confederation to federal government under the Constitution, and Washington was sworn in as the first president on April 30, 1789. An era of better management of foreign affairs loomed ahead, but the French Revolution began a few months later, unleashing a chain of events that halted the ransoming process and, together with problems of communication, frustrated the effort to resume negotiations on a peace with Algiers. As a result, no American negotiator reached Algiers until 1795, more than nine years after Lamb's departure. Meanwhile, prisoners were dying of the plague and other ailments.

The Mathurins

On learning of Lamb's failure, Jefferson turned to the Mathurins and met with the general of the order early in 1787. The general offered to do all he could, but would expect Jefferson to have the money ready to pay the ransom as soon as the deal was made. In that regard, he said that the price paid in the last Mathurin-arranged redemption was 2,500 livres per man ($500) and he doubted that they could redeem American captives as cheaply. This proposition was submitted to Congress in February, and Jefferson received instructions to go ahead with the Mathurin proposal on September 19, 1787.

Jefferson informed the Mathurin general immediately, but said he did not want the order to make any commitments until he had the money in hand. The funds were not deposited in Paris until a year later, and Jefferson then authorized the Mathurins to offer up to 3,000 livres or $555 per man, a figure that was still unrealistic, given what was reportedly being paid by the Spanish, the Neapolitans, and the Russians at the time. Meanwhile the general of the Mathurins recommended that in order to avoid giving the impression that the U.S. government rather than the Mathurins was ransoming the captives, the relatively comfortable allowance that the captives were receiving via the Spanish consul in Algiers should be stopped and they should be put on a much more modest dole from the Mathurins. This might persuade the Algerians that they were objects of charity from whom not much could be expected. It might then be possible to get a lower ransom. The general suggested a figure of about three cents per captive per day, less than half of what they had been receiving. Jefferson gave him "full powers as to the amount and manner of subsisting them."[1] He explained to Congress that he had agreed because "this being the first instance of a redemption by the United States, it would form a precedent, because a high price given by us might induce these pirates to abandon all other nations in pursuit of Americans."[2] Jefferson said that "to destroy, therefore, every expectation of a redemption by the United States, the bills of the Spanish consul at Algiers, who had made the kind advances before spoken of for the sustenance of our captives, were not answered. On the contrary, a hint was given that these advances had better be discontinued, as it was not known that they would be reimbursed." According to Cathcart, this allowance, which we have earlier seen amounted to 7½ cents per day, was not stopped until September 1789. The Spanish evidently continued it for some eighteen months after the Americans dropped their hint. This may have been a private charity by the Spanish consul, but one wonders what the Spanish thought of Jefferson's cheeseparing and his ungentlemanly refusal to reimburse them.

One would like to believe that such a callous action by a modern American politician would be unthinkable. Jefferson said this decision had caused much distress to the captives, and himself, but he seems to have had no afterthoughts as to its correctness. Perhaps he rationalized that the Mathurins made him do it. It is questionable, however, whether their rationale was correct as far as influencing the Algerines was concerned. The idea that the United States would improve its negotiating position by abandoning its people and pretending that it was unwilling to ransom them while at the same time preparing to make a new offer assumes a naïveté on the part of the Algerines that was not realistic.

In any event, the Mathurins were dispossessed by the French Revolution in 1789 before they had time to do anything for the captives, and that was the end of that. In his report to the House of Representatives of December 30, 1790, Jefferson explained that he had been unable to tell the Congress earlier about these negotiations for fear that to do so would jeopardize their chances of success.

While the swearing-in of Washington as president presaged a new era of more effective government, it was a while before it took effect. The immediate impact abroad was a downgrading of American representation. Jefferson left Paris in September 1789 and returned to the United States to become secretary of state, while John Adams, who had left London in early 1788, became vice president. William Short served as chargé in Paris from April 1790 to June 1792 and was succeeded by Gouverneur Morris, who had royalist sympathies and whose recall was requested by the French government in April 1794. He was succeeded by James Monroe, who was perhaps too republican, in August 1794. In London there was a hiatus of four and a half years until Thomas Pinckney presented his credentials as minister in August 1792. In Lisbon, which became the post responsible for negotiations with Algiers, David Humphreys presented his credentials as the first minister resident in May 1791. Only in Madrid was there continuous representation throughout the period from 1785 to 1795, in the person of William Carmichael, who served as chargé from 1783 until September 1794, when William Short presented credentials as minister resident.

Casualties and Costs

Meanwhile, five of the American captives died during the plague epidemic of 1787–88, and Captain Zachaeus Coffin, the passenger on the *Dauphin,* died of consumption in 1787, while one seaman, a "Scotch boy" (Charles Colvil), was ransomed by the British for $1,481. As of July 9, 1790, fourteen captives remained. Three of these subsequently died in captivity, while another three were ransomed by friends. The remaining eight eventually made it home, but not for another six years.

Various persons estimated the cost of ransoming the remaining men. In appendix 7 an extract from Jefferson's letter to Congress of December 30, 1790, shows the figures ranging from $1,200 to $2,920 per man, for a mean of $2,060. This, however, did not take into account the cost of a peace treaty, which would be separate from the ransom and would cost upwards of $300,000, according to various estimates.

The Senate resolved sometime between December 30, 1790, and February 22, 1791, that the president should take such measures as he thought necessary to redeem the captives for a sum not to exceed $40,000, which would have been enough to free the fourteen survivors.[3] But no action seems to have been taken for eighteen months, in spite of various indications that the timing might be propitious. The old dey, Muhammad bin Uthman, died in 1791 and, as noted earlier, his successor Hasan was reported to be well disposed toward the Americans. In particular, O'Brien seemed to have developed a friendly relationship with him through their common interest in maritime matters and repeatedly said that the proper choice of an agent and payment of bribes could assure a reasonable settlement. Failure to move quickly to exploit the new situation was to have tragic consequences.

John Paul Jones

On May 8, 1792, President Washington having asked how much he could pay for peace and ransom, the Senate authorized $40,000 for a peace treaty and $25,000 a year thereafter for its continuance, plus the $40,000 for ransom authorized earlier.[4]

On June 1, Jefferson wrote to John Paul Jones, naval hero of the Revolutionary War, who was living in Paris, informing him that the president had decided to appoint him peace commissioner and consul in Algiers, apparently on the reasonable assumption that as a former naval warrior Jones would be able to influence the Algerians. Jones had written to John Jay in 1787 suggesting that a fund be raised by public subscription to ransom the captives, and this may have led to his selection for the job.[5] In a remarkably long and detailed letter, Jefferson summarized what had happened since 1785 and gave the background of the various possibilities suggested by O'Brien and others. Jones was instructed to bargain and authorized to spend up to $27,000 for ransom, or $13,000 less than the Senate had voted, and $25,000 for a treaty, with the hope he would get both for less. Jefferson's decision not to authorize Jones to spend the entire $40,000 on ransom was apparently based on O'Brien's estimate, quoted below, that the deal could be struck for 14,000 sequins.

The letter and Jones's commissions as negotiator and consul were written by Jefferson personally in order to keep word of the appointment secret: "supposing that there exists a disposition to thwart our negotiations with the Algerines, and that this would be very practicable, we have thought it advisable that the knowledge of the appointment should rest with the President, Mr. Pinckney [in London], and myself." The consular commission is in the Seeley G. Mudd Manuscript Library at Princeton University. One cannot imagine a modern secretary of state being able to pen anything so well, or having the time to do it. There is no indication who the supposed thwarters were, but the British would have been the most likely suspects at that point.

In his letter of instruction Jefferson complained that the well-meaning interference of various parties had conveyed a sense of anxiety on the American government's part and this had the effect of "making us at last set a much higher rate of ransom for our citizens, present and future, than we probably should have obtained if we had been left alone to do our own work, in our own way." He went on to say that Congress had authorized a fixed sum for ransom, provided a peace treaty was included in the deal, and that the United States would not pay part of the price in naval stores, as John Jay had suggested, because of the use to which they would be put, even though that might be a cheaper way to pay ransom. Thus the question of whether the United States should provide items of military utility to belligerents who could use them against itself or its friends arose here for the first time, and it became a recurring issue in relations with the Barbary states, who appreciated the quality of American naval stores and shipbuilding. It remains a recurring issue in U.S. foreign relations today, raised by such actions as the CIA's supplying of ground-to-air missiles to the Afghan mujahidin.

After a discussion of O'Brien's views on how much the United States would have to pay for a peace treaty, Jefferson told Jones:

> You will, of course, use your best endeavors to get it [peace] at the lowest sum practicable; whereupon I shall only say, that we should be pleased with 10,000 dollars, contented with 15,000, think 20,000 a very hard bargain, yet go as far as 25,000 if it be impossible to get it for less; but not a copper further, this being fixed by law as the utmost limit. These are meant as annual sums. If you can put off the first annual payment to the end of the first year, you may employ any sum not exceeding that, in presents to be laid down; but if the first payment is to be made in hand, that and the presents cannot, by law, exceed 25,000 dollars.

Jefferson went on to discuss the ransom of the remaining captives, saying "the fixed principle" with Congress was to establish the ransom as low as possible in order not to excite the

> cupidity of those rovers. . . . mere money . . . never has been nor is an object with any body here. It is from the same regard for the safety of our seamen at large, that they have now restrained us from any ransom unaccompanied by peace; this being secured, we are led to consent to terms of ransom, to which, otherwise our Government never would have consented; that is to say, to the terms stated by Captain O'Brien . . . "by giving the Minister of the Marine (the present Dey's favorite) the sum of one thousand sequins, I would stake my life that we would be ransomed for thirteen thousand sequins, and all expenses included." Extravagant as this sum is, we will, under the security of peace in future go so far; not doubting, at the same time, that you will obtain it as much

lower as possible. . . . You will consider this sum, therefore, say 27,000 dollars [about 14,500 Algerine sequins] as your ultimate limit, including ransom, duties, and gratifications of every kind. As soon as the ransom is completed, you will be pleased to have the captives well clothed, and sent home at the expense of the United States, with as much economy as will consist with their reasonable comfort.[6]

Jefferson said Thomas Pinckney, the new minister to London, would be Jones's confidential channel of communication and finance officer, spelled out his combined pay and allowances of $2,000, warned him to be careful of pirates, recommended O'Brien to him as someone who had given distinguished service, and warned him against reposing any confidence in the European consuls in Algiers. Pinckney, then leaving for London, was to effect delivery of the letter. He was instructed that if Jones, from whom nothing had been heard for a while, was unwilling or unable to act, he was to commit the mission to Thomas Barclay, who had negotiated the treaty with Morocco and was at that point serving as U.S. consul at Tangier but was actually living in Gibraltar. To that end, Jefferson had prepared a letter from Washington to Barclay, instructing him to follow the instructions to Jones as though they were addressed to himself. This letter is shown in figure 5.

Jones never received Jefferson's letter. He had died of the plague in Paris on July 18.

Thomas Barclay

On learning of Jones's death, Pinckney, who had arrived in London during the summer—he presented credentials on August 9, 1792—undertook to convey the papers to Barclay. His explanation of the delays encountered in accomplishing this were set out in a letter to Jefferson on December 13 that is a classic description of the problems of diplomacy in the pretelegraph age. Briefly, his first problem was to find out whether Barclay was in Tangier or Gibraltar. His next was to find someone reliable to take the papers to him. He decided that it had to be an American, but most of them seemed to have left the city. He finally settled on a Mr. Lemuel Cravath, a native and citizen of Massachusetts, whom he paid one hundred guineas to perform the task. Cravath had difficulty finding a ship to Gibraltar but eventually took one to "Cales" (Cádiz?), from where he was to proceed overland. He had left about a month before Pinckney wrote to Jefferson, and Pinckney now speculated that perhaps the papers had already been delivered to Barclay, who might be on his way.[7] The papers did reach Barclay, who immediately began making arrangements to go to Algiers but died on January 18 or 19, 1793, in Lisbon.

Sir
                    Philadelphia June 11. 1792.

Congress having furnished me with means for procuring peace, and ransoming our captive citizens from the government of Algiers, I have thought it best, while you are engaged at Marocco, to appoint Admiral Jones to proceed to Algiers, and therefore have sent him a commission for establishing peace, another for the ransom of our captives, and a third to act there as Consul for the U.S. and full instructions are given in a letter from the Secretary of state to him, of all which papers, mr Pinkney now proceeding to London as our Minister Plenipotentiary there, is the bearer, as he is also of this letter. It is sometime however since we have heard of Admiral Jones, and as, in the event of any accident to him, it might occasion an injurious delay were the business to await new commissions from hence, I have thought it best, in such an event, that mr Pinkney should forward to you all the papers addressed to Admiral Jones, with this letter signed by myself, giving you authority on receipt of those papers to consider them as addressed to you, and to proceed under them in every respect as if your name stood in each of them in the place of that of John Paul Jones. You will of course finish the business of your mission to Marocco with all the despatch practicable, and then

Thomas Barclay esquire.

...ceed to Algiers on that hereby confided to you, there this letter with the commissions addressed to Admiral Jones, and an explanation of circumstances, will doubtless procure you the credit as acting in the name & on the behalf of the United States, and more especially when you shall efficaciously prove your authority by the fact of making, on the spot, the payments you shall stipulate. With full confidence in the prudence & integrity, with which you will fulfill the objects of the present mission, I give to this letter the effect of a commission & full powers, by hereto subscribing my name this eleventh day of June one thousand seven hundred & ninety two.

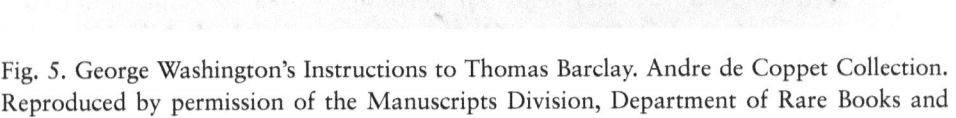

Fig. 5. George Washington's Instructions to Thomas Barclay. Andre de Coppet Collection. Reproduced by permission of the Manuscripts Division, Department of Rare Books and Special Collections, Princeton University Library.

David Humphreys

Barclay's death became known in Philadelphia on March 18, 1793, and on March 21 Jefferson sent David Humphreys a commission and copies of the appropriate papers and charged him to carry out the mission previously assigned to Jones and Barclay.

Humphreys had been one of the Connecticut (or Hartford) Wits, along with Joel Barlow, Timothy Dwight, and others. He had served as George Washington's aide during the Revolution and had accompanied him into retirement at Mt. Vernon after the war. He had been sent to Europe as a special representative in 1790, charged with reporting on the state of affairs in Europe and exploring the opening of diplomatic relations with Portugal. Washington and his cabinet had decided that the United States should maintain its diplomatic representation at the lowest possible level, appointing chargés d'affaires rather than ministers or ambassadors wherever possible. Humphreys reported that the Portuguese had already decided to appoint a minister resident to the United States and requested the appointment of someone of similar rank as the American representative in Portugal. Humphreys was accordingly named "minister resident" as opposed to "minister," one step up from chargé but without the full powers of an "envoy extraordinary and minister plenipotentiary" to negotiate on behalf of his government and commit it to observance of agreements signed.

Humphreys had thought of himself as a logical person to carry out the mission entrusted to Barclay, and had written confidentially to Washington on February 8 suggesting that the job be given to him, but the thought had already occurred to the people in Philadelphia. Jefferson's instruction of March 21 modified the instructions prepared for Jones to permit Humphreys, if it became an inescapable condition for an agreement, to offer to pay part of the sum demanded for a peace treaty in naval stores. First, however, he was to settle the accounts left by Barclay, who had also been charged with negotiating a new treaty with Morocco.

Jefferson's letter and the accompanying credentials were given to Captain Nathaniel Cutting, who was assigned to Humphreys as secretary for the Moroccan and Algerian missions. He was told to go first to London and then proceed to Lisbon without delay. He left Philadelphia for London in mid-April but did not reach Lisbon until September—a delay that had fatal consequences. Although Humphreys moved quickly and sailed for Gibraltar on September 17, arriving about a week later, time had already run out on him. On September 26 he wrote that he and Cutting were unwrapping and sorting the items Barclay had obtained as presents for Morocco to determine which of them could be used in Algiers, that he was proceeding with all diligence and planned to go to Alicante and from there to Algiers, that the plague was raging in the latter place, and that there had been no communication from the American captives since the previous winter. He recounted news of the fighting in Toulon between the French revolutionaries and British, Spanish, and royalist forces, and remarked on the need of the Gibraltar garrison for "eatables and drinkables" which the Americans could supply if they had the run of the Mediterranean.[8] As he was writing, Algerine cruisers were already setting out for the Atlantic, looking for more American ships.

The Portuguese Truce

Following the Spanish-Algerine truce and the eruption of the Algerine corsairs into the Atlantic in 1785, the Portuguese, to protect their ships coming

Fig. 6. *Colonel David Humphreys,* by Gilbert Stuart. Reproduced by permission of the Yale University Art Gallery. Gift of Mr. and Mrs. David Humphreys.

from Brazil, began to assume responsibility for guarding the Strait of Gibraltar in 1786 and had kept the Algerines bottled up in the Mediterranean. Their commitment to do so was formalized in a letter of August 2, 1787, from Queen Maria I to Congress. For this reason, and perhaps others, there had been no American ships captured since 1785, and many of them were frequenting Atlantic ports in 1793. In the absence of a peace treaty between the United States and Algiers, a truce under which the Portuguese allowed the Algerines out into the Atlantic would again expose American shipping to capture.

For some time O'Brien had been warning of the dangers of such a truce, and speculation about it was rife in Algiers, but Humphreys seems to have been unaware of how close such a development was. He was soon confronted with its reality. On October 6 he wrote to Jefferson from Gibraltar that a truce of twelve months' duration had just been concluded between Algiers and Portugal—the truce had taken effect on September 12, five days before Humphreys left Lisbon—and that a fleet of eight Algerine cruisers had gone through the Strait to the Atlantic. On the following day he wrote to say that the truce had been made through the instrumentality of Charles Logie, the British consul at Algiers, but he was happy to inform Jefferson that there were "strong circumstances to induce me to believe it was without authority, or even knowledge, of his own court, from which (I am most credibly assured) he has not received any direct communication for fourteen months past. This was owing to his having been recalled, and a successor appointed for that residence."[9]

The last part of that statement is literally true. The instructions on which Logie acted were addressed to his successor, Charles Mace, but the latter had stopped en route at Gibraltar because of the plague and delayed proceeding to his new post. Logie, still in Algiers, was acting in his stead and had received and was following those instructions. Details regarding the origins and negotiation of the truce may be found in appendix 8.

Edward Church, the chargé in Lisbon in Humphreys's absence, wrote on October 12 that he had been informed the day before that the Algerine fleet had passed through the Strait on October 5. He had immediately called together the American captains then in port and informed them of this development, but the Algerines had already taken five American ships by then and took another six by early November. Based on the accounts of the captives, the American crewmen on these ships numbered 108. The hostage problem had assumed a new dimension.

In this same letter Church reported that he had gone to see Luis Pinto de Souza Coutinho, the minister and secretary of state for foreign affairs, who said that the truce was as unexpected to the court of Portugal as it was to the Americans, although it was not quite as unwelcome to the former as to the latter. He acknowledged that some six months earlier the court had expressed to the courts of England and Spain a desire for their friendly cooperation to

> induce a disposition in the Dey towards the establishment of a firm and lasting peace . . . but having appointed no person directly or indirectly to negotiate in behalf of Her Majesty, they considered the business as only in embryo. But the British court, zealous over-much for the happiness of the two nations, Portugal and Algiers, in order to precipitate this important business, very officiously authorised Charles Logie . . . not only to treat but to conclude, for and in behalf of this court, not only without authority but without consulting it. . . . [The Portuguese] never intended to conclude either a peace or truce with the Dey, without giving timely notice to all their friends, that they might avoid the dangers to which they might otherwise be unavoidably exposed by trusting to the protection of Portuguese ships of war stationed in the Mediterranean.

Pinto de Souza said that a condition of the proposed treaty was that the Portuguese pay the dey one-third the amount he received annually from the Spanish. When the court learned of this condition from Robert Walpole, the British minister to Portugal, they informed him that "however desirous they might be of peace with Algiers they were so far from being disposed to submit to such a condition that it was the determination of her Most Faithful Majesty not to pay one farthing; but in the interval, the truce was signed by the self-constituted agent, Mr. Logie." Logie, meanwhile, had issued passports to the Algerine cruisers that allowed them to pass through the strait unhindered by the Portuguese fleet.

There was no doubt, Church wrote, that the object of the truce was to get at the Americans, and the fact that a truce was negotiated between Algiers and the Dutch at the same time left only the Americans and the Hanseatic League towns exposed to the Algerines. He went on to say that "it is a matter of certainty which I have received from undoubted authority" that one of the four ministers of the Portuguese government was in on the plot. He speculated that it might be Pinto de Souza himself or Martinho de Mello [de Melo e Castro, the minister of overseas affairs], but said his source suspected the marquès de Ponta de Lima, "the first minister."[10]

Humphreys had a similar conversation with Pinto de Souza on January 30, 1794. Briefly, Pinto de Souza said that the Portuguese had wanted a truce originally in order to reduce the number of vessels they had to maintain in the Strait of Gibraltar so they could employ some of them elsewhere, and had asked the British to sound out the Algerine position. On learning that the Algerines were demanding payment for a truce, they abandoned the idea, but Logie had gone ahead and concluded the truce without instructions, contrary to the wishes of the Portuguese. The Portuguese had let the Algerines know that they would pay no tribute or presents whatsoever for peace, that if a peace were concluded, there would have to be a period of three months during which the Portuguese could warn nations with which they had trade relations before the Algerines would be permitted out into the Atlantic, and that there could be no capture of vessels within a certain distance from the Portuguese coast. Humphreys commented that the Algerines would be sure to reject these terms.[11] Pinto de Souza may have been disingenuous, but there may also have been a genuine communications problem between the British and the Portuguese. The British were reporting as late as July 1795 that the Portuguese were determined to renew negotiations with Algiers.[12]

While the British probably shed no tears, and may even have rejoiced, over the capture of more American ships, the papers in the British Public Record Office do not reflect this. Logie may have been motivated by personal anti-American feelings—one of the captives who worked in the dey's palace, Philip Sloan, claimed that he had heard Logie telling the Algerine captains where they could find the American ships—but the record indicates that the initiative for the truce came from the Portuguese, as the British claimed at the time.

In this connection, it is interesting to note that the dey in his conversation with Logie on November 2, 1793, said that his corsairs were already fitting out for a cruise into the Atlantic when Logie had proposed the truce and "they were not sent there in consequence of the truce."[13] On the other hand, in a letter of March 27, 1794, to King George complaining that the British had led him down the garden path, the dey comments: "The object that lead us to resolve on this Peace was to Revenge ourselves on Yours and our Enemies the Americans in the open seas by harassing and destroying them in such a manner so as to reduce them to the necessity of submitting to being your subjects again. The utility of this was more for your convenience than ours."[14] The full text of this remarkable letter forms appendix 9.

Mace finally arrived in Algiers on January 2, 1794, and had to pick up the pieces that Logie, in the best tradition of departing diplomats, left behind. Although contacts on the subject continued well into 1794, the truce was not ratified by the Portuguese and the peace agreement that was to follow was not negotiated, apparently because of differences over whether and how much the Portuguese were to pay for it. The dey evidently was looking forward to the money and blamed the British as well as the Portuguese for his failure to get it. Logie wrote on November 6, 1793, that the dey had told him he would not do business with the Portuguese were it not for the British. (It sounds as though he was genuinely fond of Logie. He did not display the same fondness for Mace, and this may have contributed to his anger when things did not turn out as expected.)

So ends the saga of the Portuguese truce. Logie was following orders, but he went beyond them in issuing passes to the Algerine cruisers before the Portuguese had a chance to see the truce document and accept it. He was blamed for this by his successor. On the positive side, the dey's anger at the British may have opened the door to the eventual conclusion of a peace with the Americans.

Absent some document as yet undiscovered, one can only speculate on the reasons for Logie's zealousness, if that is what it was. He does not sound well disposed toward Americans, and he certainly did them a great deal of harm, but he has not been heard from in any detail on this question. He claimed he was only following orders. On the way home he stopped in Lisbon at the dey's request to try, unsuccessfully, to obtain Portuguese ratification of the truce and a peace agreement. While there, he expressed a desire to meet with Humphreys, but the latter declined because of a prior engagement.[15]

Humphreys sounds unnecessarily rigid in this instance. He might have found it useful to talk with Logie. His secretary, Captain Cutting, may have done so. He wrote from Lisbon on April 15, 1794: "The known and immediate agent in this infernal conspiracy against our peace and prosperity is at this instant walking in the garden beneath my window with all the apparent composure and self-complacency that can be inspired by successful villainy. Mr. Logie, late the British Consul at Algiers, who, unsolicited by the Court of Portugal, negotiated the fatal truce . . . He asserts that this court earnestly prest him to it; but I do not believe him."

Similarly, Lord Grenville in London assured Pinckney that England in rendering a service to its Portuguese ally had no intention of injuring the United States. Americans have long been skeptical of these assurances, but I found nothing in the British record to refute them.[16]

Navigation Resumed

Meanwhile, to make up for their dereliction, the Portuguese agreed on October 22, 1793, to escort American and Hanseatic ships in convoy "until the conclusion of the ratification of the truce adjusted between her Most Faithful Majesty and the regency of Algiers." This was done in spite of its being contrary to the provision in the truce that the Portuguese would not extend protection to any ships other than their own. The Hanseatic representatives argued successfully that they had a prior treaty affording them protection that took precedence over the truce, and the Americans argued that an exception having been made for the Hanseatic ships, one should be made for American ships as well. Church comments that the Spanish and British ministers had unsuccessfully opposed the granting of convoy privileges, and that their failure was a measure of the unpopularity of the truce in court circles.[17] The first convoy was scheduled to leave October 25. The *American State Papers* do not report what transpired subsequently in this regard, but the last capture for which we have a precise date is October 25—the brig *Polly* out of Newburyport. One ship, the brig *Minerva* of New York, was captured in early November, but no date is given in the documents.

The surviving accounts agree that these ships were captured by a combination of deception and overwhelming force. The Algerine vessel would fly a friendly or neutral flag until it was upon the American vessel and then unleash a crowd of boarders from the hold who would have no difficulty overwhelming the small American crew—the largest of the ships taken in 1793 had a crew of 18, while one had 17 men and one 12 and all the rest had crews of 9 or less—all of whose belongings and most of whose clothes they would immediately plunder. These deceitful tactics and the merciless plundering of the victims were common to privateers of all nationalities at the time, the captive crews' possessions traditionally being reserved to the capturing crew.

We know more about the *Polly* than we do about the other ships because one of her crew, John Foss, wrote a book, *A Journal of the Captivity and*

Sufferings of John Foss, Several Years a Prisoner at Algiers.[18] His description of their capture indicates that nothing much had changed since Cathcart's earlier adventure, although its strict accuracy may be open to question. Foss wrote that the *Polly* was captured off Cape St. Vincent by an Algerine brig flying the British flag. The crew were stripped of their clothing, but an old Turk gave him a shirt, "the only Mahometan I ever met with, in whom I had the least reason to suppose the smallest spark of humanity was kindled." The brig's commander told them of the Portuguese truce negotiated by Logie. On arrival in Algiers they were taken to see the dey, who said he had "sent several to our government entreating them to negotiate with him for peace and had never received any satisfactory answer from them. That he was determined never to make peace with the United States in his reign, as they had so often neglected his requests, and treated him with disdain, adding 'now I have got you, you Christian dogs, you shall eat stones.' He then picked four boys to wait upon him in the palace ... and ordered us to be conducted to the prison *Bilic [Beylik]*."

Humphreys Repulsed

In spite of the truce and the capture of additional American ships, Humphreys proceeded from Gibraltar to Alicante, it being the principal port of embarkation for Algiers. He had arrived there by November 5, when he sent his letter of credence and a "memorial" to the Swedish consul general in Algiers, Mattias Skjöldebrand, asking him to present them to the dey on his behalf and to seek permission for him to come to Algiers to discuss a peace treaty and ransom for the captives.[19] Humphreys then wrote to the secretary of state on November 19, reporting that an Algerine captain in the harbor claimed to have captured seven American ships, of which he had taken three to Algiers. He closed the letter with a postscript: "I open this letter to let you know the Dey has refused giving a passport." Humphreys would not be allowed to proceed to Algiers.[20]

Skjöldebrand, who had been kind and helpful to the American captives, replied in a letter of November 13 that he was flattered to be asked but dared not risk formally representing the Americans. He explained that the representatives of states at peace with Algiers feared becoming the next recipient of a declaration of war, because the regency could not afford to have peace with everyone—the soldiers had to have someone to plunder or they would revolt. If he were to undertake any political, as opposed to humanitarian, step on behalf of the Americans, it would immediately be reported to the courts of Europe, who would complain to the court of Sweden, and he would be in trouble. He had, however, given the task to his brother, Per Erik, who

Fig. 7. *Mattias Skjöldebrand,* by N. Lafrensen. Reproduced by permission of the Nationalmuseum med Prins Eugens Waldemarsudde, Stockholm.

was not there in any official capacity but was very familiar with political affairs and channels of negotiation.[21]

In the same mail Humphreys also received a letter from Per Erik Skjöldebrand and one from O'Brien. Per Erik said that he had received Humphreys's request on November 11 and after consulting with his brother immediately obtained an audience with the dey, at which

> on presenting him your letter of credence and your memorial, I did not neglect interpreting to him their contents with every persuasive consideration and reason, adding thereto all that I thought capable of leading him to favor your demands and propositions. He replied to me, with an unshaken firmness, that he would not make peace with the Americans, or any other nation whomsoever, at any price whatever; that there had been a time when he was well disposed to support the engagements, at half price, made by his predecessor, the Dey Mahamet Bashaw, with Mr. Lamb, an American negotiator, which you are probably acquainted with. But now, since the conditions of a peace with Holland require only to be ratified; since the Portuguese have demanded a peace, and the Dey has fixed his pretensions with the Portuguese commandant, who was here some days ago, (which amount to near three million

piasters) which the Dey expects here in a few days; since the Algerine corsairs have made ten American prizes, and one hundred and five slaves more, and the Dey has again sent his corsairs out of the straits, expecting still to add to the number; he declared to me that his interest does not permit him to accept your offer, sir, even were you to lavish millions upon him, "because," said he, "if I were to make peace with every body, what should I do with my corsairs? What should I do with my soldiers? They would take off my head, for the want of other prizes, not being able to live on their miserable allowance."

Skjöldebrand had argued vainly that the Portuguese might not accept the dey's price for peace, that the Americans had never fought nor enslaved the Algerines as the Portuguese had, although they had shown in their war with England that they lacked neither strength nor courage, that peace would already have been concluded had not two negotiators been stopped by death, and that if he feared peace he should break with some state that was less useful to him than the United States could be. The dey had responded "that he would not allow any American ambassador under any flag whatever."

Skjöldebrand counseled patience. He noted that the dey had a mercurial temperament and suggested that Humphreys remain quietly at Alicante or Lisbon for a month or two to see what developed. He had reason to believe the Portuguese would not accept the dey's terms for peace, which would enrage the dey, and that would be the favorable moment for renewing the American request to negotiate. He also suggested that the Americans switch their patronage from the Jewish house of Bassara (Bouchara), which they had been using as agents for some time, to that of Bakri. Skjöldebrand commented that the senior Bouchara "has not (although king of the Jews) either the grace or the influence of those Bacris with the Dey . . . on this occasion . . . (being afraid of failing in the business, when they thought it so near a conclusion) they [the Boucharas] have labored and supplicated the Dey on the subject of your propositions, but have received, in like manner, a decisive and less temperate refusal than myself."

Skjöldebrand went on to ask how much the Americans were prepared to pay for peace and whether they could pay 2,000 piastres (about $2,000) a man for ransom as well as provide the costly presents consuls were required to give every two years. He promised to keep their communications secret and to let Humphreys know immediately if the situation turned favorable, and said that if Humphreys decided to honor him with his confidence, he should send him "a power to make use of it."[22]

O'Brien's letter of November 12 supported Skjöldebrand's and commended the latter to Humphreys. He supplied a couple of details:

Fig. 8. *Per Erik Skjöldebrand*, by P. Krafft. Reproduced by permission of the Nationalmuseum med Prins Eugens Waldemarsudde, Stockholm.

(1) Robert Montgomery, the consul at Alicante, had written to the Boucharas "and they, without waiting to embrace a favorable opportunity, immediately made application to the Dey relative to your coming to Algiers to make peace. The Dey answered very abruptly that he would not receive you and would not make peace with America . . . that when he wanted the Americans, for nearly two years, to make peace, they would not give him an answer, which was treating him and his people with indifference." If, however, Humphreys would empower Skjöldebrand to represent him, and told him how much the Americans were prepared to pay for peace, Skjöldebrand would

> apply to Mackoiah [Micaiah] Bensahud [Bensa'ud?], one of the principal men of the house of Joseph Cowen Bockeries [Cohen-Bakri], the great Jew merchants of Algiers, and head banquiers, that has the greatest influence with the Dey. . . . And the Dey, being of a wavering unsettled disposition, those people I have mentioned being empowered, they would, when opportunity offers, embrace and secure it effectually. Then, sir, let the American ambassador come and put a finishing hand

to the whole affair.... Indeed it would not be prudent for you to come to Algiers until the foundation was laid, and the terms known.

(2) He believed the dey was "prepossessed against the Americans by the British consul, who had information of your destination by the captain of the Portuguese frigate [*Ulysses*], and by Mr. Walpole, British resident at Lisbon."

The mission of the commander of the *Ulysses,* Captain Scarniche, is not spelled out in the correspondence. He arrived at Algiers on November 2, was taken by Logie to see the dey, and sailed on the seventh. He presumably was charged with discussing the conditions the Portuguese were putting on the truce regarding the protection of vessels, notably American and Hanseatic, carrying cargo to and from Portugal. The dey made much of the courtesies that had been extended to Scarniche as evidence of his good faith in observing the truce, but the courtesies did not extend to accepting the Portuguese conditions for the truce or lowering the price. Logie reported the dey's terms for peace to be 1,076,000 sequins, subsequently increased to 1,226,000, or roughly $2.3 million, about two-thirds of what the Spaniards were supposed to have paid. A subsequent document of April 27, 1795, which Cathcart and O'Brien claimed was a copy of the dey's 1793 demands, puts the total figure for peace at $2,452,000 before redemption of Portuguese captives. O'Brien commented that "the majority of Algerine politicians" were of the opinion the Portuguese would not accept such exorbitant terms. They were correct. The truce was not ratified by Portugal.

O'Brien also commented that three Algerine cruisers were at sea looking for more Americans, and they expected to pick up another ten or so ships. They apparently were foiled by the convoys provided by the Portuguese and Spaniards.

Perhaps in the same mail, too, was a November 5 letter from O'Brien to President Washington. He reported that ten ships and 105 men had been captured, that Mattias Skjöldebrand had advanced them money "to relieve their present necessities," and that by virtue of the Portuguese truce the corsairs had become masters of the Western Ocean. He advised that the only alternative for the United States was to fit out an expedition of thirty frigates and privateers to stop the corsairs.

O'Brien further commented that the Americans should have accepted the dey's original terms (of 1786), which were

> reasonable, considering what other nations pay. But I am afraid that favorable opportunity is irrevocably lost. But depend, sir, the Dey would wish to be at peace with the United States, provided we paid equal to what the Dutch, Swedes or Danes pay. We should be at peace with the Barbary States; our colors free and respected, and no subject of

the United States slaves. You must needs think, sir, that in case of the United States fitting out this proposed fleet, that those subjects of the United States which have been nearly nine years in captivity, that they would, when redeemed, be a very valuable acquisition to the American corsairs; for by their known experience of the ways and manoeuvres of those crafty people, would in great measure depend the desired effect in capturing corsairs of this regency.

Humanity towards the unfortunate American captives I presume will induce your excellency to co-operate with Congress to adopt some speedy and effectual plan in order to restore liberty and finally extricate the American captives from their present distress.

In a postscript he noted that there were a total of 115 captives in Algiers. Only ten were survivors from 1785.[23]

In forwarding these letters to Jefferson in a letter dated November 23 from Alicante, Humphreys commented: "From these communications it will also be but too evident, that no choice is left for the United States but to prepare a naval force, with all possible expedition, for the protection of their trade; and that there is but too much reason to fear, the corsairs, under a perfect sense of security from danger, elated with impunity and success, will infest the channel of England, and even the coasts of America, in another season, unless the most vigorous and decisive measures are taken."

Humphreys remained in Alicante until December 12, when he left for Madrid and Lisbon. Before leaving Alicante he gave written instructions to Montgomery regarding expenditures on behalf of the Americans in Algiers. First of all,

> to hide the nakedness, and screen from the inclemency of the season, the poor American prisoners in Algiers, you will have the goodness to provide each one of them a comfortable suit of clothing. . . . Secondly, you will please transmit regularly by way of subsistence . . . eight dollars a month to each of the captains, six dollars a month to each of the mates, and at the rate of twelve cents a day to each of the mariners. . . . Lastly, you are requested, sir, to open a correspondence with Pierre Eric Skjoldebrand, Esq. with the object of obtaining whatever useful intelligence, and rendering whatever services to the United States, may be in your power, from your favorable local situation, and well known good dispositions.

Humphreys signs himself "Commissioner Plenipotentiary from the united States to the Dey & Regency of Algiers." He seems not to have shared Jefferson's fear of making the United States look too prosperous. This was perhaps a reflection of his military experience, which made him both more sensitive to, and more sensible about, the needs of the captives than the civilian Jefferson was.[24]

Humphreys arrived in Madrid on the twenty-first of December and wrote to Jefferson again on the twenty-fifth. (By the time the letter reached the United States, Jefferson would have been succeeded in the post of secretary of state by Edmund Randolph.) In the letter Humphreys noted that he had received a letter from the consul in Málaga, Michael Morphy or Murphy, informing him that the Portuguese, far from withdrawing their squadron from Gibraltar, had just reinforced it with "two sail of the line and three capital frigates. They are now ten sail and have orders to give convoy to all Americans going to the westward, as far as they may require to get into safety from the enemy." He had also heard from Simpson, the candidate consul at Gibraltar, that five American vessels had sailed from there under the protection of a Portuguese frigate. He also reported that the British ambassador in Madrid had told him and William Short "that the Portuguese charge had told him Portugal would not give six pence for peace with Algiers."

So ended Humphreys's efforts to negotiate personally with the dey, although he was deeply involved in subsequent aspects of the affair. That he was not allowed to proceed to Algiers set the negotiating process back two years. The United States paid dearly, both in cash and in American lives, for its inability to get a negotiator on the scene sooner.

6

Negotiations at Last

The dey's unwillingness to discuss peace with the Americans lasted almost two years. What changed his mind and made him decide to accept an American negotiator is not clear, but anger with the British over the Portuguese truce fiasco and other matters may have been a factor. Whatever the reasons, it was clear that he had become interested in peace with the United States by late 1794. Meanwhile, Congress had agreed to begin construction of a modest fleet of six frigates and to create a navy. Construction was to be stopped if peace was reached with Algiers, underlining the role of that regency as the inspiration for the decision. Once an American negotiator, a Philadelphian named Joseph McDonald Jr., arrived and the preliminaries were disposed of, agreement on a treaty was reached rather quickly. The cost was exorbitant. American willingness to pay it reflected the improved state of the national economy and the assured flow of revenue to the Treasury.

Enter Cathcart

By his own account, the negotiation logjam was broken in large part by the efforts of James Cathcart, one of the more engaging figures in the drama of the American captives. He alone among the prisoners has left a portrait and an extensive paper trail through which we can trace him until his death in 1843. His narratives give us the liveliest picture we have of what was happening inside the establishment in Algiers. He was a key player in the negotiations that eventually led to the freeing of the captives, and he takes full credit for their success. We have few means of checking the accuracy of what he says, and here and there in his narrative he may have exaggerated his role. Nevertheless, it sounds as though he was able to exploit a personal relationship with the dey, who seemed to enjoy his wit and who played the curmudgeon to him with apparent pleasure.

Already in this narrative we have had several accounts from Cathcart. They come from two sources. One is *The Diplomatic Journal and Letter Book of James Leander Cathcart, 1788–1796*. These are notes and copies of

Fig. 9. *James Leander Cathcart,* by C. Coltellini. From *The Captives,* compiled by J. B. Newkirk, 1899.

letters he kept in captivity, which were later used for his memoirs, edited and published by his daughter in 1899 under the title *The Captives*. His *Journal* was published by the American Antiquarian Society in 1955 with the comment that Cathcart or his daughter had edited the material that appears in *The Captives* to present him in a more favorable light. The *Journal* is therefore considered more reliable than the memoirs. Yet, judging by its content as published and by the fragments of a draft in the Library of Congress collection of his papers, some of its narrative portions, perhaps many, were written or edited by Cathcart well after he was freed and left Algiers. While it is almost all we have and we are forced to rely on it for many details, we should have no illusions as to its total accuracy any more than we should with regard to other memoirs written after the fact.

According to the *Dictionary of American Biography,* Cathcart was born of a respectable Scots family in Ireland in 1767 and came to America at a very early age with a relative named Captain John Cathcart. In October 1779 James became a midshipman on the Continental frigate *Confederacy* and was captured by the British and held prisoner in one of the hulks at New York under conditions that sound worse than those at Algiers. He would have been only a boy at the time. In 1782 he escaped and subsequently entered the American merchant marine, which led to his capture by the Algerines in 1785. (Compare this with the account he gives in the December 20, 1785, petition in appendix 6 in which he claims to have served in the *British* navy. Nevertheless, he was eventually awarded a U.S. midshipman's pension for his naval service during the Revolution, so his story must have been credible.)

Nothing is said in *The Captives* about his education, or where he learned the Spanish he claimed to speak when he was captured. A brief history of him in the book *Arlington Heritage: Vignettes of a Virginia County* says he learned both Portuguese and Spanish from other seamen before he was fourteen. One can imagine how much, or little, he would learn from such contact. He wrote that his responsibility at one point was to interpret for the dey all the letters that came to him from Christian powers. He implied elsewhere that he was able to translate documents from Turkish, but he confessed to the pasha of Tripoli on one occasion that he could speak neither Turkish nor Arabic well enough to conduct business. This is borne out by his transliterations of Arabic and Turkish terms. He must have had a reasonable command of lingua franca to survive, and probably knew some Arabic and Turkish but not enough to do much actual translating.

According to the *Arlington Heritage* account, Cathcart signed on to the *Maria* as second mate in 1785 for a voyage to Cádiz with a cargo of furs, lumber, and dried codfish. We have already had his account of his arrival in Algiers and his early treatment there. He worked, not very happily, in the garden of the dey's palace for about a year before being sent to the Beylical bagnio, the largest of the prisons, to his intense disgust.[1]

Perhaps because of his intelligence, certainly because of his consistent good luck, Cathcart was not sent to hard labor in the quarries but, together with an unnamed shipmate he refers to as his "companion" (who can be identified from the context as James Harnet), was apprenticed to a carpenter, "a genteel-looking Spaniard, a native of Barcelona." The Spanish prisoners tended to be either mariners captured at sea or deserters from the garrison at Oran. According to Cathcart, there were about four hundred of the former and a thousand of the latter. The Oran deserters were disowned by the Spanish government and had scant prospect of being ransomed. This turned many of them into desperate cases who were prominent in the criminal element among the prisoners. Cathcart's carpenter, on the other hand, had resigned himself to his situation and had set about becoming expert in his trade. Now considered the best in Algiers, he was much in demand for carpentry work. Cathcart was lucky to be working with him.

On March 17, 1787, the king of Naples ransomed three hundred of his subjects, creating many vacancies in the workforce. Cathcart was taken from the carpentry shop and ordered to serve the wakil al-kharj at the admiralty. He was one of six to nine Christians who waited on table, took care of the stores, and performed other domestic chores. They were well fed and received tips from visitors. This was a desirable position.

Then, when the four-hundred-odd nondeserter Spanish prisoners were ransomed under the Spanish truce, Cathcart replaced the admiralty's departing qahwaji, or coffee server. This was an even better position, because visitors were expected to fill the qahwaji's coffee cups with gold coins before they left. These were then divided among the household staff. Then, in June 1787, he was made clerk of the admiralty. He remained in that job until April 1788, when he was removed because of an altercation over the accounts and was sent to the Galera bagnio, where he occupied himself with a tavern he had acquired along the way, and where he was appointed clerk of the bagnio with responsibility for mustering and feeding the prisoners morning and evening and reporting absences.[2] The taverns sold wine, spirits, and food to the prisoners and to local residents. Cathcart farmed his out to other prisoners, who paid him so much per pipe, or cask, of wine or spirits. The taverns sound primitive but evidently were profitable, judging by Cathcart's reports of charitable actions he was able to take on behalf of the other prisoners. He claimed that none of his fellow sufferers among the original captives ever lacked a good meal while it was in his power to give them one, that he saw to it that they were attended to in the hospital when sick, that those who died were buried in a decent coffin at his expense, and that he followed every American to his grave and read a prayer over it.

Meanwhile, Cathcart said, he had never enjoyed better health. He said that during his tour as clerk at the admiralty "all the people of the Magazine, the Vikilharche [wakil al-kharj] of the Marine excepted, had died and been replaced three times" because of the plague, which raged with particular severity in 1787. Whether because of a rugged constitution or good fortune, Cathcart seems to have been sick only once, when he addressed a letter to O'Brien in 1793 as coming from "Death's Door."

On page 150 of *The Captives* Cathcart says that in July 1791 he became chief clerk to the "Prime Minister," who at that point would have been Mustafa Pasha, the khaznaji and subsequently dey. Cathcart had evidently remained clerk of the Galera bagnio up to then. Then the account becomes confused. On page 157 he says that in March 1792 he became secretary to the dey and the regency. Elsewhere he said this appointment resulted from the liberation of his predecessor, a man named Andreiss, following the Dutch treaty of April 1794. The latter date would accord better with the details of his role in the negotiations and with other aspects of his narrative.

It would also fit better with the letter Cathcart wrote on January 12, 1794, to William Wilberforce, the well-known member of Parliament, abolitionist, and philanthropist, asking for his help in raising £675 sterling for his redemption so that he could be restored to his "long lamented Patria," Britain.[3] It sounds as though it was written in an understandable fit of depression following the fiasco of Humphreys's visit to Alicante, and not like something the powerful clerk of the dey, who could easily raise £675 on his own, would be writing. Not surprisingly, there is no mention of the letter to Wilberforce in Cathcart's *Journal* or *The Captives*. The *Journal* does, however, contain the text of a 1791 letter addressed to Dr. Philip Werner, the surgeon of the British trading station in Algiers, rejecting inclusion in a British effort to redeem captives. (Cathcart could reasonably claim British nationality because of his birth in Ireland.)

The chief clerkship was a very influential position, for which Cathcart had to pay 1,000 sequins, or $2,000, to the treasury and 383 sequins as customary bakhsheesh to various officials. It is indicative of their relationship that the dey advanced Cathcart half the 1,000 sequins; the Skjöldebrand brothers put up the other half. (The Skjöldebrands had earlier lent him $5,000 with which to purchase a prize vessel loaded with wine, which he sold for enough to permit him to buy another ship in which he eventually sailed to the United States.)

Cathcart's portrait in a Revolutionary War–period uniform (fig. 9) was published in *The Captives*. It shows a full-faced, dignified young man who looks somewhat pleased with himself. I have not yet found the original.

Negotiations Resume

As chief clerk Cathcart had arrived at the position from which he played his role in the negotiations. On January 2, 1794, Congress, aroused by the Algerian seizures of American ships and impressed by Washington's statements regarding the need for the country to defend itself, approved by a narrow margin a resolution calling for creation of a navy, and in March voted to authorize the construction of six frigates for that purpose.[4] The authorization contained a provision, however, that construction of the ships would be stopped if a peace treaty should be concluded with Algiers in the meantime. A treaty was concluded in 1795, before construction was completed, but Congress compromised on continuing work on three of them after Washington pointed out the unfortunate economic effects of halting construction on all six. Work was resumed on the other three at the time of the undeclared naval war or Quasi-War with France (1798–1801).

Soon after Congress acted, there was progress on the negotiating track (no connection implied). According to *The Captives* (327), Cathcart wrote to

Humphreys in the spring of 1794—the letter is undated but it was written after the Dutch treaty—to say that "the Dey has no objection" to peace with the United States on terms similar to those concluded with the Dutch.

Meanwhile, on July 19, 1794, Humphreys was authorized to borrow in Europe up to $800,000 with which to buy peace and ransom the captives. Priority was to be given to ransoming, and he was authorized to spend up to $3,000 per captive. His instructions, contained in a letter from Secretary of State Edmund Randolph of July 19, 1794, sound wonderfully delicate today:

> It must be submitted to your discretion, upon the view of all circumstances, as well as of personal danger as public benefit, whether you will go over [to Algiers] yourself—a measure which unquestionably would enable you to seize more certainly, than when at a distance, one of those moments of good humor and caprice which the letters transmitted through you from Algiers designate as the lucky seasons for impressing the Dey, and consider as having, unfortunately for our country, escaped without being caught. If, however, you find it unsafe, or impracticable, to undertake the mission yourself, it will then be proper to use the instrument selected by Mr. [Gouverneur] Morris, and to instruct him accordingly, maintaining always, perfect cordiality and concert with the French commissioner, but, at the same time, not hesitating to follow your own ideas when they shall seem preferable, and resorting to the Swedish consul at Algiers, his brother, or any other individual, or expedient, according to your judgement, on the best means of accomplishing success.[5]

This was followed by a second letter from Randolph dated August 25, 1794, which read in part:

> I beg leave to refer to my letter of the 19th July . . . as indicative of the President's wish that you should continue in the destination for Algiers. It is too interesting to the feelings of us all, not to retain you in a mission for which your experience in the subject, and other qualities, combine to fit you, rather than any other person who could be sent.
>
> *These are the instructions of the President*
>
> 1. Ransom and peace are to go hand and hand, if practicable; but if peace cannot be obtained, a ransom is to be effected without delay.
> 2. After endeavoring to obtain a ransom, at the lowest possible rate, or at the rate allowed by Portugal, or other nations the least favored, you may if necessary go as far as three thousand dollars per man.
> 3. You will refer to the former instructions for the real wishes of the

Government as to the sum to be paid for peace; keeping in mind the preference for a larger annuity and a smaller douceur [conciliatory gift] in hand, to the reverse. But we would not break for fifty thousand dollars per annum, and two hundred thousand dollars by way of douceur, to secure a peace for a convenient term of years. But, though this form of the thing is most eligible, yet it is not judged to be a sine qua non; for, after all, what is usual and effectual must decide, and the payment in gross may be accomodated to the necessity of accomplishing the object.

4. If, however, by any other modification of the sum of eight hundred thousand dollars, a peace and ransom can be obtained, you may modify accordingly; restricting yourself, on the head of a ransom, within the above mentioned limit of three thousand dollars per man.[6]

These are very broad instructions. We had come a long way from the $200 per man Jefferson had authorized Lamb to offer. As president, Washington had obviously weighed in, and we have here an early example of the preponderant role the person in that job can play in foreign affairs, particularly after a strong secretary of state has left office.

Humphreys Goes AWOL

Humphreys evidently had not received these letters (or Cathcart's letter) before he decided rather abruptly to leave Lisbon for the United States in November 1794, finally arriving in Newport in February after a terrible voyage. His biographer, Frank Landon Humphreys, said his purpose was "to see the president and come back with full powers to enable him to prepare for whatever contingencies might arise. He courageously determined to go without leave, sure that the rectitude of his conduct would approve itself to his old general."[7] He evidently got away with this, but not without some criticism. If he had received news of the authorization of July 19, and there should have been time enough for him to do so, there would have been no real justification for his going home. The authorization gave him full powers to negotiate and enough money to buy a treaty—he had heard from Per Erik Skjöldebrand in September that peace and redemption of the captives could probably be had for six to seven hundred thousand dollars. Whatever Humphreys's rationale for what he did, Cathcart said his behavior convinced the dey that the Americans were trifling with him and further complicated the negotiations. It certainly prolonged them, and the suffering of the American seamen, by at least a year. It also deprived Humphreys of the glory of negotiating the peace treaty himself.

Encouraging Signs

Meanwhile there were continuing signals that the dey was more open to a settlement than he had been before the Dutch truce. O'Brien, in a rambling and sometimes incoherent letter of October 1794 to Humphreys, said that the dey's price had become $2,435,000, which Humphreys should reject out of hand as preposterous. O'Brien did not say how he knew these were the terms, but said they were a bargaining ploy. The dey would surely come down and would probably settle for a total of $600,000. If the dey flew into a rage and ordered Humphreys to leave, Humphreys should do so without hesitation, but should leave someone reliable, one of the Skjöldebrands or the Cohen-Bakris, with power to negotiate for him.

Cathcart sent to Montgomery in Alicante a more detailed account, dated December 22 and described as having been copied from the "Publick Register" of the regency. It said that in exchange for a hundred-year peace, the dey expected $1,080,000 for the public treasury, $540,000 for himself, $273,000 in presents to his family and various government officials, and $354,000 for ransoming one hundred captives, for a total of $2,247,000. The text of this document, an impressive list of expected bakhsheesh, is in appendix 10.

Humphreys saw Washington twice and left the United States in April 1795, arriving at Gibraltar on May 13. He was accompanied by Joseph Donaldson Jr. of Philadelphia, whom Washington had appointed "American consul to [not "in" or "at"] Tunis and Tripoli," and Philip Sloan, a former American captive who had been released at the time of the Dutch truce and was returning in the capacity of interpreter and assistant to Donaldson.[8] Donaldson had been recommended by the secretary of the treasury and may have been a treasury official himself, but I have been able to find little about his background aside from his being a resident of Philadelphia.[9] Cathcart describes him as over fifty, "of a forbidding countenance and remarkably surly." He cites various instances of Donaldson's ungentlemanly behavior in his account. The two of them did not get along well.

French Help

Unaware of the hollowness of French aid in 1785, Humphreys and Washington reportedly agreed that French help with Algiers would be important to their effort, but Humphreys's instructions were rather vague. In a letter of April 4, 1795, Randolph recommended to him that he "proceed as early as possible to France, for the purpose of obtaining the co-operation of that Government in this negotiation." Humphreys was to arrange this with the help of James Monroe, the American minister, and Joel Barlow, long resident in France and an honorary citizen of that republic, who was thought to be influential.[10] Accordingly, on arrival in Gibraltar, Humphreys sent Donaldson and Sloan on to Alicante while he went to Paris, taking a month to get to Le Havre by ship.

Humphreys, according to his biographer, had intended for Donaldson only to "ascertain facts and profit of occasions," and expected him to remain in Alicante until such time as a negotiator for Algiers could be appointed. That is not what his written instructions of May 18 to Donaldson said, however. They instructed him to proceed to Algiers without delay, to consult with the French consul, and if it appeared that a treaty could be had for a price within the sum authorized, to "proceed to arrange & agree upon a Provisional Treaty. That is to say, a Treaty providing, that the liberation of our Citizens in Captivity at Algiers shall take effect as soon as the Money can be paid." Donaldson was to proceed to Lisbon immediately after concluding the agreement in order to obtain the money stipulated in the agreement, money that Humphreys said he expected would be available by the time the agreement was concluded or shortly thereafter. Humphreys emphasized the need for haste in order to extricate the captives before another round of the plague arrived.[11] Later in the document Humphreys spoke of a treaty of peace and friendship as though he assumed that would be part of the agreement Donaldson might reach, although that was not clear from the language quoted above, which spoke only of an agreement on liberation of the captives. As we saw earlier, ransom of captives and treaties of peace appeared to be separate concepts in Algerine minds. It was conceivable that Donaldson could negotiate only an agreement on ransom.

Donaldson later complained that Humphreys had not taken the time to explain what he meant. The instructions, covering several pages, are quite detailed and explicit, but perhaps Humphreys did not discuss them as fully as he should have. He evidently was notorious in this respect. Barlow, in a letter to his wife of April 16, 1796, commented that Humphreys "seems to have too much beef in his head to be a good manager of such affairs. The most conspicuous talent that I can discover in him hitherto is that of keeping a secret, and keeping it from those whose knowledge of [it] is absolutely necessary to his success. His eternal mystery and silence (I will not say inattention and folly) will probably lose us the treaty yet."

The effort in Paris to obtain French support did not go smoothly. Monroe had been personally well received in France, but his mission was complicated by the November 19, 1794, treaty with England negotiated by Jay, by then chief justice of the Supreme Court. It dealt with various territorial, commercial, and financial issues unresolved since the Treaty of Paris and was not a treaty of alliance, but the French, who were at war with England and thought they were America's first friends, naturally resented this agreement with their enemy. Monroe persisted, however, and on August 1 reported that he had received assurances that the French would send instructions to their officials to help the Americans.[12]

I have found no reference to such instructions in the archives of the French consulate at Algiers. That does not mean none were sent, but Humphreys reported that the official to whom the instructions had been entrusted, Allois d'Herculais, did not arrive in Algiers until after a treaty had been negotiated. On the other hand, the French consul, Césaire-Philippe Vallière, had sent a friendly letter to Humphreys in December 1793 offering to help, and he and others apparently believed that the Americans wanted him to do so. He went so far as to discuss peace terms for the Americans with the dey and may have been acting on instructions generated by the efforts of Gouverneur Morris. According to Cathcart and Per Erik Skjöldebrand, however, his performance was unhelpful, and they both suspected he was trying to frustrate the American effort. Cathcart claimed that he had deliberately muddied the waters by telling the dey Donaldson had carte blanche to pay whatever was needed to get the prisoners released, and this seems to be confirmed by Skjöldebrand's letter of August 13, 1794, to Humphreys, in which he wrote, "It is true that since the French consul was commissioned in your business, the pretensions of the Dey were exorbitant."[13]

The person Humphreys originally had in mind for the job of negotiator was Colonel Benjamin Hicheborn, Barlow's partner in the shipping business in Paris. Hicheborn, who had served in the Boston Independent Corps under John Hancock during the Revolution, declined the honor, pleading poor eyesight, and the choice fell on Barlow, already well known to Humphreys. He agreed to go and had begun assembling presents to take to officials in Algiers by the time Humphreys left Paris for Lisbon via Le Havre on September 12.

While waiting for his ship to leave Le Havre, Humphreys was startled to learn that Donaldson had already gone to Algiers and negotiated a treaty without his, or French, help. When he reached Lisbon on November 17, he found that O'Brien had been waiting for him there since early October with the treaty.

The Negotiations

How did Donaldson do it? The official record is sparse, but we have a fairly full, and colorful, account from Cathcart in *The Captives*. While he perhaps embroidered here and there and magnified his own role, the basic story rings true. The following is a summary, arranged in a chronological order more precise than that followed by Cathcart, who skips about.

Cathcart starts by saying that his position as chief clerk had enabled him to counteract the bad impression created by Humphreys's unauthorized departure for the United States, but does not explain how he did this. Then he goes on to explain that it was he who devised the argument used by the dey on July 1, 1795, with his divan, the members of which were fretting over talk of peace with America. They noted that the United States had no navy to menace them, and argued that peace with Portugal would be more advantageous. The dey replied that, in the first place, the Americans would provide naval stores that would render the Algerines independent of those supplied by the Scandinavian countries and Holland, on whom they could then declare war by turns, which would be much more lucrative than war with the Americans, who would probably arm to protect themselves if their overtures were repulsed. Furthermore, the northern nations were accustomed to paying tribute and did not consider it degrading, since it was a commercial expense paid by their chambers of commerce rather than the public treasury, whereas the Americans would have to pay out of the public treasury and must first obtain the approval of Congress. How Cathcart thought this latter argument would influence the divan is not clear, but he says he managed to inculcate these ideas in the minds of the dey and others and that this was the true cause of the dey's decision to reduce the price when it came to bargaining and of his willingness to be patient when the cash was not immediately forthcoming. Cathcart felt that this was of "infinite service" to the American cause.

Donaldson reached Alicante in early August 1795, and on August 13 letters announcing his arrival there were received by the Skjöldebrands, Vallière, and O'Brien. Montgomery also sent a letter to Cathcart, who, after consulting with one of the Skjöldebrands and O'Brien, told the dey that an American gentleman had arrived at Alicante and requested permission to come and discuss terms of peace. The dey asked if he was the long-awaited ambassador, and Cathcart said he was not, the ambassador having gone to France, probably to arrange the financial details. The gentleman at Alicante was his designated precursor, however. The dey asked Cathcart if he would assume responsibility for the precursor's having full powers to negotiate. Cathcart said, on his head be it; the man had full powers but the amount he could offer was fixed. Therefore, if the dey was not prepared to lower his demands, he should not give permission for him to come.

The dey asked if the Americans expected a peace for nothing. Cathcart replied that they wanted it on the same terms as the Dutch. The dey commented that it was the Americans' fault that they had not profited from his goodwill in the past and then asked how they could expect to have peace on the same terms as the Dutch, who supplied the Algerines with so much in the way of naval stores. Cathcart asked what the Americans had ever done to the Algerines to merit having thirteen of their ships seized and 131 people imprisoned as slaves. He would nevertheless consider his ten years in captivity well spent if he could be the mediator who established peace between the two nations. The dey responded, "So you may, but you must pay for it," and his moustache curled, indicating that a squall was coming.

Cathcart countered with an oration on the contrast between the Catholic powers, who had been at war with the Muslims since the Hejira (622 A.D.), and the Americans, who gave the Muslims full religious freedom on their territory. The Algerines made the Catholic powers pay high because their hostility had obliged them to spend millions on defense, while the Americans had never been at war with them. The dey's whiskers relaxed and he said, "Let him come."

There is no way of knowing whether this dialogue actually occurred or was invented by Cathcart after the fact, but whether it did or not, he obtained from the dey authorization to issue a special passport for Donaldson to come to Algiers and had it sent to Alicante on a Ragusan brig chartered by the Skjöldebrands for $400—all of this within six hours of receipt of Donaldson's letter. Vallière was incensed and wanted to know why he had not been consulted. Cathcart said that while Vallière had not actively opposed his efforts, the other European consuls had; he blamed the Spanish, the Danish, the Venetians, and the Chamber of Commerce of Marseille in particular. He took credit for outsmarting them and for persuading the dey to punish the Spanish for preventing Philip Sloan from embarking from Alicante immediately after Donaldson's arrival with news that an American emissary had arrived.

While waiting for Donaldson in the period August 13–September 2, Cathcart had daily discussions with the dey about the forthcoming visit of "the Ambassador." The dey was impatient and concerned that Donaldson might not come after all. Cathcart counseled patience and offered to take the dey's final offer to Alicante himself if Donaldson did not come. The dey said, "Yes, and never come back again." Cathcart pleaded the sanctity of his word. If he had wanted to escape, he said, he could have been ransomed twice by the British, but he had refused each time. He felt that this increased the dey's good opinion of him.

The dey wanted to know what terms the Americans would accept, and Cathcart said they expected peace on the same terms as the Dutch and would make the dey a private present of $100,000 plus $50,000 for his family. Cathcart thought he saw "a latent spark of satisfaction" on the dey's face and was convinced that at that moment he could have bought a peace treaty and the release of all the captives for $450,000.

Donaldson reached Algiers on September 2, in the same Ragusan brig that had carried his passport to Alicante. When Cathcart informed the dey, the dey told him to take Donaldson to the regency-owned house that had been prepared for him. As for himself, he was going to his country house to see his wife (it was a Thursday afternoon). Cathcart answered, "Her ladyship will not be forgot in the terms of the peace." The dey looked over his shoulder and smiled.

Cathcart gives us a colorful description of Donaldson's disembarkment. He was suffering from gout, and his right leg was "muffled in flannel, shod with a large velvet slipper and his right arm leaning on a crutch." He had to undergo a painful, sweaty walk over rough pavement through a curious crowd to reach his assigned residence. After a further painful trip up a flight of stairs, he finally collapsed on a couch and "uttered a string of ejaculations and execrations, so equally mixed together that I could not discover which predominated. 'What is the matter?' said the Jew [Micaiah Cohen-Bakri], with a look of astonishment. 'Nothing at all,' said O'Brien. 'The ambassador is only saying his prayers and giving God thanks for his safe arrival.' 'His devotion is very fervent,' said Micaiah."

Cathcart then had dinner, with wine, brought in. Donaldson's disposition improved, and Per Erik Skjöldebrand came by after dark to discuss the history of the negotiations to date and, one presumes, strategy for the future. It sounds very much like the arrival of today's typical special emissary at some remote post.

Although the following day was Friday and no business was normally done in the palace on that day, Cathcart managed to obtain an appointment for Donaldson to see the dey at 7:00 A.M. and to present his credentials, which Cathcart read and explained to the dey.

After a brief exchange on the subject of peace, the dey said that, it being Friday, they would talk business the next day. But he summoned Cathcart back at 9:00 A.M. and, after quizzing him again on whether Donaldson really had the authority to negotiate, told him to convey to Donaldson the terms he had ordered made out the previous year—terms Cathcart had already reported on December 22, 1794, to wit: $2,247,000 plus two frigates of thirty-five guns each, an annual donation of naval stores to the value of 12,000 sequins, and biennial consular presents such as those given by Sweden, Denmark, and Holland. Cathcart told him these terms would be rejected, but the dey commanded him to convey the offer immediately. As Cathcart went to kiss the dey's hand. his foot slipped on the pavement, and the dey said, "Can you not stand?" and Cathcart replied, "Yes, but the weight of Your Excellency's proposal made me stumble." Cathcart was told later that the dey had laughed heartily at this reply and told the members of his cabinet about it.

What is clear from this account is that the dey was anxious to conclude a treaty. It is less clear why. A need for cash is one explanation, but the details are lacking. Another is that he was doing it to spite the British, with whom he was very irritated at the time because of the Portuguese truce affair. As noted in the previous chapter, on March 27, 1794, he had written to George III a long letter of complaint about having entered into that engagement to please the British, with the understanding that the Portuguese were seriously interested in it. His disappointment at the Portuguese refusal to ratify the truce with money was to be expected. Whatever the cause, and whatever he may have said to Cathcart, the dey's behavior is understandable only if one assumes that he wanted a peace treaty with the Americans. Half the battle was won.

Donaldson reacted to the dey's proposal with despair. It had been a mistake to come, he concluded; any offer he could make in response would be regarded as an insult, so it would be better to make none. Cathcart, O'Brien, and Skjöldebrand eventually talked him out of that, and they agreed on a counterproposal of $543,000 for peace and ransom.[14]

Cathcart, accompanied by Philip Sloan, returned to the dey with the counteroffer, and a heated dialogue ensued. The dey "smiled in contempt and then broke out in a rage." He called Cathcart a liar and an infidel for claiming that Donaldson could offer no more and said he had been told by Vallière that he had carte blanche and could give what he pleased for peace. Cathcart replied that Vallière was a liar and an ignorant fellow and asked if Vallière had received orders from his government to intervene in this case. The dey said he had not, but had given him the information from motives of friendship. Cathcart remarked that Vallière was incapable of friendship and begged the dey not to listen to such malicious reports.

The dey accused Cathcart of disloyalty, saying he must have helped Donaldson draw up the proposal: "You have not been in Algiers so long for nothing. If you had not dictated those terms how should that man, who only arrived in Algiers yesterday, know how to appropriate the different terms specified in the proposal?" Cathcart replied that he was an American and obliged to give the ambassador all the information he had, but as a grateful servant of the dey he had ensured that the dey and his family were well taken care of. The dey asked him to read the proposal again, and then said, "A hundred thousand for me, and fifty thousand for my family—sequins, you mean?" Cathcart replied that he meant dollars, not sequins, and the dey said, "Go out of my sight immediately, thou dog without a soul, and never presume to bring such trifling terms in to me again under pain of my displeasure." Cathcart said this expression meant a bastinadoing at the least.

When Cathcart returned to Donaldson's house with the dey's response,

Donaldson said he had gone as far as his instructions permitted and could go no further. The others remonstrated with him and argued that a modest increase in the offer might be enough. Then at 2:00 P.M. Cathcart was summoned by the dey again for another scolding and given a third proposal of $982,000. This Donaldson also rejected, refusing to increase his offer by a single dollar. When Cathcart, having failed to change Donaldson's mind, returned to the dey with his response, the dey ordered him to send Donaldson back to Alicante at daybreak on the fifth.

Cathcart passed the dey's instructions to Donaldson, but in the following discussion it emerged that in fact Donaldson had authority to go up to $650,000. Cathcart said they could do better than that, and together with O'Brien and Skjöldebrand they worked out a written offer of $585,000. Cathcart then instructed Donaldson to make ostentatious preparations to depart the following morning and ordered porters to be ready to carry his baggage to the dock, while Skjöldebrand sent word to the Ragusan brig's agent to have the brig ready for departure in the morning. The purpose of these maneuvers was to create the impression, which would reach the dey's ears, that Donaldson was in fact leaving because he did not have the unlimited powers ascribed to him by Vallière. The next morning at 7:00 A.M. Cathcart, Sloan, and Cohen-Bakri called on the dey and presented proposal number 4. Cathcart told him Donaldson would be at sea before noon, but was making this last offer, to which he had added his entire personal fortune, in order to avoid having the negotiations broken off. The dey said the added amount was trifling and that the French consul had sent his dragoman that morning to tell him again that Donaldson had carte blanche. Cathcart told the dey he was being imposed on by Vallière. The dey replied that he had reduced his first demand by two-thirds and could go no further. Donaldson could embark when he pleased.

Cathcart said he regretted beyond measure that the United States would now be obliged to arm itself against Algiers, but the dey had promised to let the captives be ransomed, and he asked that they be allowed to go. The dey took a pinch of snuff and asked to have the proposal read over again line by line. Cathcart pointed out that the dey and his family would now get $240,000, and that the total sum was $279,500 more than the Dutch had paid.

The dey answered, "Yes, you know how to gabbar," using the lingua franca version of the Italian *gabbare*, to cheat or deceive. "Should I now reject your terms and send your ambassador away, your enemies would rejoice and you would become the laughingstock of all the consuls and Franks in Algiers. Go and tell your ambassador that I accept his terms, more to pique the British, who are your inveterate enemies, and are on very bad terms with me, than in consideration of the sum which I esteem no more than a pinch of snuff," at the same time blowing away a pinch he held in his fingers. The dey then added that annual payment in naval stores and presents on the arrival of ambassadors and consuls must be paid on the same scale as paid by the Dutch, Swedes, and Danes. (The customary presents paid by these states were later calculated by O'Brien to be $16,000 biannually plus $20,000 on the arrival of a new consul.)

Continuing to keep up the pretense that Donaldson was leaving at noon, Cathcart and the others were prepared to return to the palace at 10:00 A.M. when Cohen-Bakri reappeared with a list of naval stores being demanded by the dey. There was some consternation over the problem of reconciling these with the amounts of cash being stipulated, but this was worked out—vastly incorrectly, it transpired—and they proceeded to meet with the dey, who authorized them to raise the American flag at the admiralty as a sign that peace had been agreed on. Cathcart proceeded to the admiralty, where the flag was raised at noon and received a twenty-one-gun salute, to the surprise of the inhabitants, foreign and otherwise.

The negotiations had taken less than forty-eight hours, an incredibly short time. Cathcart commented that "peace was established between the Regency of Algiers and the United States of America, to the astonishment of every person in Algiers, friends as well as foes, by a lame old man who understood no language but his own, without funds or credit and surrounded with enemies."

But their troubles were only half over. Until they found the money promised to the dey, there would be no release of the captives. The dey said he was an old man and recommended that they hurry, because his successor might not be as friendly to the Americans as he was. In the meantime, as a token of his esteem, he made Donaldson a present of a fine Barbary stallion and of Joseph Koenig, the young German captive who played a role at the palace window (see appendix 3) on the night Hasan's predecessor died.

7

Money Problems

The amount of money the Americans agreed to pay the Algerines, $585,000, was equivalent to nearly nine million of today's dollars. It was a very substantial sum for the infant republic, which had federal budget receipts of only $6,115,000 in 1795. The Algerines wanted payment in gold, not paper currency or check. The republic's credit was good for that amount in Europe: it could sell bonds (the correspondence used the term "stock," in the British sense of a fixed-interest security) on the open market, although they would be discounted. Unfortunately, war in Europe led to a shortage of gold, and the bankers wanted to discount the bonds too much. There followed a year-long saga of trying to assemble the hard cash to pay the dey the amount promised. It was finally tacked together through a series of transactions, and ended up costing close to one million dollars.

Treaty Payments

There were three separate but related financial obligations imposed by the treaty, only one of which is mentioned in that document. The first was the traditional "peace presents," which amounted to 20,016 sequins, or about $40,000 worth of jewelry, watches, textiles, and cash distributed to roughly a hundred officials—everyone from the dey to the baggage handlers, passing by the head cook and the dey's barber. The dey, for instance, was given a ring, a watch and chain, a snuffbox, a ring for his wife and one for his daughter, 16 pieces of gold brocade, 82 pieces of broadcloth, 3 pieces of damask, and 4 of linen for a total value of 10,359 sequins, or about $21,000. These presents were provided by Micaiah Bakri and were passed out in the days immediately following the treaty signing. Donaldson eventually paid Bakri for them from Livorno in the spring of 1796. The business of supplying these presents to foreigners at grossly inflated prices was an established racket engaged in by the bankers and other merchants of Algiers, the recipients often selling the present back to the banker at a discount and the object in question being recycled to be presented again, perhaps to the same person. Thus, Donaldson suspected that the dey had owned his ring before.

These presents should not be confused with the consular presents that were expected every two years or when a new consul arrived. Cathcart's journal contains a list of presents given by the Danish consul in 1792 and 1794. There are 116–plus recipients on the list, including two brothers and an uncle of the dey.

The second obligation was the annual payment of 12,000 sequins mentioned in the preamble of the treaty, which stipulated that this could be paid in cash or kind. (The original translation of the treaty stipulates "Algerian sequins" but the revised translation of 1930 speaks of "gold pieces.") The Algerines wanted naval stores, and the final cost of the items requested under that heading for the first two years was estimated by the Americans at $144,246, or roughly 75,000 sequins, more than triple the stipulated payment. The treaty stated that in such cases the excess could be carried over as a credit against future payments. The Americans tried to get out of paying in kind whenever possible because of the trouble and expense involved in procuring and shipping various items, large masts in particular. Delays and disagreements over quality and kind lasted for the life of this "annuity" or tribute, which was not ended until 1812, when Consul General Tobias Lear left after a dispute regarding payment and the dey declared war on American shipping. In 1815, under duress, the Algerines agreed to a new treaty that contained no provision for tribute. These events are discussed later.

The third obligation was the $585,000 that was the price for redeeming the captives and for peace. How much for peace and how much for ransom does not seem to be specified officially, but in his account book in his papers at the Houghton Library, Barlow lists an amount of $215,052.80 that he paid for redeeming 105 prisoners, four of whom were not American mariners but whom he had to ransom anyway at the dey's insistence. (This was well below the usual extra ransoms imposed by the Algerines, according to Barlow.) A fifth man was Richard Hales of Marblehead, who had been arrested for smuggling at Cádiz some eight years earlier and sentenced to life at Oran, from which he had escaped. He had tried unsuccessfully to get the British to ransom him, and had then turned to the Americans. There were thus 100 American officers and seamen ransomed by Barlow at a price of about $2,000 per head. The correspondence mentions no calculation based on so much per officer and so much per seaman, and the distribution seems to have been arbitrary, with the dey trying to get a maximum total figure for himself and not worrying unduly about the allocation of the rest, once obtained.

To the Americans in Algiers, unaware of the complications that the gold shortage would cause, the job looked simple. To get the money, someone would have to go to Lisbon with the treaty and give it to David Humphreys, who would forward it to President Washington for ratification and who had the authority to draw on the $800,000 credit that Congress had authorized. The gold should be available in London from Baring and Company, the bankers who were to raise the money through the sale of six-percent bonds issued by the Bank of the United States.

Cathcart fancied himself for the job of carrying the treaty to Lisbon, but O'Brien persuaded him that he was needed in Algiers and his patriotic duty was to remain there. Cathcart claimed that O'Brien had first gone behind his back and prevailed on Skjöldebrand's dragoman and Micaiah Bakri to suggest to the dey that he, O'Brien, be sent. The dey had responded that Philip Sloan could do the job. O'Brien had then come to Cathcart for sponsorship. When Cathcart went to the dey with some reluctance on the evening of September 6 and pointed out to him how useful it would be to send someone who understood the quality of naval stores the Algerines wanted, the dey readily agreed that O'Brien should go, but Cathcart left O'Brien in suspense for some time to punish him for his duplicity.

On the afternoon of September 7, Cathcart received the Turkish text of the treaty from "the Secretary of State," Osman Khoja, and took it, with a translation that he claimed he made himself, to Donaldson. This translation was reexamined in 1930 and "considerable differences" between it and the original Turkish were found.[1] The text was similar to, but not identical with, the Swedish-Algerine treaty of 1723 as amended.

On September 8 the gifts acquired from the Bakris were distributed to Algerine officials. On the ninth Per Erik Skjöldebrand chartered a Portuguese brig to take O'Brien to Lisbon, but according to Cathcart, Donaldson refused to pay the $20 premium that would have been required for the direct voyage, and O'Brien, who left the afternoon of the eleventh, was forced to take a Spanish boat to Malaga instead, and to go overland from there to Lisbon, which he reached on October 1. (Why O'Brien, Cathcart, or one of the Skjöldebrands did not come forward with the $20 is a mystery. Perhaps the amount is wrong.) In addition to the treaty, O'Brien carried Donaldson's dispatches and a golden yataghan or sabre sent by the dey to Humphreys as a mark of esteem.[2] It would be a long time before the captives would hear from O'Brien again.[3]

After O'Brien left, Cathcart and Donaldson dined together and considered that the affair was settled and there would be no alterations until they heard from Humphreys. Donaldson said Humphreys had told him a great part of the funds in question were available in Lisbon. He and Cathcart accordingly expected the transaction to be completed within two to three months. Cathcart claimed that, had he been authorized to do so, he could have raised the cash himself with bills on London, Marseille, or Livorno, but he did not trust Donaldson enough to run any more risk than he had already, especially since Donaldson did not seem to appreciate what he had done to date. The record does not show that he made any offer to do this.

On September 13 Donaldson retired to the Swedish consul's country house, which Cathcart says was four miles from the city (according to a map in Playfair's *The Scourge of Christendom,* it was south of town), and did not return until November 1, when he came down with "bilious colic," followed by the gout, which kept him confined for a month. Cathcart meanwhile was badgering the dey to arrange a truce with Tunis, which was nominally subordinate to Algiers, and reported that on November 8 he "procured a truce with Tunis for eight months, guaranteed by the Dey of Algiers, translated it and took the original to Mr. Donaldson, who kept his bed with the gout and the colic." This truce, the text of which forms appendix 12, was not recognized by the bey of Tunis when the time came, as we shall see.

According to Cathcart, on November 20 "the mates and seamen from the American ships laid siege to his [Donaldson's] chamber and insisted on his procuring them leave to stay in town" instead of the bagnios. Donaldson, who had declined an offer from the dey to let the men out of prison at the time the treaty was concluded, said he could do nothing for them at present. They "cursed him for an old hickory face, etc. and hoped that he would be brought up standing before another month and left him." They were back on January 1 to besiege him again. They occupied his house, said it was American property, and refused to leave. Donaldson had to summon the guards, who beat the men and chased them away. The dey wanted to put the men in chains, but Cathcart interceded on their behalf. The men did not appreciate that, however, and also called him names.

Meanwhile Cathcart reported that he was being abused daily by the dey because of the delay in news from Lisbon. On January 3, 1796, the dey ordered Donaldson to freight a sandal to Spain to find out why the money had not been forwarded.[4] He promised to wait until the sandal returned, but said that if the stipulations of the treaty had not been met, at least in part, by then, along with some assurance he could rely on about the rest, he would expel Donaldson, cut off Cathcart's head, and then make peace with Portugal in order to be able to send his cruisers out against American shipping again.

The sandal was chartered, and Donaldson provided a certificate, authenticated by the various consuls, that she was employed as a packet, i.e., a mail and passenger ship, by the American "ambassador" at Algiers. A health certificate was issued to her as the *Independent,* Philip Sloan master. Flying the

American flag, she sailed on the fourth with a crew of twelve "Moors" carrying a letter from the dey to Humphreys—which Cathcart had written but did not reveal to Donaldson—and with orders to remain in Alicante for a fortnight, or as much longer as the American consul might decide to retain her. The sandal made a speedy crossing and arrived in Alicante on the sixth. Montgomery then went off to Lisbon, carrying the dey's letter and Donaldson's dispatches.

Meanwhile the Spanish packet (there was an intermittent mail service between Algiers and Alicante) arrived in Algiers on January 28 with a letter from Humphreys, dated December 14, reporting that the funds could not be obtained in Lisbon and that O'Brien was going to London to try to raise the money there. The dey responded the next day with a threat that if the money was not forthcoming in one month he would declare the treaty void and cut off Cathcart's head. Donaldson pretended to relish the prospect of the latter operation.

Three weeks later, on February 21, there was a scuffle among Captains Wallace, Furnace, and Williams, who evidently were drunk. Wallace and Furnace fell from the gallery of the house they were occupying, and Wallace, master of the schooner *Despatch,* was killed on the spot. The dey commented that it was a judgment from God because the Americans did not honor their engagements.

By February 25 the dey's abuse of Cathcart was "unbearable," but no heads were cut off, nor was Donaldson expelled. The dey was displaying remarkable patience, all things considered. It was almost five months since the treaty was signed, and he had not seen any money.

Barlow to the Rescue

Meanwhile, after an unhurried trip through France and Spain, Joel Barlow arrived in Alicante on February 8, carrying with him 162,530 livres (about $30,000) worth of consular presents for the dey and other officials. (Barlow later wrote in his notebook that the presents, which included a shotgun formerly belonging to Louis XVI, had been badly chosen and half of them were unusable in Barbary.) His initial reaction, on learning of the money problem, was that he should not go to Algiers until there was some better news on that front, but as he learned how the dey's wrath had intensified, he changed his mind and decided that perhaps the delivery of the presents would help. He chartered the *Sally,* an American brig that happened to be in port, sailed on the first of March, and arrived at Algiers three days later after a tempestuous voyage. The weather was so bad that he could not land until the following day, "weakened by the most violent sea-sickness I ever suffered."

Fig. 10. *Joel Barlow,* by Charles Willson Peale. Courtesy of the U.S. Department of State.

He told Cathcart, who escorted him ashore, that he did not yet have his consular commission, although he expected to have one soon. Because of his lack of credentials, the dey refused to receive him when he requested an audience on March 8.[5] Ramadan began on March 9, and the dey's disposition worsened. Barlow wanted to give him some of the presents he had brought, but the dey refused and said he would not accept any presents from agents of the United States and would send them all packing as soon as the embargo on the port (because the corsairs were out cruising) was lifted. Cathcart commented that if Donaldson had not been so miserly with presents, Barlow would not have had such a difficult time. As it was, little business was transacted for the rest of Ramadan.

Spite and Pettifog

On March 21 Donaldson asked Cathcart why he had not been informed of the dey's letter to Humphreys that had been sent on the sandal. Cathcart replied that Donaldson had chided him for not being able to keep a secret back in October when he had shared one with him, so how could he expect him to perform otherwise now? Cathcart's account is full of acerbic exchanges of this sort between himself and Donaldson, and it is clear that both of them had difficult personalities. Cathcart makes Donaldson sound ungracious, rude, and grasping—and himself sound officious, spiteful, and pettifogging. After one satisfying dinner, Donaldson said he hoped Cathcart would visit him at his boat club on the Schuylkill, but such moments of grace seem to have been rare.

Barlow was more charitable than Cathcart. In a letter of April 3, 1796, to the secretary of state he said that Donaldson "merits confidence as a man of talent & integrity . . . [who] conducted himself with firmness & prudence and a man of more integrity could not have been found for the business." He was less flattering about Cathcart. In his letter to the secretary on May 4 he said, "I am told that Mr. Cathcart has hopes of obtaining the consulate for this place. He has neither the talents nor the dignity of character necessary for the purpose, though I sincerely wish that he might be employed in the business of the peace present and tribute, in which I think his intelligence and industry would enable him to render essential service."

On the other hand, he gave a very flattering appraisal of O'Brien in a letter of October 18 to the secretary, saying that

> a more suitable person than he probably cannot be found to be placed here as consul for the United States. He enjoys the esteem and confidence of the Dey, of other officers and consuls, to a degree perhaps unequalled by any foreign agent in the place. He has a singular talent for what is called Algerian management. The blemishes that arise from a defect in the rudimental arts of education will appear only in his correspondence, the jargon of this country called "lingua franca" in which all business is done by word of mouth, puts the scholar & the sailor on a level, and the University of Algiers is better for certain purposes than that of New Haven.

His appraisal of Micaiah Bakri is also favorable, although it reflects the casual anti-Semitism found throughout American writings of the period. In a letter of April 3 to Humphreys he said, "Baccry the Jew is likewise a warm friend. He appears to be a man of uncommon merit for one of a race so degraded and debased as the Jews of Algiers."

Sloan's Return

On March 28, three weeks into Ramadan and almost three months since his January 4 departure for Alicante, Philip Sloan arrived by land from Cherchel, some fifty-five miles west of Algiers, where the sandal had been forced by contrary winds. Montgomery had held him in Alicante until word came that O'Brien had returned to Lisbon from London without the money. Sloan had brought with him Humphreys's answer to the dey's letter, and he and Cathcart went to see the dey. The latter asked him if he brought the money or "any account of it." Cathcart told him of Humphreys's "disappointment" and asked permission to read his letter. He hoped thereby to introduce information the Bakris had given him that Montgomery had brought back to Alicante from Madrid a credit for the necessary funds but the Spaniards would not permit their exportation, and that unless the dey wrote to the king of Spain, there was no hope of getting the money to Algiers. Cathcart only managed to get the first part of his message out when the dey, infuriated, called both Sloan and him "dogs without faith," slapped him on the cheek, and threw Humphreys's unopened letter out of the room. Cathcart tried to argue with him, but the dey drew his yataghan and the two of them fled, Sloan scooping up the letter on the way out. Cathcart said the letter was returned unopened to "our agents" and never opened subsequently.[6]

The Frigate

The general outline of what happened next is reasonably clear, but details are sparse and sometimes contradictory. According to Cathcart's journal, he wrote to Barlow and Donaldson on April 1 to say that "with the most poignant grief" he must inform them that the dey had decided to dismiss them from the city as soon as the embargo on the port was lifted. Cathcart suggested they try to raise the cash locally. They followed his advice, but the Skjöldebrands replied that everyone was afraid to lend the Americans money. Then on April 3 the dey refused the traditional end-of-Ramadan presents that were proffered by Barlow and Donaldson and gave them eight days to leave the country.

Barlow, on the other hand, said in his letter of April 2 to his wife that the dey had let them know that they would be sent away in eight days and that war would be declared at the same time, but that thirty days' grace would be given before prizes were taken. He was perhaps reacting to Cathcart's message of the previous day. The day after, he gave a slightly different account in a letter he and Donaldson sent to Humphreys, which can be read to say that war would not be declared until the thirty days were up.

It is clear from Barlow's April 3 letter to Humphreys, which is eleven pages long, that he thought the delay in receipt of the money was due to Humphreys's unwillingness to send it until the Senate ratified the treaty—which had occurred on March 2, in any event. He seems to have had no idea of the trouble Humphreys was having, and his letter is a rather petulant complaint. He does "not know what instructions you [Humphreys] have received and therefore cannot tell how you have acted or intend to act relative to paying the money." He goes on to explain that this treaty is not like others, but is a purchase agreement. Therefore the U.S. should be prepared to pay immediately, because the treaty is "as good as could be obtained." He remarks that peace was obtained because of the rupture between the dey and the British, and he defends Donaldson against Humphreys's complaint that he did not confer with the French consul before negotiating, saying that it was not Donaldson's fault and that, in any event, neither France nor her consul enjoyed credit with the dey at that moment. He sounds unhappy and irritated.

On April 5, however, a meeting with the dey was arranged by Micaiah Bakri in which it was agreed that in exchange for an additional present of a frigate of 36 guns to the dey's daughter, Barlow and Donaldson would have a three-month grace period to procure the money.[7]

Cathcart says he was present as interpreter at the April 5 meeting but gives no details, and the fullest account we have is a letter of April 5 to Humphreys signed by both Barlow and Donaldson. It reports that, thinking the dey would be in a better humor because his cruisers had brought in some Danish ships, they instructed Bakri

> that if he could engage him in conversation on his cruisers and prizes, he might offer him a new American-built ship of twenty guns, which should sail very fast, to be presented to his daughter, on condition that he would wait six months or longer for our money. The Jew observed that we had better say a ship of twenty-four guns, to which we agreed. After seeing him three or four times yesterday under pretence of other business, without being able to touch upon this, he [Bakri] went this morning and succeeded. The novelty of the proposition gained the Deys attention for a moment, and he consented to see us on the subject. But he told the Jew to tell us that it must be a ship of thirty-six guns or he would not listen to the proposition. We were convinced that we ought not to hesitate a moment. We accordingly went, and consented to his demand, and he has agreed to let everything remain as it is for a term of three months.

They then reveal that

> In order to save the treaty, which has been the subject of infinite anxiety and vexation, we found it necessary some time ago to make an offer to the Jew of ten thousand sequins ($18,000), to be paid eventually if he succeeded, to be distributed by him, at his discretion, among such great officers of state as he thought necessary, and as much of it to be kept for

himself as he could keep with success. The whole of this new arrangement will cost the United States about fifty-three thousand dollars. [Did they mean to say sixty-three?] We expect to incur blame because it is impossible to give you a complete view of the circumstances, but we are perfectly confident of having acted right.

Donaldson's instructions were broad enough to have covered the $18,000 to Bakri, but not the commitment of a frigate, although one could argue that it simply meant paying part of the treaty price in kind rather than cash, as with the naval stores already agreed to. Barlow in a letter of April 8 to the secretary of state said, "It is difficult, Sir, to give you a proper view of the weight of embarrassment under which we consented to the present arrangement of the affair. I shall be extremely unhappy, but not at all surprised, if the president should think we went too far. . . . if any blame is to be attached to us, I think it ought to fall principally on me. Not that there was any difference of opinion. He [Donaldson] was as convinced as I was that what we did was absolutely necessary to save the treaty. . . . But without me he would not have run the risk."

Barlow then referred to his enclosure number 6, which gave details, but that document does not seem to be in the archives. So we are left with Cathcart's brief description and the fuller one given by Barlow and Donaldson above. A description of the atmospherics of the meeting with the dey would be interesting, but that does not seem to exist.

When he learned of the frigate offer, Humphreys was very displeased, according to Barnby, but it was accepted with equanimity in Philadelphia, and the government proceeded quickly to have the frigate constructed according to Algerine specifications. It was delivered, as the *Crescent*, early in 1798.

Barlow and Donaldson had considerably underestimated the cost of the frigate, which they put at $45,000, whereas its real cost proved to be $99,727. Similarly, the naval stores that were to be delivered as part of the "peace present," which had been agreed to by Donaldson at the time of the treaty signing, had been estimated by Cathcart and the Algerines at $60,000, but the actual cost including freight was $174,413.[8] This, plus Humphreys's personal expenses and miscellaneous charges by Donaldson, brought the final cost of the treaty to $992,463.25, according to the secretary of the treasury in 1797. That sum was almost 12 percent of federal receipts in 1796. The U.S. government nevertheless proceeded to deliver the goods without balking and without repudiating its negotiators, even though they had more than used up all the $800,000 allotted for treaties with Tunis and Tripoli as well as Algiers. The government's attitude may have been conditioned by the fact that in 1796 there was a budget surplus of $2.65 million.

Barlow showed considerable courage when it came to expenses. He obviously knew that he was sticking his neck out, and he was at some pains to persuade Philadelphia that his liberality with the public purse was really canny bargaining. Thus in a letter of April 18 to the secretary of state he dwells on the profitability of the Mediterranean trade and estimates: "The money for freights taken by Swedish ships alone in the Mediterranean, even in times of General peace, amount to Twelve Hundred Thousand Dollars a Year. Those of the Danes must be considerably more. During the present European War these Profits I presume have doubled." Then, in enclosure number 5 to his letter of April 20 to the secretary, he goes through a set of calculations to show that the advantage of maintaining peace with the Barbary states will amount to $990,000 a year after deducting treaty costs.

Things Are Looking Up

Donaldson sailed on April 6 for Livorno to negotiate bills of exchange for the ransom and the peace settlement. There was an important Jewish colony in Livorno that had close family and business ties with the Bakris and other Jewish families of Algiers and other trading centers around the Mediterranean. Gold bullion was available there, and the family ties facilitated the transfer of credit and commodities. In Livorno Donaldson found himself dealing with Micaiah Bakri's cousin Solomon. He left copious descriptions of his transactions in his often irritated and illegible letters to all and sundry, but he was not able to accomplish a great deal, because of complications arising from the French invasion of Italy, discussed below.

By late April Barlow's sunny disposition was triumphant. In a letter of April 17 he said he had received "a new commission as a sort of temporary consular agent" from Humphreys and had told Cathcart to tell the dey he was now a consul (was he referring to Cathcart's doing so on April 6?). On April 26 he wrote to his wife that nothing had been received from Humphreys later than his letters of February 7 "and then and before then as good as nothing"—this is where he remarked that Humphreys had too much beef in his head—but "here it is a very good society, if I had time to enjoy it, and a charming country to promenade. . . . the Dey has given me a very fine horse. We are going to make a little journey one of these days. The two Swedes and the French Hercules [Herculais] are charming lads. And there are some very good Christian women, who expect my wife here to embellish the party."[9]

By May 8 Barlow had taken a house in the country and was contemplating working in the garden. His initial, very unfavorable impression of Algiers, revealed in detailed letters to his wife and the secretary of state in which he complained about the unimaginable discomfort of the town, had softened, and his early culture shock had worn off. Henceforth he seemed to enjoy the job most of the time, although he complained of overwork after Donaldson's departure. He did not explain what that work was, beyond saying that he was writing all the time. The consular files do not contain that much in the way of paper, but from his notebooks it is clear that he was assembling data on Algiers. Perhaps he was planning to write a history or description of the place and of the negotiations. There are the beginnings of such a book in his notebook, but it never saw the light of day.

Exit Cathcart

Meanwhile on April 29 the dey had summoned Cathcart and told him to get his vessel ready to sail on the first fair wind, as he intended to dispatch him with a letter to President Washington.[10] The letter said, briefly, that eight months having elapsed since the treaty was signed without one article in it having been complied with, he was sending Cathcart with a list of the items the regency wanted, so that Barlow could be provided with them as soon as possible. Cathcart immediately busied himself readying his ship and preparing the list of naval stores (the final version of which is in appendix 11). It is interesting both because of its magnitude and as an indication of the sort of things the Algerians needed in an age of sail and naval warfare.

Cathcart, free at last, sailed on May 8 at noon, after what he described as moving farewells with Barlow, the Skjöldebrands, and his brother captives. His polacca, the *Independent* (that name was popular with the Americans), was manned by three Christians and seven "Moors." In his journal he comments that during his ten years, nine months, and fourteen days of slavery he had gone through scenes the remembrance of which made him tremble with horror and lament the situation in which he was leaving his brother prisoners. He went with a one-year Mediterranean passport from the dey plus letters of recommendation from Barlow to everyone up to and including the secretary of state. Barlow also gave Cathcart a letter of instruction stating among other things that he understood Cathcart had agreed to make this journey at his own expense in return for being released from captivity sooner than he otherwise would have been. In his reporting on the Cathcart voyage, Barlow made much of this clever saving to the U.S. government, but Cathcart complained in his journal that Barlow did not seem to appreciate the expense that he was incurring, that he could not carry a cargo because he was honor bound in return for the dey's passport to go directly to Philadelphia, and that he would have to sell the ship to pay for the trip. (It does not sound as though he actually lost any money when all the accounts were in. He perhaps made some on the sale of the ship in Philadelphia.) In any event, he said he made the sacrifice willingly, proud to have left no stone unturned to serve his country.

Cathcart did not realize that his departure was the result of a Machiavellian plot by Barlow. The latter, obviously pleased with himself, explained this in a letter of July 12, 1796, to the secretary of state:

> A few weeks after the arrangement made in April, having heard nothing from the funds, and foreseeing that they probably would not be here by the time, I thought it highly expedient to engage the Dey in a step of his own by which he should be insensibly brought to consider the peace as established on a footing different from that of the punctuality of a moment in the payment of money. Mr. Cathcart, from the office he held, enjoyed a portion of his flighty confidence. I thought it probable that if he [the dey] could be engaged, as from his own mere motion, to send this man to America on the subject of the peace presents and annual tribute it would give a new turn to his contemplations. He would be looking to America for answers and arrivals, instead of counting the days in which he was looking to me for money. . . . But it was necessary that neither he nor Mr. Cathcart should know that the idea came from me. And even his Jew broker, who was the only man who could engage him in this business, must not know my real motive.
>
> The Jew hated Cathcart and wished him away. This was sufficient for the Jew. And I engaged him to hint the matter to the Dey in such a manner as that he should conceive the project to be his own. . . . The plan was properly managed at the time, and Cathcart was sent . . . without expense to the U.S. . . . I believe that it is in a great measure owing to the circumstances of this mission that we are now at peace with Algiers.

It does not appear that Cathcart ever learned about this letter in his subsequent career in the government. At least, he does not mention it. It was not published in the early state papers series, and Cathcart would have had to dig to find it. He may not have had the sort of access that would permit him to do that, and may not have had any interest in doing so, not suspecting an underhanded move by Barlow.

We will return to Cathcart later. It is indicative of Barlow's self-confidence that he felt able, indeed eager, to dispense with the services of the most knowledgeable American in Algiers. One would have expected him to value the contact Cathcart gave him at the highest levels of the local establishment. Barlow evidently considered him an irritant in the peace process, but he had no one to put in his place, and the next Christian secretary was not an American. A modern management expert might give Barlow a D, or maybe an F, for treatment of subordinates in this instance. On the other hand, he did procure Cathcart his release from captivity earlier than would have been the case otherwise and may have saved him from becoming a victim of the plague, which broke out again in early May and took away six of his compatriots.

Follow the Money

So far, none of the money promised in the treaty and no naval stores had reached the dey. The reader will recall that O'Brien had set off for Lisbon with the treaty in September 1795 and arrived there on October 1. Humphreys did not arrive back from Paris until November 17. Had Humphreys gone directly to Lisbon from Gibraltar in May instead of going first to Paris, he could have obtained the $800,000 in gold quickly from Baring and Company in London. He would then have been in a position to pay the agreed sums immediately after the treaty was signed. Unfortunately, by the time he returned from Paris and wrote to the Barings, the situation had changed. Large amounts of bullion had begun to leave England for the Continent to support governments opposing the French, and there was none available in London. Baring, in a long and detailed report of August 29, 1796, said their troubles began by the time they received Humphreys's letter of November 29 (with no indication when that was). They had thought that the problem was only temporary, but it lasted longer than they had expected.

Humphreys decided soon after his return to Lisbon to send O'Brien to London to get the money, using the U.S. brigantine *Sophia,* which evidently was assigned to him more or less permanently for transport and courier service.[11] Penned in by the weather, O'Brien could not leave Lisbon until the day before Christmas. By the time he arrived in London, Baring and Company could supply no gold on the spot. It was suggested that he should go to Hamburg and try there, but that did not work either. He returned to Lisbon with word that there was no gold to be had. As we have seen, Humphreys next asked the Spanish if they would permit the export of gold and was turned down. Baring then reported that gold was available, for a price, in Livorno. When Humphreys learned that Donaldson had gone to that city, he instructed Baring to issue him a letter of credit for $400,000 with which to buy gold. This was promptly done. At about the same time, he sent O'Brien off to Philadelphia in the *Sophia* to discuss the specifications and delivery of the promised frigate. O'Brien arrived there by June 1796, and impressed government officials favorably with his competence and understanding, leading to his further employment with the U.S. government.

Donaldson in Livorno

The $400,000 letter of credit was duly received by the Baring representative in Livorno, and Donaldson used it to pay off the $20,000 he owed the Bakris for the presents purchased and distributed to Algerine officials at the time of the treaty signing and to purchase a total of $100,000 in gold that he placed on a ship belonging to the Bakris. The Bakris refused to send the vessel to Algiers, however, until they had assembled a cargo for it. The Baring agent suggested that Donaldson should accept payment in bills of exchange drawn on the Bakris which the latter would undertake to pay in Algiers, but Donaldson refused because he wanted gold and was concerned about the exchange rate, which he said the Bakris were manipulating. Then, to complicate matters, the French seized Livorno on June 27 and the House of Baring agent left. Under British law, bills of exchange drawn from Livorno under enemy occupation could no longer be paid in London, and the British squadron blockading Livorno (commanded by Horatio Nelson) would not permit the Bakri ship to depart for Algiers if it carried anything other than Donaldson's gold. (Nelson's letter of September 26, 1796, to Donaldson to this effect is in the archives of the Historical Society of Pennsylvania.) An early Catch-22 situation, but Donaldson eventually arranged for $106,000 to be transported to Algiers in November 1796 on a ship that by its name, the *Jack,* was perhaps American.

Redemption

Release of the prisoners was arranged, however, well before anything had been received via Donaldson or Humphreys, when Barlow suddenly acquired $200,000 in gold in early July and paid it to the dey. When the dey asked where the money came from, Barlow said the Bakris had lent it to him. The dey said he would free the prisoners only if the Bakris would accept responsibility for the total treaty debt, which the Bakris agreed to do. This was a truly remarkable display of trust, and it is testimony to the power of Barlow's personality that he obtained it.

John Foss, one of the prisoners, described what followed:

> On the 9th of July, we were informed by a letter from Mr. Barlow that we might expect to be at liberty within three or four days. But advised us not to put too much dependence, for says he, "the heart of Pharaoh may be again hardened." . . . What a joyful night was this. We passed it with praises to our kind deliverer. And sanguine expectations of ensuing freedom. Our stoney floors on which we were laid, were apparently softer than beds of down. The chains on our legs were seemingly of no

weight. Our cruel task-masters now looked on us, with smiling countenances, and congratulated us, on our good fortune in the following singular manner: "Sanzafidas, droak imche il blaedic, ila kelp ou Romi."[12] Which in English is thus, You unbelievers, now you are going to the country of Christian dogs.

On the 10th at day break in the morning all hands were called as usual. And a few minutes before the time, that the doors are opened for the slaves to go out to work; we were notified by the bagnio-keeper that all the people taken under the American flag must stay in the Bagnio, and hold themselves in readiness to go to the Dey's palace, and receive our tiskaras [tadhkirat], or pass-ports from the Dey; and that we should be embarked the next morning. However it so happened, that the Dey could not attend, to give us our tiscaras that night, though he received the money. This long and tedious night was spent, in anxious expectation of hearing the sweet sound of Liberty echo in our ears, on the approaching morning. And, O glorious event, this was the ultimate night we spent, in that gloomy dungeon, that horrible mansion of wretchedness and misery.

On the 11th we were again notified by the Bagnio keeper, that we must be ready to go to the Dey's palace, for our pass-ports. A short time after the slaves of other nations had gone out to work we were called out of the Bagnio, into the street, where we were received by the Dey's chief clerk, who conducted us to the palace, and there each man received his tiscara from the Dey. The sweeper of the palace at this time, being a Venetian, he was liberated according to custom. At 9 o'clock, A.M. we all embarked on board a ship belonging to Mr. Macchio Baccri.... On board of this ship were also forty eight Neapolitans, who had been ransomed a few days before us. Oh! what a glorious sight, now could we behold the stripes and stars flying with honor, where they had so often been hoisted with contempt. Every tongue was uttering, long live the humane benevolent Barlow. O! Happy day, O! Happy day.

While we were enjoying the fruits of this happy event, there was nothing to be heard, from the slaves of other nations, but the most bitter curses heaped upon their governments, and Sovereigns. They being chiefly of the Roman Catholic Religion, are taught, that they are the only true Christians, and having now seen the Dutch, and Americans liberated, and they neglected, it exasperated them to such a degree that they would exclaim in the most violent language against their Priests, Sovereigns, and religion. "Why," said they, "are we, who are true Christians, unnoticed by our country, and suffered to remain here in slavery, while the Protestants, (who are no more than degenerate

Christians) are daily emancipated, and are not suffered to wear the yoke of slavery." They would say to each other, "Behold what examples of humanity, are now set by the Protestants, and how little they are noticed by the Roman Catholic governments. . . ."

On the 12th we received the provision on board, and got the ship ready for sea. On this day Joseph Rogers, belonging to Salisbury, on Merimack river, paid the great debt of nature. He was attacked with the plague on the 10th and remained in the hospital on shore.

On the 13th at 5.a.m. we got under way and stood to sea, at 7 a.m. we found a Neopolitan below sick with the plague, we then tacked and stood into the bay again, and made signals for the harbour master to come on board. He boarded us at nine and took the sick man on shore; we then tacked and stood to sea again with a fresh breeze from the eastward, destined for Leghorn. At 4 P.M. to our great joy and satisfaction, we lost sight of the Barbary shore.

On the 14th, another Neapolitan was attacked with the plague, and died on the 16th. On the 15th Captain Samuel F. Bailey, was attacked with the plague. Finding the plague beginning to rage on board the ship, we directed our course for Marseilles, this being the nearest port in the Mediterranean, wherein we should be permitted to perform quarantine with this contagious disorder on board. On the 17th Capt. Bailey died, whom we committed to his watery grave in as decent a manner as our present situation would admit. On the 22d, all hands, except twelve, who remained on board to take care of the ship, went on shore to the Lazaretto, where we performed a quarantine of eighty days.

Barlow sent the following description to his wife on September 1. The original is in French. No explanation is given for the delay.

> The Danish consul said the other day in the company of some people "The American agent is not a man, he's an angel that God has sent here to save the interests of his country." And our poor slaves . . . what moving scenes at the moment of their departure! What blessings, what tears of recognition. All of them said that without me and without the operations that astonished them, they all would have perished in slavery. Because if this treaty had been broken it would have been impossible to conclude another for several years and without spending three times, perhaps ten times more money.
>
> I still remain without means and without credit. . . . I act without orders and without money. Nothing equals the negligence of our public agents except the folly and culpable temerity of our mariners . . . to have

come into these waters before peace was concluded everywhere [referring to the *Eliza,* captured by the Tunisians in June; see chapter 8].

The bulk of the prisoners left Marseille for Philadelphia on a Swedish ship, the *Jupiter,* on November 13 and arrived on February 9, 1797. Their homecoming is discussed in chapter 10.

How Did He Do It?

On July 12, as the prisoners were about to leave, Barlow wrote the long letter to the secretary of state in which he explained how he had arranged Cathcart's departure, and then went on to describe how he had managed the redemption in spite of receiving no cash:

> My being able to procure the liberation of the people at this time has been owing to an accident. From some circumstances in the commercial speculations in this place it has so happened that money has been exceptionally scarce here for several months past. The Jew House who serve as our Brokers here, and who do the greater part of the business of the place, have had their funds for some time in the hands of the French Government to the amount of half a million dollars. The operations of some other houses for a year past have centered nearly in the same point, so that there was no money left except in the public Treasury. Though I had so far gained the confidence of the Jews that they declared to me that they would advance money to the amount of the Redemption, it could not be raised. . . . The plague broke out in the end of May and very much increased my anxiety for the fate of our people. . . . Some time in June a new French Consul[13] arrived and by some brilliant presents revived the influence of the Republic with the Dey so far as to borrow from the public treasury about 200,000 dollars, which he paid into this Jewish House [Bakri]. I immediately insisted that they should prove the sincerity of their friendship by lending me that sum and as much more as the redemption would come to, for which I would give them my bill on Mr. Donaldson at Leghorn. They at first agreed to it, but afterwards raised difficulties on account of the risque of transportation. . . . as they wanted the money here they said they must have the bills at about 3 percent below the usual exchange (that is at 33 masoons of Algiers for the piece of eight of Leghorn. The usual exchange is 34). I absolutely refused to give the bills at a farthing below the usual exchange, as I would not set such an example for American transactions here, though I knew that the Dutch, the Danes and the Venetians had gone to 32 and even to 31 in some of their late public payments. . . . It is finally settled at 34.[14]

Barlow had been well advised to fear the plague. When it first broke out, he had asked permission to move the men to a house outside the city, but the dey had refused, saying they remained slaves until they were liberated. Five of them had died by July 12, a sixth had to be left behind because he was sick, and another died before the ship reached Marseille. The longer the men remained in Algiers, the greater the chance of their succumbing, particularly if they lived in the bagnios, where sanitation was the worst and fleas the most common. Barlow got them out just in time.

O'Brien's Return

The dey learned soon after the prisoners departed that he had been paid with his own money, and he was very angry. At the same time, the Bakris were getting cold feet about their commitment to cover the entire U.S. obligation. Barlow lay low, hoping something would turn up, and it did. O'Brien had been appointed captain of the *Sophia* at $200 a month and sent back from Philadelphia to Lisbon in her. He arrived there on July 19 just as Cathcart, who had arrived on June 27, was leaving for Philadelphia. Cathcart immediately turned about and spent four days with O'Brien before resuming his journey. In the meantime, Humphreys's prospective father-in-law, the British banker John Bulkeley, had managed to raise $200,000 in gold in Lisbon. This was promptly loaded on the *Sophia,* which set off for Algiers on August 2. The cargo was not insured against all risks because O'Brien was confident that, with the Mediterranean passport the dey had given him, there would be no problem with corsairs. He was wrong, and was captured by a Tripolitanian cruiser under the Scottish renegade Peter Lisle and taken to Tripoli. There, after some delay and an abortive unloading of his cargo, the pasha of Tripoli, Yusuf Qaramanli, realized that he would be in trouble if he took the dey's gold, so he loaded it back on the ship and sent O'Brien on his way. O'Brien reached Algiers with the gold on October 1. The dey was overjoyed to see it and apologized to Barlow for being angry with him: "I have long admired your constancy and courage. I now find you are true to me, as well as to your country. I have treated you with great severity, but you must allow that I have had uncommon patience; for I always felt something at the bottom of my heart which told me that man cannot lie. God has rewarded you for all your sufferings. We will be friends forever. If you have any favors to ask, let me prove my sincerity."

Even before O'Brien arrived with the gold, Barlow had been the toast of Algiers because he had managed to liberate the prisoners. He was dubbed Abul Qanasil, the Father of Consuls, and treated with great respect. His colleagues' admiration was not unalloyed, however. He wrote to the secretary of state on August 18, 1797, from the quarantine station at Marseille:

The Danes, Venitians, & probably the Swedes, have already suffered greatly by our success. It is certain that the Spanish Consul in Algiers had orders during the whole of last year to drive me from that place if it could be done for $50,000. The sum was not sufficient. Herculais told me, before he left Algiers, that the French never would have suffered us to get a footing in Barbary, had they not supposed that it would be under their wings, but since they found we had done it without their aid, and found too that our commercial relations were likely to be strengthed with the English & weakened with them, they certainly would force us out of Barbary very soon; and it was his opinion that they ought to do it.

This was the beginning of European complaints of Americans overspending abroad and ruining the game for the others.[15]

The *Fortune*

The captives left Algiers on the *Fortune,* a British vessel that had been captured by the French and sold as a prize at Algiers, where she was bought by the Bakris. She was thus an Algerine vessel, but she was flying the American flag and had been given a passport as an American vessel by Barlow. He explained to the secretary of state in a long letter of August 24, 1797,[16] that it had been necessary to get the prisoners out of Algiers because of the plague and that the only available ship was the *Fortune,* which was already scheduled to take fifty just-released Neapolitan prisoners to Livorno. Because Tuscany and Genoa were at war with Algiers, he thought it might be "inconvenient" for the American passengers to be sailing under the Algerine flag. He therefore obtained from the Bakris a fictitious bill of sale for the ship in his own name, gave her the American flag and appointed Captain Calder of Gloucester to command her as far as Livorno (he doesn't mention the passport). He gave Calder the bill of sale and written instructions to burn it as soon as he arrived in port, explaining that he had obtained it for no other reason than to secure the ship's passage against the enemies of Algiers, and that he did not and would not own any part of the vessel. He had written to the same effect to Donaldson, who was still in Livorno. The Bakris obviously had conspired in this scheme in the belief the American flag would protect their vessel.

On arrival at Marseille, Calder complied with his instructions and burned the bill of sale, but at some point between then and October 7, when the travelers were released from quarantine, the fictitious title to the ship, with her home port listed as Philadelphia, was acquired by Donaldson in Livorno, presumably with the connivance of the Bakris. Donaldson's motives were not clear. He said it was all due to a misunderstanding, but it seems likely that Solomon persuaded him they could make a good return on importing wheat from Algeria to France and that American "ownership" would protect the vessel from capture by states at war with France or Algiers.

Michael Smith, who had been first mate of the *Polly*, was given command and John Foss signed on as first mate. (Foss says in his journal that the ship's name was changed to the *Fortune*, but Barlow referred to her by that name at the time of departure.) If the account in the *Philadelphia Gazette* is correct, some thirteen other ex-prisoners, including Moses Brown of the *Polly*, signed on with him. Foss does not say who the other men were. He mentions five of them by name in one passage, but only two of them are among those he lists as arriving at Marseille.

The ship sailed for Bona in eastern Algeria—today's Annaba, formerly Hippo, where St. Augustine was bishop and wrote his *Confessions*—on November 17. She arrived there on December 7, took on a load of grain, and sailed for Marseille on January 17. A week later she was stopped and boarded by a British vessel and allowed to proceed. Then, about nine leagues out of Marseille on February 5, she was taken by two British ships, which took all the crew but Foss on board and sent the *Fortune* with a prize crew to Portoferraio on the island of Elba, where she was adjudged good prize by a British admiralty court. One of the crewmen, George Tilley of the brig *George*, was impressed on the pretext that he was an Englishman, and three others signed on board a British transport, but the rest, including Foss, "being determined not to enter in the British service," found passage to Livorno, whence Foss eventually sailed for Philadelphia on a Ragusan polacca. It is indicative of the dangers and uncertainties of sea travel in that period that the polacca was boarded five times by naval vessels and privateers of various nationalities before clearing Gibraltar, and boarded twice in the Atlantic.

According to the Bakris, who came forward after the vessel was captured, the *Fortune* and her cargo were still theirs. Barlow noted in a letter to Donaldson that the

> universally established rule in the Barbary states is that the flag shall protect the cargo. In consequence of this rule, when any property of the Dey or his subjects, having been shipped on a vessel belonging to any of his friends is taken or turned from its destination he requires the nation whose vessel it is to pay the value of the property at the port of destination. On this principle the Danes and Swedes have had a number of cargoes to pay for to Algerine subjects during the present war. And then they make their reclamations on the captors or their government. The

Danish consul told me lately that the English had already refunded all the money that he had paid for property taken by them, which had amounted to at least 200,000 dollars.

The dey, irritated by the delay in arrival of the promised naval stores, ruled in favor of the Bakris and against the Americans. Barlow was forced to leave a promissory note with the Bakris for $40,387, the estimated value of the ship and her cargo, to be paid by the United States within six months. In return, the Bakris told the dey that the bill had been paid, and Barlow was allowed to depart for France.

Barlow sailed from Algiers on July 19, 1797, and arrived on July 30 in Marseille, where he had to undergo forty days of quarantine. Thus ended his Algerine adventure, but not his story.

The Sequel

The U.S. government had been giving thought to its representation in North Africa for some time, and in 1796 it had asked Barlow to stay on when Per Erik Skjöldebrand declined the honor of appointment as consul. Barlow had been eager to return to Paris after the prisoners were released, but agreed to stay on until the treaties were negotiated with Tunis and Tripoli. Before leaving Algiers, he appointed one George Clarke, Esq., not otherwise identified, to be in charge of the affairs of the United States until his successor arrived. Clarke remained at that post until 1798.

The government had been concerned that a legal limitation of $2,000 a year on a consul's salary would make it difficult to find someone capable for the job. It resolved the problem by declaring the post a supervisory consulate general with $4,000 per year for salary and expenses and by giving the post to O'Brien, whose abilities had impressed people in Philadelphia as well as Barlow. We do not have O'Brien's personal reaction to this, but it would have meant a considerable elevation in his fortunes, and he must have been pleased and flattered to have been picked. He arrived in January 1798 on board the frigate promised the dey, the *Crescent*, whose specifications he had carefully monitored.

The dey had also ordered a brig and a schooner at his own expense, and these two, the *Hasan Pasha* and the *Skjoldebrand* (the Americans didn't use the umlaut) respectively, were completed in 1798 and delivered in February 1799. Also delivered at the same time were the schooner *Lalla Aisha* and the brig *Hamdullah*, which were provided as a substitute for the naval stores requested by Algiers. The ship *Hero*, loaded with naval stores in payment of treaty obligations, was supposed to arrive at the same time but was delayed and initially presumed lost. According to O'Brien's report of March 1799,

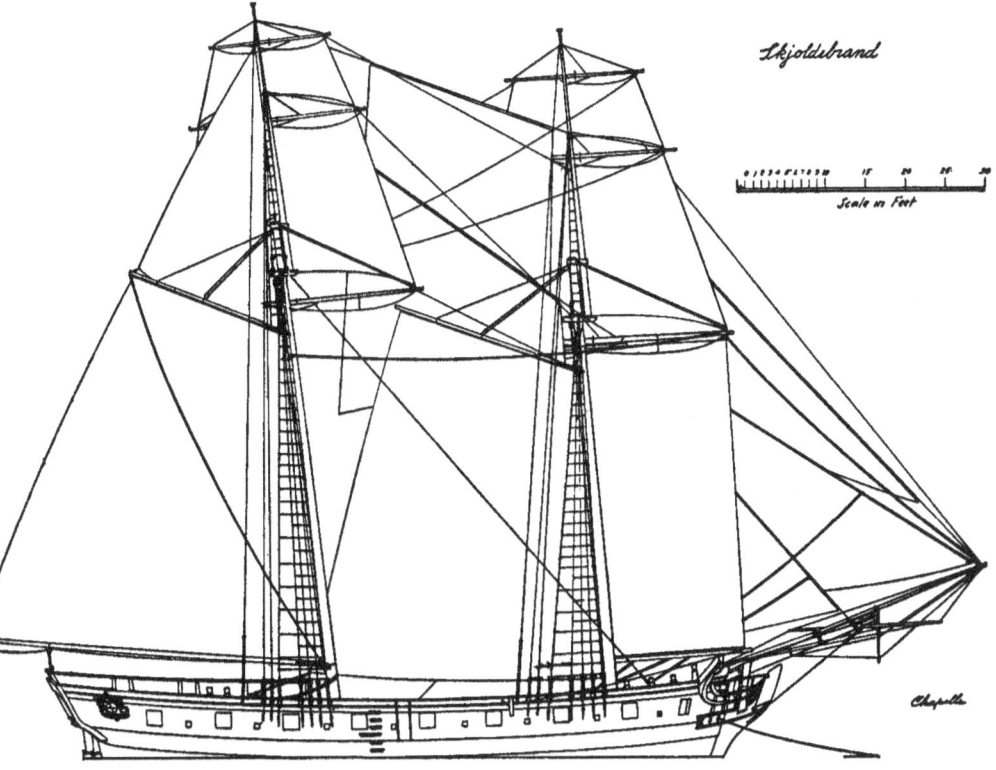

Fig. 11. Sail Plan of the *Skjoldebrand*. SI Warship Plan 147. Reproduced by permission of the Smithsonian Institution, NMAH/Transportation.

the Americans valued the *Hasan Pasha* at $49,000, the *Skjoldebrand* at $28,000, and the *Lalla Aisha* at $21,000, for a total of $98,000. (On page 277 of *The Captives* Cathcart says the three vessels were valued at $78,639.38 at Philadelphia.) The amount was to be credited to U.S. treaty payments. The *Skjoldebrand* obviously was named by the Americans for Per Erik and Mattias Skjöldebrand in gratitude for their help with the negotiations and their aid to the captives. The record does not indicate whether the Algerines retained the name, but it seems unlikely. The *Hasan Pasha* was named for the dey, of course, and Lalla [Lady] Aisha was probably his daughter.[17]

Hasan Dey never saw this contingent of vessels. He had died in 1798 and been succeeded by Mustafa, the khaznaji. Al-Zahhar describes him as Hasan's nephew and says he was a good man—"gentle, generous, attached to the ulama and reconciliation, merciful to the poor and the orphans, loving the mujahidin and raids and courageous." William Eaton, who, together with Cathcart, was taken by O'Brien to an audience with Mustafa, gives a very uncomplimentary description of him, calling him a "huge, shaggy beast sitting on his rump," which has been repeated by most American writers on the subject. It sounds like a stereotypical reaction to a strange culture. On the other hand, in his treatment of the Americans Mustafa could be difficult.

The first serious problem came in September 1800 with the arrival of the first American man-of-war to enter the Mediterranean, the *George Washington*, commanded by Captain William Bainbridge. Mustafa wanted to send an impressive tribute, including a hundred slaves and various livestock and zoo animals, to the Ottoman sultan, whom he had angered by concluding peace with France while Napoleon was occupying Egypt. He insisted that he wanted the tribute to be taken on an American naval vessel, refusing an offer he had at first accepted of a British warship. To make a long and painful story short, O'Brien and Bainbridge decided that they had no reasonable alternative but to accede to the dey's demand. Refusal would mean war, and the *Washington* was anchored under the guns of Algiers. Escape would be dangerous if not impossible. More important, the numerous American ships then in the Mediterranean would be subject to capture by Algerine corsairs, and the prisoner saga would begin all over again. As the final indignity, the Algerines insisted on flying their flag at the *Washington*'s main topgallant masthead. American anger was general; there were fulminations from all quarters, the administration in Washington took it seriously, and the incident was long remembered as a humiliation that would not be forgiven. James Madison, the secretary of state, wrote to O'Brien on May 20, 1801:

"The sending to Constantinople the national ship of War, the George Washington, by force, under the Algerine flag . . . has deeply affected the sensibility, not only of the President, but of the people of the United States. . . . the indignity is of so serious a nature, that it is not impossible that it may be deemed necessary, on a fit occasion, to revive the subject."

When the *Washington* arrived at Istanbul, the Ottomans, who had not previously heard of the United States, were much impressed by the vessel, the commander, and the crew. Bainbridge had what must have been a pleasant stay, being entertained and generally admired by both Europeans and Ottomans for his bearing and conduct and the condition of his ship. On departure he was given a *firman* or letter of safe-conduct by the kapudan pasha or admiral of the Ottoman fleet. It served him well when he reached Algiers in January 1801. The dey wanted to make him return to Istanbul with a message for the sultan, but Bainbridge refused and said he would risk war rather than comply. The dey grew angry, but settled down when Bainbridge produced the firman. The next day, in compliance with the wishes of the sultan,

Algiers declared war on France and the dey ordered the entire French community, some fifty-six men, women, and children, put in irons and held for ransom of $1,000 each. O'Brien and Bainbridge, his influence increased by the kapudan pasha's firman, persuaded Mustafa to relent and to give the fifty-six permission to leave the country. No other vessel being available, Bainbridge took them on board the *Washington,* although the Quasi-War with France was not yet over, and delivered them to Alicante, for which he received the thanks of Napoleon. Such occasional acts of civility show that the age of chivalry was not yet entirely past.[18]

O'Brien was succeeded by Tobias Lear in November 1803.[19] Mustafa, who was murdered in 1805, was succeeded by Ahmad Khoja, who had been one of the four clerks who controlled the military pay records and tax receipts. Lear described him as being mild and reasonable in his manners and conversation, but not to be trifled with.[20] Al-Zahhar gives us no personal details about him.

Not long after Ahmad Khoja's accession to power, the American naval presence that had been built up during the war with Tripoli (1801–1805) was reduced, owing to rising tensions with the British and to Jefferson's economizing measures. In 1807 the fleet was withdrawn from the Mediterranean. Seven of the country's thirteen frigates were decommissioned and the remaining ships were manned by two-thirds of their wartime crews. The officer corps was reduced to 9 captains, 36 lieutenants, and 150 midshipmen.

In October 1807 Ahmad Khoja demanded immediate delivery of naval stores that, under the treaty with the U.S., were then two years overdue. When Lear was unable to comply, the dey sent his cruisers out to look for American shipping. They captured three American vessels, two of which were retained until Lear managed to settle the dispute by borrowing money from the Bakris to make a cash payment in lieu of the naval stores. The third vessel, the schooner *Mary Ann* of New York, was retaken by her crew. The captain, Ichabod Sheffield, reported to the U.S. naval agent in Naples that they had been seized by a 44-gun frigate on October 26 "within the straits" (presumably of Messina), that three of his six-man crew had been taken, and a prize crew of eight men and a boy had been put on board. Three days later, near the North African coast, he and his remaining crew had retaken the vessel, thrown four of the prize crew overboard, and set another four adrift in a boat. He had kept the boy on board. A copy of the November 9 report of this affair from the naval agent at Naples was forwarded to Washington by the naval agent at Marseille, Stephen Cathalan, who appended a dry note: "Captain Sheffield retook his vessel with three men and a boy."[21]

Although the dey promised Lear on December 17, after payment of the tribute, that the *Mary Ann* incident would not affect their relations and no more American ships would be taken, in March 1808 he demanded $18,000 as compensation for the eight Algerines who had lost their lives as a result of the retaking of the vessel. Lear resisted payment, even after being threatened with physical violence, but paid up when the dey threatened war.

Ahmad Dey was murdered in November 1808 and was succeeded by Ali Pasha, who lasted four months and was himself murdered, to be followed by Haj Ali, who initially showed a friendly disposition toward the Americans. There were no further major problems until July 1812 when, following a dispute over the amount of tribute, Haj Ali declared war on the United States and ordered Lear to leave. A letter to Ali from the Prince Regent, later George IV, saying that the British were the "masters of every sea and the terror of all maritime states" and asking the dey not to permit those who were the enemies of Great Britain to lessen the harmony then prevailing between them, may have influenced him to act against the Americans, although he probably was not yet aware that the United States had declared war on Britain on June 12. He sent his cruisers out against the Americans, but most of them were already bottled up by the British at Gibraltar, and the ensuing war kept American shipping in the Mediterranean to a minimum. The Algerines did manage to catch one American vessel, the brig *Edwin* of Salem, Captain George C. Smith and a crew of ten. Two members of the crew were eventually ransomed, but the rest remained prisoners in Algiers until 1815.

On March 2, 1815, the United States Congress, following ratification of the Treaty of Ghent ending the war with Britain, finally reciprocated by declaring war on Algiers and authorizing the fitting out of the ships thought necessary to the task. Two squadrons were formed, one under Bainbridge and one under Captain Stephen Decatur. The latter, consisting of three frigates, two sloops, three brigs, and two schooners, left first and arrived at Gibraltar on June 15. Decatur went looking for the redoubtable Rais Hamidou (Ahmad), the most famous of the Algerine corsair captains, and caught up with his frigate the *Mashuda* on June 17 off the coast of Spain. In the ensuing battle Hamidou and some thirty of his men were killed, while four Americans died. The Americans next caught up with and captured an Algerine brig, the *Estedio,* which they sent into Cartagena along with the *Mashuda.*

Decatur then made for Algiers, where he and William Shaler, designated as peace commissioners to negotiate with the Algerines, dictated the terms of a treaty of peace that provided for the abolition of tribute, the release of American prisoners, the payment of an indemnity of $10,000 for seizure of the *Edwin,* the restoration of other American property in the hands of the Algerines, and, in the event of future hostilities, the treatment of captives as

Fig. 12. *U.S. Squadron Before the City of Algiers, June 30, 1815.* Drawing by N. Jocelin, New Haven, Conn. Courtesy of the Naval Historical Center, Washington, D.C.

prisoners of war rather than as slaves. As part of the agreement, the Americans promised to return the *Mashuda* and the *Estedio*.

Decatur next proceeded with his squadron to Tunis and Tripoli, where the authorities had allowed the British to retake prizes that the American privateer *Abaellino* had brought into local ports. At Tunis he demanded $46,000 as compensation. After an attempt to delay, Mahmud Bey, Hamuda's successor, paid up. Decatur followed the same procedure at Tripoli, demanding $30,000 but agreeing to reduce it to $25,000 in return for the release of ten Christian prisoners. The Americans then sailed away to rendezvous at Gibraltar with Bainbridge and his squadron, which had also made a tour of the three capitals to impress the local populations with American naval strength. The two captains sailed home with most of their squadrons, leaving two frigates and two sloops of war to protect American interests.

Shaler, who had been a special diplomatic agent in Mexico and had participated in negotiating the Treaty of Ghent, stayed behind in Algiers as consul general. He remained there in that capacity until 1828. His *Sketches of Algiers* is one of the more useful books on the period.

The Algerines were unhappy with the 1815 treaty and sought to amend it. As part of their justification for seeking to declare the treaty void, they alleged bad faith on the part of the Americans in not arranging the return of the *Estedio*, which the Spanish had refused to release because she was captured in Spanish waters. A prolonged contention ensued, and the issue was not resolved until December 1816, when the dey finally agreed to an American "ultimatum," presented by Shaler, that defended American conduct in the *Estedio* matter, denied the dey the right to void the treaty, rejected a provision in the Algerine version of the treaty that would have obligated the Americans to pay a consular present when a new consul arrived, and provided for most-favored-nation treatment of the U.S. with regard to prizes brought into Algiers.

The American position had been strengthened by the British-Dutch bombardment of Algiers in August 1816. It so severely damaged the lower town of Algiers that the dey moved his palace to the citadel at the top of the Qasbah, where it remained until the coming of the French in 1830. (The move also had the advantage of making him less accessible to the janissaries of the ojak and thus more able to resist them.) The British admiral, Lord Exmouth, imposed on the Algerines at this time the release of some 1,200 prisoners and the cessation of Christian slavery in Algiers.

There were no more serious problems with the Algerines. Shaler became an honored figure on whom the Algerines relied for advice and judgment on diplomatic matters, and the Americans were in good odor until the end of the ojak with the French conquest of 1830.

8

Tripoli, Tunis, and Morocco

With the conclusion of treaties with Tripoli and Tunis, the United States was at peace with all the Barbary powers, but its diplomatic troubles were only beginning. The primary focus of this book is on Algiers, and there is not space for full treatment of the other capitals, but the reader will want to know something about what happened there. This chapter is a summary of events in Tripoli, Tunis, and Morocco. Each of these deserves a separate study by itself.

At the end of the eighteenth century there was a significant change in the American posture that was to have notable impact on relations with Barbary—the creation of the United States Navy. As noted earlier, construction of the six frigates authorized by the law of 1794 was to have been terminated if peace was reached with Algiers, but a compromise was made in 1796 when Congress, with some skillful urging by George Washington, authorized completion of three of the six, the *United States,* the *Constellation,* and the *Chesapeake.*[1] They were launched in 1797. The remaining three—the *Constitution,* the *Congress,* and the *President*—as well as a number of other vessels for a total of forty-five were added to the fleet during the undeclared naval war or Quasi-War with France (1798–1801). The nineteenth century thus began with a new naval power on the scene. The Americans were no longer defenseless against Mediterranean piracy. In theory this should have greatly facilitated maintenance of peaceful relations with the Barbary states, but sea power did not prove to be an automatic remedy. It may have worked in Morocco, it did not work at Tripoli, and it came to a draw at Tunis. It changed the elements of the diplomatic equation, but that did not necessarily make it any easier to solve.

The conclusion of peace treaties made it appropriate to assign consuls to all the states in question. James Simpson, a British subject residing in Gibraltar, had been appointed consul in Tangier in 1794. He moved to Tangier in 1797 and remained at that post until 1820, when he died of apoplexy. Compared to the others, he had a peaceful time of it, relations with Morocco being reasonably good most of the time. In 1797 William Eaton was appointed consul in Tunis, and James Cathcart was appointed consul in Tripoli. Eaton was a classic political appointee. Cathcart was picked because of his experience and knowledge of the area. Together with O'Brien, they had many difficulties with the rulers of their host countries, who complained about the amounts and nature of American payments.

One troublesome issue was the continued requests, particularly from Algiers, for payment of tribute in naval stores such as masts and lumber rather than in cash. The quality of American timber for shipbuilding was evidently appreciated. Perhaps more important, it provided an alternative to reliance on the Dutch and the Scandinavians, the primary suppliers in the past, making it less costly to declare war on them in order to capture their ships. Procurement and shipment across the Atlantic of heavy items such as masts was expensive and complicated, and the Americans sought to avoid it. They had only limited success.

Of the three rulers of the Ottoman regencies, Yusuf Qaramanli of Tripoli was clearly the most difficult. Cathcart's letters describing his encounters with him bring to mind the problems of dealing with certain modern autocrats, such as Slobodan Milosevic and Saddam Hussein, but the reports of others make him sound more reasonable. Although Hamuda Bey of Tunis was a cut above his colleagues in Tripoli and Algiers in terms of culture and understanding, the Americans found him difficult too, and in some of the correspondence he does not sound very amiable. Compared to the others, Mustafa Dey of Algiers initially sounded positively benevolent, although we saw in the previous chapter how difficult he could be.

The Consuls Arrive

Eaton and Cathcart arrived at Algiers on the *Sophia* on February 9, 1799. They stayed for a brief period and then moved on to their posts. Cathcart had with him a wife, Jane Woodside, whom he had married while in Philadelphia. She had with her a twenty-year-old female companion, an Englishwoman named Betsy Robinson, who fell out with the Cathcarts during the voyage and sought refuge with, and later married, O'Brien after their arrival in Algiers. This understandably angered Cathcart, who accused O'Brien of seducing Miss Robinson, and led to permanent hostility between the two men.

Eaton, a Dartmouth graduate from Mansfield, Connecticut, had a checkered military career behind him. An irascible protégé of Timothy Pickering, the secretary of state, he had no North African or diplomatic experience and quickly concluded that force was the only language the Barbary powers understood. A man of proven courage and limited tact, he must have been a trial to the Tunisians. He and Cathcart both found O'Brien too conciliatory in his approach to the Algerines, but they were both object lessons in the drawbacks of the stiff or confrontational approach.

Tripoli

The saga of America's war with Tripoli has been told and retold over the years, with most attention paid to the naval campaigns. A number of these accounts are listed in the bibliography. The following is focused on the diplomatic details in an effort to give a coherent summary of the little-understood negotiations that followed the Tripolitanian declaration of war against the United States in 1801. A fuller treatment can be found in Ray Irwin's *Diplomatic Relations of the United States with the Barbary Powers*.

If Algeria was a pirate republic, Tunis and Tripoli were pirate principalities. Local dynasties had sprouted in both places. Tripoli had been taken from the Knights of St. John by the Ottomans in 1551 and was governed by pashas—*bashaws* to the Americans at the time—and janissaries sent out from Istanbul until 1711. In that year a kouloughli cavalry officer, Ahmad Qaramanli, seized power while the Ottoman governor was absent. He massacred three hundred janissaries, swore loyalty to the sultan, and established a dynasty that ruled under the title of pasha until 1835, when Istanbul resumed direct control. Yusuf Qaramanli, the pasha with whom the Americans had to contend, was Ahmad Qaramanli's great-grandson.

Tripoli controlled loosely the area occupied by northern Libya today, stretching some 1,000 miles along the coast from Tobruk in the east to the border with Tunisia, about 150 miles west of Tripoli. Although certain coastal areas had been prosperous under the Romans, who developed an impressive system of rainwater cisterns to cope with the arid climate, there was not enough water to support a large population. There are no reliable figures, but a French estimate at the end of the seventeenth century put the population of the town of Tripoli at around 40,000, broken down as 3,500 Turks and koulouglis, 35,000 Arabs, and 2,000 Christians, including slaves. Privateering was an important source of income, and there were some agricultural exports in good years.

The town was walled and well defended. It was protected by 115 guns and a substantial garrison. Of lesser importance economically and politically than Tunis or Algiers, it nevertheless had a small corsair fleet with the potential to cause considerable damage to American shipping, and peace with Tripoli was important to the future of American trade with the Mediterranean region.

An initial peace treaty was negotiated quickly and rather easily by O'Brien, who was sent there by Barlow in October 1796.[2] He arrived on

November 1 on the faithful *Sophia* and three days later had concluded a treaty that he estimated cost a total of $56,486. Yusuf had wanted equal treatment with Tunis, which he had heard was to receive $60,000 in addition to naval and military stores, but O'Brien told him that the amount promised was far less and that, since the dey of Algiers was responsible for Tunis, there was no telling when if ever the Tunisians would receive their money. On the other hand, he had $40,000 with him and could hand it over immediately on the signing of the treaty. He threw in another $12,000 in lieu of naval stores and consular presents plus $1,000 for the chief officer of the Tripolitanian navy, Peter Lisle. Yusuf settled for the bird in hand, but later claimed that O'Brien had promised him the *Sophia* as part of the deal. O'Brien denied this, but the misunderstanding, if that is what it was, left a sour taste in Yusuf's mouth. He later accused O'Brien of making false promises and spreading allegations that he was subordinate to the dey of Algiers. Articles 1 and 12 of the treaty, which provided that the dey of Algiers should guarantee preservation of the treaty and should aid in the resolution of disputes that might arise under it, obviously bothered him. His anger may have been increased by the wording of article 11 that is described in note 2, and certainly would have been increased when he learned how much the Americans finally paid for a treaty with Tunis. It is not clear why, if he resented the dey's claim to seniority so much, he agreed to articles 1, 11, and 12 in the first place. He may have been illiterate and unaware of the significance of what he signed.

O'Brien returned to Algiers with the treaty. Barlow and the dey endorsed it and sent it on to Humphreys, who did the same and forwarded it to Philadelphia. It was ratified by the Senate on June 10, 1797.

Cathcart was the first duly commissioned American consul assigned to Tripoli. He arrived there in April 1799 and was in difficulty from the beginning. There is not space here to reproduce his lengthy letters describing his travails, but some of them can be found in volume 2 of *American State Papers* and in *Naval Documents*. One cannot help wondering whether someone less officious and less given to sermonizing might not have done better. There were occasions when a more accommodating attitude on his part might have averted the gathering storm. But it might not. Yusuf sounds very disagreeable. In a ruthless struggle to gain power, he had first murdered his eldest brother in front of their mother. Then he fomented a rebellion against his father and blockaded Tripoli, facilitating the bizarre takeover and eighteen-month misrule of that city by Ali Burghl, the Algerine adventurer we last saw in appendix 3 leaving Algiers under a cloud. The Tunisians intervened to oust Ali and install Yusuf's elder brother Ahmad—Hamet to the Americans—as pasha in January 1795, giving Yusuf the post of bey, or commander of the troops. Yusuf promptly used his new office to oust Ahmad and usurp power.

He was an effective, if troublesome, ruler and remained on the throne until 1834 in spite of, or perhaps because of, being the first head of state the United States tried to unseat.

In addition to his discontent over the nondelivery of the *Sophia,* Yusuf had been unhappy from the start with the amount of money he was receiving from the Americans. In February 1801 he demanded that the United States pay him $250,000 for a new treaty plus an annual tribute of $20,000. Cathcart managed to stall for a while, but on May 14 Yusuf declared war on the United States and signaled this decision by having the flagpole of the American consulate chopped down. Cathcart was told he could stay, but he chose to leave ten days later for Livorno with his wife and their first child. He left U.S. interests in the hands of the Danish consul, Nicholas Nissen, who was eventually rewarded for his much-appreciated efforts with a silver snuffbox and some heartfelt letters of commendation.

Meanwhile, because of the threatening sounds from Tripoli and uncertainty about the attitudes of the other North African governments, President Jefferson, newly in office and reflecting his long-held views that a forceful response was called for, had already decided to send a squadron of three frigates—the *President,* the *Essex,* and the *Philadelphia*—and a schooner, the *Enterprise,* under Captain Richard Dale as commodore to the Mediterranean to protect American shipping. Dale was given a letter from President Jefferson to Yusuf and $10,000 to offer as an inducement to maintain the peace. He arrived at Tripoli on July 24 to find that war had already been declared. In response, he imposed a blockade on the port. Yusuf invited him to come ashore and negotiate a peace, but Dale said he did not have the authority to do that; he could only negotiate a truce. There seems to have been no response from Yusuf. The first action of the Barbary Wars occurred a week later, when the *Enterprise* under Lieutenant Andrew Sterett captured the polacca *Tripoli* after a famous three-hour battle that demonstrated the superiority of American gunnery and tactics.

Dale remained at Tripoli for another ten days and then went to Malta for water. En route back to Tripoli he stopped and searched a Greek ship which had on board forty-one Tripolitanians, including an officer and twenty soldiers. On arriving back at Tripoli he proposed an exchange of prisoners, there being three or six, depending on the source, American prisoners in the town. Yusuf agreed to let the Americans go in exchange for all of the Tripolitanian military personnel. He showed little interest in the civilians but did express an interest in negotiating a truce. Dale declined to discuss it and, after putting his prisoners ashore, departed for Gibraltar on September 3.

At Gibraltar Dale learned that the crews of two Tripolitanian vessels that the *Philadelphia* had been guarding in the harbor there had escaped. The

Philadelphia was relieved of guard duty and sent to Tripoli, where she patrolled the coast briefly in September. The rest of the squadron continued to guard the two Tripolitanian vessels at Gibraltar and to convoy American merchantmen, which had returned to the Mediterranean in numbers on news that peace treaties had been negotiated with all the Barbary states. Their captains and owners did not seem greatly concerned that Tripoli was no longer at peace.

So ended the first campaign season against Tripoli. The *Enterprise* captured another Tripolitanian vessel and the navy successfully convoyed a number of merchantmen to and from South European ports, but the taking of the *Tripoli* was the principal accomplishment of Dale's tour as commodore. The administration in Washington made the most of that victory publicly, but knew that it represented little progress in solving the problem with Tripoli. A more forward policy was adopted in the following year.

Dale returned to the United States in the spring of 1802 and was succeeded as commodore by Captain Richard V. Morris, who was given instructions to support Cathcart, then at Livorno, in negotiating a peace with Tripoli. For his part, Cathcart was told by Secretary of State Madison in a letter of April 18, 1802, "The disposition to peace expressed by the Bashaw of Tripoli, on the appearance of commodore Dale before that place, with the impression which it is hoped has been made on him by the course and circumstances of the war, have lead the President to conclude that the time is come when negociations may advantageously take place.... The President confiding in your capacity, experience and faithful regard to the interest of the United States has thought proper that you should be charged with the negociation." He was instructed that he could accept deletion of the offending words about Algiers in the treaty but that he must "in the most preemptory manner stifle every pretension or expectation that the United States ... will make the smallest contribution to him [Yusuf] as the price of peace." Nor would the customary presents on arrival of a new consul be made once relations were restored, since it was Yusuf who had broken relations so unjustifiably, but if Cathcart thought it expedient, he could "send any little gratification along with the consul." This language implies that Jefferson and Madison were so impressed by the exploits of the *Enterprise* that they thought Yusuf would be too, and would therefore be willing to forget his earlier insistence on more money. This expectation was not met, although a peace feeler made through the Tunisians in May 1802 indicated that there was indeed some interest in peace on Yusuf's part.

The same letter informed Cathcart that he had been designated to succeed O'Brien as consul (not consul general) in Algiers, and his commission was attached. This must have been heady stuff and may explain the haughty tone some of his subsequent correspondence took.

Cathcart boarded the *Chesapeake* at Livorno in mid-October and was in Malta by November 25, when he wrote a stern letter to O'Brien worded as though he were already in charge of the post at Algiers. He evidently was unaware that the dey had written to Jefferson on October 17 to say that he would not receive Cathcart as O'Brien's replacement because "his character does not suit us as we know wherever he has remained he has created difficulties and brought on a war."

Morris tried to take Cathcart to Tripoli in February 1803 but was prevented from doing so by stormy weather. In his *Diplomatic Negotiations of American Naval Officers, 1778–1883,* Charles Oscar Paullin, relying on the papers of Captain Morris, reported that Cathcart had nevertheless managed to communicate with Yusuf through the Danish consul in Tripoli and made an offer that was rejected. Paullin wrote that the precise terms were not known, although Cathcart had previously offered $40,000 for a ten-month truce and $20,000 annually for a permanent peace. This would have been double the amount he was authorized to offer by his second set of instructions from Madison, dated April 9, 1803, which contradicted the instructions of a year earlier. He was now being authorized to pay Tripoli $20,000 for peace and $8,000 or $10,000 a year thereafter. The same instructions authorized payment of $10,000 a year to Tunis.[3] In short, in spite of our determination not to pay tribute to Tripoli and Tunis, we had authorized Cathcart to do just that.

Morris, perhaps feeling his oats with instructions giving him a "superintending agency" in all negotiations with the Barbary states, and perhaps aware that the Tripolitanians had indicated that Cathcart was persona non grata there, shipped Cathcart back to Livorno in April, saying he would send for him if he needed him. He then went to Tripoli in May without him, much to Cathcart's distress.

After an inconclusive engagement with Tripolitanian gunboats and shore batteries on May 28, a performance for which he was later criticized, Morris opened negotiations on May 29. He went ashore on June 7 and met with Muhammad Dghies, the pasha's prime and foreign minister, but not with Yusuf. Dghies offered peace in exchange for $200,000 plus the expenses of the war. Morris offered $15,000—$5,000 as a consular present and $10,000 after five years if Yusuf kept the treaty faithfully. (He seems not to have been aware of Madison's instructions of April 9, which probably had not reached either Cathcart or him.) The Tripolitanians understandably refused to accept his offer, and Morris was told to leave.

Morris, who had his wife and young son with him on the *Chesapeake*,[4] spent more of his time convoying American merchant ships and lying in port than blockading Tripoli. He was relieved of his command in the summer of 1803 and returned home to face a court of inquiry that censured him for his "indolence and incapacity." He was succeeded temporarily by Captain John Rodgers of the *John Adams* and permanently as commodore by Captain Edward Preble, a renowned, crusty disciplinarian who arrived in the Mediterranean on the *Constitution* in September 1803. His squadron included the frigate *Philadelphia* and four smaller vessels. After dealing with the then current crisis with Morocco that is discussed later and after a detour to Cádiz to pick up supplies, he sailed up the Mediterranean toward Tripoli, dropping off Consul General Tobias Lear and wife in Algiers en route.

Preble had arrived in the Mediterranean confident that if he was given the ships he asked for, he would render the purchase of peace or the payment of tribute totally unnecessary.[5] Off the coast of Sardinia on November 24, however, he learned that on October 31 the *Philadelphia* had run aground on a reef at Tripoli and had been surrendered by her captain, William Bainbridge, he of the trip to Istanbul in 1800. Bainbridge and 306 men were prisoners in Tripoli, and the Americans had lost one of their prized vessels to the Tripolitanians, who had quickly refloated her. Relations with Tripoli had suddenly become more complicated. Preble subsequently tried to make up for the loss of firepower by renting mortar and gunboats from the Kingdom of Naples, but they were not a fully effective substitute for the *Philadelphia*.

Meanwhile, after establishing his supply base at Syracuse, Preble wrote to Muhammad Dghies on January 4, 1804, to propose an exchange of prisoners—the Americans held sixty at that point, taken from the Turkish ketch *Mastico* captured by the *Constitution* on December 24—but his letter did not reach Tripoli until after the destruction of the *Philadelphia* on February 16 (see below) and was rejected out of hand. In the interim, the Tripolitanian agent in Malta, Gaetano Schembri, had put out a peace feeler through a British intermediary, and on January 17 Preble wrote to the secretary of the navy, Robert Smith, "that I have had indirect proposals from the Bashaw for a peace. He is willing to restore the Frigate Philadelphia if we will give him a schooner and he will give up the officers and men for five hundred Doll: each. I believe that on these terms he would make peace but he demands an annual stipend for keeping it, such as the Sweeds And Danes pay him amounting to———doll: p^r annum payable———[spaces left blank in the original] This we never ought to accede to, as it would stimulate the avarice of the other Barbary powers and probably induce them to make war upon us." Preble then turned to his plans to acquire mortar and gunboats to use against Tripoli when the weather was more favorable "in a way that will lessen Yusuf's demands" and commented that Yusuf "seems already to be convinced he has something to dread, or he would not propose accepting One hundred and fifty Thousand Doll: for what not long since he expected to receive Three Millions."[6]

On January 20 Preble wrote to Smith again, saying, "I have received further indirect proposals from the Bashaw. He appears to be willing to give me as many of our officers and men as I have Tripolines in exchange. For the remainder I suspect he is willing to take 400 dollars for each, and make peace without any considerations or annual Stipend or Tribute and give us the Frigate for a Schooner. These terms will be thought favorable to the United States. I shall send a vessel to Col: Lear to consult him and in the meantime take the necessary steps for lessening the Bashaw's expectations."[7]

On January 31 Preble wrote to Lear saying that Yusuf's agent in Malta had made an offer of peace for $500 per man after an exchange of sixty prisoners plus a schooner for the frigate. "This would gain peace on terms more reasonable than expected by our government:

300 Americans captured
-60 Tripolines
_____
240 @ $500 = $120,000

What sum will you authorize me to pay for the ransom of the officers and men?"[8]

Lear did not receive Preble's query, via the *Vixen,* until March 15. He responded with a long letter in which he said he had no special authority on the subject and could only say that "I should not hesitate to take upon myself in behalf of the United States to pay at the rate of 600 dollars for each (exclusive of what might be exchanged) . . . if the Bashaw will make peace without . . . any Annual tribute, or Consular present, excepting a small present on the reception of the first Consul that is appointed." He said he was sending O'Brien up the Mediterranean on the *Vixen* and that "His knowledge of the language, Manners, and Politicks of these Regencies, must be highly useful to you."[9]

In the interim, the course of negotiations had been altered by the spectacular destruction of the *Philadelphia* in Tripoli harbor by Stephen Decatur and his men on board the *Intrepid* (the ex-*Mastico*) on February 16, 1804. This is one of the more famous exploits in American naval history, but it did not restore the vessel to American control or seriously threaten Yusuf's control of the city. It did make him angry, however, and less amenable to American propositions.

Finally, direct negotiations were opened through the French chargé d'affaires in Tripoli, Bonaventure Beaussier, the Danish consul having excused himself. Preble called at Tripoli in the *Constitution* on March 26 and sent an officer ashore with a letter to Beaussier from Talleyrand, the French foreign minister, informing him of Napoleon's interest in the fate of the American prisoners and instructing him to help Preble in his negotiations.[10] Preble invited him to come on board for dinner, which Beaussier did on the twenty-seventh, after first meeting with Yusuf. Preble gave him a five-gun salute and sent him ashore at 5 P.M. The next day Beaussier wrote Preble a long letter detailing developments back on shore.[11]

In his audience before going out to the *Constitution*, Beaussier had informed Yusuf that Napoleon hoped to hear soon that the prisoners had been released following conclusion of a solid peace that would be advantageous to both parties. Yusuf had responded that he was delighted (*charmé*) at Napoleon's intervention and for his sake would not press all the advantages that the fortunes of war had given him. He recommended that Preble send ashore the prisoner taken on the *Philadelphia* so that he could question him freely as to how he and his comrades had been treated, in order to destroy the general opinion that they had all been massacred. (He was referring to an exchange of letters between Preble and Dghies in which the latter had accused the Americans of mistreating prisoners and Preble had responded that he had on board "the prisoner taken on the *Philadelphia*," who had been wounded but whom the Americans had treated kindly and who was "well in health." Dghies had asked that he be sent ashore so the Tripolitanians could assess his condition themselves, but Preble had refused to do so in the absence of a "cartel"—a written agreement—on prisoner exchange.)

Yusuf had been "astonished" that Beaussier did not return ashore with the prisoner in question, and Beaussier dilated at some length on how useful the release of the man would have been to the American cause. He reported that Yusuf was not impressed with the formidable force Preble had, or with the American project, revealed by Preble to Beaussier, to install Ahmad in Benghazi (Yusuf said he was a drunk who was incapable of raising support). Nor did he seem to be impressed with Beaussier's statement that the Americans would pay ransom only and would not pay for peace, and that they would sacrifice the prisoners rather than accept conditions incompatible with the honor and dignity of their nation. To Beaussier's comment that exaggerated demands by Tripoli would displease Bonaparte, Yusuf had replied that he did not think Napoleon would want to deprive him of the advantages acquired by the fortunes of war.

Beaussier concluded that whatever the success of Preble's efforts to punish the Tripolitanians, the Americans would add much to the expense without securing release of the prisoners, who were locked away securely in the castle, and that the greater the damage done to Tripoli, the higher the price would be. Beaussier does not mention any offer from Yusuf, but speculates that he would not settle for less than 500,000 piastres fortes, which would be about $500,000—double the estimate Beaussier had given Preble during their conversation on the twenty-seventh, according to Preble's report.

A sudden gale having forced Preble to leave Tripoli on March 28, he did not receive Beaussier's letter until shortly before his return on June 12. He had been preoccupied with events in Tunis and Naples in the interim. He was joined by O'Brien at Malta on April 12 and on May 13 was informed that the Kingdom of Naples would rent him the gun and mortar boats he had requested. He was thus ready to try his own experiment in diplomacy backed by force.[12]

On June 13 he sent O'Brien ashore at Tripoli with his first direct offer—$40,000 for the ransom of the officers and crew of the *Philadelphia* plus $10,000 for Prime Minister Dghies and other senior officials. He would not pay anything for peace but would stipulate a consular present of $10,000 by the first consul appointed to the post and another consular present after ten years. O'Brien met only with Dghies and was not allowed to see the prisoners or other consuls. The offer was rejected scornfully, and Dghies later pointed out to Bainbridge that Holland had paid $80,000 and Denmark $40,000 for peace, and neither of them had prisoners to ransom.

O'Brien also carried with him a letter from Preble to Beaussier acknowledging recent receipt of the latter's letter of March 28, copies of which he would send immediately to his government and to Robert Livingston, our minister in Paris, "so that they may be acquainted that the intervention of the First Consul [Napoleon] through the chargé d'affaires of the French Republic in Tripoli is not likely to have the effect which (I believe) they might have expected. I cannot but suppose the First Consul will feel somewhat mortified that through his influence you have not been able even to obtain permission to land the necessary clothing & Stores which the Americans are suffering for want of. It is probable the First Consul expected his meditation would have had more weight with the Bashaw of Tripoly than it appears to have had."

Preble's tactless remarks presumably reflected his conclusion, noted in his diary on March 28, "that the French, English and Swedish consuls are all in the Bashaw's interest. We must therefore depend on our own exertions for effecting a peace, which can only be done by the increase of our force." His letter brought a stiff response from Beaussier, who said he had been doing his best to prepare the Tripolitanians to negotiate seriously, and complained that O'Brien had not consulted with him before going to see Dghies. He termed the offer that O'Brien carried "truly ridiculous."

The blockade of the port by the brigs *Siren*, *Argus*, and *Scourge* and the schooner *Vixen* continued while Preble left for other parts. He returned on

Fig. 13. *Commodore Preble's Squadron Engaging the Gunboats of Tripoli, August 3, 1804.* Engraving by Charles Denoon. Reproduced by permission of the Huntington Library, San Marino, Calif.

July 25 with the schooners *Nautilus* and *Enterprise* plus six Neapolitan gunboats and two mortar boats to join the blockade. He was ready to begin the assault with a total force numbering 1,060 officers and men. The Americans attacked on the afternoon of August 3 with a heavy bombardment of the town and a series of hand-to-hand battles on Tripolitanian gunboats boarded by the Americans, who demonstrated their superiority at that sort of combat. Thirteen Americans were wounded and one, the younger brother of Stephen Decatur, was killed. The action was impressive, but Yusuf remained uncowed.

On the following day Preble wrote to Beaussier that his offer still stood but that he expected the arrival of another four frigates and at that point would not pay a cent. Yusuf responded that he sincerely desired peace but not on such dishonorable conditions.

Preble attacked again on August 7, with most of the action being directed at shore batteries. The Tripolitanians responded in kind and at least fourteen Americans were killed. That evening the frigate *John Adams* arrived with the news that Preble was to be replaced as commodore by Captain Samuel Barron, who would be arriving with four frigates and who was senior to Preble in the service. This was a great disappointment to Preble, and he redoubled his efforts to "reduce" Tripoli before Barron arrived.

On August 10 Preble sent O'Brien ashore with a new offer—$80,000 for ransom and $10,000 for a consular present. In a letter dated August 9 he told Beaussier that four more frigates were arriving to reinforce the American fleet and would "enable us to destroy all the Sea Port towns in Tripoly. After their arrival it will not be in my power to offer a single dollar either as ransom or peace.... I now propose my last offer which I most solemnly assure you I will never transcend ... Eighty thousand for ransom ... and ten thousand dollars as a consular present."[13]

Beaussier responded on August 10 that he thought the latest offer "Still inconsiderable" but had discussed it with Dghies, who said it would be a mistake to present such an offer to Yusuf in his present state of mind: "Your first attack ... intimidated him a little, but the second encouraged him." Dghies thought, however, that he could get him to settle for $150,000.[14]

Preble recorded in his journal on that date that he had received a message from Beaussier asking for authorization to offer $100,000 for ransom and $10,000 for a consular present. "These terms were rejected." The documents show, however, that on August 10 he wrote again to Beaussier, offering $100,000 plus $10,000 for a consular present and that he wrote a second letter on the same date offering an additional $10,000 for the prime minister and other dignitaries who had been helpful.[15] Thus, he had upped his offer to $120,000.

Beaussier did not respond until August 30, with a letter he had begun writing the day before. He said he had discussed Preble's offer with Yusuf on August 12 and was about to

> reply in a manner which would perhaps have been satisfactory to you, and to make a Signal for you to send [someone] on shore, when this prince formally required me to suspend my answer until he had witnessed the effect of the third attack—this took place in the night between the 23 and 24 instant [August], and you, sir, must be sensible that it was perfectly null.... not a single bomb was thrown beyond the forts [into the town]. The attack between the 27th and 28th was more serious ... [but] the Bashaw seems to care little about the injury to the houses by the shot [solid cannonballs].... the [explosive] shells only, which he fears may burn and destroy his town, give him some uneasiness and revive in him the desire for an accomodation.... in the actual state of things I think it best to leave the Bashaw to his own reflections—He is naturally dark, mysterious and unconfiding....

I had written thus far when to my great astonishment and regret I heard that a brig of your squadron was advancing to parley [to offer an exchange of prisoners].... I cannot but view this step as most impolitic as well as detrimental to the interests of your country, because at this moment it must be construed to your disadvantage and tend to raise the pretentions of this regency.

On the thirtieth Beaussier saw Yusuf, who rejected the idea of a prisoner exchange and demanded $400,000 in ransom as well as the usual presents. He said he was keeping the price low out of respect for Napoleon. Beaussier advised Preble to keep attacking the town, and particularly the castle, unless he felt able to meet the pasha's terms. "You must persevere until the pasha, harassed at all points, will himself ask for a parley."[16]

Beaussier's letter was referring to the night attacks of August 24 and August 28 in which extensive use was made of the gun and mortar boats rented from Naples. The first attack seems to have had little effect, but the *Constitution* took part in the second, and Preble believed that heavy damage was done to the town.

Beaussier wrote again on September 1 to say that Yusuf was convinced that an American gunboat had exploded with great loss of life in the second attack and was puffed up by that. Beaussier, however, had reason to believe he would settle for $300,000. Preble does not seem to have replied. The fifth and last attack was made on September 3, with large quantities of shot and shell fired into the town but no word that Yusuf's position had softened.

The tragic finale of the active naval campaign against Tripoli was almost as spectacular as the destruction of the *Philadelphia*. The *Intrepid*, the ketch captured earlier from the Tripolitanians and used by Decatur for his assault on the *Philadelphia*, was packed with explosives and combustibles and sent into Tripoli harbor on September 4 to be blown up and destroy the Tripolitanian fleet. Unfortunately, it exploded before reaching its target; whether accidentally or intentionally has never been clear. All thirteen officers and men on board were killed. A number of bodies burned beyond recognition were washed up on the beach. At least one of them must have been a Tripolitanian, because Jonathan Cowdery, a surgeon's mate from the *Philadelphia*, reported that fourteen bodies were buried by the prisoners. Beaussier, in a last letter to Preble dated November 1, said that this effort had been fatal only for the Americans. An "infinity" of bodies and body parts had been found on the beach, the fortifications had not been touched, and the explosion had only caused a general commotion in the town and the countryside around it. In his own case, he had lost all the windows of his house.

Five bodies were eventually transferred to the Protestant cemetery east of town, where a small monument to the crew of the *Intrepid* was erected. In the period of diplomatic relations with Libya (1951–80) American ambassadors used to lay wreaths there on Memorial Day. They will probably renew the practice when relations are restored, if the monument is still there.

A few days after the *Intrepid* tragedy, Captain Barron arrived at Tripoli with reinforcements on the frigate *President*; Tobias Lear and his wife as well as William Eaton were also on the vessel. Preble relinquished command on September 10. The squadron sailed away to winter quarters at Syracuse, and Preble returned home to Portland, Maine, amid general regret by his subordinates and the public, by whom he had been widely admired. He had been ill intermittently for some time and died three years later.

Preble's inability to force Yusuf to sue for peace has been attributed to the modest forces at his disposal, particularly after the loss of the *Philadelphia*, but we will never know how much difference the presence of that vessel would have made. Preble's tactic of bombarding and then making an offer was criticized by Beaussier, with reason. But if he had been able to bombard more effectively, if the bombs supplied by the Neapolitans had not been full of duds or he had had another frigate or two, his negotiating tactics might not have mattered.

Another unanswerable question is whether a less stubborn attitude regarding ransom payment might have enabled Preble to settle the issue peacefully before incurring the expenses and casualties of his naval campaign. Although various persons offered opinions that Yusuf would settle for various amounts within the limits of Preble's authority to pay, the only figure directly attributable to Yusuf that we have is the $400,000 mentioned by Beaussier in his letter of August 30. Preble was not authorized to go beyond $180,000.

There were no further bombardments under Barron, who was sick most of the time, or under his successor, John Rodgers, who assumed command on May 22, 1805. Bainbridge and his men remained prisoners in Tripoli until peace was negotiated by Lear and Rodgers for $60,000 in June 1805, following an indirect approach from Yusuf through the Spanish consul. Five of the men had died and five "turned Turk," i.e., converted to Islam. Of the survivors, the largest contingent to return home consisted of Captain Bainbridge, 17 of the officers, and 101 of the crewmen, who reached Hampton Roads on September 10, 1805, on the *President*.

The Shores of Tripoli

Credit for bringing Yusuf around to a much lower figure must go in large part to William Eaton, the former consul in Tunis. He had developed, and received qualified official approval of, the plan mentioned earlier to organize a military campaign to restore Ahmad to power and bring down Yusuf. Secretary of State James Madison's comment on this proposal sounds apt today:

> Although it does not accord with the general views of the United States, to intermeddle in the domestic contests of other countries, it cannot be unfair, in the prosecution of a just war, or the accomplishment of a reasonable peace, to turn to their advantage the enmity and pretensions of others against a common foe. How far success in the plan ought to be relied on, cannot be decided at this distance, and with so imperfect a knowledge of many circumstances. (ASPZ:701)

In the spring of 1805, Eaton led a group of four hundred armed men, including Ahmad and a suite of ninety, plus a Navy midshipman and eight U.S. Marines, some five hundred miles across the Western Desert from Alexandria to Derna, in what is now eastern Libya. Eaton showed great courage and tenacity, but he had much difficulty keeping his motley army together and preventing the timorous Ahmad from quitting. His journal makes stirring reading, and this ranks as one of the most remarkable marches in American military history.

Eaton's little army reached Derna on April 25. Supported by three vessels of the U.S. Navy—the schooner *Nautilus,* the brig *Argus,* and the sloop *Hornet*—they attacked on the morning of the twenty-seventh and had captured the town by 4 P.M. The gallantry of the marines, led by Lieutenant Presley O'Bannon, and of the naval personnel was exemplary. This was the "shores of Tripoli" of "The Marines' Hymn." It was a far cry from Desert Storm, but was more heroic in terms of individual exploits. Eaton stood on the road to triumph. Tripoli was still some eight hundred miles to the west, but with support from the navy, a little added money—he had spent only $30,000 thus far and thought a few thousand dollars more would suffice—and a few more marines, its conquest was now feasible. Dissident tribes would rally around their standard, and it would all be over for Yusuf.

Or so Eaton thought. But the tribes did not rally to Ahmad, and a detachment of Tripolitanian horsemen soon appeared on the scene and laid siege to Derna. They were unable to retake the town, but neither was Eaton able to disperse them. He and his men found themselves in a precarious position. Then, on June 11, the *Constellation* arrived with news that Tobias Lear and Commodore Rodgers had reached agreement with Yusuf on a peace treaty on June 4. The terms—$60,000 for ransom, no tribute payments, and treatment of captured Americans as POWs rather than as slaves—were considered favorable to the United States, but they meant the abandonment of Ahmad as well as of Eaton's glorious plan. Although this was advertised as an honorable and advantageous peace, and obtaining release of the *Philadelphia*'s crew was obviously a major consideration in the minds of Lear and Rodgers, they were much criticized at home for undercutting, not to say betraying, Eaton and Ahmad.

On June 12, Eaton and the American and European members of his force, plus Ahmad and his retinue, embarked on the *Constellation* under cover of darkness, leaving the rest of the four hundred men to their fates. Eaton went home a bitter man. Ahmad went into impecunious exile, and Yusuf remained in power for another twenty-seven years.[17]

The capture of Derna influenced Yusuf to be more reasonable in his negotiations with the Americans, and in that respect it was a success. But it was also a sad example of what happens to dissidents who rely on a foreign power to support them and then are abandoned when the going gets tough or a better offer turns up.

Tunis

Tunis had a long history of independent rule behind it and boasted a prosperous economy, cultural institutions such as the famous Zitouna University, and a sense of national identity that Algiers and Tripoli did not have. In 1534 it was occupied by the Ottomans, who already controlled Algiers and Tripoli and who took advantage of dissension within the Arab ruling family to take over the country. The Spaniards responded by seizing Tunis in 1535 and a thirty-nine-year struggle between Spain and Turkey for control of the country ensued, finally being settled in Turkey's favor in 1574.

Like Algiers, Tunis underwent a shift from direct rule by Istanbul to rule by leaders from among the janissary garrison. In 1705, however, Tunis went a step further when an officer named Husayn bin Ali assumed power and established a dynasty that was to rule under the title of bey, or prince, until the coming of the French in 1881.

For the rulers of Tunis, managing relations with their bumptious neighbor to the west was an enduring preoccupation. Although the dey claimed to be senior to them (the bey of Tunis sent him an annual tribute of olive oil) and sometimes gave them orders, his pretensions were deeply resented and his orders were not necessarily obeyed. The ruling bey at the time of our story, Hamuda (1782–1814), was noted for his skill in handling this problem. Generally considered an enlightened ruler who focused on agricultural and political reform and maintained Tunisia's independence, he was a sharp bargainer who did not manifest great interest in developing diplomatic and commercial ties with the United States. Like his colleagues in Algiers and Tripoli, he was still involved in the corsair trade. The raid on Carloforte mentioned in chapter 1 and the prolonged bargaining over the release of the captives taken there occurred during his reign.[18]

As noted in chapter 6, Cathcart claimed to have negotiated a truce with Tunis at the time of Donaldson's negotiations with the dey in the fall of 1795. The translated text, from his papers in the New York Public Library, is in appendix 12. Dated November 8, 1795, it was issued by the dey, who is quoted as ordering Hamuda not to attack American vessels for a period of eight months. The translation says that it was signed by Haj Ali, the Tunisian wakil or chargé d'affaires in Algiers (who had arrived with the annual tribute of oil). The dey had earlier proposed to Cathcart a payment to Tunis amounting to $51,650 in cash and naval stores, but Donaldson had refused to consider it, saying he did not have the authority to negotiate another treaty. He seems to have had second thoughts subsequently, because he and Cathcart called on Haj Ali on October 28 with presents to a value of 925 sequins, and Ali promised to do all he could to befriend the Americans when he returned to Tunis. Cathcart does not mention any discussion with him of the larger sum proposed by the dey. When Barlow heard these details from Cathcart and Donaldson, he assumed the truce was in effect, but he understood that it was only temporary and that he would have to negotiate a more lasting agreement.

Barlow also counted on the Algerines to help him, but the dey was overly free with assurances of Tunisian conduct and of his ability to command it. When Barlow finally appeared in October 1796 with the gold O'Brien had been carrying on the *Sophia,* the dey said he would write to the bey of Tunis immediately telling him to conclude peace with the United States. He evidently kept his word and also sent a similar letter to Tripoli, which seems to have had some effect, but Tunis was a much more complex affair.

To begin with, five months earlier, on May 22, 1796, Barlow had written, on Herculais's recommendation, to a French merchant in Tunis named Joseph Etienne Famin, authorizing him to negotiate a treaty of peace and commerce, informing him that a truce already existed but was due to expire in July, and saying the United States could not go beyond 20,000 piastres ($20,000) for peace—15,000 in cash and the remainder in jewelry and the like. He enclosed a letter of credence for Famin.

Famin's motives were subsequently questioned and Herculais apologized for recommending him,[19] but Barlow commented in a letter of August 17, 1797, from the quarantine station at Marseille that the apology was a little late and noted that Herculais had told him it was his duty as a French citizen to oppose the interests of the Americans because of the "attachment of their government to the British interest." The implication of Barlow's remark is that Herculais's recommendation of Famin was not intended to be helpful.

For his part, Famin was reportedly threatened with boycott by other members of the French community if he continued to represent American interests, and it must have taken some courage on his part to continue doing so.

Barlow described Famin as the right-hand man of Yusuf Khoja (Clerk Joseph), a "Georgian renegade"[20] who was the *sahib al- tabi'* or keeper of the seal (usually written "sapatapa" in American documents of the period, although both Eaton and Cathcart wrote it "sahibtappa," which is closer to the original). Yusuf was very influential with the bey and eventually became chief minister. One sign of his importance is his seal on the *tadhkirat* or passports issued to corsair vessels leaving Tunis. He is the most frequently mentioned personality, other than the bey, in the American documents of the period. Judging by the correspondence, he was not very helpful to the Americans, but his motives were perhaps more financial than political.

Famin wrote to Barlow on June 17, 1796, to report that on June 13 he had met with the bey, who was pleased that Barlow wanted to negotiate with him directly rather than relying on the dey to impose a treaty. The bey had told him to return in two days to discuss terms. When Famin then suggested prolonging the eight-month truce negotiated by Cathcart, he was surprised by the bey's response that no such truce existed, that it was true Haj Ali had proposed a peace treaty to him, but there had been no follow-up, and that if he had agreed to a truce, he would have signed the document, which he had not done in this case.

Two days later the bey told Famin that his price for peace was 50,000 "piastres fortes d'Espagne" (roughly $50,000) plus the customary bakhsheesh for the various officials and a present of jewelry for himself. Pending agreement, he was agreeable to a six-month truce from that date, and one was written and signed on the spot. The original is in the National Archives.

At this point the imprudence of American travelers intervened in the form of the schooner *Eliza,* with a cargo of brandy, which was taken by a Tunisian galiot—a small, open-decked galley—two days out from the French port of Sète, on June 14, 1796. The schooner's owner, Edward Brand, who was on board, wrote a lament to Barlow from Tunis on June 23 in which he noted that the *Eliza* had been taken a day before the Famin-negotiated truce went into effect and that the bey considered the vessel good prize and the crew slaves. He had not put them at hard labor, however, pending a response from Barlow and had allowed the crew to remain on board the ship because the plague was then raging in Tunis. The bey set ransom for the *Eliza* and her cargo and crew at $10,000.[21]

On August 2 Barlow wrote to Famin that in exchange for peace he was willing to pay 4,670 Venetian sequins (about $10,000) for the *Eliza* and her crew, and to give Yusuf Khoja 6,000 piastres and the bey 20,000 as well as the "customary" donations in the amount of 20,000. He hoped the entire deal could be concluded for not more than 50,000 piastres and commented that there was no question the truce had been negotiated by Haj Ali nine months earlier and signed by the dey, who was accustomed to giving orders to the bey. If the latter did not accept Barlow's offer, he might have to settle for only 20,000 piastres.

This threat did not have much effect. O'Brien, passing through Tunis en route to Tripoli in October, was told by the bey—who probably knew at that point how generous the Americans were being with the Algerines—that his price had gone up to $140,000. When O'Brien countered that the U.S. might possibly pay $101,350, the bey reduced his price to $107,000. Subsequently Barlow made a counteroffer of $80,000, which the bey rejected.

At this juncture the dey, who had made various extravagant promises of support to Barlow, decided to make war on Tunis. Barlow wrote to his wife on December 30 that the "Dey has sent fifty thousand ambassadors on horseback, well armed, to negotiate my affairs in Tunis. These good negotiators ought to bring the head of the Bey to me and his treasures to the Dey."

The dey's warlike gesture had little effect. His troops were soon recalled because of snow in the mountains, and although he promised Barlow that the campaign would resume in the spring, no more was heard of it and the Americans capitulated to Hamuda's demands. Barlow commented that he wished he had accepted the bey's first offer. Famin eventually negotiated a treaty on August 1, 1797, and on February 28, 1798, the Senate committee considering the matter reported:[22]

> a peace with the Bey of Tunis, after a variety of difficulties, and a tedious negotiation, has been at length concluded on the following terms, viz:
>
> | | |
> |---|---|
> | In money | $50,000 |
> | In naval stores, called regalia | 35,000 |
> | In peace presents | 12,000 |
> | In consul's presents | 4,000 |
> | In sackatappa, or secret service money | 6,000 |
> | | 107,000 |

The Senate consented to ratification of the treaty on condition that article 14, which would entitle goods coming from Tunis to enter the United States for a duty of only 3 percent, be suspended. It recommended that the United States enter into "friendly negotiations with the Government of Tunis, on the subject of the said article, so as to accomodate the provisions thereof to the existing treaties of the United States with other nations." The instructions sent to Humphreys in Lisbon pointed out that the provision in article 14 would be ruinous to the United States, which depended on customs revenues for the greater part of its budget. Under its various most-favored-nation agreements with other states, it would have to give all of them the benefit of the lower tariff granted the Tunisians. Barlow suspected that Famin had put that provision into the treaty in hopes of benefit from it himself by shipping goods to the United States.

The Americans also objected to article 11, which required the United States to give the Tunisians a barrel of gunpowder for every gun fired in saluting American warships, and article 12, which permitted the bey to commandeer American vessels at will and use them as he saw fit. Indeed, Barlow said that the language in articles 11 and 14 had not appeared in the draft of the treaty Famin had sent him in April 1797, although it must have been in the final version that Humphreys passed on to Washington.

Revision of the treaty was negotiated in early 1799 by Eaton and Cathcart, who went to Tunis from Algiers to discuss the offending provisions—issues that were still contentious in 1805, according to the bey's letter of August 31 of that year to President Jefferson—and the treaty was ratified by the Senate in 1800. The negotiations were made difficult by Hamuda's unhappiness with the nonarrival of promised items of "regalia" and his complaints that the Americans were treating the Algerines better than the Tunisians. Eaton's account of the negotiations in his report of April 15, 1799,[23] is a classic description of the problems encountered by American negotiators over the years in the Middle East and North Africa. Hamuda's complaints and threats to send his cruisers out against American shipping if his demands were not met continued after the treaty was ratified, and Eaton, who was not a tactful or patient man, had a difficult time dealing with him. Eaton's attitude came through clearly when he wrote to the Department of State at one point in 1800:

> It is certain that there is no access to the permanent friendship of these states without paving the way with gold or cannon balls; and the proper question is which method is preferable.... They are under no restraints of honor nor honesty. There is not a scoundrel among them, from the prince to the muleteer, who will not beg and steal.... The United States set out wrongly and have proceeded so. Too many concessions have been made to Algiers. There is but one language which can be held to these people, and this is *terror*.[24]

Eaton was also exasperated by Famin, whom he publicly horsewhipped in 1800.[25] He was called before the bey for this, but his behavior was excused after he described Famin's misdeeds, and the bey gave his hand a "cordial squeeze," according to Eaton. Eventually, however, his quarrels with the bey became too serious and he was ordered out of the country in March 1803 under humiliating circumstances—he was $22,000 in debt to a Tunisian official, and the commodore of the American fleet, Captain Morris, had to bail him out. At one point during the proceedings Captain Morris was arrested by the Tunisians as security for the money owed by Eaton, at which the Americans took great umbrage. Eaton was replaced by Dr. George Davis, surgeon of the U.S. Navy schooner *Enterprise,* who was designated by Morris to act as consul. Eaton returned to the United States and was subsequently appointed U.S. Navy agent for the Barbary states. He then reappeared to capture Derna.

On August 1, 1805, following the end of the war with Tripoli, the most serious incident ever in U.S.-Tunisian relations occurred. Hamuda was demanding compensation for a Tunisian cruiser and her two prizes intercepted during the American blockade of Tripoli. Davis, the consul, reported that the bey was threatening war if his demands were not met. In response, most of the U.S. Mediterranean squadron—five frigates, two brigs, two schooners, one sloop, and eight gunboats—sailed into Tunis harbor under a flag of truce and took up a line that "stretched athwart the harbour from one end to the other."[26] After taking up this warlike position, the squadron commander, Commodore Rodgers, asked the bey in a somewhat truculent letter to declare whether he wanted war or peace and gave him thirty-six hours to reply, failing which Rodgers would commence "both defensive and offensive operations against your regency." This was the second earliest example (the first being at Tangier in 1803) of American gunboat diplomacy.

The ultimatum expired with no result, but eventually Hamuda responded by appointing an ambassador, Suleiman Mallimalli or Mellimelli, to Washington to negotiate a resolution of the points at issue between the two countries.[27] Hamuda sent with Mellimelli a diplomatically worded letter dated August 31 complaining of the "too martial temper of the aforementioned Commodore Rodgers, very imprudently stirred up and supported by the Chargé d'affaires, George Davis, whose equivocal conduct has deserved examination, just as it caused me extreme surprise," and saying that he had authorized Mellimelli to "treat with you and terminate everything."[28]

Tobias Lear was with Rodgers on the *Constitution.* The bey had initially refused to receive him, but after Lear sent him a copy of his special credentials from Jefferson, he welcomed him and they had two long and cordial discussions. Lear's detailed report of their meetings quotes Hamuda, who was indignant at Rodgers's display of force, as asking if Lear thought he was a fool and as saying he had never said he was going to declare war on the United States as Davis had reported.[29]

Fig. 14. *Tunisian Corsair Boarding the Ship* Mercury *of Boston off Sardinia*. Attributed to M. Corne. Courtesy of the Naval Historical Center, Washington, D.C.

Hamuda's remarks imply that Davis had misunderstood or distorted what he was told by Hamuda and by Yusuf Sahib al-Tabi'. Davis sounds from the correspondence as though he was unhappy in Tunis, and this may have influenced his judgment. On the other hand, he sounds quite restrained in a note he sent to Rodgers on August 4, saying that "an imperious sense of duty to my Country . . . urges me to recommend a suspension of any hostile operation, until advice can be obtained from His Excellency the President of the United States.—No material injury will arise from the delay—our situation will not be rendered worse; & that of the Enemy will not certainly be bettered."[30] He may have had in mind a less bellicose show of naval strength.

Rodgers, who had a very long and distinguished naval career, also had a reputation as a rigid disciplinarian. In the correspondence to be found in *Naval Documents* he sounds preemptory in manner and quick to take offense. At this remove, his ultimatum to the bey reads like a message from someone who was looking for a fight.

This incident is usually seen by American writers as a victory of diplomacy backed by force,[31] but that view was not unanimous at the time. There is in the Tunisian state archives a letter of June 28, 1806, from Jefferson, countersigned by Secretary of State Madison, to Hamuda Bey that puts it in a rather different light. Jefferson seems to sympathize with Hamuda and writes:

> I learned with great concern that the Commander of our Squadron in the Mediterranean, Commander Rogers [*sic*], deeming it his duty to ask explanations of menaces understood to have been signified towards the United States, had done this in a manner not consisting with the respect due to your Excellency's character, nor with the friendship which I bear you. In this, be assured that he was not governed by his instructions, which have inculcated, on all occasions, the greatest respect for your person and Government, and a spirit of conciliation in the execution of all his duties. Of this he will be made duly sensible on his return home, now daily expected.[32]

Someone, perhaps Lear, may have given Jefferson an unfavorable report on Rodgers, but Lear's detailed report on the incident in *Naval Documents* praises him, saying, "The moment was peculiarly happy for us, and the judicious and decided measures taken by Commodore Rodgers made so powerfull an impression on the mind of the Bashaw, that the negociation afterwards became easy and unembarassed." Perhaps Jefferson was reacting to the letter Mellimelli sent him on December 31, 1805, spelling out the Tunisian position.[33] It is a model of clarity and may have been the first occasion on which Jefferson had a clear picture of the Tunisian point of view.

Whatever his source of information, it is evident that Jefferson did not approve of Rodgers's tactics. Paullin in his biography of Rodgers notes that "Jefferson's friendly yielding to the demands of Mellimelli is one of many indications that he did not enter into the commodore's plans and wishes to discipline the bey of Tunis by the use of force. In his annual messages he made no mention of the Tunisian expedition. He did not publicly commend Rodgers for his efficient services in ending the war with Tripoli and in humiliating the bey."[34] The implication is that "disciplining" the bey should have been commendable.

Mellimelli departed Tunis on the *Congress* on September 1, accompanied by Lear and a retinue of ten that, according to the list in Arabic and English in the Tunis consular documents, included a secretary, a barber, a cook, a steward, and three slaves—plus four gift horses for Jefferson, which the president could not accept for himself, but whose stud fees paid for part of their upkeep. Mellimelli arrived in Washington on November 30. The first ambassador from the Muslim world, he created a sensation with his exotic garments and retinue and was an instant social success. But he was a tenacious bargainer and insisted that the United States should replace the Tunisian cruiser and her two prizes seized by the Americans—the principal contentious issue in the bey's mind.

Judging by the remarkable comments about his tenacity and zeal in the second paragraph of Jefferson's above-mentioned letter of June 28, 1806, Mellimelli irritated people a good deal by his stubbornness. His exoticism palled after a while, and there was criticism of the expense of maintaining him—host governments fed and housed foreign ambassadors in those days—and of the nature of the hospitality extended to him, including the services of "Georgia, a Greek," evidently procured to relieve his need for female company.

Accordingly, there was relief in the capital when, in May 1806, Mellimelli set off on a tour of Philadelphia, New York, and Boston with Cathcart as his escort. In Boston, Mellimelli refused to accept the first vessel offered in exchange for the captured cruiser, because it had previously belonged to the bey. Madison, evidently worn down by the continuing dispute, ordered another prepared and, loaded with the commodities bought by Mellimelli for resale in Tunis—including 673 bags of coffee, 132 barrels and 39 boxes of sugar, and four containers of cochineal, according to the ship's bill of lading—it was sent off as a present to the bey with Mellimelli on board. He and Cathcart parted with mutual recriminations.

Mellimelli arrived home in December 1806. The eventual impact of this first mission seems to have been beneficial, because Tunisian-American relations remained relatively noncontentious after January 1807, when the bey finally agreed to settle his claims for $10,000. The bey sent Jefferson a warm letter on February 27 thanking him for the polite reception he had given Mellimelli, praising the "reasonableness and tact" of Tobias Lear, who had visited Tunis in January 1807 and explained the mutual misunderstandings that existed between the two countries, and vowing that relations would be founded on principles of "entire and perfect reciprocity."[35] On March 1, 1807, Lear wrote from Tunis to John Ridgely, the acting consul in Tunis, as well as to other consuls in the Mediterranean, informing them that "the differences which existed between the United States of America and the Regency of Tunis . . . are now happily and honorably settled" and trade with Tunis could be "carried on with as much security and advantage as that of any other nation with whom the Bey is in friendship."

Morocco

Unlike the three regencies, Morocco had been an independent country governed by a succession of Arab and Berber dynasties since 788. Ottoman rule did not extend that far, and although Spain and Portugal managed to establish a few presidios at various points along the Atlantic and Mediterranean coasts, Moroccan sovereignty was never seriously in question until the coming of the French in 1912. The current Alaouite dynasty has been on the throne since 1688.

Sidi Muhammad bin Abdallah, the sultan who had concluded the peace treaty of 1786 with Barclay, died in 1790. His son and successor, Moulay (My Lord) Yazid, died in 1792 during a power struggle with two of his brothers and was succeeded by a third brother, Moulay Slimane, or Sulayman, who reigned until 1822. The change of rulers necessitated renewal of the 1786 treaty. Congress had appropriated $20,000 for the necessary gifts in 1791, following Sidi Muhammad's death, and Barclay was appointed to go to Marrakesh and negotiate the renewal. But he had to postpone his visit because of Moulay Yazid's death and died himself before he could resume the effort following Moulay Slimane's accession to power.

In June 1795 James Simpson, the consul in Gibraltar, went to Morocco with a present of armament consisting of twenty 6-pounder iron cannon and ten 4-pounders, with powder, tools, shot, and carriages for their installation on ships, with a total value of $3,912. He was received by Moulay Slimane, who asked him how much the United States was prepared to pay in exchange for renewal of the treaty. Simpson said he was certain they would not pay anything, with which Moulay Slimane told him he might as well go home, but Simpson received permission to remain for another six months while waiting to hear from Humphreys on the subject. He reported that the idea the United States would pay tribute was suggested to the Moroccans by John Lamb, our first negotiator to Algiers, who was in the country on a horse-buying trip.

Something or someone changed Moulay Slimane's mind, because soon thereafter, being required to go elsewhere and put down a rebellion, he summoned Barclay and told him he was ready to renew the treaty with no tribute, saying, "The Americans, I find, are the Christian nation my father most esteemed. I am the same with them as my father was, and I trust they will be so with me."[36]

In 1802 Moulay Slimane asked permission to ship grain to Tripoli on the *Mashuda*, a Tripolitanian cruiser commanded by the notorious Murad Rais that had been caught at Gibraltar the previous year while en route to the Atlantic in search of American prey. The *Mashuda* had been blockaded by the Americans ever since. Moulay Slimane claimed that the ship was now his. The commanders of the American forces, Captain Dale and his successor Captain Morris, both refused permission on the grounds that it would make a mockery of the blockade of Tripoli. The Moroccans then declared war on the United States. Simpson learned of it in Tangier on June 22. He immediately departed for Gibraltar but was then allowed to return to Tangier for six months, during which period settlement of the dispute could be discussed. Accordingly, he returned, and peace was declared soon after he informed Moulay Slimane that the president had decided to send him a hundred gun carriages as a gift.

In 1803 the *Mashuda* was allowed to depart from Gibraltar, following Simpson's receipt of instructions that the vessel should be released if there was proof that she really belonged to the Moroccans. She sailed for Tripoli but was intercepted by the Americans and taken to Malta. Moulay Slimane was reported to be infuriated by this, and in July the two frigates of his navy, the *Mirboka* or *Mirboha* (Mabruka? Mirbuha?) and the *Miamona* (Ma'munia?), sailed with orders issued by the governor of Tangier to intercept and capture American vessels as well as those of states having no peace treaties with Morocco. The *Mirboka* soon captured the brig *Celia* out of Boston with a crew of eight, but was herself intercepted by the *Philadelphia* under Captain Bainbridge and taken to Gibraltar, where the Moroccan crew were detained as prisoners of war.

At this juncture, the new commodore of the Mediterranean fleet, Edward Preble, arrived in the *Constitution* with the new consul general to Algiers, Tobias Lear, and his family on board. First stopping at Tangier on September 12, Preble fired a gun, the signal for the appropriate consul to send out a boat, but there was no response from the American consulate. Fearing something was amiss, he repaired to Gibraltar where he learned from Bainbridge that two Moroccan cruisers had been sent out with orders from the governor of Tangier to capture American vessels, implying that Morocco was at war with the United States. Preble decided on a tough approach and had the means to put it into effect. By September 13 there were six American warships at Gibraltar. After a series of visits and exchanges, the *Constitution* and the *Nautilus,* cleared for action, anchored at Tangier on October 4, to be followed by the frigates *New York* and *John Adams* two days later. Moulay Slimane arrived in Tangier on October 5, and in succeeding days the Moroccans, evidently impressed by the American show of force, explained that it was all a mistake and blamed the governor of Tangier. There was an impressive exchange of courtesies, the Moroccans supplied the Americans with a quantity of livestock, and the treaty of 1786 was reaffirmed.[37] Far less threatening than the display of force by Commodore Rodgers at Tunis in 1805, this was the first use of gunboat diplomacy by the Americans and was the last trouble of any account with Morocco until the Perdicaris affair in 1904.[38]

9

Relevance

The events of September 11, 2001, brought home to the American public the importance to their daily lives of attitudes in the Muslim world. What relevance does our first encounter with that world have to today's events? Are there lessons from that experience that should be applied today? How did our diplomacy and naval force work back then? To what extent have these events influenced American attitudes two centuries later?

Policy Implications

Since September 11 a number of commentators in the media have cited the U.S. experience with the Barbary corsairs as an example to be followed in dealing with Usama bin Laden and al-Qa'ida. The speakers or writers often are unaware that in Barbary the United States was dealing with recognized governments, not autonomous terrorists, and they misunderstand the position the United States took on the questions of ransom and tribute. They have the war with Tripoli in mind when they speak or write and usually do not know how it ended or how we solved our hostage crisis with Algiers.

Some of the commentators have quoted the phrase "millions for defense but not one cent for tribute" as the precedent to be followed today. The literate may think that Jefferson said it with regard to the Barbary states. Those who have bothered to look it up in Bartlett will respond that it was not Jefferson but Charles Cotesworth Pinckney of South Carolina who said it to Talleyrand's emissary when he suggested that a bribe might avert a war. In fact, it seems that it was neither Jefferson nor Pinckney but South Carolina congressman Robert Goodloe Harper, who said it in a toast proposed at a congressional dinner for John Marshall in 1798. It had no connection with the Barbary crisis or hostages. But Jefferson did say something to the same effect about Barbary, and the expression did become a popular rallying cry in the Barbary crisis of the early nineteenth century.[1]

Not paying blackmail, nor dealing with those demanding it, remains fixed in the minds of American officials as a basic policy, both for practical reasons and as a matter of principle. Few officials today realize that business ethics and expediency triumphed over principle in our initial resolution of the problems with the Barbary corsairs—that the United States paid tribute to Algiers for years, and that it ransomed its citizens from Algiers for a princely sum that, if converted to a percentage of the national budget, we cannot imagine the United States government paying today. Rather, Jefferson's view—"we prefer war in all cases to tribute under any form and to any people whatever"—is the accepted wisdom, and knuckling under to the bandits is unacceptable.

Thus, a special task force on terrorism chaired by then Vice President Bush in 1986 came to the conclusion that the United States must not negotiate with terrorists or pay them ransom for the release of hostages. This was and is an uncontroversial policy, but, like many such principled positions, it has been violated in a major way more than once, as in the Reagan administration's Irangate affair. Furthermore, no one has prescribed how the United States is to extricate its citizens from captivity against the wishes of their captors in the absence of a negotiated settlement. The possibilities will depend on the circumstance in each case, of course, but the implication of a policy of no negotiations or concessions is that if ultimatums fail and rescue is not possible, the hostages may be sacrificed to the national interest or to political expediency, depending on one's point of view. That has happened at least once in recent memory.[2] (The Bush doctrine has since been amended to permit negotiation with captors.)

Fortunately for the Algiers captives, John Adams's view prevailed in 1795 and the navy did not have to rescue them. A rescue attempt at Algiers would have been a bloody affair, with little or no chance of success, and the captives would have been killed rather then rescued. There was probably no serious consideration of such an operation in any case. For one thing, the navy did not yet exist when the captives were freed. For another, what Jefferson and others had in mind as the appropriate naval action was a blockade and a reduction of the corsair fleet, not an amphibious landing. Whether that would have freed the captives is problematic. The blockade strategy was tried at Tripoli and was not very effective.

The Algiers problem foreshadowed a dilemma that has confronted the United States repeatedly over the years—how to deal with a leader, or state or organization, that does not accept the Western rules and is beyond American reach, even with force that is overwhelming. The hostage crises in Iran and Lebanon come to mind immediately. Although in 1980 the Americans thought they could rescue the hostages in Tehran with a military action, their luck ran out and the operation was a disaster. The captives were finally released as a result of negotiations in which the Algerians played a key role and that gave Iran satisfaction regarding some of its financial claims against the U.S. government, while a mechanism was established for paying U.S. claims against Iran. In other words, there was a quid pro quo. (When the Reagan team came into office in 1981, it was convinced the Carter administration had paid ransom to Iran and wanted to abrogate the Algiers agreement. It was persuaded not to do so.)

The Lebanese captors wanted their relatives held prisoner in Kuwait released. There was never much chance of rescuing the hostages, because their locations were unknown, and there was no way military pressure could have been applied effectively. Asking the Kuwaitis to release their prisoners was an unacceptable alternative, both as a matter of principle and because the prisoners had been involved in acts of terrorism against the Americans as well as others. A large amount of money properly distributed might have helped. That was not tried. (Or was it?) The bizarre attempt to trade weapons for hostages that was part of the scandal known as Irangate led to further seizure of hostages. Release came very slowly as a result of realization by the Iranian sponsors of Hizballah, the Lebanese faction that was holding the prisoners, that the prisoners were not an effective asset for them. Otherwise, the hostages would probably have died in captivity. In both Iran and Lebanon it was diplomacy, not force, that eventually secured the release of the American prisoners.

Diplomacy Backed by Force

The advocates of the diplomacy-backed-by-force approach can find plenty of examples to cite in our dealings with North Africa—the display of naval strength at Tangier in 1803, the more threatening display at Tunis in August 1805, the naval and land operations against Tripoli from 1801 to 1805, and Decatur's sweep in 1815. But the record shows that the American navy, for all its exploits, did not "overawe" the regencies until Decatur's sweep after the War of 1812. It garnered some respect, but it did not frighten Yusuf Qaramanli in Tripoli, and at this late date it is impossible to calibrate with precision what impact it had on Algiers, Tunis, and Morocco.

Nevertheless, whatever one makes of the navy's operations, it is certainly true that before they had a navy the Americans were not taken seriously by the regencies. If they had had a navy, they might not have had a hostage crisis in the first place, although the experience of the European powers showed that the mere existence of a navy was not always sufficient to protect a state's shipping. Only the British and French were able to secure meaningful and reasonably durable treaties with the Algerians, and that only after a good deal of naval action. The lesser European powers were unable to pose a serious threat to the regencies and were in constant danger of having their treaties disregarded in spite of their navies.

In the absence of a navy, however, the Americans had no alternative to paying up if they wanted to see their men again and to insure the safety of their trade with the Mediterranean ports. From the very beginning, before there were any hostages, they knew that they would have to pay for peace and the only question was how much. It rankled nevertheless. The Europeans treated their tribute payments as necessary commercial expenses and did not worry unduly about principle, but the Americans were more sensitive about being respected than the Europeans were, and the national humiliation of paying tribute grated on their nerves. In terms of expense to the taxpayer, they would have been better off had they agreed to pay the Tripolitanians as well as the Algerines what they asked for in the beginning, but this would have gone against the grain.

Except in the case of Morocco, there seemed to be no prospect at the end of the eighteenth century for a stable relationship with the states of North Africa based on commerce, mutual interest, and respect. The rough soldiers who ruled from Algiers to Tripoli did not display interest in international respectability or trade with America. They preferred booty and tribute. "The Algerines are a company of rogues, and I am their captain," one of the deys is alleged to have said to the British consul in the late seventeenth century.[3] That they got away with their roguishness as long as they did was due to the toleration, and sometimes encouragement, extended to them by the European powers, and Britain and France in particular. Whoever was to blame, the Americans had to treat with the Algerines on their own terms, and the Algerines' independence and imaginary impregnability shielded them from the ordinary inducements and blandishments of international intercourse.

The ability to project military power in order to deal with such states is one of the essential attributes of American politico-military policy today, and impressive displays of this capability have been given in places like Libya, Lebanon, Bosnia, and Kuwait as well as Afghanistan and Iraq. But the difficulty that conventional military forces have in dealing with irregular situations, such as that in Algiers in 1795 or Lebanon in 1983, raises questions as to how effective the military force behind the diplomacy will be in practice. The U.S. military were quite effective in Lebanon in 1958, when their landing in the midst of serious unrest—one hesitates to call it a civil war given the much grander conflagration twenty years later in the same country—served as a deus ex machina that permitted a return to normal political life. In fact, it was too successful, encouraging policy writers to think that limited warfare was an approach that should be tried more often, and that we could get away with it in Vietnam. People overlooked the fact that the Lebanese population was largely unarmed in 1958 (there were few rifled weapons in private hands) and no one shot at the Americans, who were welcomed as liberators. In 1982–83 the situation was entirely different, with large quantities of arms of all descriptions in private hands. The Americans made the mistake of taking sides, and the gunmen soon discovered that the marines were just as mortal as everyone else. Somalia in 1991–93 was another case where military force was supporting diplomacy and came up against a determined local resistance that was beyond its ability to contain. All of which is to say that while Diplomacy Backed by Force sounds like a redoubtable slogan, and it echoes others, such as Teddy Roosevelt's Big Stick, that have caught the popular fancy over the years, it is not a reliable indicator of how things will work out when the crisis comes. When things go wrong, as they often will, it may help to remember that George Washington saw nothing immoral about buying our way out of a fix in 1795.

The Diplomatic Experience

North Africa was a field of pioneering endeavor for American diplomacy. While a number of notable individuals—Benjamin Franklin, Thomas Jefferson, John Adams, John Jay, and David Humphreys—had diplomatic experience negotiating with the Europeans, the non-European world was terra incognita to them. There was no U.S. official representation whatever in the great arc from Morocco to Japan when the *Maria* and the *Dauphin* were seized in 1785. The United States had no organized diplomatic service and would not have for many years to come, and there was no one in the United States who had meaningful experience in dealing with the North Africans. John Lamb, a Connecticut horse trader, passed for an expert. At the same time, with the exception of Thomas Barclay and Tobias Lear, the Americans on the ground in North Africa had no exposure to the trade of diplomacy before finding themselves negotiating with foreign leaders on matters of high importance. This was a learning experience in very difficult circumstances, and the marvel is the confidence with which these men responded to it.

O'Brien and the others showed no hesitation about writing directly to the president of the republic or the secretary of state and making policy recommendations, most of which were sensible and some of which were prophetic. They carried out their instructions in a professional manner with little guidance from home, and were able to improvise when the occasion demanded it. Their self-assurance and pride of country were shared by their naval colleagues, who did not hesitate to decide on and take military-diplomatic moves that today would have to be cleared at the highest level of the government.

In search of verdicts on the performances of these men, I looked to see what other diplomats had to say about them—were they considered inept and awkward or, perhaps, bold and skillful? Unfortunately, the other diplomats seem to have been quite discreet, judging by the consular records of the British and French. A concerted search might turn up more morsels, but aside from some complimentary remarks about Barlow from the dey and the Scandinavian consuls in Algiers, all I have found to date are a few remarks such as those of the French consul in Algiers, de Kercy, that Lamb was not made for diplomacy, seconded by unfavorable remarks about him from Expilly, the Spanish representative. There were also disparaging references to Cathcart by Logie, and by each of the rulers of Algiers, Tunis, and Tripoli. The bey of Tunis called him a troublemaker, which may have been unjust but would not be inconsistent with the image he projected in his writings. The Algerines were put off by the sad state of Donaldson's clothing, according to Cathcart, and Hamuda Bey must have complained a good deal about Eaton as well as about the tone of "hauteur" that he claimed the acting consul, Dr. George Davis, had used toward him. In general, however, the other officials do not seem to have devoted much time to critiquing the American performance. The Americans were not that important.

The Americans themselves were another matter. They were very free with their comments about each other. Cathcart and Eaton disparaged O'Brien as soft on the Algerines and in thrall to the Jewish bankers; Eaton raged about Lear; Donaldson execrated Humphreys as incompetent; O'Brien and Cathcart were very uncomplimentary about Lamb and about each other;[4] Barlow got rid of Cathcart; and so forth. Such backbiting was to be expected, given the tensions arising from a difficult and often unpleasant situation and the difficulty of communication, but in spite of their individual shortcomings, these Americans did rather well—much better than one would expect from a group of people with similar backgrounds thrown into such a situation today, even with their cell phones and e-mail.

Lamb was nevertheless an unfortunate choice as negotiator. It is unlikely anyone else would have done much better with what he had to offer the dey, but had he gone to Paris as Jefferson requested in his letter of June 20, 1786, and had he given Jefferson a fuller and more coherent account of what had taken place in Algiers, perhaps Jefferson and Adams would have found a way to keep the negotiations going. In particular, a better understanding of what had taken place could have prompted a response to the February 1787 message from Hasan, the wakil al-kharj, asking that Lamb be sent back (chapter 4). An answer to that invitation to dialogue might have led to settlement on terms more favorable than those finally accepted. The lack of response was evidently offensive to Hasan and was one reason he did not think the Americans were serious when Humphreys tried to go to Algiers. The Lamb mission was thus an object lesson in the importance of timely and clear communications, and of answering the mail when it comes in.

In terms of human lives and expense, the Americans would have been better off had they ransomed the original twenty-one prisoners for the $48,300 the dey reportedly agreed to with Lamb, which was not out of line with what others were paying. Jefferson and Adams had already determined to exceed the terms of their original authorization when they decided to use money designated for the purchase of peace treaties to pay ransom. The $80,000 they were authorized to spend for peace with all of Barbary, a sum that was quite unrealistic for that purpose, would have covered the ransom demanded in Algiers plus the $20,000 cost of the Moroccan negotiations and left a balance of $10,000—not enough to buy peace from Tunis and Tripoli, but they could have asked for more.

They would have been criticized for exceeding instructions, but had they done so, a number of American lives would have been saved. Then too, without the encumbrance of a hostage situation, negotiation of a peace treaty at an earlier date might have become possible. It is unlikely that the large amount of money eventually paid for a peace with Algiers would have been forthcoming as long as the United States was being governed under the Articles of Confederation, but who knows what a skillful and personable emissary might have accomplished with a good deal less money, particularly if he did not have to worry about the fate of hostages?

Jefferson made it clear that his policy was being guided not by the money but by concern about being tagged as an easy mark. A fear of paying too much, of being outsmarted in bargaining, is a recurring theme in American dealings with this region down to the present and reflects permanent stereotypes about Arab and Middle Eastern business practices, character, and reliability. Barlow, for instance, should have accepted Hamuda Bey's first proposal, but that would go counter to his ingrained beliefs on how to bargain. The Americans' purported skill at horse trading and poker does not seem to be of much help in such situations abroad, where different cultures produce different recipes for successful bargaining. Not much has changed in this respect over the past two centuries. Today the stakes are not money but political support, and the Americans (and others) are still misjudging reactions in the Middle East.

Resolution of the Algiers hostage problem took eleven years. Many hands were involved before it was over. Some of the hands were helpful, particularly those of the Skjöldebrand brothers and Micaiah Bakri, but in the final analysis the Americans had to make the necessary decisions on their own. They were a mixed bag. Donaldson was intemperate and coarse, judging by Cathcart's comments. Perhaps he agreed to pay too much, but he does not seem to have had much choice. It was either that or no peace. He was honest and intelligent and did his best. He does not sound like a great personality, but he succeeded in getting a treaty where others had failed.

Barlow did a magnificent job of getting the captives released in advance of paying for them. He had little to work with except his personality, and his success illustrates the importance of that factor in diplomacy. He would have been in trouble in today's Foreign Service for freewheeling in the matter of the frigate and the *Fortune,* but under Washington he got away with it. (Washington's large view of such matters is refreshing. He rarely appears in the narrative, but he must have played a critical role at certain points in the process, as in the decision to pay the large amount needed for peace with Algiers. This was an early example of the critical importance of executive leadership in determining the direction and outcome of diplomacy.)

In terms of background and previous experience, Lear was the best prepared. He had many detractors, but he seems to have had a level head, and he remained on the job longer than any of the others. He was able to get along with the North African rulers, and that was not a mean accomplishment. He may have thought that Captain Rodgers's truculent stance at Tunis in August 1805 was unnecessary, but he may not. The published record does not tell us. His negotiation of the 1805 peace with Tripoli was mightily criticized at the time and will continue to be cited as an example of the civilians pulling the rug out from under the military. His concealment of his acceptance of Yusuf Pasha's refusal to allow Ahmad's family to rejoin him immediately was unforgivable, but otherwise the treaty he negotiated was reasonable, and the American prisoners from the *Philadelphia* were ransomed for a modest sum by prevailing standards. (But note that they were freed by paying ransom, not by military force, although force was obviously a factor in bringing the Tripolitanians to the negotiating table.) With the argument that Lear should have concentrated on supporting Eaton rather than negotiating a treaty, one enters the realm of the hypothetical, where diplomats are not supposed to tread, but one cannot help feeling sorry for Eaton, who was deprived of the glory that would have been his if his expedition had been completed successfully.

It is noteworthy that two men who had been very close to Washington, Humphreys and Lear, occupied key positions at critical times in our early dealings with the North Africans. Humphreys had been Washington's aide de camp and carried the British flag from Yorktown to Congress in one of the favorite scenes of the Revolution. Lear had been Washington's secretary and was with him when he died. Both men were the object of complaints, and Humphreys's unauthorized leave of absence in the midst of the crisis was very unfortunate, but both showed a good deal of common sense most of the time.

Eaton was a disaster as diplomat, but as coup leader he was outstanding. His efforts were not entirely in vain. His capture of Derna did influence the outcome.

O'Brien gives the impression of being a dependable, rather taciturn person who would wear well. It is too bad he left no journal and we do not know more about him—although he did send in a lengthy report on the negotiations in which he was involved. He evidently tired of the job of consul general in Algiers and wanted out, although he seems to have done the job well.

Cathcart, on the other hand, sounds officious and smug, passing judgment on the others as though he was convinced that he was indeed holier than they. He does not seem to have been popular with his fellow prisoners in spite of his charitable exertions on their behalf, and he was criticized for his arrogance by Lear, Bainbridge, and others. Nor did he seem to have a gift for getting along with the North Africans, although he evidently had a good working relationship with the dey of Algiers. Whatever his shortcomings, he played a critical role in the treaty negotiations in Algiers, and his survival skills were impressive.

O'Brien and Cathcart were both accidental diplomats; the rest were political appointees. While some had more defects than others, these men were models of perseverance and courage under challenging conditions. None of them flinched, although each must have felt desperate at times.

Communications

Throughout this story, communications between the government and the negotiators in the field were abysmal. In an era of instant, wireless communication from the remotest parts of the world, it is difficult to appreciate fully the unreliability and slowness of communication in the era before steam navigation and the introduction of the telegraph in the mid-nineteenth century. (The first Atlantic crossing by a steam-propelled ship, the *Savannah*, occurred in 1819 and took 29 days and 11 hours. The first permanently successful submarine cable across the Atlantic was laid in 1866.) There was no regular mail service across the ocean, and letters of the period are full of introductory or closing statements that the writer is seizing the opportunity of the departure of some vessel to send his dispatch. On some occasions, when a particularly critical piece of information was to be conveyed, as in the case of the Portuguese truce of 1793, the writer reports that he is chartering a ship to carry it. In either case, arrival at the intended destination was subject to the winds and weather and quite unpredictable. Thus Secretary of State Pickering, in a letter to Barlow dated December 3, 1796, acknowledges "receipt of your several letters numbered from 1 to 5, of which the duplicates were received together on the 25th of July, the originals (of nos. 1 and 2) through Mr. Monroe [via Paris] on the 13th of August, and the triplicates on the 18th of October." Humphreys's three-month voyage from Lisbon to Newport in 1794 was an extreme case but not unique. Six weeks for the transatlantic passage seems to have been regarded as normal. That meant three months for a single exchange of communications.

This was also before the creation of the typewriter and carbon paper, not to mention the computer and the Xerox machine, or the scanner. All communications had to be written painstakingly by hand. Copies could be made with a letter press, if one was available—not very likely in North Africa. Sometimes the consul would have an assistant with good handwriting, but more often it was up to him, and few of them wrote well. Reading O'Brien's letters, or Donaldson's from Livorno, for instance, is an exercise in cryptanalysis.

Encryption was by codes, using a key in which groups of numbers or letters represented words. De Castries's letter in appendix 5 is an example. (The reader may wish to try to find the key.) The key could be changed only by providing the recipient with a new list of words and their equivalents, a process that could take months. Such codes were relatively easy to break and therefore not very secure, but this method was still in use by the Department of State as late as World War II for less confidential communications on subjects such as commercial or personnel matters. The "brown code," so called because it was in two large brown volumes full of words and their equivalents, was still on the shelf in the American Consulate General in Sydney when I arrived there as a young vice consul in 1949.

All of the above meant that there could be none of the micromanaging from the home office that is standard in today's diplomacy. There was no way the officials in Philadelphia or Washington could know of developments in Algiers or Tunis until weeks or months after they happened, and the man on the spot was very much left to his own devices within the rather broad limits of his instructions. This is not always an unenviable situation. There are occasions today when the diplomat abroad, chafing under the kibitzing of unimaginative drones at headquarters, would welcome some of the isolation that Barlow enjoyed. Barlow, who complained of his lack of instructions, would have found modern communications priceless, but they would certainly have restricted his freedom of action. He would not have been able to offer a frigate to the dey on his own.

Modernity does not mean that elaborate communications systems always work. Reliable 99 percent of the time, they have a way of failing when most needed. When the American hostages were seized in Tehran in 1979, Washington had no communication with them and had to depend on the Swedish embassy, which overlooked the American compound, for word of what was going on. During the hostage crisis in Khartoum in 1973 a sandstorm blotted out all communication for a considerable period. The more complex and rapid our communication facilities become, the more disastrous the occasional breakdown. (At this writing, June 2003, the State Department is still having trouble receiving mail through the postal system because of the anthrax scare, and its diplomatic pouch system for communicating with the field was suspended for many months in 2001 and 2002 while all the pouches and mail rooms were screened and disinfected. For a period, the Department was almost totally dependent on electronic communications of one kind or another. This is, of course, the only practical means of communicating in the fast-moving situations that the United States finds itself in continuously, and the mail system is purely secondary, but not everything needs to be communicated instantaneously, and some things cannot be. The lack of mail service is always troubling, and total reliance on electronics has its risks.)

The Naval Role

The important, and sometimes independent, diplomatic role of the U.S. Navy in the North African saga, inaugurated by the voyage of the *George Washington* in 1800, is striking. From 1801 to 1805 naval commanders played a dominant role in a series of negotiations with Tripoli as well as in dealings with Tunis and Morocco. They also engaged in gunboat diplomacy on their own. Most striking to a bureaucrat, they even assigned naval officers to act as consuls at Tunis and Tripoli in the absence of regularly appointed officials, a sacred plot of turf the modern Department of State would be very reluctant to cede to one of the armed services.

There was a naval hiatus from 1807 through the War of 1812. At the end of that war, in 1815, as we have seen, the navy returned in a big way with Stephen Decatur and imposed new peace treaties, ending the payment of tribute and the enslavement of American seamen. It continued to maintain an intermittent Mediterranean presence, and to play an occasional political role, throughout much of the nineteenth century and into the twentieth.[5]

The naval historian Charles Oscar Paullin says:

> the traits of character that distinguish the naval officer, simplicity, candor and directness, affect his negotiations and give them a sort of unity. The sailor-diplomat is pre-eminently a "shirt-sleeve" diplomatist. He is a stranger to the devious and tortuous methods which so long disfigured international statecraft. Being a fighter by profession, he does not underestimate the importance of a display of force when temporarily filling the peaceful office of a diplomat. . . . A naval officer rather than

a civilian was chosen for such diplomatic tasks because he could best unite force with persuasion, a combination always regarded as a requisite in dealing with these peoples.[6]

While the qualities Paullin describes may be admirable, even in a diplomat, effective diplomacy also demands imagination, understanding of foreign cultures, comprehension of the national interest, and subordination of personal conviction to that interest, i.e., discipline. Preble's gallant performance at Tripoli contributed much to his stature as a naval hero, but he was a failure diplomatically. As Beaussier pointed out, his tactic of bombarding and then making an offer conveyed the impression that he was anxious to settle. He would have done better to continue bombarding without making an offer. If he was going to make an offer, however, he should have been more realistic and started with a sum the Tripolitanians might have considered seriously, not with a ridiculous offer of $50,000 when the going price for ransom of an ordinary seaman was $500 or $600. By stubbornly ignoring the authorization that would have permitted him to pay the going price, he maintained his reputation for resoluteness, but he prolonged the conflict a year at a cost of at least thirty lives and, by my estimate, $500,000 in additional expense.[7] Our honor was intact, and politically it was worth the price at home, but this was not an example of effective diplomacy on the ground. (It would be interesting to know to what extent O'Brien, who did the actual negotiating, supported or opposed Preble's tactics.)

Similarly, Rodgers at Tunis in August 1805, perhaps spoiling for a fight after being deprived of one at Tripoli, sounded unnecessarily bellicose and preemptory. While he may have impressed the bey with his strength and determination, he did not solve the problem or improve relations. His challenge to the bey did lead to the sending of a Tunisian ambassador whose mission was eventually successful, but credit for thinking of that should go to the bey, not Rodgers. More persuasion and a less threatening attitude on the commodore's part would not have been out of place, and he set an unfortunate example of how one is supposed to deal with Third World potentates. Indeed, running through the literature of and about the period, including today's output, are repeated expressions and observations, such as Paullin's above, to the effect that the rulers of Barbary could best be brought to reason by force, or threats of same, applied by stalwart Americans. One did not apply this formula to Europeans, of course, but only to denizens of the Third World. (Paullin, the reader may recall from note 1 to chapter 1, thought the North African rulers had minds that were physically different from our own.)

The term *gunboat* did not enter the written language until 1793, according to the *Oxford English Dictionary*, and the first citation it gives for the term *gunboat diplomacy* is the February 1927 issue of the *Proceedings* of the

Naval Institute at Annapolis. The concept that when a hostile people were thought to be impervious to diplomacy, one subdued them by shelling or threatening to shell their towns from offshore, sometimes using shallow-draft vessels mounting a few guns, was well established long before that, however. The ship in question did not necessarily do any firing. Sometimes its presence in the harbor and the threat of bombardment was enough to discourage unruliness.

As noted in the previous chapter, the first instance of American resort to this tactic, at least in the eastern hemisphere, was at Tangier in 1803, when the fleet under Preble in the *Constitution* sailed into the harbor in reaction to a Moroccan declaration of war that may or may not have been real. The Moroccans said it was all a mistake, blaming the governor of Tangier, and relations improved markedly. The operation was therefore successful, and the navy took full credit for a judicious use of force. An undated résumé of this incident prepared in 1806 or 1807 reads: "Rodgers and Preble having taken their measures, sailed from Gibraltar for Tangier October 6 and laying their ships before the town on the 12th of October, compelled the Emperor to sign the Treaty of 1786."[8] We are unlikely ever to know for certain what was in the Moroccan sultan's mind, but he might have been surprised to learn that he had been "compelled" to do something he did not want to do. "Persuaded" would have been a better word. This may seem like a distinction without a difference, but the word choice reflected a dangerous and unwarranted belief in the efficacy of a show of force.

The navy, as we have seen, played its role with confidence. The various commanders showed no inhibition about taking actions that could have serious consequences, acting under their broad set of instructions. Like the diplomats, they were far from home and free from supervision. They took advantage of that freedom and did not shrink from doing what they thought necessary, with results that were not always happy. There is not space here to go into the details of their instructions and their decisions, but it is something that is worth further study. How fully did the naval commanders understand the potential consequences of their actions? Were they too concentrated on their tradecraft and honor to think much about the political repercussions?

From today's vantage point, the naval officer's confidence sometimes looks like arrogance. A belief in American moral superiority and future glory that seems somewhat naive today pervades the correspondence of the time and is often reflected in modern writings on the period. The early Americans, military and civilian, were proud of their country's unique past and promise, and pride sometimes led them to be extraordinarily quick to take offense, to feel that their person or their country or their ship had been insulted, and to resort to arms to maintain their honor.

Midshipmen were taught that they must defend their personal honor by force if necessary, and dueling among gentlemen was accepted practice, provided the rules were followed. *Naval Documents* lists five duels among officers of the Mediterranean squadron in the period January 1802–August 1803. Three officers and the governor of Malta's secretary were killed. The duel was often fought with pistols at four paces (presumably four by each man for a total of eight, or about twenty feet). How anyone could miss at that range is not explained. Officers with so intense a need to preserve their honor may be likely to take and give offense when they encounter a culture they do not understand. Thus, Captain Rodgers's communications about the bey of Tunis sound as though he was unable to comprehend the bey's unwillingness to accept the rules of blockade, a Western concept that was foreign to him. One senses little empathy in Rodgers's character. Perhaps empathy should not be expected from a military officer, but it is necessary to successful dealing with other peoples and to creating mutual respect, without which peace cannot be permanent. This does not mean that military men cannot be good diplomats, but diplomacy is not part of their normal occupational skills.

Faith in the importance of the navy's diplomatic role nevertheless persists among today's officials, who see demonstrations of strength as a way to influence events on the ground. The use of the battleship *New Jersey* to bombard targets in Lebanon in 1983 carried that concept to an extreme, and it did not work. Indeed, it is worth noting that naval bombardment alone does not seem to have been very effective in the Mediterranean, at least not along the southern or eastern coasts. Preble's mustering of all his forces to bombard Tripoli did not have much effect, and Algiers was unbowed by a series of naval attacks over the years. Decatur's most effective action was the destruction of Algerine shipping, not bombardment of the shore, and the city was finally taken by the French in 1830 from its land side, not from the sea.

American Attitudes toward the Muslim World

I started this inquiry persuaded that the Barbary experience made an important contribution to the negative attitudes Americans have toward Arabs and Muslims today. There has been much writing on the subject of those attitudes in recent years, and a few of those works are listed in the bibliography. The classic explanation starts with the hostility engendered by the eighth-century Muslim invasion of Spain and southern France, followed by the Crusades and the Jihad in response, the Turkish destruction of the Byzantine Empire and conquest of much of southeast Europe, the warfare between Christians and Muslims along the line of confrontation in Spain and North Africa, and the depredations of the Barbary corsairs, all contributing to a Western communal memory of perpetual hostility. This perception is supported and amplified by a body of travel and romance literature that portrays Muslims and Arabs in an unfavorable light, with stereotypes abounding.

Unfavorable perceptions of Muslims in general, and of Arabs in particular, are widespread in the United States.[9] The role of Islamic fundamentalists in acts of terrorism, and Arab and Islamic hostility to the United States for its support of Israel, appear to some as validation of Samuel Huntington's thesis in *The Clash of Civilizations* that a conflict between the Christian West and Islam is inevitable. This perception has been heightened by the events of September 11.

But we cannot identify the contribution of the Barbary crisis to these attitudes. Most Americans have only the vaguest ideas about the Crusades and the Turks and know nothing at all about the identity of the Barbary pirates, who are likely to be seen as romantic figures on those rare occasions when they do exist in the popular imagination. More recent events, including the Arab-Israel conflict and the violence and polemics it has engendered, are more likely sources of current attitudes toward Arabs and Muslims. Events two centuries ago have undoubtedly contributed to the cumulative negative image, but we cannot measure with any precision the impact of that contribution today.

Summation

This first series of crises with the Muslim world lasted off and on for thirty years, from 1785 to 1815. While the outcome is enshrined in American history as a triumph of American virtues and arms, common sense and diplomacy counted for more than valor in actually finding solutions much of the time. Decatur's victorious progress of 1815 put an end to the problem as far as the Americans were concerned, and it demonstrated the usefulness of force properly applied, but the original crisis with Algiers and the war with Tripoli were settled in the end by diplomacy. Diplomacy was also required to give practical effect to Decatur's victory over Hamidou and to his demonstrations of force at Tunis and Tripoli. It is possible for diplomacy to work without force, but force will not avail much in the end if it is not backed up by effective diplomacy.

Postscript

Return of the Natives

George Washington's second term was drawing to a close when the *Philadelphia Gazette and Universal Daily Advertiser* of February 7, 1797, reported on page 1:

> A Swedish barque [*Jupiter*] in 70 days from Gibraltar, that touched at Marseilles has arrived at Marcus-hook; we have peculiar satisfaction in announcing to the public, the arrival in this vessel of our countrymen who were so fortunate some time since to obtain their release from slavery in Algiers.[1]

On February 10 the paper reported:

> Our late captives of the Algerines arrived in this city yesterday afternoon under an escort of several hundreds of their sympathetic fellow citizens of both sexes, who had gone to meet them on the road to town; upon their reaching the Indian Queen Tavern the crowd was so considerable as to render their passage difficult, and on their entering the house an ardent acclamation expressed the satisfaction of the people at their happy extrication and safe return.
>
> It appears that a captain and 14 seamen of the released captives entered in an American ship in Marseilles, to go up the Mediterranean on a trading voyage; the remainder have arrived safe, excepting only the 3 that died soon after their release & before they had reached Marseilles; after they had performed quarantine at Marseilles, they went on shore at that city, and had an allowance of 35 cents a day for each seaman, 50 cents for each mate, and 120 cents for each captain, to live upon; and each was supplied with a suit of wearing apparel by the Consul of the United States.

At the tavern the men were perhaps given a drink or two and a meal, although the *Gazette* does not mention it. They then vanish from the *Gazette* and we do not know much about what happened to them afterward. Mention of their return is made here and there in newspapers, but with rare exceptions they left no discernible trace of their adventure or their existence beyond, perhaps, entries in the vital records when they married or died or had children.

There is no mention of official participation by the federal government in the welcoming celebration, but at least one of the returnees, Captain Newman of the *Thomas,* saw a representative of the Department of State in Philadelphia and gave him a letter from Barlow to the secretary:

> Algiers, 12 July, 1796
> Sir,
> This will be presented to you by the remnant of our captive citizens who have survived the pains and humiliation of slavery in this place; after effecting their deliverance, in the manner which I state to you in my letter of this day, without funds, or any direct intelligence that they are soon to be expected, I have another task to perform, in which it is impossible to promise myself success: it is to embark them without the infection of the plague. ·
>
> Five of their fellow sufferers have died of that contagion within a few weeks; and another who is attacked must be left behind. It rages with such violence in the town, that although they cannot embark without risk, yet it is much more dangerous for them to stay longer here, in any situation where it is possible for me to place them in this most incommodious of all conceivable abodes.
>
> If they escape infection, we shall be much indebted to the attention of Capt. Calder, who commands the ship, and to the careful assistance of the other captains who inspect the embarkation as well as to the harmony and good understanding which prevail among all the crews.
>
> When we reflect on the extravagant sums of money that this redemption will cost the United States, it affords at least some consolation to know that it is not expended on worthless and disorderly persons, as is the case with some other nations, who, like us, are driven to this humiliation to the Barbary States. Our people have conducted themselves in general with a degree of patience and decorum which would have become a better situation than that of slaves; and though after they are landed in their country, it would be useless to recommend them to any additional favours from government, yet I hope they will receive from merchants that encouragement of their professional industry which will enable them in some measure to repair their losses, and from their fellow Citizens in general, that respect which is due to the sufferings of honest men.

Several of them are probably rendered incapable of gaining their living; one is in a state of total blindness; another is rendered nearly the same; two or three carry the marks of unmerciful treatment, in ruptures produced by hard labor; and others have had their constitutions injured by the plague. Some of them are doubtless objects of the charity of their countrymen, but whether this charity should flow to them through the channel of the federal government, is a question on which it would be impertinent for me to offer an opinion.

I am, sir, with great respect,
Your obedient servant, JOEL BARLOW[2]

This letter was evidently circulated in printed form, and the *Salem Gazette* of February 24, although it did not print the text, commented:

Barlow's letter respecting our Brethren lately returned from their captivity in Algiers arrests the public attention. While everything honorable to the prisoners is expressed, the cruelty of their captivity is sufficiently described to convince us that they were proper subjects of public commisseration. We are reconciled to the payment of the enormous sum, exceeding 600,000 dollars, because it is a tax paid to these barbarians by the most powerful nations of Europe, perhaps for want of an enlightened policy, by which they might cooperate against an enemy bought and sold to add dangers to Commerce and to aggravate the calamities of War in Europe.

So the payment of what seemed an enormous sum was accepted by at least some of the public as inevitable.

Who Got Home When?

There are fragments of information indicating that some, perhaps most, of the men went directly home, and we know that some of them picked up where they left off and resumed their maritime profession. Here are a few of the fragments:

Four of the crew of the *George*, a Newport vessel, had reached home before February 20 on the *Juliet*, according to the *Newport Mercury*,[3] and are referred to (but not by name) in the February 21 issue of the paper, which carries the *Philadelphia Gazette* story verbatim, with one significant difference—an added two paragraphs about the number of captives and their treatment.

On the same page of its February 24 issue with its comment on the Barlow letter to the secretary of state, the *Salem Gazette,* describing the toasts and orations at the celebrations marking Washington's birthday on February 22, reported that "after the festivity was closed, another contribution was made, in behalf of an Algerine prisoner, just returned from his captivity, and who was present." So we know that at least one of the men from Salem had reached home by February 22.

On the third page the paper carries the same detailed list that was in the Philadelphia and Newport papers of payments made by Barlow totaling $625,000. Below it, in the same column, is the text of a moving letter to Barlow from eight of the ships' captains:

> Algiers July 10 [or 16?], 1796
>
> We the subscribers, American masters and late captives in Algiers, think it a duty incumbent on us, in behalf of ourselves, our officers and crews, to acknowledge in a most grateful manner our sincere and cordial thanks to you for the particular care and attention we have received from you since your arrival in this city, in your public and private character, during our unhappy slavery, & bringing about that happy redemption so much sought by us and our beloved country—a business which to all people seemed impossible, but by your particular care and attention has been brought about, that a life so ever beloved by us may be long continued is the sincerest prayer of
>
> J. Newman
> Isaac Stephens
> William Furnass
> Samuel Calder
> James Taylor
> Moses Morse
> William Penrose
> Michael Smith

A preliminary reconnaissance in the records of Essex County, Massachusetts, from whose ports four of the ships came, shows that among the returnees who reached home were Samuel Calder of Gloucester, master of the *Jay*, and Moses Morse or Morss of Haverhill, master of the *Jane*. Local records at historical societies and libraries in these communities give a few traces of both of them. Calder was the subject of an item in the *Massachusetts Mercury* of February 28, 1797, under the heading "PRESIDENT'S BIRTHDAY from Gloucester" which read:

> To complete the joy of the day at which harmony and decorum presided on the arrival of their respectable fellow townsman, Capt. Samuel Calder, from distressing and tedious captivity in Algiers, the company repaired in procession to his house to greet and welcome him to his native country. He expressed in the most lively sense, his gratitude for

their affection & attention, and each one retired to his house, to reflect on the pleasing occurences of the auspicious era.

In the files of the Sargent House Museum at Gloucester is a ship's manifest dated July 20, 1797, that shows Calder as master of the ship *Flora*, David Pearce owner (he had also been owner of the *Jay*). The ship was bound for Europe with a cargo of white and brown sugar. Calders appear in the Gloucester city directory until World War I, when they disappear.

Moses Morse of Haverhill appears in the town records for a while after 1797. He is listed as a member of the Fire Club, a gentlemen's volunteer firefighting and social club, in 1800, and the Haverhill public library has a photocopy of his inscribed copy of John Foss's narrative. One of his two sons, Hazen, became a well-known silversmith, engraver, and artist, and one of Hazen's eight children, Henry, born in 1826, moved to Boston and was a well-known, skilled diamond cutter. Moses himself died intestate at some date prior to December 27, 1803, and is not listed as being buried in the town, which suggests that perhaps he died at sea.

The records contain surprisingly little trace of John Foss of Newburyport, a mariner on the *Polly* and the only one of the returnees who published an account of his captivity and of his return home. His *Journal of the Captivity and Sufferings of John Foss* was published by Angier March, Middle Street, Newburyport, in 1798. There were at least two editions of it, but queries on two separate occasions indicate that it is unknown in Newburyport's Main Street bookstores today.[4] Foss also had two works published while he was abroad, a "Letter from Algiers" in the *Salem Gazette* of August 11, 1795, and a "Solemn Call to the Citizens of the United States" in March 1797. After his return, his poem *"The Algerine Slaves"* was published in 1798.

Foss was included in the general redemption of 1796, but he was one of the seamen who signed on to the *Fortune* after she had unloaded the captives at Marseille, and was therefore not among the returnees to Philadelphia on February 9. He landed there on July 25. He records meeting up there with some of his companions in captivity, including Moses Brown of Newburyport. He arrived back in Newburyport, where he was reunited with his family and friends, on August 23. Foss's journal ends there, and the published version gives no indication of what happened thereafter.

Moses Brown was perhaps the son of Captain Moses Brown, an officer in the naval forces during the Revolution and the subject of a 1904 biography by Edgar Stanton Maclay.[5] Page 632 of the deaths list in the Vital Records of Newburyport carries Moses Jr. as "died at sea" on December 22, 1797, indicating that he had resumed his maritime vocation after his return from captivity. The same page, however, also lists a Moses Jr., Capt., "washed over at sea, Sept. 1798," another Moses Brown, Capt., "at sea, Jan 1, 1804" (this was the father of our Moses Brown and the subject of Maclay's biography), and a third Capt. Moses Brown lost at sea at the age of forty-one in 1818. There was no shortage of Moses Browns in Newburyport.

Judging by the paucity of information about them in the records, the returnees of Essex County made no lasting impression on communal memories. Their adventures were unknown to the current librarians and local historians I have consulted. There are no monuments to them. They have left a few traces in the vital records, but none of them appears to have been locally famous for very long if at all. None of them seems to have made a great fortune or to have built a great house overlooking the port. The same is true of the returnees from Newport. They have left no readily visible trace.

A more profound study would perhaps uncover descendants living today. It would be interesting to learn whether they preserve any recollections, written or oral, of their ancestors' stories of Algiers, and whether they have any idea what they went through.

Charitable Actions

In spite of his disclaimer, Barlow may have hoped the government would do something for the men, but I have come across no indication that there was any general, organized effort on their behalf after their return. On the other hand, his hope that the returnees would "receive from the Merchants that encouragement to their professional industry which will enable them in some measure to repair their losses, and from their fellow citizens in general that respect which is due to the sufferings of honest men" was not entirely unrealistic. The following public acts of philanthropy on behalf of the men are mentioned in the records, and a concerted search might turn up more.

(1) In box 1 of the Cathcart papers at New York there is an undated letter from Robert Montgomery, the consul in Alicante, to Mattias Skjöldebrand authorizing him to distribute $900 among the officers and crews as a "donation from friends of America at Lisbon."

(2) Item 41 in roll 1 of the Algiers consulate papers is a letter of May 10, 1794, perhaps to the secretary of state, Edmund Randolph, reporting the deposit of $887.28 "collected Wednesday night at a benefit given for the Relief of the American Prisoners in Algiers, received from Charles Stuart Powell, manager of the Boston Theatre." The signature is illegible.

The intended distribution of the money was detailed three years later on page 4 of the March 15, 1797, issue of the *Portsmouth Oracle*:

Salem, Feb. 21, 1797

The subscribers in whose hands were lodged Eight Hundred and Eighty Seven Dollars, 28 cents, being the proceeds of a Benefit Night, at the

Boston Theatre for the relief of the American prisoners in Algiers, have directed the following distribution of it to be made, viz,

To Captains	Dls.	Cts.
James (Isacc) Stevens of Concord	65	
Moses Morss Haverhill	50	
William Furnass Berwick	50	
Samuel Calder Gloucester	50	
Timothy Newman Newburyport	50	
Michael Smith do.	50	
To Mates		
Alex. Forsyth of Boston	42	28
Edward Harwood Salem	35	
John Walker Cape Ann	35	
Benjamin Edwards Newburyport	35	
John Foss do	35	
Privates		
James Pease of Salem	30	
Samuel Henry do	30	
Thomas Simmons, Jr. Haverhill	30	
Benjamin Lunt Newburyport	30	
John Earl Berwick	30	
Daniel Fall do	30	
Nathaniel Keen Kittery	30	
Peter Page do	30	
Thomas Manning Cape Ann	30	
John Edwards Manchester	30	
Benjamin Ober do	30	
Walter Gibbons do	30	
Moses Brown (?) Maine	30	
	887	28

The above persons are notified, that by calling on any of the subscribers, they will be immediately furnished with a check on the Union Bank, for the amount respectively set against their names. [The five names subscribed are only semilegible but seem to be:

Peter Hinton
Henry Johnson
Thomas Danforth } Trustees
Samuel Smith
Thomas Greenleaf

The list is of the men from New England, excluding Rhode Island, who arrived at Philadelphia on February 10, with three exceptions. Michael Smith, John Foss, and Moses Brown were not on the *Jupiter*. Three returnees from Boston were excluded, as were one from Salem and one from Portsmouth. The language of the announcement makes it clear that the money had not yet been distributed, so this should not be read as a list of those who had reached home, something Foss would not do for six months, and one can only speculate how his name, Michael Smith's, and Moses Brown's (if it is in fact his) got on the list in advance of their return.

Captain Stephens and Alexander Forsyth, both of the *Maria*, were presumably given slightly more than the others because they were the only ones in this group who were among the prisoners of 1785. Michael Smith presumably was promoted from mate to captain by reason of his taking over the *Fortune*. Similarly, Foss was only a seaman at the time of his capture but was treated as a mate because he had served in that capacity on the *Fortune*.

(3) Item 42 in roll 1 of the Algiers consulate papers is a letter of June 7, 1794, from someone in Philadelphia to Randolph reporting an unsolicited gift of £350 sterling "for the unfortunate prisoners at Algiers."

The Officials

We know a good deal about some of the civilian officials who were in Algiers. Barlow was the subject of several biographies. Cathcart wrote a journal and was the subject of a biography. So was Lear. All have been mentioned in some detail in the correspondence that is the official record. Here, briefly, is what happened to them after Algiers.

Barlow

After returning from Algiers in 1797, Barlow remained in Paris, living at 50 rue de Vaugirard, until the summer of 1804, when he and his wife left for the United States. In 1807 he came to Washington at Jefferson's urging and bought a house he called Kalorama, or "fine view" in Greek. He paid $14,000 for the house and thirty acres of land. During the four years Barlow lived there, the house was famous for its hospitality and the social grace of its owners.[6] In 1811 Barlow was sent back to France as minister, with the twin tasks of pressing claims regarding American shipping and establishing normal trade relations between the two countries. The French played a delaying game, but on October 11, 1812, Barlow was invited by the foreign minister to come to Napoleon's winter headquarters at Vilna to conclude negotiations on a treaty of commerce. Barlow made the difficult trip with considerable misgivings, arriving on November 18.

Barlow did not get to meet with Napoleon. By the time he arrived, the latter's Russian campaign was already in trouble, and by early December the French troops and the diplomats at Vilna were in full retreat in the terrible Polish winter. Barlow got only as far as Zarnowiec, a small village near Krakow, where he died of pneumonia on December 25 or 26 at the age of fifty-eight. He was buried in the village churchyard and was never disinterred, but his grave's location is unknown today. His is the second name on the bronze plaque in the Department of State's entrance lobby commemorating diplomatic and consular officers who died abroad.

O'Brien

After being succeeded at Algiers by Tobias Lear in 1803, O'Brien served for a while as an adviser to Commodore Preble. With his wife and infant child, he returned to the United States with Preble in 1805. He first lived in Philadelphia and became a member of the state legislature in 1808. State Department personnel records list him as consul at Cagliari, in Sardinia, from 1809 to 1812, but this seems to be an error. There is no mention of him during this period in the correspondence of the consulate there, which was open only from 1802 to 1825. O'Brien eventually settled in Carlisle, Pennsylvania, and remained there until his death in 1824. By then he had managed to obtain just under $68,000 from the U.S. government as compensation for his services and expenses in Barbary.[7] There are no known descendants in the Carlisle area today.

Cathcart

Cathcart had the good fortune to write a journal and to have a published biography, written by his daughter. We therefore know a good deal about what happened to him. After being declared persona non grata in the three regencies—perhaps a record in the American service—he and his family left Livorno for the United States in 1805, arriving in Washington on April 1. By this time his wife had borne another three children. They lived on West (now P) Street in Georgetown until May 1807 when, with another son added to the family, they left for Madeira, where he served as consul for more than eight years and had three more children. In 1815 he was assigned to Cádiz as consul and served there until 1817, when he returned to Georgetown. They had one more son in Cádiz and two more in Georgetown, for a total of eleven children by my count.

Cathcart was next employed by the navy either in Louisiana or in Florida, depending on the source, and then, from 1823 until his death in 1843, was a clerk in the "Second Comptroller's Office" in Washington. His daughter said that he was so faithful to his country and his family that he never took a summer vacation until the year he died. His wife died less than three months after he did.

In Cathcart's papers at the New York Public Library are his will and the plans for a house, called Cathcart's Retreat, to be built at La Porte, Indiana, with the money from his claim against the government for $46,448 for expenses in Barbary and for escorting Mellimelli. He had collected some $30,000 before his death, according to Wright and Macleod's *First Americans in North Africa*. The house at La Porte seems never to have been built, but his son Richard owned a farm in Arlington County, Virginia, and there are descendants in the Washington area today.

Lear

Tobias Lear, accompanied by his wife, who had been with the fleet during his adventures in Tripoli and Tunis, returned to Algiers in November 1805. They remained at post for another seven years, evidently enjoying the comfort of their house in the country and the social life that Algiers provided.[8] They arrived back in New York on April 9, 1813, comfortably off as far as money was concerned. After visits to Washington and Portsmouth, Lear was assigned the task of negotiating a prisoner-of-war exchange with the British at Champlain, New York, which he accomplished. He arrived back in Washington to take up a job as accountant in the War Department just in time for the town's burning by the British in August 1814. He committed suicide in October 1816. Exactly why has never been established, but criticism of his role in the peace treaty with Tripoli may have been a factor.[9]

Humphreys

David Humphreys went on to become minister to Spain (1797–1801), returning to Connecticut in 1802. In an effort to improve New England's breeding stock, he imported from Spain a hundred Merino sheep, a breed that came originally from Morocco and was highly prized for the quality of its wool and for its hardiness. He later established a woolen mill at Seymour, Connecticut, known for its paternalistic community for orphan boy laborers. There is a museum devoted to him at Ansonia, Connecticut.

Appendix 1

The Procession of the Tribute

The following description of the triennial tribute ceremony, from Ahmad al-Zahhar's *Mudhakirat* (36–48), with scattered details about the powers and duties of the leading officials, gives some idea of the ojak's obsession with tradition and form and, most important for our story, the institutionalization of 'awa'id—the customary gratuities that were accorded to the holders of government positions on ceremonial occasions. In reading this account one must keep in mind that Turkish officials in Algiers, even the dey, received only a soldier's pay and rations. For anything beyond that, they were dependent on what they could extort or squeeze by virtue of their positions.

Al-Zahhar was only four years old at the time of the 1785 ceremonies he purports to describe in such detail. It is unlikely that he actually witnessed the events in question, and he would not have been old enough to remember them if he did. This is either a secondhand account or a description of a later ceremony that has been grafted onto the past. It reads rather like a chief of protocol's scenario, with a few explanatory notes about the characters involved. It is not without touches of humor—al-Zahhar was an Arab writing about Turks.

I have taken liberties with al-Zahhar's erratic use of verbs and the definite article, as well as his terminology, to make the narrative more readable and comprehensible. I have put much of it in the historical present.

Text

Then [after establishing the three beyliks or governorates] the Turks built a citadel at Sibaw and installed a commander there, but he was not called a bey. The three beys paid tribute every three years, and their deputies paid it twice every year. When the beys paid tribute, their deputies did not.

The presentation of the tribute by the beys of Titteri and of the East and by the commander of Sibaw fell in the spring. That of the bey of the West occurred in the fall. The commander of Sibaw had no deputy as the beys did.

Collecting taxes: The deputies did this in the spring, accompanied by their mahalla [a roaming encampment of officials and troops] to extract the kharaj, the zakat, and the 'ushr [traditional Islamic taxes]. They began with the legal taxes and then sent out the troops to extract the fines and unjust exactions and to plunder the wealth of the Muslims. . . .

The mahalla of the West went out in April and operated for four months. That of Titteri went out in the summer for three months, and that of the East went out on the first day of summer and stayed for six months. As for the commander of Sibaw, he had no mahalla, but if there was a rebellion among his charges he was given a special mahalla to do with as he saw fit and then return. This did not happen every year.

Between the Beys and the Amir [dey]

Every bey had an agent in Algiers who had a place of business near the house of the dey, and if a courier came to Algiers from the bey, he would stay at the agent's shop and give him the letters he was carrying. The agent would read the letter to see what was in it in order to know what to say to the dey. Then he would take the letter and the courier to the dey. When they entered the dey's presence, the agent would give him the letter and stand there. They would be permitted to sit down. When they sat, the dey would ask them about the bey, and they would convey his greetings, and if they had some matter to bring up they would speak of it. He would give them coffee, and when they had drunk it and the conversation had ended, they invoked [from God] his safety and left. After leaving the dey, the agent would give to the ministers the letters in their names and the courier would spend the night in the house of the dey.

The Tribute [danush] of the Bey of the West

When the truce with Spain occurred [in 1785], as we mentioned, the time of danush came. It was presented by the bey, Muhammad, and he brought with him much in the way of presents and wealth, and gifts of noble horses, slaves, jewelry, and splendid furnishings. He left his headquarters, Mascara, and brought with him a numerous army of followers and principal tribal shaykhs plus commanders and aghas dressed in splendid clothes and riding horses with golden saddles.

The bey had with him his big treasure. . . . As he left Mascara his people were firing their weapons, while flags fluttered and drums sounded around him until they reached the stopping place for the night, where they put up their tents and built their colored [?: wa banu fasatinahum al-mulawwana] and spent the night eating and drinking. They were rejoicing at their approach to the dey. After they reached morning safely and performed the morning prayer, they mounted and went forth, with gunplay the while, and people met them with presents for the bey. He would recompense them according to the occasion. To him who deserved a horse he gave a horse, and to him who deserved a slave he gave a [slave] mother and child, and to him who deserved clothing he gave Zaghdani burnooses and red haiks of Tlemcen work. Sometimes he would give the horse, the slave, and the clothes to those who had noble rank or were close to the government and [then?] light upon the poor from among the soldiers and others. Most of them were Turks. Their number grew each day and they did not leave him. And each day when they arrived at the stopping place for the night, he distributed dirhams to them, and some took a riyal or two riyals. It was thus every day until he reached Algiers, and especially when he was two or three days out. Meeting him created increased greed. When he approached the city, he sent his head courier with a letter asking permission to enter, and the dey replied giving him permission to enter and fixing the day for it.

Then the agha of the Arabs, the second-ranking minister of the pasha, goes out with his troops and commanders and flags and drums, and they meet at a place called Bou Farik, between Blida and Algiers. The bey and the agha dismount at a place before Bou Farik called Ain al-Sha'r and exchange greetings. The agha gives the bey the dey's greetings and congratulates him on his arriving safely. Then he gives the bey a costly present from the dey—a horse with a golden saddle and a pair of pistols and a golden sword and musket. The bey accepts the present and invokes a blessing upon the dey. They continue to exchange felicitations while they drink coffee. Then they remount and ride out together with their troops displaying the weapons in their hands and the people in the field engaging in powder play. They arrive at their overnight accommodations in Bou Farik, where they lodge, with their escorts, separately from each other.

At sunset the agha sends for the bey and invites him to be his guest, and the bey mounts and rides to the agha's tent. When he comes, the agha greets him at the door of the tent and they exchange greetings and sit down together. Then the call to the sunset prayer is given and the agha's imam comes to lead the prayer. Rugs are spread out for them and they pray inside the tent. When the prayer is finished, they return to their seats and dinner is served to them and to the commanders and aghas who came with the bey. The agha's retinue remains standing. After they finish eating and drinking and having coffee, the bey gives the customary presents to the agha's servants. Then the bey goes to his tent to rest, and after resting he sends their presents to the officers and ushers of the agha. Among them are people of the horse, like the senior commanders and ushers, to whom he sends horses and Zaghdani burnooses, and he gives slaves to those who are slave people and so forth until the gift giving is completed. To the others, like the zarnajiya [flute players] and the drummers and lesser servants of the bey and the Mamluks, he gives money. Then he gives to the people who take alms from him every day, and when he has finished with that, the Turkish and local musicians come and the dancers and singers. The latter strike their tambourines at the door of the tent and leave after the bey has rewarded them. Then the Turks come and play their mazamir [oboes] a little. The bey rewards them and they leave. Then come the owners of the Algerian [Andalusian] instruments, and they sit in front of the bey and play on the rebec, the fiddle, and the lute. When the session is finished, he rewards them and they leave and everyone sleeps.

The next morning after the morning prayer, the bey and the agha mount up with their followers and ride together toward the saha [not otherwise identified], where they take leave of each other. The agha takes the road to Algiers, while the bey goes to his enclosure and naps there. They dye their horses with henna, then eat and then ride, the bey and his representative in Algiers [wakil], to a place near the sea half an hour from Algiers called Ain al-Ribat, which is where the mahallas dismount on leaving Algiers. The mahalla gathers here and spends the night. The bey of Titteri also spends the night here, but the bey of the East overnights at the bridge of al-Harrash and at the end of the night he comes to Ain al-Rabat and performs the morning prayer there.

When the bey arrives at Ain al-Ribat as we mentioned, supper is provided for him from the house of his wakil. In the morning, after prayers, the bey sits in a [certain?] place there. There are buildings and a large basin of water. His wakil then leaves and goes to the dey, gives him the bey's greetings and tells him that the bey has arrived at Ain al-Rabat and spent the night there and awaits the order to appear before him [literally, between his hands]. Then the dey orders the khaznaji and the agha and the khazinedar [steward] to go to meet the bey and accompany him. With that, the khaznaji and khazinedar mount up and leave the king's house. The flags and drums go with them. When they arrive at the jurisdiction of the agha of the Arabs, he mounts and rides with them to Ain al-Rabat. When the bey sees their vanguard, he mounts and rides to meet them. Then he and they dismount and greet and embrace each other, then they ride to the place where the bey was waiting, dismount, sit down, and are given coffee. The cavalry performs before them, and there is powder play for about a quarter of an hour. Then they excuse themselves to ride off to meet the dey. They all ride together and enter the city.

And from the time the bey rides into the city, he is throwing money right and left to the poor and others. Some beys throw gold sultanis [worth about $2.00] while some throw silver and some throw dubloons [gold coins worth $15.00]. The divan precede them like salukis with feathers on their heads dressed right and left.

The barrah [crier] calls out the prayer for the Prophet, may God pray for and protect him, when the shawush al-salam [greetings usher] is before the bey. He greets the people to the right and left. Forty mules precede the procession, each carrying 2,000 riyals [presumably the riyal buju or pataqa gorda, worth $0.60] for a total of 80,000 riyals, and forty prized horses, a caged lion, a tiger, a wild cow, and other animals. All of this is for the beylik [government].

When he reaches the Dar al-Imara [House of the Principality, or palace] the bey enters on horseback until he meets the dey, who is seated on the royal seat, then he dismounts and goes in walking deferentially and humbly. He kisses the dey's hand and tarries a bit and the dey orders him to sit on his right about a spear's length away. When he sits, the dey turns to him, praises God for his safe arrival, and asks how his people are. They give him coffee. Then the bey presents his aghas and commanders and village notables, and they kiss the hand of the dey while the bash siyyar [chief courier] stands nearby and introduces the people. When the greetings are finished, the bash siyyar steps back and the khaznaji advances and stands before the king and takes the khil'a [ceremonial robe of investiture] from the chief clerk of the Turks, who is called the bash khoja, and presents it to the bey, who receives it politely, humbling himself to its owner, His Majesty the sultan. Then the khaznaji bestows it on the bey, who puts it on and comes forward to kiss the hand of the dey. Then he stays with him for a while before leaving.

The bey leaves and goes to the house where he is lodged. The band plays behind him, and notables of the military divan directly precede him. When he reaches the house, he sits on a chair in the middle of it and the band plays around him. When the band finishes, the king's protocol usher arrives and gives greetings at the top of his voice to those present, then the bey goes up to his sitting room at the top of the house and takes off the robe of honor. The chief usher of the Arabs takes it and takes his gratuity and goes with the robe to the Dar al-Imara to put it with the Ottoman robes. The bey then gives gratuities to those who are entitled to receive them [ashab al-'awa'id], and after that the amir's servant, who is called the dey's biskri [porter] comes and invites him to lunch.

When the bey arrives at the dey's house, there is a guard called the onbajiya—forty men carrying silver yataghans, twenty on the right and twenty on the left. Their leader is called the agha, and there is his kahya [deputy] and the khoja [clerk]. But neither the agha nor his kahya commands the guard. Rather it is under the control of the clerk, who is called the khojat al-bab [clerk of the gate]. When one of the ministers comes, he stands in the middle of the guard and shouts the greeting and enters. The guard detachment answer him at the top of their voices and they call for his success, also at the top of their voices. This wish for success is used much by the Turks and I knew it well.

So the bey stops in the detachment's midst and they exchange greetings, and they call for his success as with the ministers. Then the khojat al-bab comes to him and he takes his yataghan from his waist. The ministers are here for lunch. It was the custom of the ministers to lunch every day at the dey's house. And the khojat al-bab would take the gold yataghans and put them in a room, and they would lunch together in another room. The dey's chief cook would lunch with them. The junior cook, who wore a golden apron, would stand by their heads and order the servants to bring them different sorts of food and fruit. When they had finished eating and had drunk coffee, they all went out to the saqifa [vestibule] of the king's house and they would put on their yataghans and leave, except for the khaznaji, who went to his place of government. He did not go out with the ministers except on Tuesdays and Fridays. It was the habit of the ministers to meet the dey every morning to greet him. Then they would go to their places called the 'ulliyat [the upper gallery of Algerian houses]. On Tuesdays they would go to their gardens in the morning and come to their places of government at noon. As for Fridays, they did not go out. Each one remained in his place and invited his friends to lunch.

The dey's present: When the bey leaves after lunch on the first day, he goes to his house and prepares the dey's gift: in money, about twenty thousand douros [$24,000], jewelry worth about half that, four mature horses, about thirty big and twenty small [child?] slaves from the Sudan, haiks died red with kermes from Tlemcen and the beloved silk haiks of Fès, and golden bilaghi [slippers] and ruwahi [fans?] and golden ishtrambiyat [?], about twenty hundredweight of wax, and similar quantities of honey, clarified butter, and walnuts.

When he had prepared the above, a messenger from the dey would come to invite him to the saraya [palace] to meet him alone without the ministers. The bey goes with the messenger, accompanied by his wakil, and when he reaches the palace of the dey he greets the guards and they respond in kind. The clerk of the gate advances and takes his yataghan from his belt and they go to the saraya where he asks and is given permission to enter. The wakil enters first and greets the dey and kisses his hand and waits. Then the bey enters and greets the king as the wakil has done and kisses his hand and waits. The dey asks both of them to sit, so they sit with bowed heads. The dey welcomes them and asks the bey how he is and asks them to sit more restfully. And he says to them in Turkish, "Rahat attar" [Make yourself comfortable]. They then rise and the Mamluks take the present from the hands of the bey's servants and followers. The money and precious objects are both taken to the same room and the other things to another place. Then the khazinedar takes out the money and distributes it to the servants of the dey and then goes back in accompanied by the chief clerk and they greet the dey and stand there. They are given coffee, and when they finish, the cups are taken from them but the bey fills his cup with gold pieces, and then the wakil and the khazinedar and the chief clerk exit and the bey remains alone with the dey. Even the Mamluks of the dey distance themselves from them and remain facing their master.

The dey and the bey speak for about an hour, and when they finish, the dey says in Turkish, "Allah khayr war." That is the signal to leave him, and the bey kisses his hands, tarries briefly, and leaves.

Visits with the ministers: After that the bey goes to the house of the khazinedar and sits there for about a quarter of an hour and gives him two bags containing a thousand douros to be distributed by the khazinedar to the Mamluks. The wakil and the dey's chief clerk enter and salute him and the two go out with him and go to the head cook's place, where the bey sits briefly and gives a gratuity to the servants and then goes to his house to rest. No one goes in to him except with his permission and there is a guard detail on his door from the palace guard detachment, changing from hour to hour, to guard and serve him.

When the noon prayer is called, the man who precedes the ministers, and who is called qa'id al-zibl ["commander of the garbage"—the officer in charge of municipal sanitation], goes with him to the palace, where he goes through the greeting ceremony with the guard and enters. He sits in the dey's vestibule with the khojat al-khayl, because the latter is the third-ranking minister and that was his place of business, so he sits with him a while exchanging felicitations and then he goes into the khaznaji's office, which is near the treasury, facing the dey's chair, and he sits with him briefly, and they both are given coffee, which they drink. Then he goes out to the vestibule, where he sits with the khojat al-khayl. Then the clerk of the gate comes and he gives him a burnoose, then he goes out from there to the office of the agha, which is called hanut al-agha [the agha's shop]. The agha is the second-ranking minister. He stays with him a while exchanging felicitations, and from there he goes to his lodgings and rests.

The khaznaji's present: The bey performs the afternoon prayer; sometimes he prays in the mosque with the agha. He orders the sending of the present to the khaznaji. So they send it to him, and its value is about a thousand douros, plus jewelry and other valuables—horses, slaves, clothing, kermes haiks, Zaghdani burnooses, silk haiks, wax, honey, and rice without limit. When sunset approaches, the aforementioned qa'id al-zibl comes from the khaznaji and greets him and invites him. The bey goes with him, the present following behind him. His clerks and commanders and Mamluks are with him.

Every minister has a house he stays in—I mean the 'ulliya—when he leaves the palace. They sit there for their rest and work. They do not go to their harims until after the evening prayer, and every minister goes to his 'ulliya before the morning prayer. From there he goes to the Dar al-Imara [palace]. Every minister has in the 'ulliya a wakil al-kharj [steward], an imam, Mamluks, cooks, and servants.

When the bey arrives at the khaznaji's 'ulliya, he is met by the steward, who welcomes him and takes him up to his master. He arrives and meets and greets him and goes with him to his place in the 'ulliya and they sit together. Then the clerks and aghas and commanders enter and greet the khaznaji and he tells them to sit with him and the bey. The others go elsewhere.

Then the servants of the bey come in with the present, put it before him facing the room, and leave. The khaznaji welcomes everyone according to his rank, and when the call to prayer sounds, the imam comes in and leads the prayer. The servants put [additional] rugs before the bey and their master, while the others pray on the original rug. When the prayer is finished, they sit and he gives them supper. There is an indescribable variety of dishes. He presents one dish after another until they are surfeited and no longer stretch out their hands for the food he presents and there remains nothing of the good things except what is before them. Then the table is taken away and they wash their hands and are given coffee. They drink it and the cups are taken from their hands. Then the clerks and the aghas rise and thank the khaznaji and go down to the courtyard and the wakil is with them. The bey remains with the khaznaji for a while and then goes down to the courtyard, where a chair is provided on which he sits and distributes gratuities to the servants of the khaznaji. He gives first to the steward, who takes his present and leaves, and he gives to the imam, and he too takes and leaves, and he does the same with all the servants of the khaznaji according to their rank, and he gives to each that which is appropriate, and when it is done he returns to his house, and the qa'id al-zibl, the agha al-qawl [adjutant major], the mizwar [provost], and the barrah [crier] are before him and before them the qawljiya [guard detachment]. The guard disperses the people who come every night for alms. The bey enters the house and sits and gives gratuities to the qa'id al-zibl and the mizwar and their servants every evening until he leaves. As for the qa'id al-zibl, he gives him a gratuity every time he enters and departs, and he gives money to the wakil and to his ushers to distribute to the alms people. And after that he goes to sleep.

Gratuities of the chief clerk and the clerks: The following day the qa'id al-zibl appears before the morning prayer to escort the bey, with the ministers, to greet the pasha. After that, and after performing the prayer, he returns to his house until the lunch hour, and does the same every day until his departure. The following day the agha invites him, and the bey gives him presents as he did the khaznaji, and perhaps more. On the third day, after greeting the dey and drinking coffee, all the ministers go to their posts and the [bey's] bash katib [chief clerk] enters with the steward and the servants and they carry dirhams to the place of the chief clerk of the pasha, and the bey goes there and sits, with the chief clerk facing him. At the bey's side is his own chief clerk. A leather tray is put down and the dirhams are poured out onto it, while the sipahis [cavalry troopers] stand at the door. The chief clerk opens the register and the dispensing of gratuities begins. These are called the gratuities of the third day, because this is the third day since the bey put on the sultan's robe of investiture. Each of the workers takes what is his due, including the clerks and servants of the tribunal and the rest of the divan, including the ushers who wear the tartur [conical hat] that is shaped like an inverted V. The dirhams remaining after this distribution are given to the grand chief clerk [of the beylik]. If what remains is too little, the bey adds to it. After this the bey goes to his house and rests a little.

Then the messenger comes to announce lunch, and he goes and lunches with the ministers as we have said before. Then he returns to his house and prepares other gifts, money and jewelry. The messenger of the dey comes and asks the bey to follow him. His wakil and ministers and his chief clerk precede him and they enter into the dey's presence in the manner we have mentioned earlier. The bey stays with the dey for about an hour, discussing conditions in the country and the community as well as other matters. When he leaves the dey, he goes to the house of the khazinedar and gives money to the servants as he did the first time. Then he enters the house of the chief cook and distributes money there too. Then he returns to his house and rests a little and orders distribution of major gifts to the people of the government, the clerks and dragomans, the stewards and sipahis and the cook and his assistants and the steward and the clerk of the gate. He had given them money before he entered Algiers, contrary to the practice of the bey of the East, who does not give them money until the third day. As for this bey, the bey of the West, he distributes only slaves, haiks, silk, wax, honey, clarified butter, and rice, and nothing else. So everyone receives his due. Then the noon prayer sounds and the qa'id al-zibl arrives. The bey goes out to the palace where he sits a little with each minister and returns to his house before the afternoon prayer and gives presents to the ushers.

The ushers' gratuities: After the conclusion of the afternoon prayer and after the band has played, they leave the palace; their number is seven ushers. These are the grand ushers, not the junior ones who come to him the morning of the fourth day before the dawn prayer. Three are the ushers of the Qasbah: one wears a tartur, one wears al-'amama al-mubrija [a melon-shaped turban] which the people of Tunis call al-riza [grain of rice?], and the third wears a shashiya [North African felt cap]. They all wear caftans of green cloth and big red shoes with pieces of iron nailed to the soles. The usher of the agha of the soldiers, called "the saddler," is dressed like the others except that his caftan is pomegranate red in color. He comes with the seven big ushers and they sit with the bey and drink coffee. After this the junior ones among them get up and place a big, round cotton cloth on the floor. The bey gives an order to his khazinedar, and he pours out on the cloth dirhams from a sack in the amount of more than a thousand douros, and their heads are bent to the ground like oxen learning to plow.

After a while the head usher raises his head and says in Turkish, "Savandar, effendi" [Make us happy, sir], and the bey responds, "Baraka" [That's plenty]. With that, the rest of the ushers raise their heads and the head usher says, "Yes, plenty, but we are seven and we have many expenses in this service." (Because every year four of them go on mahallas that we have mentioned, two to the mahalla of the East, one to the mahalla of the West, and one to that of Titteri. They receive gratuities that exceed their expenses ten times, but they are a people who are insatiable.) So the bey orders that the amount be increased by what he had first given them, more or less, and they are silent for a while, and then the head usher's deputy speaks, "Savandar, effendi!" and the bey responds, "Baraka." They continue to press him, and then they bring out the snuffbox and give it to him, saying, "Jak barnut, effendi!" [Take some snuff, sir]. And they continue to press him, entreating in the name of the head of the dey and of the sultan, and he increases the amount by a third of what he has already given. This continues until they reach four thousand douros, when they divide the money without counting it. Each one puts his share in a handkerchief and stows it inside his caftan. After that the one called the saddler advances and puts a kerchief between the hands of the bey, who orders that he be given [more?], and the saddler importunes him to increase it, and he increases it. Then the other ushers speak on behalf of their companion, and he increases until he has given him seven hundred douros or more. Then they open the door for him and they leave the room after kissing his hand. They stand in rows in the courtyard and cry out at the top of their voices, and it is like the braying of a donkey, only more so, and say in their tongue, "Allah as'aluk, effendi" [perhaps *allah ismarladik*–may God be with you], and prolong doing so until they go out the door. Then they go to the house of the agha of the soldiers, which is called the serkeji [vinegar seller's]. This is the place of military judgement. He who deserves execution by them, they kill here, and he who deserves beating gets it here [apparently a reference to punishments meted out to members of the ojak, who in this respect are treated differently from nonmembers]. Those ushers go there every day after the afternoon prayer to eat their evening meal with the agha. This house has both a cook and a steward. After they eat they disperse.

The yearly advancement of the ushers: It is the custom of these ushers that every year the head usher steps down and his deputy succeeds him. Thus each one advances every year, and the deputy becomes head usher of the Qasbah. He takes off the melon-shaped turban and puts on the tartur, and he of the shashiya puts on the turban and the usher of the sipahis puts on the caftan and the shashiya, and so forth. When the new head usher puts on the tartur at the palace, he goes to kiss the hand of the dey. The other ushers are standing by, and when he has kissed the hand of the dey and tarried a bit, they pursue him and run after him with whips and he flees in front of them until he arrives at the place they call Hanut al-Shawash [the ushers' shop].

As for the shawush al-salam [greetings usher], he advances to the rank of usher of the sipahis, and the steward of the serkeji takes his place. The usher who wears the turban is the one who carries the dey's slippers when he enters the mosque for the Friday prayers, and puts them back on again when he leaves. I saw him one day when the dey was coming out of the mosque, presenting his slipper to him while he was bending over and holding the edge of the slipper with his fingers. When the dey inserted his right foot, the usher let go and went away as fast as he could.

The present to the khojat al-khayl: As for the bey, when the ushers leave him, as we mentioned, he prepares the present for the khojat al-khayl, who is the third-ranking minister. It amounts to half what he gave the other two ministers. The messenger comes for him before the evening prayer and he goes with him to the khojat al-khayl. They dine together and he tips the khoja's servants as he did the others and then returns home. He tips those who went with him as well as the alms seekers and then goes to bed.

The customary [gratuities] of the rest of the men of the ojak: At the end of the night, before the morning prayer, the three ushers of the Qasbah mentioned earlier come to him and do the work of their friends who are coming. [?] He tips them and they tarry and two ushers wearing the qat [an Algerian costume of Turkish origin] of red cloth. On their heads are red shadud [?]

with gold embroidery. The first of them is the usher of the sipahis and the second is the greetings usher. They take their gratuities, and after them come the cook and the wakil al-harj of the serkeji, then all of them go away.

On the fourth day the bey dines with the wakil al-kharj and gives him a present like that he gave to the khojat al-khayl. On the fifth day he dines with the wakil bayt al-mal [custodian of forfeited and intestate property] and gives him less than he did the other ministers. The remaining three nights the bey is a guest at his wakil's place and gives him a gratuity of about one thousand douros [$1,200], plus slaves, haiks, and wax. He rewards him as he does the other ministers. He gives the wakil's clerk one-third of what he gives the wakil, and he gives presents to the servants of the wakil.

The farewell of the bey and the present given to him: On the seventh day, which is the eve of his departure, a messenger comes from the dey, and the bey goes to the palace and sits with him. He urges the amir to take care of his subjects and counsels him on the affairs of the bayt mal al-muslimin and other matters. The amir leaves and returns to the house where he is staying. The dey sends him a present: two horses and a kohl pot of gold, a gold dagger and gold-embroidered clothes and two pieces of jewelry with precious stones. After the afternoon prayer the ministers send their presents of horses and arms and gold-embroidered robes.

On the morning of the eighth day the bey goes to greet the dey and drink coffee with him. The dey girds him with a golden belt and wishes him godspeed. The bey mounts his horse inside the palace and exits riding, the band playing behind him. The agha, I mean the second minister, leaves with him to see him off to Ain al-Ribat. The agha returns, and the bey goes to his enclosure where he spends the night. The wakil and his clerk are with him, and they settle accounts for what the wakil spent on him. The following morning they say farewell and the bey departs while the wakil returns.

Cathcart's Version

[The following is a much briefer description of the tribute procession of the bey of the East (Salah Bey) in 1788 as recorded by James Cathcart in his journal. As one of the clerks in the dey's palace at that point, he was in a position to witness the ceremony. His description of the ritual aspects of the visit, while giving a different perspective, conforms generally with that of al-Zahhar and provides a few explanatory details missing from the latter's account. Cathcart's spelling is preserved throughout.]

Commencing May 1788; This morning at 5 A.M. the Algerines Piratical Flag was Displayed on all the Marine Fortifications, The Christian Vessels then in Port paid the usual Compliment on such Occasions by Hoisting their Colors.

The whole Divan of Algeirs the Dey Excepted went out to receive the Bey—or Sheik of Constantine and to accompany him to the Deys Pallace—as he had Pitched his tents in the Rebata or Plain the Night Before. These Plains are distant from the Gate of Bebazon four miles. The Laga [agha] or Commander in Chief of all the Military Forces of Algiers and Superintendent of Every thing that is transacted within the Rejency of Algeirs, this City Excepted, went out the Evening before in Order to Confer with him on the State of the Deys Cabinet and other important Affairs.

At 6 A.M. the Bey was met by the Divan all Mounted on fine Arabian Coursers Richly Caparison'd, and after the Usual Ceremonies were Paid they Proceeded towards the City in the following Order—First the Aga of Spahias with the Beys Guards about thirty in Number, secondly fifty Mules loaded with Money . . . [the equivalent of $75,000]—and forty fine Barbarian Horses. This is what is customary to Pay the Rejency every three Years, besides his Caliph [khalifa or deputy] is Oblig'd to bring the half of that sum Every Six Months, next followed Six Mules—Loaded with Gold to be Distributed to the Dey and Divan as presents and Amounts to about 24000 Algerian Sequins [$48,000]. . . .

Next followed Several Horses Richly Caparison'd Designed for Presents to the Great Men, attended by many of the Beys Guards and Spahias. The next that Presented itself to our View was Seven Stand of Colours Carried by Seven Ianyiacgies [janissaries] standard bearers a Horse back a band of Moorish Musick three Holy fools or Maraboots Proclaiming the Beys arrival and then Deys Hampa or Body Guards all Ridiculously dress'd in Brass Caps and adorn'd with feathers to make them appear more Foolish.

Then followed the Bey riding on the Hasnagis Left Side, behind them the Laga and the Hodge of Cavallos or Clerk of the Cattle belonging to the Rejency, which is a birth of the greatest Consequence and the fourth of the Divan, behind him came the Vikilhadge or intendant of the Marine,—followed by a number of others of Inferiour Rank. At 7 A.M. Entered the Gate of Bebazon and was Saluted by all the Marine Fortifications and likewise all the Batteries they Past before they Entered the City.

On the Beys arival at the Pallace he was disarm'd for fear of his Proving Disaffected and try to Assassinate the Dey–then he and the Hasnagi Rode into the Pallace yard and alighted in the presence of the Dey and the other great Men alighted without side of the pallace Gate. On his paying his Respects to the Dey he Kisses his Hand and Sits Down Opposite to Him Disscourses about an Hour, Drinks a Dish of Coffe and fills the Cup with

Manboobs [mahbub = $1.35] this is the Perquisite of the Christian Slaves in the pallace, who seldom fail to bring the largest Cup they can get in order for the Bey to fill it. He then kisses the Beylique or Deys Hand and is attended by ... several others and Conducted to his own Pallace. The Divan then Sits and if his Conduct is approved of the Caftan [the khil'a] is sent him by the Deys Head Christian or his first Christian Servant that Attends his own Person, if not it is not sent but the next time that he comes out of his House to go to the Deys Pallace he is Seiz'd and led to the Aga d'Baston's Prison and Choak'd immediately without a tryal, as Delays may prove Dangerous. . . .

During the Beys stay here which is eight Days he generally Visits the Dey twice a Day Tuesdays and Fridays Excepted. With the Bey came 17 Christian Slaves his Attendants—Most part Genoese and Neapolitans Likewise a Free Surgeon Native of Marseilles. . . .

The Bey had brought with him Eleven Desperados that has Reneagued their faith as they Despaired of Ever being redeemed they being Deserters from [Oran] a Spanish Garrison on this Coast, 80 Leagues to the Westward of Algiers. . . .

When the Bey is in his own Province he resides at a City of the Same name [Constantine] where he lives in great Splendour. Eight Days is the Limited time for his Stay here if he stays any longer he incur's the Dey's Displeasure. When he leaves Algeirs he Returns to the Eastern Province pretty well strip'd of his ill acquired Wealth. He commences very soon to Plunder the Unfortunate and Wretched Arabs and by that means as soon as Possible makes up his losses sustain'd during his short stay at Algeirs at the Cost of those Miserable Wretches whom Almighty Providence has pleas'd to place under his Jurisdiction and Government.

Notes

I have translated both *khoja* and *katib* as "clerk," even though the first means a teacher or learned person, because the context indicates that people holding both these titles have clerical or office functions and al-Zahhar seems to be using them interchangeably.

I have translated *shawush* (pl. *shawash*) as "usher" throughout, because that is the way the term is used today, although there are places where terms like "sergeant at arms" or "chamberlain" might be more descriptive of the man's function.

Throughout the text, al-Zahhar usually calls the dey *amir* (prince), *malik* (king), or pasha interchangeably. He uses the word *dey* very rarely. To avoid confusing the reader, I have sometimes used *dey*.

For a guide to the value of the coins mentioned above, see appendix 2.

Appendix 2

Algerian Coinage

A wide variety of coinage circulated in eighteenth-century Algiers, the unfamiliar terms for which are mentioned frequently in the literature of the period, often with whimsical transliteration of the Turkish or Arabic nomenclature. The following table is based primarily on equivalents given in Cathcart's *Journal*, Barlow's notebook, and Ahmad Tawfiq al-Madani's *Muhammad Uthman Pasha*, plus Nasr al-Din Sa'iduni's two volumes cited at the end of this appendix. The U.S. values are from Cathcart's *Journal*, except where otherwise indicated.

The basic unit of account was the muzuna (Arabic *mawzuna*, Turkish *mevzuna*, meaning "weighed" and implying full weight), variously transcribed as meson, messoon, mazoon, and mesouna. Cathcart and Barlow both give it a value that works out at 40 to the dollar, but the reader will note that Barlow bragged about getting 34 to the dollar in his $200,000 exchange transaction with the Cohen-Bakris in June 1796. This is confirmation, if any was needed, that these values are all variable.

Copper	U.S. value
12 aspers (Ottoman *akce*, connoting "white"— originally a silver coin of about 1.03 grams that was the basic unit of Ottoman currency) =	$0.01
29 aspers = 1 muzuna =	$0.025

Silver	
1 riyal dirham or pataqa chica = 8 muzunas =	$0.20
1 riyal buju (10 gr.) or pataqa gorda = 24 muzunas =	$0.60
1 duru (duro) jaza'iri (20 gr.) or piastre = 48 muzunas =	$1.20

Gold	U.S. value

al-Madani

1 mahbub = 3 riyal bujus = 72 muzunas
1 sultani (3 gr.) = 108 muzunas = 4½ riyal bujus

Cathcart and/or Barlow

1 manboob (mahbub) = 54 muzunas =	$1.35
1 sequin = 72 muzunas =	$1.80
1 Spanish dollar = 40 muzunas =	$1.00
1 Spanish doubloon (doblón) =	$15.00
1 Portuguese Joannes (Joe) =	$15.50–16.00
1 Venetian sequin = 11G pataqas chicas =	$2.10–2.25

Notes

Pataqa

Regarding *pataqas chicas* (small) and *gordas* (big, fat), *pataqa* (Fr. *pataque*) perhaps comes from the Spanish *patacón*, a coin of 5 pesetas. The Spanish dictionaries agree that *patacón* comes from the Arabic *abu taqa*, meaning Father of Window, because "los Moros" took the Pillars of Hercules shown on the coin to be a window. This suspicious folk etymology is attributed to Reinhart Dozy (1820–1883), author of *Spanish Islam,* who cites travelers' accounts in his *Glossaire des mots espagnols et portugais dérivés de l'arabe.* Franz Pick and René Sédillot in *All the Monies of the World,* 2d ed. (New York: Pick, 1971), 413, show it as equivalent to the Spanish duro of 8 reales or riyals.

On the other hand, *patacca* is Italian for a false coin or a large coin of slight value. Italian dictionaries say its etymology is uncertain, but Giacomo Devoto in his *Avviamento alla Etimologia Italiana* (Florence: F. Le Monnier, 1966) says it comes from the old Provençal *pataq*.

Meanwhile, the French dictionary *Le Robert* says *pataque* is an ancient Italian coin used in the sixteenth century in the Kingdom of Naples, where it had a value of 5 carlini. Take your choice.

Al-Madani writes it in Arabic as *bataqa* or *bitaqa,* which means "ticket" or "letter" in Arabic and Turkish and comes from the Greek, according to Redhouse and Lane, while Sa'iduni, who is perhaps more authoritative, writes it as *badaqa.*

Pataca is still in use in Macao, where it is a coin worth 100 centavos. Barlow reports that the *pataqa chica* was a unit of account and that no such coin was in circulation in his time in Algiers, but Sa'iduni's second volume has a picture of one on page 265. He describes it as the universal unit of account for financial transactions.

Duro

The duro or douro was a Spanish silver coin introduced following the discovery of America. It became the prototype silver coin of the region and was given a weight of 27.06 grams in 1772 (versus 24.06 grams for the American dollar of 1792). It is still in use as a unit of account of differing values in some areas of North Africa. This presumably was the coin referred to by the captives as the "Mexican" silver dollar and was also the "hard" piastre mentioned in the negotiations with the Tunisians.

Sequin

There was an Algerian as well as a Venetian gold sequin. The Venetian sequin, or ducat, weighed 3.56 grams, which would make it worth $2.22. (The gold content of the U.S. dollar as of 1792 was 1.6038 grams.) This accords with Cathcart's valuation. The Algerian sequin or sultani, according to al-Madani, weighed 3 grams, which would give it a value of $1.87, but Sa'iduni pegs it at 3.4 grams (for a value of $2.12) until the devaluation of 1823. On the other hand, Krauer and Miche's *Catalogue of World Gold Coins* (Iola, Wisc.: Krauer, 2000) shows the sultani as having a gold weight of 3.25 to 3.40 grams in the period 1785–1807. It is difficult to tell from the accounts of the negotiators which sequin they are using, and I have assumed a value of roughly $2.00, except where the Americans pegged it at $1.80.

Livre

The *livre tournois* was a French unit of account from the thirteenth through the eighteenth centuries. Its exchange value was $0.20. It was supplanted by the franc, with the same value, during the French Revolution.

Mahbub

The mahbub was a Turkish gold coin of the eighteenth century originally having a value of 25 piastres. Al-Madani calls it an Egyptian coin and gives it a value of 72 muzunas. That would make it worth $1.80. Barlow and Cathcart peg it at 54 muzunas or $1.35.

Buju

The meaning of the non-Arab word *buju* as in riyal buju is uncertain. Of the various explanations offered by Daniel Panzac and experts at the American Numismatic Society, a deformation of the Turkish *buçuk,* meaning half, seems the simplest and most likely, the riyal buju being half a duro.

Current Values

For an approximation of current (2003) equivalents of the dollar sums mentioned in this account, I have consulted table A-3 in John J. McCusker, *How Much Is That in Real Money?* and am using a multiplier of 15.

Additional Sources:

Nasr al-Din Sa'iduni. *Al-Nizam al-mali li al-Jaza'ir fi fitrat al Uthmaniyya, 1800–1830* [The financial system of Algiers in the Ottoman period, 1800–1830). Algiers: SNED, 1979.

———. *Al-Nizam al-mali li al-Jaza'ir fi awakhir al-'ahd al-Uthmaniyya, 1792–1830* [The financial system in Algeria in the late Ottoman period, 1792–1830]. Algiers: SNED, 1985.

Appendix 3

Hasan Dey's Accession and Related Incidents

The Strangling of the Khaznaji

Version of al-Zahhar (*Mudhakirat*, 49)

Summary: Salih, the bey of Constantine, in the summer after the truce with Spain [1785 (?)], came to Algiers with his triennial tribute and the dey asked him why he had permitted grain to be shipped from his region to France in spite of the dey's instruction not to do so. Salih replied that he had received instructions from the khaznaji to allow shipments by those who had special permits from him. The dey was angry with the khaznaji and told the wakil al-kharj, Hasan, who was the khaznaji's son-in-law, what the khaznaji had done and said he was concerned about how to deal with this insubordination. Hasan told him not to worry: on the next day, God willing, he would be executed.

Hasan then gave orders to the head shawush to arrest and strangle his father-in-law early the next morning. [There is no mention of indictment or other legal process.] The dey then appointed Hasan khaznaji, making him his putative successor. He also appointed Ali Burghl, another son-in-law of the defunct, as wakil al-kharj in place of Hasan.

The strangled khaznaji's daughter, Hasan's wife, blamed Salih Bey, not her husband, for her father's death and eventually had her revenge against him when her husband became dey. Salih was executed in turn, also without legal process, but not before some bloody fighting had occurred.

Version of Cathcart (*Journal*, 310–11)

[Cathcart, who by his chronology was clerk of the Galera bagnio at the time of this incident, had a tendency to embroider and may not have witnessed much of what he describes so graphically, but he perhaps reported accurately the account that was circulated among palace servants. Except for the chronology, its details track with those in al-Zahhar's account.]

Monday the 26th of May 1788. This morning the Hasnagie as is his Customary came to the Pallace Door and sat at the outside until the Port was oppen'd between the Hours of four and five A.M. Accompanied by the Laga [agha] and Hodge of Caballos [khojat al-khayl]. The Bash Chau's [shawush or head usher] as is his Customary came to pay him his Respects, and the Hasnagi offer'd him his Hand to Kiss, the Chaw Abruptly Pushed his Hand away Seizes him and with the Help of two more Chauses Disarms him Strips him of his turbant and Burnuse and Hurries him away to the Laga of Bastons Prison. During the time of Securing him he asked of the Laga the Reason he was so used, the Laga said he knew not but it was the Dey's Orders and must be Obey'd. As the Chauses Drag'd him under the Deys Window he called Aly Aly! [Allah, Allah?] what have I done! is there no Person that will Plead my Cause or interceed for me in the Moment of impending Danger. Oh! Aly my Wife my Children don't let them Suffer. The Laga asured him he would befriend them all that lay in his Power while he Lived. This unfortunate Great Man with haste was Conducted to the Place of Execution. The first Cord that was used to Strangle him by some means broke when he was about Half Dead upon which another was brought which effectually Done the Business. This Ambitious Man Died Piti'd by all but Lamented by none but the turks of his own party. This once Great and Respected Man was carried by four Pisqueras [Biskris] to his own New house and laid out in the Porch, and no Person was let to Visit him under Pain of Disobedience to the Deys Orders. His house was then shut up and no Person allow'd to enter without the Deys Orders. The family of the Deceas'd being at the Garden [presumably the khaznaji's country house] and hearing of the Unhappy Event, made Ready to come to town but was Prevented by the guards that was sent from town to take care that none of the Deceasds Property should be taken out by any of his Friends, about two Hours afterwards the Wife of this Unfortunate Statesman went on the terrace of the House and would have thrown herself Down had she not been Prevented by one of her Attendants. She Requested in a very pathetic manner to be permitted to go to town to have one more View of her Dear Lord, before his Remains was interred. Her Request was granted. She immediately goes to the House where her Husbands Corps was laid, but Ahlas! no Entrance was for her, but immediately was ordered away from the Door in a Rough manner by the guards which set the unhappy woman almost Disstracted.

At 2 P.M. was Carried by four Pisqueras the Corps of this once Dreaded Minister attended by not one turk as previous to his interrment the Dey gave orders for not a turk to attend his Funeral under Pain of death. He was buried at Bebal Weyd [Bab al-Wad] in his own Burying Ground without the least Ceremony leaving his Wife and Children to bewail his Untimely Fate.

Hasan's Accession to the Deyship

[Hasan's accession to power was not automatic, even though the tradition was that the khaznaji be the successor.]

Version of al-Zahhar (*Mudhakirat*, 51)

Muhammad Pasha fell ill in his palace and when his end was near Ali Burghl, the dey's khazinedar,[1] spoke with Hasan, the khaznaji, and told him that when the dey died he would send for him secretly to come to the palace and assume power in accordance with the custom, and this was to be done without the knowledge of Ali Agha [of the Arabs].

On the thirteenth of Dhu al-Qa'da of the year 1205 [July 12, 1791] the ministers came as usual to the palace, where they were met by the wakil al-kharj [Ali Burghl]. They asked him how the dey was and he said that he had found rest during the night, when in fact he had died that night, may God have mercy on him. So they asked him to give the dey their greetings and he said he would do so. They returned to their homes.

Ali Agha, known as al-Qahwaji [the coffee maker], wanted to become pasha on the amir's death, contrary to the customary practice which was that when the amir died the khaznaji would take his place and the agha would become khaznaji. But Ali Agha wanted to precede the khaznaji because he saw himself as brave and strong.

Ali Agha's house adjoined that of the dey. The khaznaji's house was nearby, so that if the khaznaji went to the palace he would have to pass by Ali Agha's house. At first light, when the wakil al-kharj had ascertained that all the ministers were sleeping in their homes, he sent secretly for Hasan the khaznaji to come to the palace. The messenger found him ready and they went together. When they passed Ali Agha's door, the latter's servants saw them and told their master, who got up, carried small guns [banadiq sghira–pistols?] under his outer garment and followed them.

When the khaznaji entered the palace, he called the commander of the guard and told him to arrest Ali Agha if he came, take his arms away, and hold him until further orders. He then went before the dey's seat and sat there. He then summoned the ministers, the ulama, and the notables of the town. When they arrived, he informed them of the dey's death and that he had entrusted him with the succession. So the people who bind and loosen [the notables] swore allegiance to him and he put on the sultan's robe and raised the flag on the palace. The band played and the cannon were fired, while the criers in the markets announced pardon and protection, the death of the amir and the succession of Hasan Pasha.

As for Ali Agha, when he followed the khaznaji he was arrested and imprisoned in a latrine/bathroom,[2] then the amir ordered his exile to al-Qala'a, where he lived until he was found slaughtered. It was said that he killed himself, and it was also said Hasan Pasha ordered that he be killed.

[Al-Zahhar was ten years old at the time and obviously is repeating the version of events in circulation when he wrote, some years later. There are problems of chronology with it, but his description tracks more or less with Cathcart's.]

Version of Cathcart (*Journal*, 315)

Monday the 11 Day of July 1791. Departed this life Mahomet Bashaw Dey of Algiers at a few minutes past five in the Evening after an Illness of Several Days. This was kept a Profound Secret by Ciddi Alli [Ali Burghl] Vichelharche of the Marine and Ciddi Mahomet Hasnadar or Deys Chamberlain until the same night when Ciddi Alli went over the [roof] terrace of the Pallace and tap'd at the Hasnagies or Prime Ministers Window and was answered by a Christian Slave [identified by Cathcart elsewhere as Joseph Koenig, a German]. Ciddi Alli told him to call his Master and inform him he had some Letters of importance for him from the Bey of Constantine and beg'd he would come to the Window immediately, he accordingly came and was inform'd of the Dey's Death and that he was appointed by the late Dey in his Will to supply his place. Ciddi Hasan Hasnagi thanked him for his information and beg'd of him to use the greatest Precaution and take all Necessary Steps to prevent Opposition on the next Day. Ciddi Alli told him that he expected no opposition but from the Aga or Generallissimo of the Rejency.

Version of Charles Logie, British consul
(PRO FO 3/7 Algiers 13 July 1791, quoted in Barnby, *Prisoners*, 97)

Mahomet Basha, Dey of Algiers, died 12 July 1791 between the hours of seven & eight, much regretted by his subjects. Hassan Basha, the Hasnagi, appointed Dey within half an hour without tumult.

[Logie said he had been the first consul allowed in to congratulate the new dey and remarked that the new man had a large family and the traditional congratulatory presents would be more expensive than they had been with his predecessor, who had no family members in high office.]

Hasan, Ali Burghl, and the American Ships

Version of al-Zahhar (*Mudhakirat*, 61–63)

[This confused account is the only remotely contemporaneous Algerian description I have found of the capture of American ships in 1793. It should not be taken too seriously, except as an illustration of what some Algerians may have thought happened.]

In Safar 1206 [1791] the truce with Sweden expired and he [Hasan] ordered the consul of the Americans to pay what they owed in the way of financial obligation, and gave them a delay of twenty days.[3] If they did not pay what they owed, on the twenty-first day he would take American ships found at sea. When the period of the delay elapsed, he ordered the ships of the jihad to be readied. On the day of departure, al-Haj Muhammad al-Qabtan and the other captains went up to take their leave. He bid them farewell and they tarried with him. Then he called al-Qabtan over and whispered in his ear, "If you find American ships after so much [time] then take them."[4]

It was the custom of the jihad captains on the day of departure to take their leave of the dey and after leaving him to visit the tomb of the sound intercessor, the eminent source of good counsel, Sidi Abd al-Rahman al-Tha'alabi, whom God has availed to us. Then they went to visit the tomb of the sound intercessor Sidi Ali al-'Abassi, whom God has availed to us, Amen. And from there they went to Bab al-Jihad, where they took their leave of the wakil al-kharj and then went to their ships.

When al-Haj Muhammad al-Qabtan took his leave of the wakil al-kharj [at that point Ali Burghl, Hasan's coconspirator], the latter asked him what the amir had ordered him to do. Al-Qabtan said, "He ordered me if I met American ships after my journey by thus and so, to take what we found of them." The wakil al-kharj said, "Take what you find of them and don't observe the delay. Don't do what the dey ordered." Al-Qabtan replied, "I hear and obey." He thought the wakil al-kharj was speaking in disobedience to the dey and [or?] that the latter had changed his mind after they parted.[5] He went to his ship and left immediately. After three or four days he encountered an American ship and captured it and returned to Algiers. When he arrived the captain of the port went out to him and he informed him that this ship[6] was American booty which he had captured in the west [the Algarve?] and he had brought it [them?] back to harbor and was going to return to complete his voyage. The captain of the port went to the dey and informed him. The latter became agitated and angry with al-Qabtan and ordered his arrest.

When they went to arrest al-Qabtan, the wakil al-kharj heard about it and went up to the palace, met with the dey, and said to him, "I heard that you were angry with al-Qabtan and ordered his arrest. I am here between your hands, do with me what you will, for I am the one who ordered him to take the ships of the American, thinking we would win by taking them before they gathered their ships."

As for the man who went to arrest al-Qabtan, when he arrived at the ship's side he ordered him to come down to see the dey. All of the raiding party spoke to him and said, "The captain won't come down because we are sailing now, so go back to the dey and give him our regards and ask him to wish us well and when our voyage is completed and we return al-Qabtan will meet with him." So the messenger went to see the dey, told him what happened, and gave him the crew's greetings. The dey silenced his rage at al-Qabtan and increased it at the wakil al-kharj.

The ship sailed at that hour, and the wakil al-kharj returned to his office. The following day the dey ordered him exiled to Turkey on a ship that was leaving that day, and gave him all the wealth in his [the wakil's] house.[7] When he had left Algiers and was some distance from its harbor, the dey thought to kill him, so they began making signals from the lighthouse, not by fire [but by flags?], for the ship to return. But the ship did not turn back and it did not respond to the signals. So they fired a cannon without shot and the ship kept going. Then they added a cannon with shot, but it kept on going and did not return. Ali arrived at Istanbul and was well received there. After that he went to Tripoli.[8]

. . . There was no captain like al-Qabtan in the annals of jihad. . . . after taking many American ships and others he returned to Algiers with a booty that was uncountable and entered Algiers on a famous day, filling the hands of the raiders with money and goods.

At the end of the year [1208?—1793] the Americans asked for peace with the dey through the mediation of other people. The dey asked for three million douros and ships for the jihad [about $3.6 million]. There was mediation to get him to lower the price by half a million douros, and he agreed to that. In addition to the money, three ships for the jihad. Peace was concluded on that basis and a period was set for coming with the money and the ships. When the period was approaching its end, the money and the ships were paid: a frigate and a blandira and three sakakin, with their armament.[9]

Notes

1. This is inconsistent with al-Zahhar's earlier statement that Burghl was made wakil al-kharj, and with Cathcart's account that he had been the chamberlain and governor of the palace (i.e., the khazinedar) but was made wakil al-kharj when Hasan became khaznaji in 1788. In any event, he seems to

have been in the palace with the khazinedar (Muhammad) on the night of Bin Uthman's death.

2. "Mathara" in the text, "ghurfat istihmam" in al-Madani's notes.

3. There is no further mention of the Swedes. There was no American consul in Algiers at the time, nor was there any agreement on financial obligation of the Americans to Algiers prior to 1795.

4. "Ida wajadtum marakib al-Amirkan ba'd kida fakhaduhom."

5. This would make more sense if it read "He thought the wakil al-kharj was speaking in *obedience* to the dey" but the Arabic seems clear: "wa qad zanna qabtan inna wakil al-kharj takallam *bimarad* al-amir."

6. "Hadhihi al-marakib." It is unclear throughout whether he is talking of one ship or more: he constantly uses the plural *marakib* and refers to it, or them, as *ha*.

7. Allowing an exile to take his wealth was contrary to normal usage.

8. Ali passed himself off in Tripoli as the sultan's new governor and instituted a bizarre period of misrule.

Cathcart in his Library of Congress manuscript says that Ali Burghl was so-called because burghul (bulgur) was what he fed his people, and that his departure from Algiers referred to here was by Spanish brig on February 7, 1793.

9. The blandira is described in al-Madani's footnotes as a light craft armed with cannon that went swiftly to meet the enemy at a distance. In other words, a gunboat. Elsewhere it is described as having been adopted from the Spanish. Venture de Paradis describes it as a bomb vessel. *Sakakin* looks like the plural of *sikkin*, meaning knife, but evidently is a type of vessel, perhaps a *saetia* or *saettia*, a lateen-rigged vessel with a long sharp prow. The reference is perhaps to the three ships supplied by the Americans in 1799 that are described in chapter 7.

Appendix 4

The American Prisoners and Their Ships

Judging by the accounts of James Cathcart and John Foss, as well as the reports of O'Brien and others, the total number of captives taken from American ships from 1785 to 1793 was 132, although a State Department study of 1987 concluded that there were only 130, of whom 40 died. (Foss and Cathcart list only 29 deaths.) Four of the men were Spaniards. One was French. Two had what look like Italian names. Eleven claimed to be British. Five men were ransomed by friends or family, and three—O'Brien, Cathcart, and Philip Sloan—were released in advance of the general redemption.

Of the total, 88 were included in Foss's list of redeemed prisoners who should have arrived at Marseille. Of these, 65 (two of whom were not on Foss's list, indicating that his total should have been 90) arrived in Philadelphia on board the Swedish ship *Jupiter* on February 9, 1797, according to the list in *Naval Documents,* the handwritten original of which is in the National Archives.

Twenty-five men dropped off at Marseille, including the Spaniards and Italians, who evidently chose to remain in Europe. Some men signed on to other vessels. John Foss and his friend Moses Brown from Newburyport, for instance, signed on to the ill-fated *Fortune,* with Michael Smith, former first mate of the *Polly,* as master (see chapter 7).

In the lists below, an asterisk before the name indicates that the man arrived in Philadelphia on February 9, 1797; the home port is as shown in *Naval Documents* under "Where belonging."

The Prisoners of 1785

Schooner *Maria* of Boston

*Isaac Stephens, captain, Boston	general redemption, 1796
*Alexander Forsyth, mate, Boston	general redemption, 1796
James Leander Cathcart	left with despatches, May 8, 1796

*Thomas Billings (John Gregory) Boston	general redemption, 1796
James Harnet	died in madhouse, 1793
George Smith	redeemed by friends, 1793

Ship *Dauphin* of Philadelphia

Richard O'Brien, captain	left with treaty, Sept. 1795
Zachaeus Coffin, captain	(passenger) died of consumption, July 2, 1787
Andrew Montgomery, mate	general redemption, 1796
Philip Sloan	redeemed by Dutch, 1794
James Hull	general redemption, 1796, but taken by a Neapolitan cruiser
Charles Colvil	redeemed by friends, 1790
John Robertson	redeemed by friends, June 12, 1791
William Patterson	redeemed by friends, Jan. 3, 1794
John Doran	died of plague, July 1, 1787
William Harding	died of plague, June 6, 1788
Peter Loring	died of plague, June 27, 1784
Robert McGinnis	died of plague, 1787
Edward O'Reilly	died of plague, May 8, 1788
Peter Smith	died of plague, July 18, 1787
Jacob Tessanaer	died of plague, July 13, 1793

Those who signed the April 3, 1786, petition to George III, claiming to be British subjects, included all four seamen (but not the officers) of the *Maria* and more than half the crew (Sloan, Colvil, Robertson, Patterson, McGinnis, O'Reilly, and Smith) of the *Dauphin*.

Sloan was included in the Dutch redemption package of 1794 because he was "sweeper" of the dey's palace and by tradition the man in that job was included in each general redemption, the redeeming nation being required to pay his ransom to the dey.

It is noteworthy that Harnet was the only fatality among the crew of the *Maria*. Of the fifteen men on the *Dauphin*, seven died of the plague, and only Montgomery and Hull were included in the general redemption of 1796.

The Prisoners of 1793

John Foss, at the end of the narrative in his *Journal*, lists the following men from the captures of 1793. The names are as given in the second edition, which differs slightly from the first. Names in parentheses are as they appear on the list of men arriving in Philadelphia.

Ship *President* of Philadelphia, captured October 23, 1793

William Penrose, captain	general redemption, 1796
*Peter Barry (Barny), mate, Philadelphia	general redemption, 1796
*James Allen, 2d mate, Philadelphia	general redemption, 1796
*John Dix (Dicks), Baltimore	general redemption, 1796
*Henry Pilson (Pitson), Philadelphia	general redemption, 1796
*Anthony Russell, Philadelphia	general redemption, 1796
Isaac Brooks	general redemption, 1796
John Higdar	general redemption, 1796
John Jones	general redemption, 1796
Nicholas Box	died of plague July 22, 1794
John Thomas	died of plague June 18, 1794
Nicolo Francisco, supercargo	general redemption, 1796, Spaniard

Brig *George* of Newport, captured October 11, 1793

*James Taylor, captain, Newport	general redemption, 1796
William Prior, mate	died of plague, July 3, 1794
*Gideon Brown, Newport	general redemption, 1796
*Benjamin Church, Newport	general redemption, 1796
*Stanton Hazard, Newport	general redemption, 1796
Abraham Flagg	general redemption, 1796
George Tilley	general redemption, 1796
Richard Witton	died of consumption, April 24, 1794

Schooner *Jay* of Gloucester, captured October [?], 1793

*Samuel Calder, captain, Gloucester	general redemption, 1796
*John Walker, mate, Gloucester	general redemption, 1796
*Thomas Manning, Gloucester	general redemption, 1796
John Edwards	general redemption, 1796
Walter Gibbins	general redemption, 1796
Benjamin Ober	general redemption, 1796
Abraham Simmonds	died of plague, June 8, 1796

Ship *Minerva* of Philadelphia, captured October 10, 1793

John McShane, captain	died of plague, June 16, 1794
Samuel Millborne, mate	died of smallpox, March 1, 1794
*John McFarland, 2d mate, Philadelphia	general redemption, 1796

*Thomas Barton (Budding),
  Philadelphia   general redemption, 1796
*Thomas Burgess, Norfolk   general redemption, 1796
*Joseph Deitz, Philadelphia   general redemption, 1796
*Jean Fogereaux (Fitzgerald),
  Philadelphia   general redemption, 1796
*William Grafton, Providence   general redemption, 1796
*Charles Smith, Norfolk   general redemption, 1796
*John Sutton, Philadelphia   general redemption, 1796
*Jacquin (no first name, not on
  Foss list), Philadelphia   general redemption, 1796
Abel Willis   general redemption, 1796
Giovanni Romero   general redemption, 1796
Barralami Gazona   general redemption, 1796
Vincent Romes, Spaniard   general redemption, 1796
Juan Segrane   general redemption, 1796
Joseph Rogers   died of plague, July 12, 1796
John Mott   died of smallpox, Sept. 13, 1794

Brig *Jane* of Haverhill, captured October 11, 1793

*Moses Morse (Morsse), captain,
  Haverhill   general redemption, 1796
*Edward Harwood, mate, Salem   general redemption, 1796
*Thomas Fry, Salem   general redemption, 1796
*Samuel Hendrick (Henry), Salem   general redemption, 1796
*James Pease, Salem   general redemption, 1796
*Thomas Ximenes (Simmons),
  Haverhill   general redemption, 1796
Abraham Burril   general redemption, 1796
John Ramsay   died of plague, May 17, 1796

Ship *Thomas* of Boston, captured October 8, 1793

*Timothy Newman, captain,
  Newburyport   general redemption, 1796
*George Wells, mate, Norfolk   general redemption, 1796
*John Woodman (Woodmansee),
  2d mate, Boston   general redemption, 1796
*William Dunbar, Philadelphia   general redemption, 1796
*Peter Larne (Pedro Laman),
  Boston   general redemption, 1796

*Barney McLaughten (McGlothering),
  Boston   general redemption, 1796
*Rufus (Rosmus) Morton, Baltimore   general redemption, 1796
Benjamin Bishop   general redemption, 1796
Richard Harris   general redemption, 1796
Antonio Salamer, Spaniard   general redemption, 1796

Brig *Polly* of Newburyport, captured October 25, 1793

Samuel E. Bayley, captain   died of plague, July 17, 1796
Michael Smith, mate   general redemption, 1796
*Benjamin Edwards, 2d mate,
  Newburyport   general redemption, 1796
John Foss, Newburyport   general redemption, 1796
Moses Brown, Newburyport   general redemption, 1796
Nicholas Hartford   died of plague June 2, 1796
Walbert H. Poel   died of plague July 16, 1794
Enoch Rust   died of plague July 7, 1796
Thomas Stafford   died of plague July 13, 1794

Ship *Hope* of New York, captured October 1793

John Burnham, captain   ransomed for $4,400 by James Duff, British consul in Cádiz
*William Dixon, mate, New York   general redemption, 1796
*Peter Ingram, 2d mate, New York   general redemption, 1796
*James Byrne, New York   general redemption, 1796
*Martin Duart (Deswart), New York   general redemption, 1796
*James Fox, New York   general redemption, 1796
*John P. Kickuer (John Frederick
  Ackhert), New York   general redemption, 1796
*Harmon Oldstick (Alike), New York   general redemption, 1796
*Peter C. Brier (Brior), New York   general redemption, 1796
*John F. Ricard (Rickway),
  New York   general redemption, 1796
*Benjamin Lunt, Newburyport   general redemption, 1796
*Jacob Skoomaker (Shoemaker),
  New York   general redemption, 1796
*Cornelius Tondroton (Fanviform),
  New York   general redemption, 1796
*Peter Vantorn (Vandertown),
  New York   general redemption, 1796
*Cornelius Westerdunk, New York   general redemption, 1796

Peter Sandie   general redemption, 1796
Christian Hannes   general redemption, 1796
John P. Peterson   general redemption, 1796

Brig *Olive Branch* of Portsmouth, N.H., captured October [?], 1793

*William Furnace (Furnass),
    captain, Portsmouth   general redemption, 1796
Richard Wood, mate   died of smallpox, Feb. 6, 1796
*George Bachanan (Buchanan),
    Portsmouth   general redemption, 1796
*John Earl, Portsmouth   general redemption, 1796
*Nathaniel Keen (Kein), Portsmouth   general redemption, 1796
Thomas Furnace   died of plague, Feb. 12, 1794

Schooner *Dispatch* or *Despatch*, of Richmond or Petersburg, Va., captured October [?], 1793

William Wallace, captain   died in fall, Feb. 1796
Joseph Keith, mate   general redemption, 1796
*James Hughes (Huse), Philadelphia   general redemption, 1796
*John Lemmon (not in Foss),
    Lancaster, Pa.   general redemption, 1796
*George Osborne, Philadelphia   general redemption, 1796
*Peter Page, Portsmouth   general redemption, 1796
Daniel Gullings   died of plague, Aug. 1, 1794

Brig *Minerva* of New York, captured November 23, 1793

Joseph Ingraham, captain   general redemption of 1796
*Edward Smith, mate, New York   general redemption, 1796
*Philip New, New York   general redemption, 1796
*John Parplin (Pamplin), New York   general redemption, 1796
John Cooper   general redemption, 1796
Charles Polley   general redemption, 1796
Scipio Jackson   died of "cholic," Jan. 30, 1796

On release of the captives, Captain Ingraham of the brig *Minerva* remained in Algiers, hoping to find direct passage to Spain. No passage appearing, Barlow sent him to Tripoli to help O'Brien after capture of the *Sophia* by the Tripolitanians. Barlow praised his performance in Tripoli highly. He remained there as acting consul until Cathcart's arrival in 1799, according to Department of State personnel records. Captain William Penrose of the *President* also dropped off somewhere, perhaps at Marseille.

Casualty Figures

Looking at the lists, note the difference in casualty rates among the crews. All of the crews of the *Hope* and the *Thomas* survived, and fourteen of the eighteen men on the *Hope* returned to Philadelphia together. Five out of nine men on the *Polly*, including the captain, died of the plague, and only one of the remaining four was on the *Jupiter* at Philadelphia. What made the difference? One can only speculate at this remove that factors such as morale and discipline had a role in crew survival.

The American Vessels Taken in 1793

The first detailed news from the captives taken in 1793 was a letter of November 13 from Captain John McShane of the ship *Minerva* (out of Philadelphia, owner William Bell, carrying sixteen men and a master, according to his letter, to which number the otherwise unidentified "Jacquin" seems to have been added by the time the survivors reached Philadelphia) reporting that his and nine other vessels had been taken and that he was in the "marine" at Algiers at hard labor on bread and water. He gives the following list of those in the same situation as himself:

Schooner *Despatch*, Gallas and Freeman, Richmond, Va.—William Wallace master and six crewmen

Brig *Jane*, Moses Moss [Morse] and Samuel P. Kidder, Newburyport (Haverhill)—Moses Morse master and seven crewmen

Brig *Polly*, Bailey and Noyse, Newburyport—Michael Smith master and eight crewmen [Smith was the first mate. The master of the *Polly* was Samuel Bayley.]

Brig *Olive Branch*, Col. Jonathan Hambleton Jr., Portsmouth, N.H.-- William Furnace master and six crewmen

Ship *President*, John and James Craig, Philadelphia—William Penrose master, ten crewmen and one passenger

Brig *George*, Gibbs and Channing, Newport, R.I.—James Taylor master and seven crewmen

Schooner *Jay*, Ebenezer Pass, Gloucester, Mass.—Samuel Calder master and six crewmen

Ship *Hope*, [owner not listed], New York—John Burnam master and eighteen crewmen

Ship *Thomas*, Thomas Adams, Boston—Timothy Newman master and ten crewmen (The actual count was nine crewmen according to Foss.)

Missing from the list is the brig *Minerva* of New York, Joseph Ingraham master and six crewmen. I have found no information regarding her owners.

Note that the term *ship* as used here means a relatively large, square-rigged, three-masted vessel having a bowsprit and with each mast composed of a lower mast, a topmast, and a topgallant mast. *Schooner* means a fore-and-aft-rigged vessel, relatively small and probably two-masted in this case. *Brig* means a relatively small, two-masted, square-rigged vessel.

Four of these vessels were in the coastal trade: the *Thomas* was captured on October 8 off the Atlantic coast of Portugal while en route from Cádiz to Amsterdam with a load of sugar; the *Jane* was captured October 11 en route from Cádiz to Hamburg with a cargo of hides and other items; the *Hope* was bound from Rotterdam to Málaga in ballast; and the *Despatch* was en route from Cádiz to Hamburg with sugar, indigo, and sarsaparilla. There were six vessels clearly in the transatlantic trade: the ship *Minerva* was en route from Philadelphia to Barcelona; the *President* out of Philadelphia was bound for Cádiz with a cargo of grain and flour; the *Polly* was also carrying flour to Cádiz, from Newburyport; the *Olive Branch* was carrying grain from Virginia to Lisbon; the *Jay* was carrying raisins, figs, wine, and grapes from Málaga to Boston; the brig *Minerva* was carrying wine and brandy from Livorno to New York. The brig *George*'s destination is not given, but she was reportedly carrying a cargo of grain and Indian corn from Lisbon, presumably to another European port.

Calder of the *Jay* gives a full description of his vessel's cargo in a letter of December 4, 1793, to David Pearce Jr., evidently the owner's son, in "Colchester" (a misprint for Gloucester). Calder says he was carrying a cargo of 650 casks of raisins, 20 casks of wine, 30 jars of raisins, 3 jars and 40 boxes of grapes. The "gross sales" of the cargo was 68,000 *Rvns* (*reales de vellón* or copper reals worth $0.05 each). That would make the cargo worth roughly $3,400. In a notarial of May 8, 1794, however, David Pearce estimated the value of the cargo at £1,974.5 and the value of the ship at £400.

Calder is very gloomy about his prospects and ends with the comment "I am very sorry for your misfortune, but my Own is so much greater than yours that there is no comparison" (*NavDocs*, 1:58). He had reason to be despondent: he had disregarded the warning of the consul in Málaga and sailed after it was known the Algerines were cruising for Americans.

There are two contemporary documents from Algiers that mention some of these ships and their cargoes. One is the *Registre des Prises Maritimes,* translated by Albert Devoulx and described by him in *La Revue Africaine* 15 (1869). He does not say where he found it, but says it was the record kept by the corsairs themselves on prizes taken in the years from 1765 to 1830. It lists prizes and what they fetched at auction in Algiers, and indicates the value of individual shares of the participants in the corsair venture. It is incomplete. Devoulx says it was a loose-leafed document and some of the leaves were missing. Neither of the American ships taken in 1785 is listed, and only four, possibly five, of the eleven taken in 1793 can be identified with any certainty. Other, unlisted vessels may have been taken to European ports and sold, as the *Dauphin* was in 1785. There must have been a procedure and a set of rules for recovering the proceeds of such sales, but no light is shed on it by the *Registre*.

The second document is the *Picciolo Libretto* [Little Booklet] in Italian that is among the papers of James Cathcart in the New York Public Library. Its eight pages, 23.5 x 17.2 cm, are formed by two large sheets of paper folded and bound at the fold by string. It purports to list the prizes taken into Algiers port and sold from 1787 to June 19, 1794. It is even more incomplete than the *Registre*, which lists fifty-four prizes for that period while the *Libretto* lists forty. It lists no prizes at all for the years 1790 and 1792, whereas the *Registre* lists four and six respectively. The *Libretto* lists only two American prizes, one of which, a vessel captured on October 4 by the "little xebec" of the wakil al-kharj, was bought by the Swedish consul for $9,000. The other was sold by a Spanish merchant for $4,000 to an unspecified buyer. Neither vessel is identified by name, but the $9,000 paid by the Swedish consul would not be far off the owner's declared value of the *Jay's* cargo.

According to Devoulx, the *Registre* lists the proceeds of the cargo, presumably including the human cargo sold as slaves, not the value of the vessel. The latter was the property of the beylik, which either sold it or took it over for its own use. The *Libretto*, on the other hand, does not indicate whether it is giving the sale price of the vessel or its cargo or both. It often describes the cargoes of the vessels sold, and these sound very ordinary—barrel staves, flour, lumber, pots.

The American ships that we can tentatively identify from the *Registre* are no. 255, the *President*, whose cargo of wheat and flour was sold for 76,947 pataqas chicas or about $15,000; no. 257, the *Polly*, whose cargo of flour fetched $11,381; no. 258, the *Hope*, in ballast, which brought in $2,425; and no. 259, the *George* or the *Olive Branch*, loaded with wheat, worth $21,365.

A fifth vessel listed in the *Registre* as no. 262 of January 1794 was a ship loaded with wool with fifty-five "American Christians" aboard. It was perhaps one of the ships taken in 1793 on which prisoners from other ships were transported to Algiers. None of the American vessels in question had a crew that large. Its cargo sold for $137,182, presumably reflecting in part the value of the Christians as slaves ($137,182 divided by 55 works out at some $2,500 a head, which was about what the Americans ended up paying for their men, although the market price for an ordinary seaman at this point seems to have been closer to $500).

Appendix 5

The De Castries Letter

The following is the text of the sealed letter from the marquis de Castries, minister of the navy, given to Lamb to carry to the French consul, Jean-Baptiste Michel Guyot de Kercy, in Algiers. It instructs de Kercy to do all he can to help Lamb. Next is a cryptogram followed by its clear text, referring to the letter given to Lamb and instructing de Kercy to go through the motions but not to help him in any significant way, instructions that de Kercy carried out successfully.

Text of de Castries's Letter

[The photocopy of the document carries no dateline, but the index published by the French Ministry of Foreign Affairs states that it was dated October 23, 1785, at Fontainebleau.]

> Mrs Adams et Jefferson, Monsieur, ministres des Etats unis prés Sa M^{té} ont en vertu de leurs pouvoirs, délégué Mr. Jean Lamb pour aller avec la qualité d'agent de cette puissance, négotier, rédiger, et signer préliminairement avec le Dey d'Alger un traité don't le Congrés veut que l'exécution deffinitive le soit par Mrs Adams et Jefferson.
>
> Vous savés, Monsieur, que par la convention du 6 fevrier 1778 le Roy a promis aux américains leurs offices auprés des régences de Barbarie.
>
> Sa M^{té} vous charge en conséquence de rendre à Mr. Lamb tous les services qui dépendront de vous et que comporteront la nature de leur propositions et leurs prétentions de la régence. Je ne doute pas de votre empressement á ne rien oublier pour faciliter, autant que vous le pourrés, le succés de la négotiation de Mr. Lamb.
>
> Je suis trés parfaitment, Monsieur, votre trés humble et trés obeissant serviteur.
>
> le M^{ar} de Castries

Translation

Messrs. Adams and Jefferson, sir, ministers of the United States to His Majesty, have by virtue of their powers delegated Mr. John Lamb to go as agent of that power to negotiate, edit, and sign preliminarily with the Dey of Algiers a treaty of which the Congress wants the definitive execution to be by Messrs. Adams and Jefferson.

You know, sir, that by the agreement of 6 February 1778 the King has promised the Americans his good offices with the Barbary regencies.

His Majesty therefore charges you to render to Mr. Lamb all the services which you can and which comport with the nature of their propositions and claims to the regency. I do not doubt your eagerness not to forget anything to facilitate, to the extent you can, the success of Mr. Lamb's negotiations.

I am very perfectly, sir, your very humble and obedient servant.

the Marquis de Castries

Cryptogram dated Fontainebleau, 31 October 1785

162. 294. 45. 361. 23. 222. 103. 291. 379. 405.
17. 405. 589. 224. 480. 694. 395. 607. 98. 257. 341.
447. 361. 560. 169. 47. 222. 294. 206. 17. 566. 79.
664.

664. 354. 294. 341. 563. 503. 113. 110. 461. 273.
594. 591. 322. 548. 647. 674. 17. 539. 207. 236.
294. 502. 169. 377. 246. 273. 109. 108. 361. 351. 589.
88. 664. 664. 587. 502. 22. 294. 341. 532. 164. 337.
539. 137. 17. 539. 454. 566. 150. 110. 664. 361. 79.
294. 341. 281. 426. 207. 165. 17. 620. 109. 609. 605.
331. 545. 407. 220. 9. 113. 589. 207. 208. 341. 503. 275.

314. 77. 239. 379. 664. 278. 158. 341. 404. 254. 455.
398. 12. 664. 9. 248. 545. 294. 341. 673. 197. 607.
222. 239. 502. 269. 12. 607. 294. 109. 670. 566.
328. 55l. 131. 103. 113. 207. 575. 103. 143. 351. 169.
240. 628. 214. 222. 589. 369. 461. 273. 594. 591.
327. 258. 288. 273. 142. 294. 175.
. . . . . . page 2 . . . . . .
638. 195. 307. 498. 545. 673. 197. 420. 222. 2. 545.

407. 545. 351. 589. 265. 9. 392. 131. 361. 12. 576. 222
273. 545. 110. 664. 628. 294. 341. 17. 580. 448. 118.
341. 405. 589. 224. 480. 128. 250. 187. 68. 128.

Je suis trés parfaitment, Monsieur, votre trés humble et trés obéissant serviteur.

le M^{ar} de Castries

French Clear Text of the Cryptogram

Fontainebleau le 31 8ber 1785

J'ay rémis le 23 de ce mois à M. Lamb agent des Etats unis prés le Dey dAlger une lettre de Recommandation pour vous.

Vous sentirés aisément que nous n'avons point d'avantage a leur procurer une navigation tranquille dans la Mediterrannée—vous vous bornerés donc a leur rendre satisfattion autant que vous pourrés les servir pour vous d'acquitter exterieurment de la promesse du roy, mays vous n'irés pas plus loin, & vous eviterés surtout des demarches & des requisitions efficacement prononcées dans une negociation au succés de laquelle nous n'avons rien moins q'un intéret réel.

Je compte surtout [sur] votre dexterité dans la conduite amicale & prudente que vous aurés a tenir envers M. Lamb.

Translation

On the 23d of this month I gave Mr. Lamb, agent of the United States to the Dey of Algiers, a letter of recommendation for you.

You will easily sense that there is no advantage to us in procuring for them [the Americans] a tranquil navigation in the Mediterranean. You will therefore limit yourself to giving them satisfaction to the extent that you can serve them to acquit yourself outwardly of the king's promise, but you will not go further, and above all you will avoid démarches and demands effectively pronounced in a negotiation in the success of which we have no real interest.

I count above all on your skill in the friendly and prudent conduct which you will need to maintain toward Mr. Lamb.

Source: The first text is listed in Even, *Papiers,* as vol. 13, fols. 198–99. The cypher and its translation are fols. 200–201. The originals of the documents are maintained at Nantes.

Appendix 6

The Sailors' Petition

[This is the text from the Public Record Office at Kew (FO 3/6, pp. 172–73) of a petition to King George III sent by eleven of the American captives in Algiers claiming British nationality and begging the king to intervene on their behalf. The petition was dated 20 December 1785 by Consul Logie and was received in London on April 3, 1786. I could find no indication of a follow-up. The photocopy is badly discolored and impossible to read in some spots.]

To the Kings most Excellent Majesty

The Humble Petition of the Underwritten Eleven of his Majestys subjects Taken under American colours and at present miserable slaves at Algiers Humbly [——] that the[y] were captured in the Month of July 1785 On Board the ship Dauphin of Philadelphia Richard OBryen Master and Schooner Maria of Boston Isaac Stephens Master, and sent to the port of Algiers where the Vessels were Condemned and We as Part of the Crew maid slaves.

Your Majestys most humble and miserable Petitioners beg to lay at your Majesty's feet the separate Circumstances that Obliged them Unfortunately to serve under American Colours. In proof that they have Ever been your Majesty's Dutifull and Loyall Subjects.

1. First. Charles Colvil Humbly states that he was born and served his time as a ships Carpenter to William Stormount in the town of Dundee N. Britain.

2. Secondly Peter Smith states that he was born in Dublin and served his time in the Ship Nanny[?] Belonging to John and James Watt Merchants in Liverpoole and was in 1784 cast away on the Island of Anianga[?] and was taken from thence by an American Vessel—where on his arrival in Philadelphia he was obliged to ship on board the Ship Dauphin.

3. Thirdly Philip Sloan born and served his time out of Liverpoole in the Ship Nanny belonging to John and James Watt. And in 1764 belonged to the Ship Favourite [John?] of [——] John Hughes Master was left sick in the hospital in Philadelphia and obliged to ship in American ships—having no money [——] served on board his Majesty's ships during the war.

4. John Robertson born in Glasgow in January 1764 belonged to the Ship M[——] Capt Spears Commander bound for Jamaica and was discharged in Kingston when after he shipped on a Brig belonging to Kingston and said Brig was sold in America and was obliged to ship in an American ship. Having served your Majesty During the Late War.

5. Edward A. Reilly born in Dublin & served on board his Majestys Ships during the Late War and unfortunately took passage in July last from [——] on board the Ship Dauphin & lost his passport when Captured by the Algerines—

[end of page]

William Patterson Humbly states that he was born in King Edwards Parish N. Britain and served his time in [——] to Thomas [——], Cooper and worked for James Scott in Horsleydown Lane, London, after [——] was discharged and unfortunately was a passenger on board the ship Dauphin from Dunkerque having a Certificate that he was a passenger and a British Subject, but his chest and passport being left on board could not come at them and is maid a slave of in Algiers.

Robert McGinnis [——] garrisoned at New Providence [Nassau] when General Maxwell was Governor of the Island—his father was sending him to Charlestown S. Carolina to school but the Vessel was taken by an American Privateer and brought into the Havanna where he was going to prison but was taken from there by Capt OBryen. About the same time the Spaniards took New Providence and his father being sent to England had no opportunity of going to his father.

George Smyth Humbly states that he was born in the Manor of Firth Ports[——] and served his time on board the Brig Jennut[?] John Wiseman Master belonging to Keith—and was unfortunately on board the Schooner Maria & is at present a miserable Slave in the Deys house in Algiers.

John Gregory Humbly states that he was born in Liverpoole and served his time out of said port & belonged to the Ship Willson of sd. port Charles Thompson Master & in 1784 was discharged being sick in New Yorke. Having served your Majesty during the late war—& is & unfortunate miserable slave to the Dey—of Algiers.

James Cathcart humbly states that he served his time on board the

Duke of Savoy a port Victualler Capt. Richard Harman Commander and served on boarde your Majestys ship the Enterprise Capt. John Willet Paine & on board the [——]—[——] in Plymouth and unfortunately was on board the Schooner Maria & was taken by an Algerine Cruiser.

James Garnett humbly states that he was born in the County of Cork & served his time in the Newfoundland Trade. He belonged to a small boat which by bad weather was obliged to go to Salem and was condemned and was obliged to ship on board the Schooner Maria & is an unfortunate Slave.

[end of page]

1st Charles Colvil aged 24 years was born in N. Britain in Dundee—
2d Peter Smith aged 23 years was born in Dublin—
3d Philip Slone aged [30?] years was born in Liverpoole—
4th John Robertson aged 20 years was born in Glasgow—
5th Edward ORielly aged 25 years—was born in Dublin—
6th William Patterson, aged 24 years—was born in King Edwards Parish N. Britain
7th Robert McGinnis aged 17 years was born in [——]
8th George Smith aged 17 years was born in the Mnr. of Firth N. Britain
9th John Gregory aged 20 years was born in Liverpoole–
10th James Cathcart, aged 20 years, was born in Ireland and served his time out of London
11th James Harnett aged 19 years was born in the County of Cork in Ireland

Your Majestys Humble Petitioners lay at your Most Gracious Majestys Feet their Deplorable and Miserable state of Slavery Imploring Your Majestys Mercy to Relieve them & they As in Duty bound will Even exert themselves in Defence of their King and Country—

Of these eleven men, only Thomas Billings, also known as John Gregory, was among the redeemed who arrived in Philadelphia on February 9, 1797. The fates of the others were:

Redeemed by friends: Charles Colvil, John Robertson, William Patterson, and George Smyth or Smith. Colvil, Robertson, and Smith were subsequently reimbursed by the U.S. government for their ransoms. Colvil received $2,269.53, Smith $874, and Robertson $2,271. (Did the U.S. government realize they had claimed to be British?)

Died in prison: Peter Smith, Edward O'Reilly (however spelled), Robert McGinnis, and James Garnett or Harnett.

Released before the general redemption of 1796: Philip Sloan and James Cathcart. (Did Cathcart actually serve in the British navy as claimed?)

Appendix 7

Jefferson to Congress, December 30, 1790

[On December 30, 1790, Washington presented to Congress a detailed report by Jefferson as secretary of state on the prisoners at Algiers and efforts to secure their release (see *ASP,* 1:100–108). By this time a number of estimates and statements of the cost of redemption had been communicated to the Americans from various sources. They are here summarized by Jefferson.]

In 1786 the Dey of Algiers demanded from our agent 59,496 dollars for 21 captives, which was 2,833 dollars a man. The agent [Lamb] flattered himself they could be ransomed for 1,200 dollars apiece. His secretary informs us, at the same time, that Spain had paid 1,600 dollars [a man].

In 1787 the Russians redeemed at 1,546 dollars a man.

In 1788, a well-informed inhabitant of Algiers assured the minister plenipotentiary of the United States at Paris [Jefferson] that no nation had redeemed since the Spanish treaty, at less than 250 to 300 pounds sterling, the medium of which is 1,237 dollars. Captain O'Brien at the same date thinks we must pay 1,800 dollars and mentions a Savoy captain just redeemed at 4,074 dollars.

In 1789, Mr. Logie, the English consul at Algiers, informed a person who wished to ransom one of our common sailors that he would cost from 450 to 500 pounds sterling, the mean of which is 2,137 dollars. In December of the same year, captain O'Brien thinks our men will now cost 2,920 each, though a Jew merchant believes he could get them for 2,264 dollars.

In 1790, July 9, a Mr. Simpson, who at some particular request had taken pains to find for what sum our captives could be redeemed, finds that the fourteen will cost 34,792.28 dollars, which is 2,485 dollars a man. At the same date, one of them, a Scotch boy, a common mariner [Charles Colvil], was actually redeemed at 8,000 livres, equal to 1,481 dollars, which is within 19 dollars of the price Simpson states for the common man; and the chargé d'affaires of the United States at Paris is informed that the whole may be redeemed at that rate, adding fifty percent on the captains, which would bring it to 1,571 dollars a man.

It is found then that the prices are 1,200, 1,237, 1,481, 1,546, 1,571, 1,600, 1,800, 2,137, 2,264, 2,485, 2,833, and 2,920 dollars a man, not noticing that of 4,074 dollars because it was for a captain.

In 1786 there were 2,200 captives in Algiers, which, in 1789 had been reduced by death or ransom to 655. Of ours, six have died and one has been ransomed by friends [which would leave fourteen American prisoners].

From these facts and opinions some conjecture may be formed of the terms on which the liberty of our citizens may be obtained.

Appendix 8

The Portuguese Truce

Expilly Again

The first mention of the truce that I have found in the PRO files is in a letter of June 9, 1792 (FO 63/15), from Robert Walpole, the British minister in Lisbon, to Lord Grenville, the foreign minister, in which he reports:

> A Monsieur d'Espilly,[1] who Negotiated the Peace between Spain and Algiers is here; and has given in some proposals for a Negotiation of the same nature between this Court and Algiers; but his plan as yet seems too incorrect to be attended to by the Ministers of this Court.

Ten days later Walpole wrote (FO 63/15) to say:

> Monsieur d'Espilly who had been employed by the Court of Spain in the Negotiation of a Peace with Algiers, having stated in a long memorial which he presented to Monsieur de Mello the great advantages that Portugal might receive from a Peace with Algiers; and as an inducement to the success of his plan, having represented his own great consequence and consideration with the Grand Signor [the Ottoman sultan], and his Credit at the Court of Spain to which last he referred for a particular information of his merit there, which had been rewarded with pensions to himself and family . . . Monsieur de Mello in his conference with him upon this subject . . . acquainted Monsieur d'Espilly that his memorial, however plausible it might appear, did not contain any Arguments to induce this Court, to enter into a Negotiation with a person who had not been invited by this Court to confer upon that Business, and was not authorized, as he himself had confessed, by the Powers in question, to enter into a Negotiation on that matter, and having appeared without any avowed recommendations whatever, he could not be looked upon in any other light than as an

adventurer; and Monsieur de Mello therefore recommended him as such to the Lieutenant General of the Police; Monsieur d'Espilly was accordingly soon after taken into Custody, although he had been in this City for several weeks, without having been molested; and I believe he has been, after some confinement, obliged to leave this Country; during his imprisonment he applied to the Spanish Ambassador, but this Minister did not think him in any ways entitled to the Spanish protection.

British-Portuguese Cooperation

The British correspondence does not mention peace with Algiers again until France declared war on Spain and England in early 1793. The British sought Portuguese participation in their efforts against France and in particular asked that the Portuguese navy cooperate with theirs against the French fleet. The Portuguese responded positively, but they had a request. They wanted the British and Spanish to help negotiate a peace with Algiers so that their ships in the Brazil trade would not be exposed to the depredations of Algerine cruisers if their blockading squadron was removed from the Strait of Gibraltar. On March 31, 1793, Walpole, who had just returned from leave, reported (FO 63/16) that he had met with Pinto de Souza the day before and, the latter had said,

> Directions had already been given to the Commander of the Portuguese Fleet at Gibraltar, which consists of a Ship of the line, Four Frigates and other small armed Vessels to co-operate with the British Admiral stationed there, in any manner, that he should judge expedient for the service of the common cause; provided that such service required from the Portuguese Ships, should not be of a nature, which might expose the Portuguese Brasil Ships to be captured by the Algerines and Tunisians (the latter having lately threatened to attack the Portuguese) who might be induced to venture into the Ocean in search of them; in case the Portuguese fleet should be removed from their present Station, where they have for many years kept the Ships of the Algerines from passing through the Straits into the Ocean. That the circumstance of this War with the Algerines, depriving them of the free use of that part of their Marine; in the present Situation of Affairs, it was to be wished, that the Courts of Great Britain and Spain, could suggest, or take upon themselves some Measure with those Regencies [Algiers and Tunis], which might secure the Portuguese from being captured by the Algerines; and Mons. de Pinto alluded to the proposition of a truce being entered into between the Portuguese, Algerines and Tunisians, under the Mediation of Great Britain and Spain.

On April 13, Walpole reported (FO 63/15) that de Mello had subsequently "communicated" to him a letter from the Portuguese admiral at Gibraltar

> stating the Agreement which had been concerted between him and our Admiral, in regard to their jointly cruizing at a certain distance from Gibraltar, in such a manner that the British Ships should not give any protection to the Barbary Cruizers; and that the Portuguese Ships should give all their Assistance to the British in their pursuit of any French Ships.

Then, on April 15, Walpole wrote (FO 63/17) that the British ambassador at Madrid, Lord St. Helens, had reported that the Portuguese ambassador had been instructed to solicit the good offices of Spain in

> negotiating a peace between Portugal and Algiers, as I had observed to Your Lordship was the wish of this Court, or I suppose, as Mons. de Pinto mentioned to me, a Truce during the circumstances of the present War with France, in order to give full liberty to their force at Gibraltar.

Barring the discovery of a document showing that the British somehow planted the idea in their heads, there seems to be no doubt that the initiative for concluding the truce came from the Portuguese, and according to Logie's report of July 11, 1793, quoted below, they had been seeking one since 1786. The British were perhaps overzealous in carrying out the Portuguese request, but that the latter were also applying to Spain for help in the matter indicates that their request was serious, and the British cannot be faulted for taking it as such.

On April 29 an instruction from the Foreign Office (FO 63/17, pp. 90–93) addressed to Mace, Logie's designated successor who was evidently thought to be at Algiers, told him:

> From the enclosed extract of a letter from Mr. Walpole, you'll use your endeavors to accomodate the difference which has arisen between the Portuguese and the Regency of Algiers in order that the former may not be prevented from cooperating with the British Admiral for the service of the common cause. So His Majesty commands that you'll not fail to make use of the influence you may derive from the character with which you are invested in order to obtain so desirable an object as that stated in the extract in question either by means of a truce or by any other secure and satisfactory mode.

Mace, however, was stranded at Gibraltar, as noted, and Logie therefore received the instruction and acted on it. On June 25 he wrote to Dundas (FO 63/17, p. 101):

I had the honor to receive Your Excellency's letter of 29th April addressed to Consul Mace, containing His Majesty's commands on the subject of the inclosed extract of a letter from M. Walpole to Lord Grenville. I beg leave humbly to state that to obtain either a peace or a truce with this Regency, the negotiator must have powers, to promise that on the ratification the customary presents and all other sums stipulated shall be distributed, and if a truce, the periods it is to commence and end. The Neapolitans in the year 1786 through very large presents made a truce with the Algerines for three months, a few days after the same was ratified, the cruisers sailed and captured a number of Neapolitan vessels long before the truce expired. Her Faithful Majesty [Maria I, the queen of Portugal] at that time had a Negotiator here to treat for Peace, but the Demands of the Algerines were so exorbitant that he was obliged to return. Every other Nation but the British that has Peace with Algiers obtains it by very considerable Presents and yearly Tributes; taking all these difficulties under consideration with the offence the Algerines complain of, that of the Indulgences granted the Portuguese Squadron at Gibraltar after [their] having burned their [the Algerines'] cruizer, any application made to the Regency by His Majesty's Consul would have no good effect, on the contrary be of great prejudice to any future Negotiations her Faithful Majesty might wish to enter into.

Truce Concluded

In spite of this negative initial response, Logie wrote from Algiers two weeks later, on July 11, that he had asked the dey if he was disposed to receive a proposal for peace with Portugal. The Dey replied that "for upwards of two years past He has been repeatedly applied to by the Count d'Expille to Negotiate a Peace with the Portuguese, with offers of the same terms he had Negoceated the Spanish Peace, but that the Count was of a character he would transact no business with. That if I had any offers to make He would readily attend to them, and should not ask above two Thirds the Sum the King of Spain paid." Logie commented that since the Algerines were at war with the Dutch, they had no interest in a truce with any power "out of the Mediterranean." He also reported that "the Spanish Consul assured me that he had no instruction from his court to be a mediator on this subject" (FO 63/17, p. 113). This letter was passed to the Portuguese on August 27. In a note of October 9, Pinto de Souza expressed appreciation for Logie's efforts, but said the dey's terms were not "convenient" for Portugal (FO 63/17–50969). By this time, however, a truce had already been negotiated by Logie.

On September 27 Logie wrote (FO 63/17, p. 117) to Dundas:

> On the 11th of this month, the Dey concluded a truce with the Dutch for six months. So I profited from the occasion to propose a truce with Portugal and I succeeded in concluding a truce of one year, starting the 12th, September. Here I send you a copy, and a letter to Walpole who will convey the original to Portugal so that no break of peace will occur out of ignorance. Since I had no credentials I could not extend the negotiations [to discussion of peace terms].

A second letter of the same date enclosed a translation of the truce agreement, which Logie hoped the queen would ratify as soon as possible, and suggested she send "a person of respectable character (not like the previous one) [a reference to Expilly?] to negotiate a peace and ransom of her subjects." Logie noted that he had already given certificates to Algerine cruisers "that they should be allowed to pass freely and urged that since the Dey is so disposed to H.M. influence, peace should be negotiated as soon as possible" (FO 63/17, p. 121).

Walpole gave Pinto de Souza a copy of Logie's September 27 letter on October 11, and he received a formal rejection of the terms of the treaty in a seventeen-page (in translation) note from de Souza dated October 19. The note (FO 63/17–50969) says d'Expilly was acting without authorization from Lisbon, which had turned him away, chides the British politely for Logie's proceeding to implement the truce without waiting for Lisbon's ratification, and discusses the importance of maritime commerce for Portugal, which was dependent on food imports from America and the Hanseatic ports, and the need to protect ships in that trade. The note concludes with a proposal to modify the truce to commence with a four-month period during which the Algerines would not attack ships trading with Portugal, after which period they would continue to let ships carrying Portuguese cargo pass, whatever their nationality. If the Algerines accepted, the Portuguese would send someone to discuss terms for peace. If the Algerines did not reply by January 19, 1794, they would be considered to have rejected the terms and the Portuguese would issue orders to their navy to seize Algerine vessels.

The dey rejected these terms when they were presented to him by Logie on November 2, saying that he was going to honor his commitment and the Portuguese should do the same. He suggested they send someone to negotiate the terms of peace, at which time they could talk about protection of Portuguese cargoes. He then presented his own list of gifts and gratuities expected, which amounted in final form to about $2,300,000.

Note:

1. This is the "Comte d'Expilly," described as the Spanish consul, who was so helpful to the Americans in Algiers in the 1780s. Judging by the correspondence, he was a valued contact of the American chargé in Madrid, William Carmichael, who regarded him as very influential and intelligent. John Lamb, on the other hand, wrote to Jefferson on May 20, 1787, that Expilly was a "vile" man who had deceived Carmichael and been deported from Algiers and that "we have not had a worse enemy" there (EN, 3:515). The dey's unfavorable comment about Expilly's character reported by Logie on July 11, 1793, would tend to support Lamb's opinion, although Expilly does not seem to have been deported as Lamb claimed.

It seems clear that he was involved in the Spanish-Algerine truce of 1785 and the subsequent peace settlement. He was reported to be French by nationality and had a wife with him in Algiers who, remarkably, had a private audience with the dey to discuss her business affairs (AE B1 142, p. 178). She returned to Spain in 1786 with Lamb.

Charles-Roux reports in his *Travaux d'Herculais* that Herculais (discussed in chapter 7) had accompanied d'Expilly to Algiers, but neither he nor anyone else gives us Expilly's first name, date of birth, background, et cetera, and I have so far been unable to discover who he was, or what happened to him after he was expelled from Lisbon, or why the Spanish ambassador would not support him. He sounds like a diplomatic entrepreneur who hoped to make a commission on another peace treaty.

The French and Spanish biographic dictionaries are no help. They both list Expillys, but none whose details correspond with what we know about this one. I am still questing.

Appendix 9

Hasan Dey of Algiers to George III, March 27, 1794

Your late Consul having announced to us that the Queen of Portugal had interceded with Your Majesty to become a mediator in order to obtain a Peace or a Truce with us the Algerines and he the Consul was commanded by You to notify us that it would give your Majesty pleasure if we consented to make a Peace with the Portuguese or a Truce for one year, that during that time a Peace might be Negotiated between us and them. To this we answered that to oblige our good Friend the King of England we consented to make a peace upon those terms, through the mediation of England. After we had agreed to this a Portugese vessel arrives some days past from Portugal and notifies us that all the articles agreed upon between us, and your consul, the Court of Portugal will not accept of, as the English made them to please themselves, that they have no idea of such proposals, are not contented with or will admit them. If your consul had not announced to us, that You was mediator, and requested it of us in Your Name, we never should have thought of give [sic] any answer respecting a peace with Portugal.

The object that led us to resolve on this peace was to Revenge ourselves on Yours and our Enemies the Americans in the open seas by harassing and destroying them in such a manner so as to reduce them to the necessity of submitting to be your subjects again. The utility of this was more for your convenience than ours.

If Portugal according to the report of your Consul is not contented with and will not accept a Peace, Henceforward according to ancient custom, we do not permit the Portuguese ship to enter the Port of Gibraltar or block up the Strait. But if you should say that the Portuguese are your Friend and that you will not [sic] their entrance into Gibraltar and being supplied with the necessities they want, are we not your Old Friend and have an equal right to impartiality, the Friends ought not to wish for or promote injury to their Friends, those that do so are not to be named Friends, as they act contrary to Friendship.

The Portuguese some Years past Burnt and Destroyed One of Our Cruisers, at another time One of Your Cruisers fired Shott into one of Our Vessels and damaged her, and not long ago One of Your Ships with English Colours having fired Shott into one of Our Vessels, upon being asked why they did so, answered for their pleasure.

All this we have suffered from Our Friendship toward you being immutable.

Let us now leave what has passed. But [if] after the accept of the reasoning before you, You are to receive in the Port of Gibraltar the Portuguese Ships of war or supply them with the Necessaries if they come send them away. And if they have any enmity with us they may follow us into the High Seas. But if you say that as Christians you will Absolutely Protect them Your Friendship becomes useless to us. And if after the arrival of the present [i.e., after receipt of this letter] we newly learn that the Portuguese Ships have entered Your Port We will break the Peace and send away Your Consul. This act you will not lay to our charge as from the first of our Friendship neither the Portuguese nor any other Nation have Blockaded the Streights or could they do so without your consent. Without saying further then that on your receiving our letter and that We have Your Answer purporting that You impeed the Portuguese making use of Your Port Our friendship shall remain immutable.

Source: PRO FO 95 1/3, items 192 and 193. Item 192 is a formal Arabic document with the dey's *tughra,* his official signature; 193 is the translation above.

Appendix 10

The Dey's Wish List

[This list of the dey's demands for a hundred-year peace treaty, copied from the "Publick Register" of the regency by Cathcart on December 22, 1794, was reported by him in a letter of that date to Humphreys.]

The Dey demands on the part of this Regency, two Frigates sheathed with copper to mount 36 Guns, 12 pounders on the Gun deck & every way completely equipped, etc.

The Dey demands the United States of America to pay to the Publick Treasury of this Regency in Six different payments the sum of Six hundred thousand Algerine Sequins, Value in Mexican Dollars 1,080,000

The dey expects for his own private emolument three hundred thousand Algerine Sequins, equal to 540,000

The following sums (in dollars) to be paid to the Dey to be distributed by him at his own discretion:

For the Deys Wife and Daughter	60,000
For the Deys Khaznedar or Chamberlain	5,000
For the Deys two Head Cooks @5,000 each	10,000
For the two Wakil al-Kharj of the palace @3,000 each	6,000
For Haji 'Umar, first Moorish clerk	4,000
For Sidi Yusuf, second "	3,000
For the two Money Counters @3,000 each	6,000
For the Khoja [clerk] of the Palace Door	3,000
For the head Moorish Shawush [usher]	1,000
For the Moorish ushers	3,000
For 13 officers of Justice	5,000
For 62 Officers of the ancient Diwan	13,000
For 125 Cappa negroes or Officers of the pay table	39,000
	158,000

The Sum Exacted for the Ransom of one hundred American Captives is:

For 11 Masters & one Super cargo @ $6,000 each	72,000
For 14 Mates @4,000 each	56,000
For the Deys Christian Clerk [Cathcart]	4,000
For His three American pages or servants @ 4,000	12,000
For the Redemption of 70 Mariners @ 3,000	210,000
	354,000

The following sums are to be sent privately to the following Grandees Houses:

To the Khaznaji or Prime Minister	15,000
To the Agha or Generalissimo of the Turks [Arabs]	15,000
To the Khojat al-Khayl or Farmer General	15,000
To the Bayt al-Malji or "receiver de les droits d'Aubain"	15,000
To the Wakil al-Kharj or Intendant of the Marine	15,000
To the four Khojas or Turkish Secretaries @ 10,000 each	40,000
	115,000

The whole sum exacted for the Peace & Redemption of 100 American Captives is $2,247,000

Note: The above is based on the text as it appears in *NavDocs,* 1:89, and Barnby, *Prisoners,* 129, with the titles of officials put in modern orthography. The original document that Cathcart consulted (does it still exist somewhere?) presumably stated all amounts in sequins, not dollars. The document is interesting for what it says about the persons in the dey's household that he felt should be rewarded or pacified as well as for its insight into the scale of Algerine demands. Similar demands were made of the Portuguese at about the same time.

As chapter 6 indicates, the amount actually paid under the treaty of 1795 was about a third of the amount demanded originally. The contemporary account as published in the *Philadelphia Gazette* of February 10, 1797, was:

To be paid the Dey	$180,000
The Dey's family	60,000
Redemption of 100 captives	180,000
Department of Treasury	40,000
Hassan Agi [Khaznaji?]	8,000
The Chief Aga [Agha of the Arabs]	8,000
The Hadgi Cabello [Khojat al-Khayl]	6,000

The Viguel Hagi [Wakil al-Kharj] of the marine	7,000
To Sidi Adarhaman [Abd al-Rahman] [Bayt al-Malji?]	3,000
To 4 Hadgis [Khojas] of the Divan	12,000
To 2 Moorish Hadgis [Khojas]	2,000
To 2 Cantendors [?]	2,000
To the Dey's Drogoman [interpreter]	1,000
To the Dey's Viguel Hadgi [Wakil al-Kharj]	2,000
To the Hadgi [Khoja] of the Port	1,000
To the two Cooks	2,000
To the Harmadal [?]	1,000
To the Chiouz [Shawush]	1,500
To the Pertimel [?]	1,500
To the Novagees [?]	1,000
To the Casaha [?]	2,500
Sundry Officers of the Marine	3,000
To the Hadji [Khoja] of the Kappa [?]	1,000
	525,500
Additional expenses incurred by Mr. Barlow to complete the emancipation	117,000
	642,500

The paper goes on to say, "It was stipulated that the above amount should be made in marine stores in all of 1796 as follows" and appends a list of naval items demanded by Algiers that is quite different from that given to Cathcart which is described in the next appendix. It concludes, "The above was stipulated exclusive of cash; to the amount of 12,000 Algerine sequins annually was demanded in naval stores." This can be read to mean that part of the peace payment was to be made in naval stores, but the official account which can be found at note 16 of chapter 7 makes it clear that the naval stores were a separate item. The list in the *Gazette* does not appear among the documents from the consulate at Algiers.

Appendix 11

List of Naval Stores Requested by Algiers

On pages 397–99 of his *Journal* as published by the American Antiquarian Society, Cathcart states that on April 30, 1796, the dey presented to Barlow and him this list of naval stores requested as the annual gift:

1000 cwt of gunpowder
1000 pine planks from 22 to 24 piques[1] in length
1000 oak planks   "   "   "   "   "   "
10 cables of 18 inches [a measure of diameter]
10 cables of 14 inches
10 cables of 12 inches
10 cables of 11 inches
10 cables of 10 inches
10 cables of 9 inches
10 cables of 8 inches
10 cables of 7 inches
500 bomb shells of $5^{1}/_{10}$ english inches diameter and Calibro 16
500 bomb shells of $5^{8}/_{10}$ english inches diameter and Calibro 24
500 bomb shells of 6½ english inches diameter and Calibro 34
500 bomb shells of $6^{9}/_{10}$ english inches diameter and Calibro 42

On the following day, according to Cathcart, the dey summoned him and ordered him to tell Barlow not to forward the list, as "the Intendant General of the Marine was an Ideot and did not know what was wanted." On May 2 the dey gave the Americans a new list, summarized as:

35 tons of nails of various lengths from 5 to 13½ inches
34 cables of various diameters from 11 to 18 inches
2000 bomb shells of calibres 16 to 42
12 coils of white rope of various diameters from 8 to 10 inches
1000 long oars for frigates and chebeks [xebecs]
1000 cwt of gunpowder

1000 pine planks from 22 to 24 inches long [broad?] and 6 inches thick
1000 oak planks   "   "   " "   "   "   "   "   "   "   "
2000 pipe staves[2]
100 bolts of canvas
50 cwt of lead in sheets
100 dozen long tar brushes
100 cwt of white rope yarn
3000 pine planks or boards 3 inches thick

The dey said he realized that this was too big an order for one year's present, but it could be spread over several years.

Notes

1. The pic or cubit (Arabic *dhira'*) was a linear measure of variable length from 50 cm to 75 cm, depending on the locality and the commodity being measured.

2. Cathcart said he thought the number of pipe staves wanted was 20,000, not 2,000.

Appendix 12

Cathcart's Tunisian Truce

[This text, from a handwritten document in the Cathcart papers at the New York Public Library, is the translation of the truce that Cathcart negotiated with the Tunisian representative, Haj Ali, and the dey on November 8, 1795.]

In the name of the most merciful God.

In the name of God under our hands we give unto the american Ambassador a truce with our Regency for the United States of America, until he receives intelligence from America for which we allow the time of eight months by our special order unto Hamuda Bashaw, I Vizer Hassan Bashaw Dey of the city and regency of Algiers desires that he may command all the raises commanding vessels under his command and jurisdiction not to damage plunder or impede in his voyage any american vessel until the time herein specified shall be completed and they receive our second order given under my hand by order of Hassan Bashaw Dey of Algiers the 26th of the Luna Rahabia thani [Rabi'a al-thani] in the year of the Hegira 1210 which corresponds with the 8th of November 1795.

Signed Hadge Ally Vikel or Charge des affaires and agent for the regency of Algiers and Tunis.

Translated by James Leander Cathcart.

Appendix 13

Thomas Jefferson to Hamuda Bey of Tunis, June 8, 1806

[This text, with an accompanying French translation, has been provided by the Tunisian national archives.]

Thomas Jefferson, President of the United States of America
  To the Most Illustrious and Most Magnificent Prince
  the Bey of Tunis, the abode of happiness
Great and Good Friend,

I learned with great concern that the Commander of our Squadron in the Mediterranean, Commander Rogers [sic], deeming it his duty to ask explanations of menaces understood to have been signified towards the United States, had done this in a manner not consisting with the respect due to your Excellency's character, nor with the friendship which I bear you. In this, be assured that he was not governed by his instructions, which have inculcated, on all occasions, the greatest respect for your person and Government, and a spirit of conciliation in the execution of all his duties. Of this he will be made duly sensible on his return home, now daily expected.

The measure adopted by your Excellency of transferring the explanations by a special Mission, to this place, was a proof of that desire for the maintainance of peace between our two Countries which I have a pleasure of meeting and cherishing. I have accordingly received your Ambassador Soliman Mellimelli with all the cordiality and respect which a missionary from you so justly commands, and have endeavoured in all our conferences, to convince him of our sincere desire to preserve the peace and good understanding so happily subsisting between us, and of our firm persuasion that the interests of both Countries, well understood and calculated can be permanently established only by the practice of justice, equality and mutual forbearance. If the Ambassador has pressed too strongly, and persevered too inflexibly in certain demands to which we cannot accede, I have ascribed it to a laudable zeal for the promotion of your service, and a desire to merit that favor with you, to which his talents and fidelity so justly entitle him. He will be able to inform you, on the evidence of his own observation, that the character, the principles and the institutions of our Government, distinguish us essentially from the nations of Europe. Their practices can therefore be no rule for us. The law of our connection with other nations is to do justice and receive it, to ask and to yield nothing unequal. We hold particularly that nature having placed the ocean as a common highway for the intercourse of nations, all have equal right to its use, and in the maintainance of that right we calculate neither expence nor danger. For the correctness of these principles, we appeal with confidence to the known justice and high understanding of your Excellency, to whom your Ambassador has reserved the ultimate judgement on them. Colonel Lear, our Consul General for the Southern Coast of the Mediterranean, is accordingly instructed to repair to Tunis, and to confer on the affairs which touch us mutually. He will carry with him the hope of exchanging assurances that our former Treaty will continue to be the law of our observance, that the commerce and intercourse between our nations will be cherished, and that all our relations shall be founded on principles of equality and reciprocity, neither expecting to receive what he does not yield to the other.

In your letter of July 17, 1805 you reclaim a vessel which was taken, after repeated warnings, endeavouring to enter Tripoli, while blockaded by our Squadron. A nation is surely authorized, by the common reason of mankind, to restrain all persons from passing the circumvallation by which it beleaguers its enemy, whether by land or sea, and to treat the individuals or transgressors who attempt it by fraud or force. But our war with Tripoli being over, we can now relax with safety its rigorous rights, in confidence that being now better understood, they will in any future case be better observed. We take pleasure therefore in giving you a new proof of friendship by waiving the right acquired to us by the hostile act of this vessel and as, during her detention she suffered unavoidable decay, I have substituted one more worthy of your acceptance, in which your ambassador will take his passage.

I received by your Ambassador, acceptable tokens of your friendship for which I now return my acknowledgments, with an assurance that their highest value is found in the motive which offered them. Permit me, in return, to offer the same evidence of good will in such articles from our country as I have hoped would be most acceptable to you: and with these my prayers that God will have you, Great and Good Friend, in his holy keeping.

Done at Washington in the United States of America this Twenty Eighth day of June 1806.

Your Good Friend,
[signed] Th. Jefferson
By the President of the United States
[signed] James Madison Secretary of State

Notes

Preface

1. No longer in current usage, the term *Barbary* in English dates from at least the early sixteenth century. It came originally from the Arabic name for the Berbers, the indigenous inhabitants of North Africa, who called themselves by other names. It designated the area occupied today by Morocco, Algeria, Tunisia, and Libya.

2. See Sumner, *White Slavery in the Barbary States.*

Chapter 1. Algiers

1. Bauffremont, *Journal:* 43. We find the same attitude displayed 145 years later by Charles Oscar Paullin in *Diplomatic Negotiations of American Naval Officers, 1778–1883:* "The Barbary powers did not belong to the family of nations. Their rulers had little or no sense of honor, were childish and irresponsible, and possessed minds physically different from those in authority in Christian lands (8)."

2. Panzac presumably refers in the last sentence to the fact that diplomatic recognition was obtained directly by the regencies without the intermediation of the Ottoman government. Their degree of independence from Istanbul was variable. Each of the regencies had a different relationship with the central authority, and there were instances when the latter's mandate was clear and decisive, but there were others when it was ineffective or absent. For an informed discussion of this point see Shuval, "Ottoman Algerian Elite."

3. Although men from Asiatic Turkey were favored, anecdotal evidence shows that the Algiers janissary corps also recruited elsewhere in the Ottoman domains.

4. In 1786, for instance, four of the corsair ships were owned by government officials, three by the government, and the remaining four or five by individuals, according to one of the American captives.

5. When the Algerines declared war on the United States in 1785, however, there had been no prior relations between the two governments. There was, therefore, no consul to send away and no warning period. The Americans first learned they were at war when their ships were captured.

6. The Algerines were not alone in this belief. It was shared by British mariners and merchants in the early seventeenth century, according to Hebb (*Piracy,* 24), and a British naval expedition against Algiers in 1620 was quite unsuccessful. Britannia did not rule the waves in the first half of the seventeenth century, and the British had difficulty finding resources to maintain a fleet at sea for any length of time. Their first, and for many years only, real success against the corsairs was a blockade of Salé in 1637, and that succeeded only because the Moroccan authorities were willing to help subdue the Slawis (the people of Salé).

7. For full details of the raid, see Barnby, "The Sack of Baltimore."

8. The Carloforte incident was an international cause célèbre, and various foreign powers became involved in the negotiations to ransom the captives. They included the Russians, the Ottoman sultan, and the French, with Napoleon interceding personally on the captives' behalf. The final ransom price was 500 piastres, or $500, each. Salvatore Bono in *I corsari barbareschi* (329–30) records that of the 900 captives, 755 returned home in 1803. Eleven had been sold to the Algerines and 23 had been liberated previously, while some of the women elected to remain in Tunis and married eminent Tunisians. There were 117 deaths and 95 births. One of the women bore a son who became Ahmad Bey, a famous modernizing ruler of Tunisia from 1837 to 1855.

9. *ASP,* 1:29.

10. The term also occurs in French and implies a prison that is particularly disagreeable and involves forced labor. The prison called Devil's Island, for instance, was a *bagne.* While the origin of this usage is obscure, there is broad agreement that it is somehow related to the Muslim world. Bono says *bagno* came from the North African practice of keeping slaves in the baths, and the term was transported to Italy. The *Vocabulario della lingua Italiana* (Rome, Instituto della Enciclopedia Italiana, 1986, 383), on the other hand, says it referred originally to a prison in Livorno's Fortrezza Vecchia, partially below sea level and therefore damp, where Turkish captives were held, and the same term was applied to the prison at Constantinople where Christian prisoners were held before being sent to the galleys. Neither explanation is offered with any documentary evidence.

11. This was Venture de Paradis's estimate in 1789, based on the number of flour mills in the town—twenty-five, each of which could supply 2,000 people. The desire to find some reliable statistic from which to derive a total of this sort seems to have been common. Thus, Joel Barlow recorded in his notebook that there were 4,600 Jews in Algiers, a calculation based on the number of Jewish dead as recorded by a French missionary priest. The most rigorous study of the population question to date is in *La Ville d'Alger vers la fin du XVIIIe siècle,* by Tal Shuval, who points out that a population of 100,000 within the walls of the Qasbah would have given Algiers a population density of 2,174 persons per hectare, more than three times the density of central Cairo in the eighteenth century as calculated by André Raymond. Shuval thinks 50,000 would be a more reasonable maximum figure.

12. For more on this language, see the articles on lingua franca by Hugo Schuchardt in *The Ethnography of Variation: Selected Writings on Pidgins and Creoles,* trans. T. L. Markey (Ann Arbor: Karoma, 1979), and by Keith Whinnom in *Languages in Contact: Pidgins, Creoles,* ed. Jürgen M. Meisel (Tübingen: Günter Narr, 1977).

13. al-Madani, *Muhammad Uthman Pasha,* 158–59.

14. Shaler, for instance, records (*Sketches,* 16) that the dey formally convened the divan in 1816 to deliberate on the negotiations with Great Britain.

15. Barlow thought they were at the very bottom, below the Jews.

16. According to Mohamed Amine's *Commerce extérieur et commerçants d'Alger*

(see n. 20), of the total of 250 merchants in Algiers in the period 1797–1828, 173 were Jews belonging to 38 different families.

17. According to the transcript of his memoirs as edited by Ahmaf Tawfiq al-Madani, al-Zahhar spelled it in Arabic *wakil al- harj,* with an aspirated *h,* reflecting the confusion in Turkish between *h* and *kh.* This practice has been followed by those modern Algerian writers in Arabic whose works I have consulted (al-Madani, Nasr al-Din Sa'iduni, and Ali Abd al-Qadr al Halimi). The reader's confusion is increased by the fact that every military unit had a wakil al-kharj who served as quartermaster, and the term was also used for the majordomo of an Ottoman mansion or the dey's palace.

18. The spoon was but one manifestation of an intriguing culinary motif that ran through the janissary military structure. In addition to being organized by mess units, the janissaries used their cooking kettles rather than their flags as standards to rally around, and overturned them to signal revolt, while the cooks, titular and real, had an important place in the table of organization of janissary units as well as in the political structure of the Algiers ojak. The chief cook of the dey's palace, for instance, figured well up on the lists of officials to be rewarded when treaties were signed.

19. Gustave Gautherot, *La Conquete d'Alger* (Paris: Payot, 1929, 111).

20. Mohamed Amine, *Commerce extérieur et commerçants d'Alger à la fin de l'époque Ottoman (1792–1830).* An unpublished two-volume doctoral dissertation of 1991 from the University of Aix–Marseille, this is a detailed study based on the Turkish and Arabic documents on microfilm in the Archives d'Outre-Mer at Aix-en-Provence as well as the records of the French consulate at Algiers held at Aix and the consular correspondence in the archives of the Chamber of Commerce of Marseille. The Turkish and Arabic documents include five *daftars* or account books of Algiers merchants. They show a modest volume and variety of exchanges with ports ranging from England to the eastern Mediterranean.

21. Shaler comments that "it is a maxim with the Turks, to which they adhere with inflexible rigour, that what has been, acquires the force of law" (*Sketches,* 22).

22. Here, for instance, is the British consul's description of the change of regime on November 7, 1808: "the Dey in his palace was attacked by the Turkish soldiers and in endeavoring to make his escape over the terraces of the adjoining houses was shot, his body was thrown in the street, his head severed, and immediately presented to the new Dey, ordering him to look on it, threatening if he did not conduct himself better than his predecessor, a similar fate would attend him. The revolution was conducted with little or no disturbance, peace and quietness throughout the city was restored in less than an hour. Ali is the name of the present Dey of whom I have had an audience this day [November 10]" (FO 8/1).

Chapter 2. The Deys

1. Perhaps a reference to the following hadith: "Muhammad asked a man if he was married, and being answered in the negative, he said, 'Art thou sound and healthy?' Upon the man replying that he was, Muhammad said, 'Then thou art one of the brothers of the devil.'" Thomas Patrick Hughes, *Dictionary of Islam* (1885; Chicago: KAZI, 1994), 313.

2. The term *lanjur,* perhaps from the Spanish *lancha* or launch, seems to be used for a gunboat or bomb vessel.

3. The year is wrong. Cathcart records it as happening on May 26, 1788, and in a letter of August 5, 1788, the American consul in Alicante reports it as having recently occurred.

4. Barnby, *Prisoners,* 76, apparently quoting PRO FO 76/5 Tripoli 22 August 1793.

Chapter 3. First Steps

1. Bemis, *Diplomatic History,* 121, puts the cost of maintaining the navy in the Quasi-War with France, from 1798 to 1800, at $10 million, of which $6 million was for operations. He notes that they helped protect $450 million's worth of commerce which yielded an import revenue of $22 million. This would be a hundred times the $4.5 million total volume of American trade with the Mediterranean in 1770, as given in the preface, and reflects the improved economy resulting from Alexander Hamilton's guidance and the profitability of the neutral trade with a warring Europe. The potential trade with the Mediterranean from the perspective of 1776 would have been far more modest, but the cost of building and operating a navy to protect it still would have been considerable.

2. *JCC,* 5:578.

3. Irwin, *Diplomatic Relations,* 17.

4. *The Narrative of Joshua Gee* (Hartford, Conn.: Wadsworth Athenaeum, 1943).

5. Wharton, *Revolutionary Diplomatic Correspondence,* 2:731–32, 746–47.

6. *EN,* 2:358–61; Duncan, "Hostage Taking," 3.

7. *EN,* 2:529.

8. According to the records of the Stonington [Conn.] Historical Society, Lamb was born in 1740 and died in 1804 "in consequence of a wound received in a shipwreck off the coast of Spain." He probably went to sea at an early age and, judging by his writings, was poorly educated. Huntington's phrase "suffered much" may refer to Lamb's having been captured by the British while captain of a privateer in 1778. He and the crew were sent to Halifax and may have been held there as POWs. Before that, Lamb had engaged in gunrunning for the colonists. He had sailed for Gibraltar in 1774 and arrived back in Boston in December 1777, after a three-year absence, on a brig called the *Irish Gimlet* with a cargo that included "17 brass cannon with other warlike stores for the Congress" (letter book of Nathaniel Shaw, quoted in Frances Caulkins, *A History of New London:* New London, Miss Caulkins, 1852, 485, held by Connecticut Historical Society). That he had political connections is evidenced by Huntington's letter and by his correspondence with William Samuel Johnson, a wealthy statesman and jurist from Connecticut who was a member of Congress. Lamb's letters to Johnson are discussed in the next chapter. Lamb was still involved in the horse and mule trade with Morocco as late as 1795 (Irwin, *Diplomatic Relations,* 83).

9. *EN,* 2:546.

10. *EN,* 2:548–49.

11. *EN,* 2:553.

12. *EN*, 2:574–76.
13. *EN*, 2:529.
14. *PTJ*, 18:389.
15. The editorial note in *PTJ* speculates that he had delayed his departure for Europe to see if the *Alliance* transaction could be brought to completion.
16. *EN*, 2:821.
17. Duncan, "Hostage Taking," 7, quoting *JCC*, 23:419–20.

Chapter 4. The Crisis Begins

1. *The Captives*, 8–12. Cathcart's statement about the water in the kiosk of the admiralty is confirmation of the quality of the water supply that the dey, Muhammad bin Uthman, was credited by al-Zahhar with having extended to Bab al-Jihad, the admiralty gate.
2. *NavDocs*, 1:6.
3. According to Paul Randall's letter of April 2, 1786, to his father, only one of these men was actually an American.
4. Cathcart, *The Captives*, 17–18. O'Brien does not mention any humiliating circumstances of their lodging with Logie, which was a temporary situation in any event, but the story is also related in a contemporary report by the French consul de Kercy and was repeated with details by Paul Randall in his letter to his father. Given Randall's limited exposure to Algiers, his source may have been de Kercy, and his report may therefore be false confirmation. How seriously we should take de Kercy's report is hard to say. Judging by his comments about Logie and Lamb's ship, he did not like Logie and he may have been repeating gossip. The story was also reported in detail by Carmichael in Madrid.
5. *EN*, 2:852–53.
6. *EN*, 2:857–60.
7. *EN*, 2:878–79.
8. Franks (1740–1793) was a Canadian who had joined the Continental Army and served as Benedict Arnold's aide-de-camp. He had subsequently served as vice consul in Marseille and as a diplomatic courier. He appears to have been living in France.
9. Barclay's description of the treaty negotiations contains what may be a clue to the sultan's motivation: "When the proposition for an Exchange of Prisoners was read The King said 'This is not right, why are the Christian Powers so averse to go to war with me? It is the Fear of their Subjects falling into Slavery.' To which the Kings Preacher replied, 'These People deserve more indulgence from you than many others with whom you are in Alliance. They are nearer our Religion, and our Prophet mentions those who profess their manner of Worship with Respect.' Upon which the Emperor said, 'Let this article be admitted'" (*EN*, 3:319). For a different, and more detailed, explanation, see Bookin-Weiner and El Mansour, *The Atlantic Connection*, 19–29.
10. *EN*, 2:910–11. In the Cathcart papers at the New York Public Library are what appear to be the originals of letters from Jefferson (dated November 4) and Adams (dated October 5) addressed to O'Brien that Lamb was to deliver. The Adams letter merely expressed sympathy and asked O'Brien to thank Logie for his kindness. Jeffer-

son, on the other hand, said that since the commissioners had no authorization from Congress to pay ransoms, he was obliged to ask that the captains and their crews "bind" themselves to repay the costs of their own redemption if Congress required it. He further said that Lamb was instructed to "make no bargain without your approbation & that of the other prisoners each for himself." Lamb seems to have ignored that instruction and did not inform the prisoners fully of his discussions with the dey.

11. *EN*, 2:949, 3:85–89.

12. Expilly's views are in *EN*, 3:157, Vergennes's in 3:175–77.

13. *EN*, 3:137.

14. *PTJ*, 9:364.

15. It would have been a long wait. According to Ahmad Tawfiq al-Madani's *Harb al-thalatha mi'at sana* [War of three hundred years], the Algiers-Spain peace treaty was not signed until December 9, 1791, and did not enter into force until February 24, 1792, when Algerine troops entered Oran, which had been held by Spain until then. The treaty obliged Spain to pay 120,000 francs ($24,000) a year in tribute. Judging by the fact that he appeared in Lisbon in 1793 trying to sell a scheme for a Portuguese-Algerine peace, Expilly remained in Algiers until the Spanish treaty was signed.

16. *EN*, 3:192–99.

17. *EN*, 3:226–27.

18. The captives' letter is in *EN*, 3:420–23. O'Brien's account can be found in *ASP*, 1:119.

19. *EN*, 3:205.

20. Diary of Thomas Rodney, *LMCC*, 8:347.

21. *PTJ*, 10:139.

22. *EN*, 3:241–42.

23. *EN*, 3:322–23.

24. William Samuel Johnson Papers, Connecticut Historical Society, Hartford, nos. 112 and 116.

25. *EN*, 3:241.

26. *EN*, 3:435.

27. *ASP*, 1:291.

28. See, for instance, Thomas Rodney's diary for May 2, 1786, *LDC*, 23:256.

29. *LDC*, 23:223.

30. Listed as vol. 13, fols. 198, 200, 201, in Even, *Papiers*.

31. AE B1 142, fols. 178–179.

32. *NavDocs*, 1:6.

33. Playfair, *The Scourge of Christendom*, 177–79; FO 3/6 pp. 139–44.

34. FO 3/7, pp. 40–41; Mace to Dundas, January 12, 1794, FO 3/7, pp. 132–33.

35. Playfair, *The Scourge of Christendom*, 177–79.

36. *NavDocs*, 4:263.

37. McKee, *Edward Preble*, 135.

38. Barnby, *Prisoners*, 74.

39. It appears in *NavDocs*, 1:1–6, and in *EN*, 3:192–99.

40. O'Brien in this and subsequent letters reflects a conviction that peace with Algiers and the redemption of the captives could best be obtained through intermedi-

aries rather than by direct approach and that greasing the proper palms would greatly facilitate the process. In this latter regard, his attention focuses in particular on the khaznaji (the "Causenhage" in O'Brien's spelling at this point; later he is the "Noznagee") and Hasan, the wakil al-kharj (the "Micklassha" to O'Brien). According to O'Brien, Hasan chose to ignore, even though he thought it was probably true, the British report conveyed by Logie that the brig that had transported Lamb to Algiers was American and could therefore be seized. O'Brien hoped this sign of favor to the Americans would not be overlooked. Unfortunately, there was no follow-up to O'Brien's suggestions.

41. *EN*, 3:402.

Chapter 5. Things Get Worse

1. *EN*, 3:908.
2. *ASP*, 1:101. In a letter to John Jay of November 3, 1787, Jefferson commented: "My idea is that we should not ransom but on the footing of the nation which pays least, that it may be as little worth their while to go in pursuit of us as any nation, this is cruelty to the individuals now in captivity, but kindness to the hundreds that would soon be so, were we to make it worth the while of those pyrates to go out of the streights in quest of us as soon as money is provided" (*EN*, 3:643).
3. *ASP*, 1:128.
4. *ASP*, 1:290.
5. *EN*, 3:553.
6. *ASP*, 1:290–92.
7. *ASP*, 1:293.
8. *ASP*, 1:295.
9. *ASP*, 1: 297.
10. *ASP*, 1:297.
11. *LTDH*, 2:201.
12. FO 3/7, p. 188.
13. FO 63/17, 6 November 1793.
14. FO 95 1/3, 192 and 193.
15. *LTDH*, 2:205.
16. The Cutting quote may be found in Irwin, *Diplomatic Relations*, 58. The assurance from Lord Grenville reported by Thomas Pinckney in a letter of November 25, 1793 (NA London Despatches M30, roll 2), was that "with respect to the truce between Portugal and the Algerines this country [England] had not the least intention or a thought of injuring us thereby—that they had been applied to by their friend and by the Court of Portugal to procure a peace for them with the Algerines and that Mr. Logie had been instructed to use his endeavors to effect that purpose, that he finding the arrangement for a peace could not immediately take place had concluded the truce. . . . in this they conceived they had done no more than their friendship for a good ally required of them; but that the measure was also particularly advantageous to themselves as they wanted the cooperation of the Portuguese fleet to act against the common enemy, which it was at liberty to do when no longer employed in blocking the Algerine fleet. As I had stated that the Court of Portugal had promised a convoy

to the American vessels then in their harbours he assured me that they would give no opposition to that measure." Pinckney does not say whether he believed Grenville, but the tone of his letter does not imply that he was skeptical. He seems to have taken him at face value.

17. *ASP,* 1:299.

18. The full title is *A Journal of the Captivity and Sufferings of John Foss, Several Years a Prisoner at Algiers: Together with Some Account of the Treatment of Christian Slaves When Sick, and Observations on the Manners and Customs of the Algerines.*

19. Mattias Arkimboldus Skjöldebrand (1765–1813) and Per Erik Skjöldebrand (1769–1826) were the sons of Erik Brander (1722–1814), the Swedish consul in Algiers, who had been raised to the nobility as Skjöldebrand in 1767. Brander's wife, and the brothers' mother, was Johanna Logie (1740–1780), the sister of Charles Logie, the Americans' nemesis. Logie was thus the uncle of Mattias and Per Erik. This relationship is not mentioned in the published writings of the captives but was public knowledge at the time. It is ironic that the Skjöldebrands were so helpful while Logie was so unhelpful, at least in American eyes. I am indebted to descendants of Mattias now living in Stockholm for the genealogical information.

20. *ASP,* 1:413.

21. *ASP,* 1:414.

22. *ASP,* 1:414–15. By the term *power* Per Erik apparently meant credentials giving him authority to negotiate, but not appointment as an American consul or consular agent, because he declined that honor when it was offered to him. The Swedish foreign ministry informs me that there is no record of his having been offered or having accepted such a commission. He was nevertheless carried in the American records as late as 1923 as having served as consul. This, among other instances of error in the compilation *America's Diplomats and Consuls of 1776–1865* by the late Walter B. Smith II for the now defunct Center for the Study of Foreign Affairs at the Department of State's Foreign Service Institute, indicates that the Department's records of early consular appointments are not wholly reliable. Smith, for instance, found Charles Logie listed as acting American consul at Algiers in the period 1793–94!

23. *ASP,* 1:416–18.

24. Humphreys (*LTDH,* 2:196) estimated the cost of clothing an officer and a seaman:

For an officer	RV (*real vellón*)
2½ yards of cloth for a coat faced with the same 30 RV per yard	68
Pocket, back and sleeve linings	8
Buttons, hem and thread	8
1¾ yards of same cloth for waistcoat and breeches the former with hanging sleeves	52½
Lining and Buttons for ditto	16
Making coat, vest and breeches	45
1 pair of long Trousers of strong linen	22

2 pairs of stockings	32
2 ditto shoes	52
2 shirts	75
1 hat	_20_
	398½
For a seaman	
2 pairs of long trousers	44
2 shirts	70
2 pairs of shoes	50
1 hat	20
2 frocks	90
1 jacket with sleeves & a pair of breeches	_68½_
RV	342½

The *real vellón* was a Spanish copper coin worth almost 5 cents.

Chapter 6. Negotiations at Last

1. O'Brien in a letter of September 10, 1802, to the Department of State claimed that in 1787 Cathcart had been imprisoned in the dey's palace and given 500 strokes of the bastinado for "——testing with a Moorish woman" and would have lost his head but for the influence of a Captain George Smith on his behalf. (Unfortunately, the first half of the word describing his act with the woman is indistinct and Captain Smith is not identified.) Cathcart does not mention this in his narrative. O'Brien and he were on very bad terms by 1802, and O'Brien may have embroidered the account. It raises questions as to how Cathcart could have risen to the eminence he attained within the power structure of Algiers, but it would explain later Algerine refusal to receive him back as consul in 1802.

2. Cathcart owned (perhaps "leased" would be a better word) six or seven taverns by the time he left Algiers. At this point in his narrative he seems to have had three, one at the Galera, one at the Liddi Hamuda bagnio, and one at the "Madhouse."

3. PRO FO 95/1/3, 190–91.

4. The maritime states generally supported it, while the southern and inland states generally opposed it, arguing that it would cost less to pay tribute or even to hire the Portuguese to protect our shipping, and that navies posed dangers to liberties, while the cost of building and maintaining them could be a source of corruption. For a brief, detailed description of the rebirth of the navy, see Crawford and Hughes, *Reestablishment*.

5. *ASP*, 1:528. Gouverneur Morris, mentioned in Randolph's letter, was minister to Paris at the time. The French had requested his recall in April 1794 because of his royalist sentiments, but he remained at post until relieved by Monroe in August.

6. *ASP*, 1:529.

7. *LTDH*, 224.

8. Sloan is described at one point as having been one of the sweepers in the dey's palace. Elsewhere Cathcart says his job was that of "capitan a Proa." There were two of these, whose duty was "to keep the lower part of the Pallace clean to light the Dey

down the stairs in the morning ... to remove the soldiers beds that sleep at the door of the treasury and whatever the prime minister (the khanznaji) and store keepers of the Pallace should order them" (Library of Congress Cathcart Papers, reel 1, p. 20). On page 155 of the same reel Cathcart writes that the capitan a Proa's duty was to awaken the dey in the morning and that he "places himself under the Dey's window and placing his hands at each side of his mouth in order to make a conductor for his voice bawls out as loud as he can articulate Bon giorno Effendi (good morning my lord)." Venture de Paradis (*Tunis et Alger,* 213) gives a similar account of the morning ritual, but says the office holder was called *capitan prove*. The etymology is unclear. *Proa* is a Spanish term for a ship's prow. *Prove* would appear to be the plural of the Italian *prova,* meaning proof, trial, test, ordeal. In either case, the application here remains to be explained.

9. Donaldson was the third person selected to go to North Africa as consul in this period. First Jefferson had picked a merchant named I. Gabriels, who said his "experience with the coast of Barbary, from Morocco to Tripoli has been but inconsiderable as those countries are inhabited very thinly by a set of idle people, satisfied with the common support of life," to go to Algiers to negotiate a peace agreement. Then Jefferson resigned as secretary of state on December 31, 1793, and was succeeded by Randolph, who, after a cursory effort at finding Gabriels, who had temporarily disappeared (he later claimed that the letter of appointment had been misdirected), chose a Danish sea captain named Heysell to go to Algiers via Lisbon. Heysell went to Lisbon, found that Humphreys had left, and proceeded to Alicante but was not given permission to go to Algiers, and his mission died on the vine, as did Gabriels's appointment when he eventually resurfaced.

10. Born in Redding, Connecticut, in 1754 and a Yale graduate of the class of 1778, Barlow had a remarkably varied career as a military chaplain, poet, publisher, lawyer, politician, businessman, and diplomat. Along with John Trumbull, Timothy Dwight, Lemuel Hopkins, Richard Alsop, Theodore Dwight, and David Humphreys, he was one of the Connecticut (or Hartford) Wits—young men who wrote popular satiric verse on current events in the post-Revolution period. In 1788 Barlow went to Paris to promote and sell shares in a speculative land enterprise that failed. He remained in Europe until 1804, became a political journalist, addressed the French National Convention, and was made a citizen of France because of his republican writings. He ran unsuccessfully for office in the Savoy, survived the Terror, went into the shipping business, and made money through astute exploitation of American neutrality in the wars between France and her neighbors that continued intermittently from 1792 to 1812.

11. *NavDocs,* 2:98.

12. Monroe commented acidly after his recall in 1796 that Humphreys brought with him no credentials authorizing him to negotiate with the French, and the entire burden had fallen on himself.

13. *ASP,* 1:530.

14. Barnby (*Prisoners,* 177) notes that Donaldson's report of the negotiations does

not mention that the dey's first demand included two warships. Rather, the dey asked him, when they first met on Friday morning, what the United States would offer. Donaldson said it would not be proper for him to make a proposal, but he should wait to hear the dey's demands. The dey said he would have to consult the divan. Donaldson said he made the offer of $543,000 only under pressure from O'Brien, Cathcart, and Skjöldebrand and claimed that it was Bakri, not Cathcart, who presented the offer to the dey.

Chapter 7. Money Problems

1. The original (1795) and revised (1933) translations can be found in vol. 5 of *Treaties and Other International Agreements of the United States of America, 1776–1949,* comp. Charles I. Bevans, 13 vols. (Washington, D.C.: U.S. Government Printing Office, 1968–1976).

2. The gift of the yataghan was reciprocated with twenty yards of gold- and silk-embroidered muslin and two tea sets with gold spoons (*NavDocs,* 1:159). One wonders what the dey would have done with a tea set. I have been unable to trace the yataghan.

3. According to Cathcart, on the morning of O'Brien's departure he presented him, at his request, to the dey. Cathcart claimed that this was the first time O'Brien had been in the palace or spoken to the dey. This was untrue. The record shows a variety of contacts between the two when Hasan was wakil al-kharj and khaznaji. Cathcart also says that O'Brien kissed both the hands and feet of the dey, a humiliation that Cathcart did not appreciate. That does not sound like the O'Brien who emerges from the correspondence. It sounds more like payback time.

4. A sandal is a "kind of narrow boat with two masts used on the Nile and on the Barbary coast" according to Webster's Unabridged Dictionary. The word is not of Arabic origin and perhaps comes from the Italian *sandalo,* "punt or lighter," which may come from the Greek *sandal,* meaning "sandal."

5. The lack of a commission is strange, since Barlow was given Hicheborn's, with the latter's name crossed through and his written in its place, according to Barnby (*Prisoners*: 265). I have not come across this document.

6. It is not clear how, if the letter was unopened, Cathcart knew what it said. Humphreys may have sent along a copy. Barnby claims (*Prisoners,* 207) that Cathcart subsequently opened the letter and responded to it with an explanation that the dey was too illiterate and ignorant to understand Humphreys's elaborate explanation. It is clear from Cathcart's account, however, that he was responding to Humphreys's February 7 letter to himself (reproduced in his *Journal,* 377–85) rather than to Humphreys's letter to the dey. In brief, Humphreys says he has been too ill to write as much as he would like, explains the problems of distance and transit times (not to mention weather, the modest resources of the Americans, who are a race of farmers, and the effect of the war between England and France on the currency markets), notes that he has not heard from Philadelphia for seven months and London for two, says

he is doing his best, asks for patience and understanding, and commends Barlow to him.

7. The frigate is a medium-sized war vessel. Those of the period were square-rigged, larger than a corvette and smaller than a ship of the line, had a single gun deck, and carried 36 to 44 guns.

According to Barnby, the proposal to give the ship to the dey's daughter, rather than to him directly, was a dodge to get around the fact that Barlow did not yet have any official standing for dealing with the dey. I found no mention of that in the records, and according to Cathcart the dey had recognized Barlow's consular status on April 6.

8. Cathcart and the Algerines, for instance, estimated the cost of masts at $30 each, whereas the true price was $200–450, depending on quality and size, plus the expense and difficulty of shipping.

9. There is occasional mention in the correspondence that some members of the European community in Algiers had their wives with them, but few details are given. Cathcart alleged that the British doctor had a Spanish trollop with him, and Expilly, the Spanish representative, mentions his wife being with him, but Barlow's remark is the first indication in the American documents of social life among the foreigners in town. Boyer reports (*Vie quotidienne,* 255) that in the early nineteenth century there was an active social life among the consuls and their wives and children, who were numerous, and that foreign merchants might or might not be invited to participate, depending on their standing. The existence of a lively social life among the foreigners is confirmed by the correspondence of Tobias Lear, who served as American consul general from 1803 to 1812.

Barlow may have thought Herculais—Louis-Alexandre d'Allois d'Herculais (1754–1842)—"a charming lad," but François Charles-Roux in *Les Travaux d'Herculais* comments on him that it was rare to find in one man someone who was "incompétent, maladroit, brouillon, intrigant, sectaire et hypocrite." A French military officer of aristocratic birth and checkered career, he had ingratiated himself with the Committee of Public Safety, which made him a special envoy to the governments of North Africa and the Levant in September 1794. His instructions, which he had drafted himself, gave him wide latitude to interfere in and report on the operation of French consular establishments and the loyalty to the Revolution of their personnel and those of the local French "nation"—the merchants in various French *échelles* or trading stations. By Charles-Roux's account, the damage that he did, or attempted to do, to French consular personnel and French traders was atrocious, and the harm he did to French relations, particularly in Tunis, would last for some time.

10. The vessel in question was a Norwegian or Neapolitan prize that Cathcart had bought with profits from his taverns. The polacca (French *polacre*) was a two- or three-masted vessel. The two-masted or brig version was square-rigged, while the three-masted or ship version had one or two lateen-rigged sails. From his description of it, Cathcart's polacca was a ship version. Although *polacca* is Italian for polka or for a Polish woman, the name may come from the Genovese *bollaco,* meaning mast.

11. The *Sophia* is not listed in the register of U.S. Navy ships, although she was the property of the United States government. In the consular records from Algiers there

is a copy of her captain's commission, signed by John Adams as president and dated December 20, 1798, that describes her as "the armed brigantine *Sophia*." This was a good two years after the vessel was put in service as a courier and cargo vessel for American officials in the region. I can find no record of her ownership within the government, but she looks to have been the first, and perhaps only, armed vessel operated by the Department of State.

12. This is recognizably Arabic except for the first phrase, *senza fede*, Italian for "without faith."

13. Jean Bon Saint-André, whom Barlow described as having been one of the most famous satellites of Robespierre.

14. Charles-Roux's account of this affair (*Les Travaux d'Herculais*, 120–24) is somewhat different. According to him, the French government had wanted to borrow a million piastres—about $1 million—from the dey to help it pay off some of its debts to the Bakris and "Abouhaia" (Simon Abukaya?). The dey consented to lend them only 200,000, of which Herculais, not Saint-André, put half at the disposition of Paris and deposited the other half with the Bakris to permit him to pay off local debts. Barnby in his account, citing Charles-Roux, says that the dey's unprecedented generosity to the French was a response to the willingness of the Directoire to compensate a French merchant from Toulon named Meifrund or Meyfrun, an old friend of the dey (and also the brother-in-law of the French consul, Vallière), for losses suffered in being forced to flee France because he had cooperated with the British when they occupied Toulon. Barnby appears not to have read the entire passage. On page 85 Charles-Roux reproduces the text of a letter of June 22, 1796, to Herculais authorizing him to offer Meyfrun 100,000 livres ($20,000) in return for persuading the dey to lend the million piastres and forcing the bey of Tunis to pay for some French naval vessels seized by the British at La Goulette in March 1796. But on the following page he reports that before Herculais had received this authorization the dey, when he received the new consul, Saint-André, had dropped his request regarding Meyfrun and promised not to speak of it anymore.

15. NA Algiers, reel 3, p. 188.

16. The alert reader will have realized by now that the account in this chapter of the payments to the Algerines only adds up to $538,000 in cash:

$200,000 borrowed from the Bakris
$200,000 brought by O'Brien
$100,000 sent from Livorno by Donaldson
$20,000 paid by Donaldson to Solomon Bakri for presents given at the time of the treaty signing
$18,000 to Micaiah Bakri for bakhsheesh

The total cost of the treaty was some $454,000 more, according to this account submitted to President Washington on January 4, 1797, by Secretary of the Treasury Oliver Wolcott:

Payments stipulated at the time of closing the treaty, to the Dey, and the treasury, for the redemption of the captives	$525,500
For [dey's] percentage on the captives*	27,000

Peace presents, consular presents, etc	60,000
Commission to Jew broker, presents to principals, etc	30,000
Amount of money to be paid in Algiers	$642,500
Which, with the expense of remitting from London to Algiers will amount to	$702,758.81
[meaning a charge of more than 9 percent]	
To which add:	
Payments to Colonel Humphreys, pounds sterling	3,471
Payment to Capt. O'Brien	31
Sterling pounds 3,502	or $15,564.44
Naval stores stipulated	124,413
Freight of said stores	50,000
Expense of frigate promised	99,727
TOTAL	$992,463.25

*The dey customarily received 11 percent of prisoner ransoms. This suggests the price for the captives was $245,455.

I have found no mention in the consular correspondence of receipts for any of these amounts paid, either in cash or in kind, nor is there any indication when and how the $200,000 was repaid to the Bakris. Many of the papers of the Treasury Department for the period have been lost and my inquiries at the National Archives indicate that finding such receipts at this point, assuming they were there to begin with, would be a hopeless task.

17. The descendants of Mattias Skjöldebrand (Per Erik's line died out in the nineteenth century) in Stockholm were unaware of their ancestor's involvement with the Americans or the honor done them by naming the vessel until I informed them of it. Howard Chapelle's *History of the American Sailing Navy* shows the sail plan of the *Skjoldebrand* on page 138 and describes it as "of value in illustrating the American conception of a small cruiser for the Mediterranean for the period." She was designed to carry twenty 4-pounder cannon.

The *Lalla Aisha* was a smaller vessel, designed to carry eighteen 4-pounders. According to Chapelle, the most effective vessel of the lot was the brig or brigantine *Hassan Bashaw*, which proved to be unusually fast and was used as a model for the design of later vessels.

O'Brien reported in a letter of March 17, 1800, that the frigate *Crescent*, in spite of all the care that had gone into her specifications, had developed dry rot: "It is very visible to me but I am in hopes that this year she will be run on shore, or be taken by the Portuguese if so it will be rendering the united States a service and saving much difficulties." Lear reported that three of these vessels were scrapped in 1806 as unfit for service.

18. For fuller details of the *Washington* story, see Allen, *Our Navy and the Barbary Corsairs*, 75–87, from which the above account is taken.

19. Tobias Lear (1762–1816) was born at Portsmouth, N.H., son of a prosperous shipmaster. He attended the Governor Dummer Academy and graduated from Harvard in 1783. He served as Washington's private secretary from 1785 to 1792 and was

reappointed as his military secretary in 1798. He was with Washington at the time of his death and was the last person to whom Washington spoke. His close association with Washington earned him appointment in 1801 as consul in Santo Domingo, where he served with distinction during the rise of Toussaint l'Ouverture and the French occupation of the island. The French general in command, Leclerc, forced him to leave in 1802.

20. *Navdocs,* 6:493
21. *ASP,* 3:211.

Chapter 8. Tripoli, Tunis, and Morocco

1. The first six frigates produced by the Americans were of a new design, longer and heavier than the frigates used by the British and French, and were built to overcome anything the Barbary states could put in the water.

2. When the language of this treaty, along with other treaties in Arabic, was reviewed by the noted Dutch orientalist Dr. C. Snouk Hugronje in 1930, he discovered that the eleventh article, which in English stated that the United States "is not in any sense founded on the Christian Religion,—as it has in itself no character or enmity against the laws, religion or tranquility of Musselmen . . . no pretext arising from religious opinions shall ever produce an interruption of the harmony existing between the two countries," had "no equivalent whatever in the original Arabic." He describes the Arabic text at that point in the treaty as being a letter from the dey Hasan to Yusuf Pasha informing him of the peace Algiers had concluded with the Americans and recommending its observation. "Three fourths of the letter consists of an introduction drawn up by a stupid secretary who just knew a certain number of bombastic words and expressions occurring in solemn documents, but entirely failed to catch the real meaning." See volume 53 of *The Consolidated Treaty Series,* ed. Clive Parry, 231 vols. (Dobbs Ferry, N.Y.: Oceana, 1969–81). The United States in 1796 had no one literate in Arabic to call upon as a translator.

3. Irwin, *Diplomatic Relations,* 128.

4. There was a good deal of family life on the *Chesapeake.* Midshipman Henry Wadsworth, whose journal provides some of the rare light notes in *Naval Documents,* recorded that Mrs. Morris gave birth to another son on June 10, 1803. She had not been the only pregnant woman on board. On February 22, 1803, "Mrs. Low (wife to James Low, captain of the forecastle) bore a son in the Boatswain's storeroom." He mentions as also being present the wives of the boatswain, the carpenter, and the corporal, so there were at least five women on board at that point.

5. McKee, *Edward Preble,* 201. This was not the view of the Americans and foreign consuls in Tripoli. Bainbridge wrote to Lear from prison on January 14, 1804, that Yusuf "will never be forced to terms without he considers his own safety endangered; and he is only Vulnerable to the United States one way; that is by eight or ten thousand men landing near his town, which in my opinion would be an easy conquest here."

6. *NavDocs,* 3:337.
7. *NavDocs,* 3:350.
8. *NavDocs,* 3:378.

9. *NavDocs,* 4:516.

10. The French initiative was stimulated by the American minister in Paris, Robert Livingston, on his own, without instructions. Levitt Harris, the chargé in St. Petersburg, took similar action on his own and reported that the Russian minister in Istanbul had been directed to raise the matter with the Porte. His representations, if made, do not seem to have had any effect on Yusuf.

11. This account is based on the French text, as well as the English text in *NavDocs,* 3:542–44, of Beaussier's letter to Preble of March 28, 1804.

12. A request to the archives of the Kingdom of Naples (at Naples) for documents relating to U.S.–Neapolitan cooperation in the bombardment of Tripoli turned up only an exchange of internal correspondence between different Neapolitan naval offices in 1837, thirty-three years later, on the subject of the bomb vessels, gunboats, matériel, and personnel lent to Preble, inquiring whether he had ever paid for them. The answer was that the U.S. Navy agent in Naples had paid 2,961.82 ducats (about $6,000) for them in October 1804 and there were no outstanding bills due. The Neapolitans must have been scratching for funds.

13. *NavDocs,* 4:389.

14. *NavDocs,* 4:393.

15. *NavDocs,* 4:394, 397.

16. *NavDocs,* 4:481.

17. Yusuf had agreed in the peace treaty to release Ahmad's wife and children, who had been held hostage in Tripoli, but Lear unaccountably signed a secret protocol agreeing that this could be delayed four years because Yusuf feared Ahmad would try a coup against him. Revelation of this some two years later added to the recriminations leveled against Lear by Eaton and others.

18. Eaton, in a letter of April 30, 1799, soon after his arrival in Tunis, described Hamuda as "a man of good sense, penetration, much humanity and some information." For a detailed description of the government and society of Tunis in this era, see L. Carl Brown, *The Tunisia of Ahmad Bey, 1837–1855* (Princeton: Princeton University Press, 1974).

19. Barlow enclosed an extract of Herculais's letter of April 6, 1797, with his of August 17:

> I cannot, my friend, be silent to you about the behavior of Famin. It is certain that holding Naples on one side and America on the other he sacrifices one or the other in a revolting manner. For Naples, that is all very well; but for you, my dear Barlow, I'm even more angry that it is I who procured this Janus for you.

Famin evidently was representing the kingdom of Naples as well as the United States.

20. I am grateful to Leon Carl Brown for pointing out that according to volume 3 of Ibn Abi Diyaf's *Ithaf Ahl al-Zaman bi Akhbar muluk Tunis wa 'ahd al-Aman,* by Yusuf's own account he was from Moldavia (al-Boghdan). Venture de Paradis speaks very highly of Yusuf, whom he too classifies as a Georgian.

21. Brand's tale of woe concludes with an account of his voyage. He had left Gibraltar in January thinking that peace had been concluded with all the Barbary states and had gone to Barcelona where he had sold his cargo. He had set out from

there to Sete, but had been forced to take shelter from a gale at Agde, where he had been robbed of $8,000 by a group of men who came on the vessel at night. He had waited for three months at Sete hoping for an "indemnity" from the French government but had finally been informed by Monroe in Paris that it was hopeless. He then used what money he had left to buy nineteen pipes of brandy and sailed for Málaga, to be captured by the Tunisians en route.

22. *ASP*, 3:126. *Sackatappa* looks like yet another deformation of sahib al-tabi'. *Regalia* is from the Italian, meaning gift or tip, and presumably was used here to indicate that this item was considered an addition to the treaty payment.

23. T-303, roll 1.

24. Allen, *Our Navy and the Barbary Corsairs*, 68.

25. According to Wright and Macleod (*First Americans*, 70), the whipping was administered "at the Marine Gate for spreading reports of American weakness and the dependence of the United States on France for its liberty." Samuel Edwards in *Barbary General* says it was punishment for Famin's having tried to bilk an American ship's captain of $1,000. I have been unable to find an account of this event in the papers from the Tunis consulate at the National Archives, although they are full of Eaton's remarks about Famin's duplicity and unhelpfulness. Famin had hoped to be appointed consul, and had greased local palms to keep rivals out. When he was not appointed, he put in an exaggerated claim for remuneration for his efforts and expenses and seriously overcharged Eaton for housing expenses. Eaton claimed that, among other things, he had deliberately misled the Americans and Tunisians as to each other's positions in negotiations. Eaton reported that when he was called before the bey on May 28, 1800, to account for his actions, the bey had been astonished to hear what Famin had done and "had shown a manliness, an impartiality and a justice which would not have disgraced an Elsworth." Eaton's reference, misspelled, is to Oliver Ellsworth of Connecticut, a framer of the Constitution and the third Chief Justice (1796–1800).

26. Journal of Hezekiah Loomis, steward of U.S. brig *Vixen*, *NavDocs*, 6:199–100.

27. Mellimelli was Bash Hamba or chief of the palace guards, according to Panzac. Judging by his name, he was a Turk. He has descendants in Tunis today.

28. *NavDocs*, 6:256.

29. *NavDocs*, 6:264–70.

30. *NavDocs*, 6:205.

31. In *NavDocs*, 6:iii, for instance, the incident is classified as "the notably successful use by Commodore John Rodgers of diplomacy in combination with a demonstration of naval force in a crisis threatening a full-blown outbreak of war with Tunis."

32. This letter, the full text of which is in appendix 13, does not appear in either *Naval Documents* or the American state papers collections of Lowrie and Clarke or T. B. Wait, nor have I found it in any of the collections of Jefferson's writings published to date.

33. T-303, roll 3.

34. Paullin, *Commodore John Rodgers,* 168.

35. *NavDocs,* 6:508. This episode deserves a more detailed study than it has yet received, with a comparison of American and Tunisian archives on the subject. The fullest description to date of Mellimelli's adventures in America is the article by Louis B. Wright and Julia H. Macleod entitled "Mellimelli" in the *Virginia Quarterly Review,* no. 20 (1944), 555–65.

36. Irwin, *Diplomatic Relations,* 82–84.

37. Ibid., 114–16, 131–34. For more details of the *Mashuda* affair and its sequel, see McKee, *Edward Preble,* and Allen, *Our Navy and the Barbary Corsairs.* Other accounts can be found in Whipple, *To The Shores of Tripoli,* and Kitzen, *Tripoli and the United States at War.* For a very brief Moroccan account, see the article by Mohamed El Mansour in Bookin-Weiner and El Mansour, *The Atlantic Connection.*

38. In 1904, Ion Perdicaris, a prominent Tangier merchant who claimed American citizenship, together with his son-in-law, a British subject named Cromwell Varley, was captured by a Moroccan tribal chieftain named Raisuli, who demanded a large ransom, the punishment of certain local officials, and recognition of his own authority in a significant portion of northern Morocco as the price for their release. The United States held the Moroccan government responsible, urged it to meet Raisuli's demands, and sent detachments from the Atlantic and Mediterranean fleets to Tangier. The two men were released unharmed largely as a result of French mediation with the sultan.

Chapter 9. Relevance

1. According to Paul F. Boller Jr. and John George in *They Never Said It* (New York: Oxford University Press, 1989), 105, what Pinckney actually said he said was "not a penny! not a penny!" According to Bartlett, his actual words were "not *a damned penny* for tribute." For his part, Jefferson in a letter of 1791 to Thomas Barclay said, "We prefer war in all cases to tribute under any form, and to any people whatever," according to H. L. Mencken's *A New Dictionary of Quotations* (New York: Knopf, 1942). Thus the sentiment was there, even if the attribution was erroneous.

2. An example of the tough approach was President Nixon's casual press-conference statement on March 2, 1973, that the United States would not pay "blackmail" to the Palestinian organization (the PLO) that was holding Ambassador Cleo Noel and chargé d'affaires George C. Moore captive in Khartoum. This disrupted delicate negotiations for their release then in progress, and the two were murdered soon thereafter. This did not endear Nixon to the Foreign Service. See David A. Korn's *Assassination in Khartoum* (Bloomington: Indiana University Press, 1993).

3. Playfair, *The Scourge of Christendom,* 23. The Algerines may have been rogues, but they were not notably devious. Indeed, the consular reports give an impression of direct dealing, with no hidden agendas on their part, bringing to mind the song of the pirate king in *The Pirates of Penzance:* "But many a king on a first-class throne, / If he wants to call his crown his own, / Must manage somehow to get through / More dirty work than e'er I do." It was the preemptory and often unreasonable nature of their

demands, and the frequent inability or unwillingness of the other party to deliver as demanded, that made dealing with the Barbary states difficult.

4. Eaton penned a postscript to his copy of one of Cathcart's letters (dated August 8, 1799) saying that while both Cathcart and O'Brien were men of scrupulous integrity, the two hated each other "mortally."

5. The role the navy continued to play in the Mediterranean in the nineteenth century is well described by Field in *America and the Mediterranean World, 1776–1882*. For a description of the role of America's European fleet in connection with a crisis at Beirut in 1903, see the article "Gunboat Diplomacy" in the supplement to the 1985 *Proceedings* of the Naval Institute.

6. Paullin, *Diplomatic Negotiations*, 7–9.

7. The estimate is based on the figures in *NavDocs*, 6:329.

8. *NavDocs*, 3:12.

9. See, for instance, Shelley Slade, "The Image of the Arab in America," *Middle East Journal* 35, no. 2 (1981), describing a survey conducted in 1980 in which almost half the respondents thought Arabs mistreated women and were barbaric, treacherous, warlike, and bloodthirsty.

Postscript. Return of the Natives

1. On the same page was an advertisement for the sale of "An Elegant Phaeton, with plated harness for a pair of horses, belonging to the President of the United States.... It was made by one of the best workmen in Philadelphia, and has been little used." Our presidents once had to provide their own conveyances.

2. This is the text as it appears in the microfilm of files from the consulate in Algiers in the National Archives. The obverse of the original carries the notation

Joel Barlow July 12 1796

rec d open from Capt. Newman (master of the Thomas, from Boston) Feb. 9,

1797—Who said the Captives had Mr. Barlow's permission to take a copy of it,

which he said he had given to a printer to be published.

The version published in the *Philadelphia Gazette* on February 24, 1797, differs only in a few typographical details.

3. I am indebted to Bertram Lippincott of the Newport Historical Society for this information.

4. The full text of the first and second editions of Foss's journal is on M Cards 2 #33746 and #33747, respectively. Much of it is contained in Baepler's *White Slaves, African Masters*, which is much more readable than the microform.

5. Edgar Stanton Maclay, *Moses Brown, Captain U.S.N.* (New York: Baker and Taylor, 1904).

6. The house was demolished in 1889 and the large tract that went with it turned over to the developers. It gave its name to the fashionable street and the quarter that extends from Massachusetts Avenue to Connecticut Avenue, from roughly P Street to Kalorama Circle. The house was located on what is now S Street between the Textile Museum and the Myanmar embassy, formerly Herbert Hoover's house.

7. Wright and Macleod, *First Americans*, 199.

8. The house was located about three kilometers southwest of the town in a hilly region with a view of the sea. The consulates of Britain, France, Sweden, Denmark, Spain, Holland, Sardinia, and Naples also had country residences, according to the map that faces page 320 of Playfair's *Scourge of Christendom*.

9. For a readable, detailed account of Lear's life, see *The Checkered Career of Tobias Lear,* by Ray Brighton.

Bibliography

There has been much writing on the Barbary powers and their relation with the rest of the world. These works are some of the more interesting and useful.

Abun-Nasr, Jamil M. *A History of the Maghrib in the Islamic Period.* Cambridge: Cambridge University Press, 1987. A standard scholarly work on North Africa since the seventh century. Useful for background.

Allen, Gardner W. *Our Navy and the Barbary Corsairs.* Boston: Houghton, Mifflin, 1905. Scholarly and reliable, with a great many details about the navy's actions.

Allison, Robert J. *The Crescent Obscured: The United States and the Muslim World, 1776–1815.* New York: Oxford University Press, 1995. An interesting study of American public and political reaction to the events in Barbary. Illustrated.

American State Papers: Foreign Relations. Vols. 1–2. Washington, D.C.: Gales and Seaton, 1832. A collection of official documents, many relating to the Barbary problem.

Baepler, Paul, ed. *White Slaves, African Masters: An Anthology of American Barbary Captivity Narratives.* Chicago: University of Chicago Press, 1999. Extensive excerpts from the Cathcart and Foss narratives, as well as numerous others. Useful introduction. Illustrated.

Baker, Thomas. *Piracy and Diplomacy in Seventeenth-Century North Africa: The Journal of Thomas Baker, English Consul in Tripoli, 1677–1685.* Edited by C. R. Pennell. Cranbury, N.J.: Associated University Presses, 1989. An interesting firsthand account of diplomatic life among the corsairs in the seventeenth century.

Barnby, H. G. *The Prisoners of Algiers: An Account of the Forgotten American-Algerian War, 1785–1797.* London: Oxford University Press, 1966. The best single account of the capture and eventual release of the American prisoners in Algiers. Much background detail.

———. "The Sack of Baltimore." *Journal of the Cork Historical and Archaeological Society* 74, no. 220 (1969).

Bauffremont, Joseph de. *Journal de campagne de l'amiral de Bauffremont, prince de Listenois, dans les pays barbaresques (1766).* Edited by Marcelle Chirac. Paris: Editions du Centre national de la recherche scientifique, 1981. A naval officer's observations on the Barbary states.

Belhamissi, Moulay. *Les Captifs algériens et l'Europe chrétienne, 1518–1830.* Algiers: Entreprise Nationale du Livre, 1988. A study, based largely on European sources, of the treatment of Algerian captives in Europe.

Bemis, Samuel Flagg. *A Diplomatic History of the United States.* 5th ed. New York: Holt, Rinehart and Winston, 1965.

Benchérif, Osman. *The Image of Algeria in Anglo-American Writings, 1785–1962.* Lanham, Md.: University Press of America, 1997. A survey by a former Algerian ambassador to the United States. Gives a rare Algerian perspective on the subject.

Bono, Salvatore. *I corsari barbareschi.* Torino: Edizioni RAI, 1964. By the leading Italian specialist. Full of details about the Barbary corsairs and their European opponents.

———. *Les Corsaires en Méditerranée.* Translated by Ahmed Somaï. Paris: Paris-Méditerranée, 1998. Originally published as *Corsari nel Mediterraneo* (Milan: Mondadori, 1993). Deals with European as much as Barbary piracy and privateering. Full of surprising facts about the scope and nature of European depredations against Ottoman and European commerce and about European slave hunting raids in North Africa.

———. *Schiavi musulmani nell'Italia moderna.* Naples: Edizioni Scientifiche Italiane, 1999. A detailed study, based on archival research as well as published works, of the numbers and treatment of Muslim slaves captured by Italians and put to work on the galleys, on public works, and as domestic servants in post-Renaissance Italy.

Bookin-Weiner, Jerome B., and Mohamed El Mansour, eds. *The Atlantic Connection: 200 Years of Moroccan-American Relations, 1786–1986.* Mohammedia: Edino, 1990. Papers presented at a conference held at Norfolk, Virginia, in 1986.

Boyer, Pierre. *La Vie quotidienne à Alger, à la veille de l'intervention française.* Paris: Hachette, 1963. Many details on daily life in Algiers on the eve of the French conquest, based on published sources.

Brant, Irving. *James Madison, Secretary of State.* Indianapolis: Bobbs-Merrill, 1961. The fourth of six volumes in Brant's massive study of Madison. Has details about the lighter side of Mellimelli's embassy to Washington.

Braudel, Fernand. *The Mediterranean and the Mediterranean World in the Age of Philip II.* Translated by Siân Reynolds. 2 vols. New York: Harper and Row, 1973. The classic work on broader aspects of the Mediterranean. Interesting observations on the conversion of the crusade-jihad struggle into to a corsair contest.

Brighton, Ray. *The Checkered Career of Tobias Lear.* Portsmouth, N.H.: Portsmouth Marine Society, 1985. Readable account of a remarkable life.

Brown, Leon Carl. *The Tunisia of Ahmad Bey 1837–1855.* Princeton: Princeton University Press, 1974. A readable, scholarly study of Tunisia in the first half of the 19th century. Ahmad Bey was the son of one of the Sardinian women captured at Carloforte in 1798.

Burnett, Edmund C., ed. *Letters of Members of the Continental Congress.* 8 vols. Washington, D.C.: Carnegie Institution of Washington, 1921–36. Many scraps of information here.

Cathcart, James Leander. *The Captives, Eleven Years a Prisoner in Algiers.* La Porte, Ind.: Herald Print, [1899]. Compiled by Jane Bancker (Cathcart) Newkirk from her father's journal. Somewhat chaotic in organization, but an interesting read with many useful details.

———. *The Diplomatic Journal and Letter Book of James Leander Cathcart, 1788–1796.* Worcester, Mass.: American Antiquarian Society, 1955. The text of a manuscript held by the American Antiquarian Society, whose scholars considered it more authentic than the *Captives* version of Cathcart's North African experience. There are portions of an earlier and slightly different version in the manuscript collection at the Library of Congress.

Chapelle, Howard Irving. *The History of the American Sailing Navy: The Ships and Their Development*. New York: W. W. Norton, 1949. Copiously illustrated with drawings, sketches, and photographs. All you need to know about the ships of the U.S. Navy before the age of steam.

Charles-Roux, François. *Les Travaux d'Herculais*. Paris: Editions Leroux, 1929. Describes Herculais's mission to North Africa and the havoc he wrought among France's merchant and official communities there.

Cordingly, David. *Under the Black Flag: The Romance and the Reality of Life among the Pirates*. New York: Random House, 1996.

Crawford, Michael J., and Christine F. Hughes. *The Reestablishment of the Navy, 1787–1801: Historical Overview and Select Bibliography*. Washington, D.C.: Naval Historical Center, 1995.

Devoulx, Albert. *Le Registre des prises maritimes: Traduction d'un document authentique et inédit concernant le partage des captures amenées par les corsaires algériens*. Algiers: A. Jourdan, 1872. Electronic version from Bibliothèque Nationale, 1995. Described in appendix 4.

Dow, George Francis, and John Henry Edmonds. *The Pirates of the New England Coast, 1630–1730*. Salem, Mass.: Marine Research Society, 1923; New York: Dover, 1996. A useful reminder of the vicious quality of American piracy in the seventeenth and eighteenth centuries.

Duncan, Evan M. "The Barbary States and Hostage Taking, 1784–1815." Unpublished memorandum, Office of the Historian, U.S. Department of State, Washington, D.C., 1987.

Edwards, Samuel. *Barbary General: The Life of William H. Eaton*. Englewood Cliffs, N.J.: Prentice-Hall, 1968. Described on the jacket as "The Amazing Account of a Flamboyant Hero who was truly America's Lawrence of Arabia." A laudatory account with many personal details of Eaton's exploits, some of them dubious and at least one impossible.

Even, Pascal. *Papiers du Consulat de France à Alger: Inventaire analytique des volumes de correspondance du Consulat de France à Alger, 1585–1798*. Paris: Imprimerie Nationale, 1988. Very useful for the researcher. One wishes similar inventories existed for Tunis, Tripoli, and Morocco.

Field, James A., Jr. *America and The Mediterranean World, 1776–1882*. Princeton: Princeton University Press, 1969. A fascinating study of the generally unknown American roles—commercial, naval, political, diplomatic, and missionary—in the Mediterranean from 1776 to the end of the nineteenth century.

Fisher, Sir Godfrey. *Barbary Legend: War, Trade, and Piracy in North Africa, 1415–1830*. Oxford: Clarendon Press, 1957. An effort to present a more balanced picture of the North African regencies than that put forth by Playfair and others, correcting some of the misconceptions about the character of the deys and their rule. Fisher assumes a detailed knowledge of British history on the reader's part.

Foss, John. *A Journal of the Captivity and Sufferings of John Foss, Several Years a Prisoner at Algiers*. 2d ed. Newburyport, Mass.: Angier, March, 1798. Available on microfiche (MCard 2 #33747), but a much more readable version of a substantial portion of the text can be found in Baepler's *White Slaves, African Masters*.

Fowler, William M., Jr. *Jack Tars and Commodores: The American Navy, 1783–1815*. Boston: Houghton Mifflin, 1984. Many interesting details about the creation of the navy, its officers and men, and operations in the Mediterranean.

Garitee, Jerome R. *The Republic's Private Navy: The American Privateering Business as Practiced by Baltimore During the War of 1812*. Middletown, Conn.: Wesleyan University Press, 1977. American corsairs as pillars of society.

Giunta, Mary A., ed. *The Emerging Nation: A Documentary History of the Foreign Relations of the United States Under the Articles of Confederation, 1780–1789*. 3 vols. Washington, D.C.: National Historical Publications and Records Commission, 1996. A splendid collection of correspondence. Sources include British and French archives as well as numerous American manuscript collections in the National Archives and elsewhere.

Halimi, Ali Abd al-Qadr. *Madinat al-Jaza'ir* [The city of Algiers]. Algiers: Dar al-Fikr al-Islami, 1972. A look at Algiers in the period before 1830 by an Algerian university professor, drawing largely on French sources.

Hamdan Khodja. *Le Miroir: Aperçu historique et statistique sur la Régence d'Alger*. 1833; Paris: Sindbad, 1985. Description of Algeria by a kouloughli who was an official of the regency at the time of the French invasion of 1830, an event Hamdan originally saw as a possible opening to modernization along the lines of Napoleon's invasion of Egypt. This work and al-Zahhar's memoirs are our only insiders' accounts, and details are scant in both.

Hebb, David Delison. *Piracy and the English Government, 1616–1642*. Aldershot, Hants.: Scolar Press, 1994. A scholarly study based on contemporary sources, providing a wealth of detail on corsair depredations against the English in the seventeenth century and on English inability to deal with them effectively.

Hess, Andrew C. *The Forgotten Frontier: A History of the Sixteenth Century Ibero-African Frontier*. Chicago: University of Chicago Press, 1978. A historian's perspective on the contest for control of North Africa.

Hirschberg, H. Z. *A History of the Jews in North Africa, from the Ottoman Conquests to the Present Time*. 2d rev. ed. Vol. 2. Leiden: Brill, 1981. Many details about the Jewish community in Algiers.

Hoexter, Miriam. *Endowments, Rulers, and Community: Waqf al-Haramayn in Ottoman Algiers*. Leiden: Brill, 1998. A scholarly study, based on contemporary documents, of the operation and significance of the most important religious endowment of Ottoman Algeria.

Humphreys, Frank Landon. *Life and Times of David Humphreys*. 2 vols. New York: Putnam, 1917. A partisan biography, but many useful details.

Huntington, Samuel P. *The Clash of Civilizations and the Remaking of World Order*. New York: Simon and Schuster, 1996.

Irwin, Ray W. *The Diplomatic Relations of the United States with the Barbary Powers, 1776–1816*. Chapel Hill: University of North Carolina Press, 1931. The standard work on the subject. Careful, detailed, and thorough scholarship based on American archives.

Jefferson, Thomas. *Papers*. Edited by Julian P. Boyd et al. 28 vols. to date. Princeton: Princeton University Press, 1950–.

Journals of the Continental Congress, 1774–1789. 34 vols. Washington, D.C.: U.S. Government Printing Office, 1904–1937.

Julien, Charles-André. *History of North Africa*. Translated by John Petrie. London: Routledge and Kegan Paul, 1970. Has a useful survey of the period of Ottoman rule in Algiers and Tunis.

Kitzen, Michael L. S. *Tripoli and the United States at War*. Jefferson, N.C.: McFarland, 1993. A good, brief treatment.

Lane-Poole, Stanley. *The Barbary Corsairs*. Westport, Conn.: Negro Universities Press, 1970. A readable account, originally published as *The Story of the Barbary Corsairs* (New York: Putnam, 1890). Lane-Poole's scholarship is disappointing in this case.

al-Madani, Ahmad Tawfiq. *Harb al-thalatha mi'at sana bayn al- Jaza'ir wa Isbaniya 1492–1792* [The war of three hundred years between Algiers and Spain, 1492–1792]. Algiers: SNED, 1972.

———. *Muhammad Uthman Pasha*. Algiers: SNED [198_]. A history, in Arabic, of the war with Spain in the period of the first of the deys with whom the Americans negotiated.

Mariners' Museum. *Aak to Zumbra: A Dictionary of the World's Watercraft*. Newport News, Va.: Mariners' Museum, 2000. Gives names in many languages and descriptions of a remarkable variety of ships, including almost all of those mentioned in the accounts from Algiers.

Matar, Nabil. *Turks, Moors, and Englishmen in the Age of Discovery*. New York: Columbia University Press, 1999. A study, based on contemporary sources, of the interaction between the English on one hand and North Africans and Turks on the other, a relationship that was more active than is generally realized. The first Muslim ambassador to England arrived in 1551.

McCusker, John J. *How Much Is That in Real Money? A Historical Price Index for Use as a Deflator of Money Values in the Economy of the United States*. Worcester, Mass.: American Antiquarian Society, 1992.

McKee, Christopher. *Edward Preble: A Naval Biography, 1761–1807*. Annapolis: Naval Institute Press, 1972. A detailed, authoritative, and readable account, drawing on French and British as well as American archives, of the life and exploits of one of the American heroes of the war with Tripoli.

Noah, Mordechai. *Correspondence and Documents Relative to the Attempt to Negotiate for the Release of American Captives at Algiers*. Washington, D.C., 1816. Early American Imprints, 2d ser., no. 38474 (microform). Noah was American consul at Tunis 1813–1815.

———. *Travels in England, France, Spain, and the Barbary States, in the Years 1813–14 and 15*. New York: Kirk and Mercein, 1819. A thick book that needs careful reading. Many details about problems with Algiers in the nineteenth century.

Office of Naval Records and Library. *Naval Documents Related to the United States*

Wars with the Barbary Powers. 6 vols. Washington, D.C.: U.S. Government Printing Office, 1939–44. A magnificent collection of documents of all types, official and otherwise, dealing with U.S. diplomatic efforts and naval operations in the Mediterranean in the period 1785–1807.

Panzac, Daniel. *Les Corsaires barbaresques: La fin d'une épopée, 1800–1820.* Paris: CNRS Editions, 1999. A thorough, scholarly study of the last years of the corsair epoch, based on French, Italian, British, Spanish, and Maltese archives. Surprising insights into the efforts of the corsairs to turn commercial. An English translation is forthcoming from Brill.

Paullin, Charles Oscar. *Commodore John Rodgers: Captain, Commodore, and Senior Officer of the American Navy, 1773–1838.* Cleveland: Arthur H. Clark, 1910; Annapolis: U.S. Naval Institute, 1967. A full treatment of one of the navy's heroes who played an important role in negotiations with Tripoli and Tunis.

———. *Diplomatic Negotiations of American Naval Officers, 1778–1883.* Baltimore: Johns Hopkins Press, 1912. A series of lectures. Paullin starts with John Paul Jones and his negotiations with the French and gives a detailed account of the role of naval officers in the negotiations with the Barbary powers.

Playfair, Sir Robert Lambert. *The Scourge of Christendom: Annals of British Relations with Algiers Prior to the French Conquest.* 1884. Freeport, N.Y.: Books for Libraries Press, 1972. Based, as the title indicates, on documents in British archives. Many remarkable details about the travails of British consuls and merchants in Algiers.

———. *A Bibliography of Morocco, from the Earliest Times to the End of 1891.* London: J. Murray, 1892.

Riley, James. *Sufferings in Africa: Captain Riley's Narrative . . . of the Loss of the American Brig Commerce . . .* New York: C. N. Potter, 1965. The *Commerce* was wrecked in 1815 on the coast of the region now known as the Western Sahara, and Captain Riley and his crew were captured by local bedouin. They were finally ransomed by the British consul in Essaouira. This is a reprint of a portion of one of the most popular books of nineteenth-century America, first published in 1817, with twenty-two subsequent editions.

Rodd, Francis Rennell. *General William Eaton: The Failure of an Idea.* New York: Minton, Balch, 1932. A biography. Good description of the loss of the *Philadelphia* and of Eaton's discussions in Washington.

Ruedy, John. *Modern Algeria: The Origins and Development of a Nation.* Bloomington: Indiana University Press, 1992. Although Ruedy's focus is on modern Algeria, he has a useful discussion of the Ottoman period and the events leading up to the French occupation in 1830.

Shaler, William. *Sketches of Algiers, Political, Historical and Civil.* Boston: Cummings, Hilliard, 1826. Observations, dated 1825, by the American consul in Algiers from 1815 to 1828. This collection and Venture de Paradis's notes and observations described below are the clearest and most authentic firsthand accounts of Algiers, as seen through western eyes, on the eve of the French invasion in 1830.

Shaw, Thomas. *Travels or Observations, Relating to Several Parts of Barbary and the*

Levant. 3d ed. 2 vols. Edinburgh: J. Ritchie, 1808. Shaw traveled across North Africa by land in 1722 and made numerous observations about people and places he passed. He estimated the population of Algiers at 100,000 Muslims, 15,000 Jews, and 2,000 Christians.

Shuval, Tal. *La Ville d'Alger vers la fin du XVIIIe siècle: Population et cadre urbain.* Paris: CNRS Editions, 1998. A Braudelian study of the population and economy of Algiers in the late eighteenth century based on the registers of pious endowments and of estates of persons dying without heirs.

———. "The Ottoman Algerian Elite and its Ideology." *International Journal of Middle East Studies* 32, no. 3 (2000).

Smith, Paul H., et al., eds. *Letters of Delegates to Congress, 1774–1789.* 26 vols. Washington, D.C.: Library of Congress, 1976–2000.

Smith, Walter B., II. *America's Diplomats and Consuls of 1776–1865.* Arlington, Va.: Center for the Study of Foreign Affairs, 1986. A systematic catalog of America's foreign representation up to the Civil War, based on Department of State personnel records.

Spencer, William. *Algiers in the Age of the Corsairs.* Centers of Civilization series. Norman: University of Oklahoma Press, 1976. A good, readable survey.

Sumner, Charles. *White Slavery in the Barbary States.* Boston: W. D. Ticknor, 1847; Miami: Mnemosyne, 1969. An abolitionist lecture delivered before the Boston Mercantile Library Association on February 17, 1847, describing the evils of slavery that had been eliminated from North Africa but not from the United States. The future senator compares the U.S. unfavorably to the Barbary powers.

Temimi, Abdeljelil. *Le Beylik de Constantine et Hadj Ahmed Bey (1830–1837).* Tunis: Société Tunisienne des Arts Graphiques, 1978. Contains a useful summary description of conditions in Constantine on the eve of the French conquest.

———. *Sommaire des registres arabes et turcs d'Alger.* Tunis: Revue d'Histoire Maghrébine, 1979. Annotated index of the 512 *daftars* or registers of the Algiers regency government, in Arabic and Turkish, that survive from 1830. The third section of Temimi's doctoral dissertation at the University of Aix-en-Provence, this is a very useful guide for future researchers.

Thomson, Ann. *Barbary and Enlightenment: European Attitudes towards the Maghreb in the 18th Century.* Leiden: Brill, 1987. A scholarly study.

Todd, Charles Burr. *Life and Letters of Joel Barlow.* New York: Putnam, 1886. The earliest biography of Barlow. The author had first access to the voluminous writings Barlow left behind.

Tucker, Glenn. *Dawn Like Thunder: The Barbary Wars and the Birth of the U.S. Navy.* Indianapolis: Bobbs-Merrill, 1963. A very detailed and readable account beginning with the forced visit of the *Washington* to Constantinople in 1800. Based largely on the *Naval Documents.* Tucker is one of the few authors in the field who has actually visited Tripoli.

Valensi, Lucette. *Le Maghreb avant la prise d'Alger, 1790–1830.* Paris: Flammarion, 1969. Translated by Kenneth J. Perkins and published as *On the Eve of Colonialism: North Africa before the French Conquest* (New York: Africana, 1977). A highly regarded, standard work with an extensive bibliography.

Venture de Paradis, Jean-Michel. *Tunis et Alger au XVIIIe siècle.* Paris: Sindbad, 1983. A collection of observations made by a long-time (1757–99) French consular official, trained as an Arabic and Turkish interpreter, during service at Tunis (1780–86) and Algiers (1788–90). Literate and concise, these notes and Shaler's are invaluable.

Wharton, Francis, ed. *The Revolutionary Diplomatic Correspondence of the United States.* 6 vols. Washington, D.C.: U.S. Government Printing Office, 1889.

Whipple, A.B.C. *To the Shores of Tripoli: The Birth of the U.S. Navy and Marines.* New York: William Morrow, 1991; Annapolis: Naval Institute Press, 2001. A readable account of the naval and military aspects of the war against Tripoli. Not to be relied on for diplomatic details about Algiers.

Wolf, John B. *The Barbary Coast: Algiers Under the Turks, 1500–1830.* New York: W. W. Norton, 1979. A thorough, scholarly but readable account using British, French, and Spanish archives as well as a great variety of published sources.

Woodress, James Leslie. *A Yankee's Odyssey: The Life of Joel Barlow.* Philadelphia: Lippincott, 1958. Of the two published biographies of Barlow, this is probably the more relevant for the modern reader.

Wright, Louis B., and Julia H. Macleod. *The First Americans in North Africa: William Eaton's Struggle for a Vigorous Policy Against the Barbary Pirates, 1799–1805.* Princeton: Princeton University Press, 1945. A concise account of William Eaton's stay as consul in Tunis and of his subsequent efforts to overthrow the pasha of Tripoli. Draws heavily on the Eaton papers at the Huntington Library. Many insightful details. A good read. Illustrated.

al-Zahhar, al-Haj Ahmad Sharif. *Mudhakirat* [Memoirs]. Edited by Ahmad Tawfiq al-Madani. Algiers: SNED, 1980. The Naqib al-Ashraf, or leader of Muhammad's descendants in Algiers, recounts highlights of the period from 1766 to the French occupation in 1830.

Documentary Sources

United States

National Archives, 8601 Adelphi Rd., College Park, Md., 20740–6001. The excellent quality of this facility makes up for its remote location. The Department of State records, including correspondence from consular posts such as Tangier, Algiers, Tunis, and Tripoli, are stored here both on microfilm and as original documents. They provide a wealth of information about the details of relations with North Africa. References in the text are to NA followed by post and microfilm roll number, e.g., NA Algiers, roll 3.

Great Britain

Public Record Office, Kew, Richmond, Surrey. More modest than the American establishment, this facility has better service for copying and has a very cheerful and helpful staff who will look things up for you. A great deal of material from the Foreign Office regarding Britain and North Africa in the eighteenth century is available both on microfilm and in the original. References in the text are to PRO followed by document number, e.g., PRO FO 6/17, or simply FO 6/17.

France

Foreign affairs documents in France are divided among three principal depositories:

Centre des Archives Diplomatiques de Nantes, 17 rue du Casternau, BP 1033, 44036 Nantes Cedex 1. This Ministry of Foreign Affairs facility holds archives from diplomatic and consular posts throughout the world going back to the sixteenth century. (The files of the former protectorates of Morocco, Tunisia, Lebanon, and Syria are also stored here.) The comfortable reading room has a helpful staff. A substantial portion, perhaps the majority, of the holdings are documents that the posts received from elsewhere. You may have to go to the Archives Nationales in Paris to find documents sent in by the same posts. For the archives of the consulate at Algiers that are held at

Nantes for the period 1585–1798, there is an excellent index, *Papiers du Consulat de France à Alger,* by Pascal Even.

Centre Historique des Archives Nationales, 60 rue des Francs-Bourgeois, 75141 Paris Cedex 03. This facility of the Ministry of Culture has a crowded reading room with limited staff and electronic facilities. Here you can find certain documents of the Ministry of Foreign Affairs, particularly communications *from* posts in North Africa, that are not at Nantes. You will need help. Fortunately, other researchers may help you if you look sufficiently forlorn. Budget plenty of time. References in the text are to AE (for Affaires Etrangères) followed by file number, e.g., AE B1 115.

Centre des Archives d'Outre-Mer, Aix-en-Provence. The archives of former colonial possessions, including Algeria, are kept here. In the case of Algeria, the documents from the Ottoman period that the French took with them when they left in 1962 have been microfilmed and the originals returned to Algiers.

Algeria

Archives Nationales, 12 rue du 24 Février, Algiers. Because of the unsettled state of affairs in Algeria in the 1990s, I was unable to visit Algiers and search in the archives personally. A request made through the American embassy to the director of the archives in 1993 produced Arabic translations of five documents in Turkish conveying secondhand reports of Decatur's operations and the British-Dutch bombardment of 1816. A seven-volume inventory of documents held as of 1980 lists property transactions, estates, and religious endowments.

Personal Papers

A collection of Joel Barlow's personal papers is held by the Houghton Library of Harvard University, Cambridge, Mass., 02138.

There are at least two collections of James Leander Cathcart's papers, one at the New York Public Library and a much smaller one in the manuscript reading room at the Library of Congress.

Index

Page numbers for illustrations are in italics.

Actuncan
Abaellino, 129
Abolition of privateering (1856), 6
Adams, John: captives' letter to, 52; differences with Jefferson, 40–41; election to vice presidency, 68; inexperience with the Barbary powers, 65; and the Lamb appointment, 38, 39; and Lamb's mission to Algiers, 49, 51, 52, 57, 64; negotiations with the Tripolitanian ambassador, 41–42; and North African issues, xiii; as peace commissioner to Europe, 35; on redeeming the captives (1795), 159
Adja, Sidi Haji Abdul Rahman, 41–42
Afghan mujahidin, 70
Ahmad Sharif Al-Zahhar. *See* Al-Zahhar, al-Haj Ahmad Sharif (*under* Zahhar)
Alaouite dynasty (Morocco), 156
Al-Ashraf, Naqib, 17
Algiers: coinage, 197–99; description of, 3–5, 4, 12, 13, 14; economy of, xiv, 5–8, 20, 21, 80, 161. *See also* Corsairs, Barbary; Tributes
Algiers, government of: army, 14–15; the beys, 19–20; European attitudes toward, 2–3, 243n1; formalities of war declaration, 7, 243n5; international recognition of, 14, 23, 158; military establishment, 19–20, 245n18; ministers of the dey, 18–19, 22; ownership of fleet, 5, 243n4; powers of the dey, 18, 22; regency organization, 1, 18; religious judges, 17. *See also* Deys; Ottoman Empire
Algiers, history of: chronology of events, xxi–xxviii; accounts by Europeans, 2–3; British-Dutch bombardment (1816), 130; cessation of Christian slavery, 130; declaration of war on the U.S., 43; hostilities with Spain, 8, 23, 25, 27, 43; origin of name, 4; Ottoman control over, 1, 3, 5, 16, 21; reputation of impregnability, 8, 243n6; resolution of problems with the U.S., xv; shortcomings of primary sources (historical), xvi–xvii; treaties with the U.S., 102, 104, 128–29, 234; treaty with Spain (1791), 248n15; truce with Portugal (1793), 75–79, 84, 100, 225–30, 249n16; truce with Spain (1785), 8, 27, 43, 74, 225; U.S. declares war on (1815), 128
Algiers, population and social structure: Arabs and Berbers, 16, 244n15; Christian prisoners, 17; corsairs, 16; European community, 254n9; immigrants, 16; Jews, 4, 17–18, 244n11, 244nn15–16; languages, 11–12, 14; Leo the African on, 3–4; living standards of the deys, 22; local dignitaries, 17; numbers, 3, 12, 244n11; ojak, 5, 14; Ottoman domain and, 14; Turks, 14–16
Algiers in the Age of the Corsairs (Spencer), 11, 26
Ali, Haj, 128, 148, 150, 238
Ali Agha, 201–2
Ali Pasha, 128
Alliance (frigate), 38, 39
Al-Qa'ida, 158
America and the Mediterranean World 1776–1882 (Field), 40
American army, first, xvi
American attitudes toward the Muslim world, 151, 158, 164, 171–72, 261n9. *See also* Muslim world
American Civil War, privateering in, 6
American colonists protected by British treaties, xv, 33
American moral superiority, belief in, 170

American navy. *See* Navy, early American
American prisoners: captives from the 1600s, 33–34; captives from 1784, 40; captives from 1785, 43–46, 203–9; captives from 1793, 79–80, 203, 209–13; casualty figures, 214; Cathcart's description, 44–45; claiming British nationality, 220–22; conversion to Islam, 145; death of, 43, 66, 68, 90, 116, 119, 121; delays in negotiations for, 67, 69, 74, 86, 93; differences in treatment of, 46; Jefferson on ransom for, 65, 68, 70–71, 85–86, 93, 164, 249n2; Jefferson's report to Congress on (1790), 223–24; John Adams on redemption, 159; Lamb's failure to negotiate release of, 49–57; letter to John Adams, 52; Logie's involvement with, 61; names of, 208–14; Napoleon's interest in, 140–41; numbers of, 208; O'Brien as spokesman for, 43; petition to King George III (1785), 220–22; prisoners' allowances reduced by negotiations, 67; ransomed/released from Tripoli (1805), 145, 147; redemption and departure from Algiers (1796), 117–20, 122; release from Algiers (1815), 128; rescue attempt, lack of, 159; role of France and Britain, xvi, 29, 32, 35, 59–62; siege of Donaldson's chamber, 106; sold into slavery, 43; Spanish consul's help, 67. *See also* Captives, treatment of; Ransom for Americans in Algiers

American ships, capture of: al-Zahhar's version (1793), 205–6; *American State Papers* version, 78; as America's first crisis with the Muslim world, xiii; cargo, 215–16; first reports of, 39, 40, 43–46, 214–15; Foss's version, 79–80; names of ships and prisoners, 208–16; types of vessels, 215

Americans' return to the U.S., 174–82
American State Papers, xvi, 79, 134
American vessels, 62, 208, 215, 220
Amine, Mohamed, 22, 244n16
Amir. *See* Deys
Annaba, Algeria, 123
Anthrax scare, 168
Anti-Semitism in American writings, 109
Arab-Israeli conflict, 172

Aranda, conde de, 48
Argus, 141
Arlington Heritage: Vignettes of a Virginia County, 89
Army, xvi
Articles of Confederation, xv, 66, 164
'Aruj, 5
Attitudes: American, toward the Muslim world, 151, 158, 164, 171–72, 261n9; American, toward Third World, 169; British, toward America, 35; European, toward North Africa, 2–3, 24, 243n1
Aures Mountains, 16
Autocrats, modern, 132

Bagnios, 11, 244n10
Bailey, Samuel F., 119
Bainbridge, William: and Napoleon, 127; popularity at Istanbul, 126; rescue of French hostages, 127; return to the U.S., 145; surrender at Tripoli, 138; tour of North African capitals with Decatur, 129
Bakri, house of, 82–83
Bakri, Micaiah: Barlow's assessment of, 109; dislike for Cathcart, 101–2, 115; family and business ties in Livorno, 113; negotiations of treaty with Algiers (1795), 99, 101–2, 164. *See also* Treaty payments to Algiers
Baladis, 16
Baltimore, Ireland, 8
Barbarossa (Khayr al-Din), 5
Barbary and Enlightenment (Thomson), 2
Barbary corsairs. *See* Corsairs, Barbary
Barbary experience, relevance today: communications, 166–68; the diplomatic experience, xv, 160–66, 172; lessons learned, xv, 65, 164; the naval role, 168–71, 261n5; policy implications, 158–60; Western rules not always accepted, 151, 159. *See also* Diplomacy *vs.* force; Muslim world
Barbary Legend, 3, 30–31
Barbary Regencies: and America's need for a navy, 160; European attitudes toward, 2–3, 243n1; extraction of payments, 3; government of, 1–3; location, xiv, *xix*, 243n1; origin of term, 243n1; privateering procedures, 7; relationship to Ottoman domain,

1, 3; vulnerability of the U.S. to, 160; wars, formalities of declaring, 7. *See also* Algiers, government of; Morocco; Ottoman Empire; Tripoli; Tunis
Barclay, Thomas, 36, 39, 47, 48, 71, 247n9
Baring, House of, 116–17
Barlow, Joel: on Algiers, 113–14; background, 252n10; biographies about, 180; and Connecticut Wits, 73, 252n10; on d'Herculais, 113, 254n9; on Hasan Pasha, 29–30, 32; on Humphreys, 95; on Micaiah Bakri, 109; as negotiator, 32; prisoners' gratitude to, 176; review of his accomplishments, 165; on social life among foreigners in Algiers, 113, 254n9; talent in bargaining, 113; treatment of subordinates, 116; writings, xvii
Barlow, Joel (chronology): and the redemption (1796), 120–21; letter on behalf of returned prisoners, 174–75; and U.S. negotiations with Tunis, 148–51; extension of stay in North Africa, 124; purchase of privateered goods, 7; life after Algiers, 180–81; death from pneumonia (1812), 181
Barnby, H. G., xvii
Barranis, 16
Barron, Samuel, 142
Bassara, 82
Beaumarchais (playwright), 48
Beaussier, Bonaventure, 139–45
Bedistan (Slave Market), 45
Bektash, Haji, 19
Bell, William, 214
Bemis, Samuel Flagg, 6
Betsey, 40
Beylik, meaning of, 18
Beys, 19–20, 134. *See also* Hamuda Bey
Biddle, Charles, 39
Bijaya, 3
Bin Abdallah, Moulay Muhammad, 40
Bin Ali, Husayn, 147
Bin Laden, Usama, 158
Bin Uthman, Muhammad Pasha (dey from 1766 to 1791): accomplishments and descriptions of, 24–29, 32; alleged castration of, 26; al-Zahhar on, 24–26; de Bauffremont on, 26; disinterest (sexual) in women/men, 25–29; frugality/avarice of, 25, 27–29; long reign of, 18; love for jihad, 24, 25, 26; Panzac on, 26; peaceful reign of, 28; Spencer on, 26; Venture de Paradis on, 27–29

Bin Uthman, Muhammad Pasha, chronology: plot to assassinate, 27; demands for ransom, 52; prisoners, on Lamb's audiences with, 51–53, 63–64; death of, 68, 203–4, 207; and Hasan's accession to the deyship, 203–4
Blackmail, 158
Blockade of Tripoli, xiii, xv, 141–45, 159. *See also* Tripoli
Bona (Hippo, Bône, Annaba), 123
Bonaparte, Napoleon, 9–10, 127, 140–41
Bono, Salvatore, 10
Brand, Edward, 149
Brig, defined, 215
Britain: American colonies protected by, 33; blockade of Salé (1637), 243n6; cooperation with Portugal, 226–28; first success against the corsairs, 243n6; treaties with North African states, 33; unhelpful role of, xvi, 35, 60–61, 62; U.S. declares war on (1812), 128. *See also* Logie, Charles
Brown, Moses, 123, 177–78, 180, 208
Buju, defined, 199
Bulkeley, John, 121
Bulletin de nouvelles (de Kercy), 59
Burghl, Ali, 32, 134, 201, 205–6, 207
Burj Ras 'Amar, 25
Burj Sardina, 25
Bushnaq, Nafthali, 18

The Captives, Eleven Years a Prisoner in Algiers (Cathcart): Cathcart's chief clerkship, 90–91; the dey's palace, 22; the final negotiations of the 1795 treaty, 96–102; Hasan Pasha, 31–32; Lamb's mission to Algiers, 53; publication of, 88; value of the vessels for the dey, 124
Captives, treatment of: about, 6, 9–11, 17; death from the plague, 11, 66, 68, 90, 116, 119, 121; earlier captives, 33–34; by Europeans, xiv, 9–10; by North Africans, xiv, 2, 3, 9–11, 17; women, 11. *See also* American prisoners; Slaves/slavery
Captives and their ships, 208–16
Cargo of captured American ships, 215–16

276 / Index

Carloforte, San Pietro, 9, 244n8
Carmichael, William, 40, 46, 48–49, 68
Carter administration, 160
Cathalan, Stephen, 127
Cathcart, James Leander: background, 88–90; accidental diplomat, 166; Bakri's dislike for, 115; claim to British nationality, 89, 91, 222; daughter's biography of, 181; dislike for Mellimelli, 155; disparaging references to, 163; on Donaldson, 94; and Hasan Pasha, 31–32, 87, 96–102, 204; hostility toward O'Brien, 132, 251n1, 261n4; on Humphreys, 93; knowledge of languages, 89; on Lamb's meetings with the dey, 53; memoirs, xvii, 44, 87–88, 180; on palaces of the deys, 22; purchase of privateered goods, 7; review of his accomplishments, 166; rise to prominence in Algiers, 44, 46, 90; role in crisis with Algiers, 44, 87, 91; shortcomings as diplomat, 134; tavern owner in Algiers, 90, 251n2; on Yusuf Qaramanli, 132. *See also The Diplomatic Journal and Letter Book of James Leander Cathcart, 1788–1796;* Treaty payments to Algiers; *The Captives*
Cathcart, James Leander (chronology): on captives' arrival in Algiers (1785), 44–46; on captives' living conditions, 11, 44–46; and lodging with Logie, 46, 247n4; service to the wakil al-kharj, 90; Washington's instructions (1794), 92–93; and truce with Tunis (1795), 238; and final treaty negotiations with Algiers, 96–102; on the dey's request for naval stores, 236–37; Barlow's plot to send away, 115; departure from Algiers (1796), 114–15; arrival in Tripoli as consul (1799), 134; and negotiations with Tunis (1799), 151; unwelcome in Algiers (1802), 137, 181, 251n1; negotiations with Tripoli (1803), 137; unwelcome in Tripoli (1803), 137, 181; life after return to the U.S., 181; death of (1843), 87
Charles-Roux, François, 230, 254n9. *See also* D'Herculais, Allois.
Chesapeake, 131, 257n1
Christians, enslavement of, xiv, 2, 9–10
Church, Edward, 76–77, 79
CIA (Central Intelligence Agency), 70

Clarke, George, 124
Codes (secret) in communications, 167, 218–19
Coffin, Captain Zachaeus, 46, 52, 68
Cohen-Bakri, Joseph, 83
Cohen-Bakri, Micaiah. *See* Bakri, Micaiah
Coinage, Algerian, 197–99
Colvil, Charles, 68
Communications in diplomacy, 166–68
"A Concise Account of Negotiations," 53
Congress, 131
Connecticut Wits, 73, 252n10
Constantine, 20
Constantinople, Ottoman sultan of, xvi
Constellation, 131
Constitution, 62, 131
Continental Congress, 33–36. *See also* Ransom for Americans in Algiers; Treaties
Corsairs, Barbary: defined/described, xiv, 5–6, 23; capture of American ships, 33–34, 40, 43–46, 79–80, 203–16; consular passports issued to, 7; costs to other nations, 9; different from modern terrorists, xiii–xiv, 6, 7, 23, 158; enslavement of captured Christians, xiv, 2, 9–10, 130; eruption into the Atlantic (1785), 74, 84; European renegades in, 16; legitimacy of, xiv, 6, 7, 23, 158; *Les Corsaires barbaresques* (Panzac), 3, 9, 26; methods of capturing ships, 79; most notorious, 8; overcome by French (1830), 1; patriotic/religious obligation, 5; piracy/privateering, 5–11; raids, 8–9; as revenue source, xiv, 5–8, 20, 80, 133, 161; rules of operation, xiv, 7–11, 23, 122–24; the *ta'ifa,* 16. *See also* Captives, treatment of
Corsairs, European, xiv, 9–10, 16
Cravath, Lemuel, 71
Crescent, 112
Crusades, 171–72
Cryptogram, 218–19
Cutting, Nathaniel, 73, 78

Dale, Richard, 135
Dar al-Imara, 24, 187
Dar al-Jnina (Junaina), 22
Dar-al-Sultan, 19
Dar Aziza Bint al-Bey, 22
Dauphin, 20, 43, 216

Davis, George, 152, 163
Deane, Silas, 34
De Bauffremont, Joseph, 2–3, 26
De Castries's letter to de Kercy, 58–60, 217–19
Decatur, Stephen: and the destruction of the *Philadelphia*, 139; role in retrospect, 172; at Tunis and Tripoli (1815), 129; and the war on Algiers (1815), 128. *See also* Tripoli
Declaration of Paris (1856), 6
De Kercy, Jean-Baptiste, 50, 58–60, 163, 218–19
De Paradis, Jean Michel Venture. *See* Venture de Paradis, Jean Michel
Derna, xiv, 146–47
Devoulx, Albert, 20, 215–16
Deys: assassination threat to, 22, 245n22; authority of, 18; autonomy of, 5; defined, 5, 18; description by Europeans, 2; Eaton's description of, 151; ministers of, 18–19, 22; relationship to Ottoman sultans, 5; Western attitudes toward, 24, 151. *See also* Bin Uthman, Muhammad Pasha; Hasan Pasha; Mustafa
Dghies, Muhammed, 137, 139
D'Herculais, Allois, 96, 113, 122, 148, 254n9
Diplomacy: Americans' criticisms of each other, 163; conditions for early negotiators, 162; consular records about Americans, 163; demands of, 169; and executive leadership, 93, 165; inexperience with Muslim states, 162; in Irangate, 160; in negotiations with Tripoli (1801), 133; political appointees, 166; review of Americans' efforts in North Africa, 164–66, 172; role of naval commanders, 168–71, 259n31; Western rules not always accepted, 159. *See also* Barbary experience, relevance today; Diplomacy *vs.* force; Gunboat diplomacy
Diplomacy *vs.* force: Algiers, 171, 172; attitudes toward Third World, 151, 169; force as an adjunct, xv; Iran, 159; Lebanon, 159, 171; lessons to be learned, xv, 172; navy's role today, 171; Somalia (1991–93), 161–62; Tangier (1803), 160; Teddy Roosevelt's Big Stick, 162; in today's policies, 161; Tripoli (1801–05), xv, 131, 145, 159, 160, 165, 171–72; Tunis (1805), 160, 172, 259n31. *See also* Barbary experience, relevance today; Gunboat diplomacy
Diplomatic History of the United States (Bemis), 6
Diplomatic Journal and Letter Book of James Leander Cathcart, 1788–1796 (Cathcart), 87–88
Diplomatic Negotiations of American Naval Officers, 1778–1883 (Paullin), 137, 243n1
Diplomatic Relations of the United States with the Barbary Powers (Irwin), 133
Dissidents abandoned at Derna, 147
Donaldson, Joseph, Jr., 32, 94, 96–102, 164–65. *See also* Treaty payments to Algiers
Dragoman, 2, 50
Duels, 171
Duro, defined, 199
Dwight, Timothy, 73

Eaton, William: on the Barbary states (1800), 151; classic political appointee, 132, 166; diplomatic experience, 132; disaster as diplomat, 166; on Famin, 151, 259n25; on Hamuda Bey, 258n18; Hamuda Bey's complaints about, 163; on Mustafa (dey), 126; on O'Brien and Cathcart, 261n4; review of his accomplishments, 165–66
Eaton, William (chronology): arrival in Tunis as consul (1799), 131–32; and negotiations with Tunis, 151; arrival at Algiers, 132; debts, 152; ordered out of Tunis (1803), 152; attempts to unseat Yusef (1805), 145–47; battles at Derna (1805), 146; use of force over diplomacy, 131; deprived of glory, 165
Edwin, 128
Eliza, 120, 149
The Emerging Nation, xvi, 38, 41–42, 51
Encryption, examples of, 167, 218–19
Enterprise, 135, 136, 142
Essex, 135
Estedio, 130
European community in Algiers, 113, 254n9

Exmouth, Lord, 130
Expilly, count de: advises Lamb, 49; houses American captives, 46; on Lamb, 163; Lamb on, 230; and the Portugal-Algiers truce, 225, 228–30; and the Spain-Algiers truce (1785), 230

Famin, Etienne, 148–51, 259n25
Field, James, 40
Fisher, Godfrey, 2–3, 30–31
Fortune, 122, 208
Foss, John: on Americans' capture and treatment, 79–80; first mate of the *Polly*, 123; published journal of, 79–80, 180, 250n18; on redemption of prisoners, 117–19; return to the U.S., 177, 179, 180
France: perfidy of, 59–60; Quasi-War with, 91, 127, 131; unhelpful role in negotiations, xvi, 29, 32, 59–60; victory over Barbary corsairs, 1
Franklin, Benjamin, xiii, 34, 35, 39
Franks, David S., 48, 247n8
French Revolution, 66, 67
Frigate, defined, 254n7

Gautherot, Gustave, 21
Gee, Joshua (father/son), 33–34
George Washington (frigate), xv, 126, 168, 256n18
Gold, 103, 105, 116–17, 121
Good prize, 6
Grenville, Lord, 79
Gunboat diplomacy, 152, 157, 168–70

Hales, Richard, 104
Halimi, Ali Abd al-Qadr, 16
Hamdullah, 124
Hamidou Rais, 128
Hamilton, Alexander, xiii, 38
Hamuda Bey: characteristics as leader, 132, 147, 258n18; letter from Jefferson (1806), 239–41; raid on Carloforte, 147–48; and U.S. negotiations with Tunis, 151–53, 238
Harnet, James, 89
Harper, Robert Goodloe, 158
Harriss, Elizabeth, 34
Hasan. *See* Hasan Pasha
Hasan Dey. *See* Hasan Pasha

Hasan Pasha, 124–25
Hasan Pasha (dey from 1791 to 1797): accomplishments and descriptions of, 26, 29–32; al-Zahhar on, 27, 29; attitude toward Americans, 69; Barlow on, 29–30, 32; Cathcart on, 27, 31; Fisher on, 30–31; fondness for Charles Logie, 78; Jewish confidants of, 18; long reign of, 18; O'Brien's friendly relationship with, 69; relationship to Muhammad Pasha bin Uthman, 25–26; sexual proclivities, 31; wife of, 201. *See also* Ransom for Americans in Algiers; Treaty payments to Algiers
Hasan Pasha, chronology: seafaring career, 31; orders strangling of father-in-law, 201–2; accession to the deyship, 203–4; account of meeting with Lamb, 56; refusal to negotiate with Americans (1793–94), 81–83, 87; and the Portugal-Algiers truce, 78, 81–82; letter to King George III (1794), 78, 231–32; anger at the British (1794), 78, 87; wish list to America (1794), 233–35; final negotiations of the 1795 treaty, 96–102; gives horse to Donaldson, 102; threatens Donaldson and Cathcart (1796), 106–7; gives horse to Barlow, 113; death of (1798), 125
Hebb, David Delison, 9
Herculais. *See* D'Herculais, Allois
Hero, 124
Hicheborn, Benjamin, 96
Hippo (Bône, Annaba), 123
Hizballah, 160
Holroyd, John Baker, First Earl of Sheffield, 35
Hostage crises, modern, 159
Humphreys, David: background, 73; Barlow's observations of, 95; Cathcart on, 93; museum devoted to, 182; portrait, 75; return to the U.S., 180; review of his accomplishments, 165; sensitivity to captives' needs, 85–86
Humphreys, David (chronology): "minister resident" to Portugal, 74; recommendation of a naval force (1793), 85; and the Swedish consul general in Algiers, 80–81; and the Portugal-Algiers truce, 77; meeting with George Washington (1795), 94;

life after Algiers, 182. *See also* Ransom for Americans in Algiers; Treaty payments to Algiers
Huntington, Samuel, 36
Husayn Bin Ali, 147

Iceland, corsair raids on, 8
Independent, 114
Intrepid, explosion of, 144–45
Irangate, 159, 160
Irwin, Ray, 133
Islam, conversion to, 14, 16, 145

Al-Jaza'ir (the Islands), 4
Janissaries, 3, 14, 15, 16, 17, 243n3
Jansen, Jan, 8
Jay, John, 36–38, 41–42
Jefferson, Thomas: economizing measures, 127; fear of overpaying for prisoners, 65, 68, 70–71, 85–86, 93, 164, 249n2; inexperience with North Africa, 65; misquoted, 158, 260n1; *Papers*, 38; on relations with other nations, 240; on use of the oceans, 240; on war *vs.* tributes, 40, 159
Jefferson, Thomas (chronology): peace commissioner to Europe (1784), 35; and the Lamb appointment, 38, 39; correspondence with O'Brien, 44; and financial preparations for Lamb, 47–48; and Lamb's mission to Algiers, 48–50, 53–54, 59–60, 63–65; request for Spanish support, 48–49; request for French support, 47, 58; differences with Adams, 40–41; negotiations with the Tripolitanian ambassador (1786), 41–42; letters from captives to, 52; appointment to secretary of state (1790), 68; report to Congress on prisoners (1790), 223–24; instructions to Jones (1792), 71; recommendation of forceful response to Tripoli (1801), 135; letter to Hamuda Bey (1806), 153–54, 239–41
Jews in Algiers: attacks on, 18; important commercial ties, 17–18; involvement in negotiations, 52; key in release of American prisoners, 18; knowledge of foreign affairs, 17–18; Micaiah Bakri, 99, 101–2; Nafthali Bushnaq (Bu Jnah), 18; numbers of, 17, 244nn11, 16; social position, 17–18. *See also* Bakri, Micaiah
Jihad, 5, 24, 25, 26, 171
Jijel, 16
John Adams, and the blockade of Tripoli, 142
Johnson, William Samuel, 39, 55
Jones, John Paul, xiii, 69, 71
A Journal of the Captivity and Sufferings of John Foss (Foss), 79–80, 180, 250n18
Judges, religious, 17

Kabyles, 16
Kapudan pasha, 126
Karamania, 27
Khaznaji, strangling of, 201–2
Knights of St. John of Malta, xiv, 9
Koenig, Joseph, 102
Kouloughli, 15

La Grande Enclopédie (Lamiraut), 6
Lalla Aisha, 124–25
Lamb, John: background, 246n8; disparaging references to, 163; evaluating his mission, 55; failure to negotiate treaty or ransom prisoners, 49–57; lack of information about, 36; obstacles to negotiations, 64; unqualified as negotiator, 32, 37, 38, 54, 63–64, 163. *See also* Adams, John; Jefferson, Thomas; O'Brien, Richard
Lamb, John (chronology): Huntington's recommendation, 36–37; request for Spanish and French support, 49; financial preparations for negotiations, 47–48; and Paul Randall, 47, 50–51; delays in mission, 39, 49; De Castries's letter to De Kercy about, 217–19; and the wakil al-kharj, 50, 52, 54, 55–56; communication about ransom costs, 50–56; correspondence with Jefferson, 49–51, 53–54; captives' reports on, 52, 60, 63–64; communication with Jay, 54–55. *See also* Ransom for Americans in Algiers
La Revue Africaine (Devoulx), 215–16
Lear, Tobias: background, 255n19; criticism of, 147, 182; as a negotiator, 165; review of accomplishments, 165–66; on social life among foreigners in Algiers, 254n9; subject of a biography, 180, 262n9

Lear, Tobias (chronology): succeeds O'Brien in 1803, 127; negotiation of peace with Tripoli (1805), 139, 145, 146; on meeting with Hamuda, 152–53; return to Algiers (1805), 182; life after Algiers, 182; death by suicide, 182
Lebanon, 159–60, 171
Lee, Arthur, 34
Le Maire, André Alexandre, 2, 61
Leo the African, 3
Les Corsaires barbaresques (Panzac), 3, 9, 26
Letters of Delegates to Congress, 58
Levantines, defined, 3
Libya, 145
Lisle, Peter, 121, 134
Livingston, Robert, 37, 141
Livorno, 113
Livre, 199
Logie, Charles: account of the Lamb affair, 63; and America's difficulties with Algiers, 43, 58; attitude toward Americans, 78; on Cathcart, 163; on Hasan's accession to the deyship, 204–5; involvement with captives from beginning, 61; Lamb on, 50; O'Brien on, 60–61; and petition by British subjects, 62; and Portugal-Algiers truce, 75–79, 227–29; relationship to Skjöldebrands, 250n19; Sloan on, 77; and U.S. shipping disaster, 61
Logie, George, 60, 61
Logie, Johannie, 250n19
London Chronicle, 13

Mace, Charles, 61, 74–75, 78, 227–28
Al-Madani, Ahmad Tawfiq, 15
Madinat al-Jaza'ir, 16
Madison, James, xiii, 126, 136, 146
Maghrib (Occident), 1
Mahbub, 199
Mahmud Bey, 129
Malik. *See* Deys
March from Alexandria to Derna, 146
Maria, 43
La marine, 11
Marshall, John, 158
Martin, Maria, 11
Mary Ann, 127–28

Mashriq (Orient), 1
Mason, Daniel, Dr., 33
Mathurins, 57, 66, 67
McDonald, Joseph, Jr., 87
McShane, John, 214
Mellimelli, Suleiman, 152, 154, 155, 260n35
Metidja, 19
Military power in foreign relations. *See* Diplomacy *vs.* force
Military supplies as payment, 70, 160. *See also* Naval stores
"Millions for defense, not one cent for tribute," xiv, 158, 260n1
Minerva (brig), 79
Ministers of the dey, 18–19, 22
Mohamed Amine, 22
Monroe, James, xiii, 54, 68, 95–96, 252n12
Montgomery, Robert, 83, 85, 94
Moors, origin of term, 16
Morocco: Alaouite dynasty, 156; declaration of war on the U.S. (1802), 156; history of, 155–56; motivation of the sultan for peace, 48, 247n9; peace treaties with, xiv; renewal of 1786 treaty, 156–57; role of naval commanders in negotiations, 168–71; stable relationship with, 48, 161; and U.S. show of force (1803), 157. *See also* Treaties, terms of
Morris, Gouverneur, 68, 96
Morris, Richard V., 136, 137, 138
Mosque of the Sayyida, 25
Moulay Muhammad bin Abdallah, 40, 48
Moulay Slimane, 156–57
Moulay Yazid, 156
Mujahidin, Afghan, 70
Murad Rais, 8
Murphy, Michael, 86
Muslims, enslavement of, xiv, 9–10
Muslim world: America's first ambassador from, 154; America's first challenge from, xiii, 172; America's first foreign policy failure in, 36; current misunderstandings of, 158, 164, 171–72, 261n9; importance of in Americans' daily lives, 158; relevance of America's first encounter with, 158; stereotypes of Muslims and Arabs, 126, 151, 164, 171–72, 261n9. *See also* Barbary experience, relevance today

Mustafa (dey from 1798–1805), 18, 125, 127, 132

Nafthali Bushnaq (Bu Jnah), 18
Names of captured ships and prisoners, 208–16
Napoleon, 9–10, 127, 140–41
Naqib al-ashraf, 17
Nautilus, 142
Naval Documents Related to the United States Wars with the Barbary Powers, xvi, 134, 153–54, 171
Naval stores: Ahmad Khoja's demands, 127; arrival in Algiers, 124–25; costs of, 99, 112; delay in reaching the dey, 116, 124; demanded by Hasan Pasha, 97, 102, 124–25, 132, 236–37; Jefferson's position on, 70; in negotiations, 39, 102, 104, 132, 148
Navy, early American: creation of, xv–xvi, 58, 87, 91, 131, 251n4, 257n1; differences between Jefferson and Adams, 40; duels among officers, 171; early choice to forego, 33; effect on diplomacy, 131, 160; expense of, 33, 246n1; honor and pride in, 170–71; and imposition of new peace treaties, 168; need for, 160–61; role of naval commanders in negotiations, 168–71, 259n31; states' support for, 251n4; and today's Sixth Fleet, xv; traits of naval officers (Paullin), 168. *See also* Decatur, Stephen
Negotiations: difficulties with the Barbary states, 151, 260n3; early American, with Europeans, 33–34; review of Americans' efforts in North Africa, 164–66; today's policies, 159–60; Western rules not always accepted, 159. *See also* Diplomacy; Diplomacy *vs.* force
Nelson, Horatio, Admiral, 62
Newburyport Ship Registers 1789–1820, 20
Nissen, Nicholas, 135
Nixon, Richard, 260n2

O'Bannon, Presley, 146
O'Brien, Richard: on Charles Logie, 60–61, 63; as a diplomat, 162, 166; Eaton on, 261n4; friendly terms with Hasan, 69; hostility toward Cathcart, 132, 251n1, 261n4; key figure in crisis with Algiers, 44; on Lamb, 52, 63–64; marriage, 132; review of his accomplishments, 166. *See also* Ransom for Americans in Algiers; Treaty payments to Algiers
O'Brien, Richard (chronology): captain of the *Dauphin*, 44; on captives' treatment in Algiers (1786), 46; on dangers of Portugal-Algiers truce, 75; on the redemption of the captives (1786), 248n40; urges quick resolution of crisis (1793), 84; recommendations to Humphreys (1793–94), 82–84, 94; initial peace treaty with Tripoli (1796), 133–34; arrival in Algiers with gold, 121, 148; supervisory consulate general (Algiers), 124; estimates of wealth of Algiers (1802), 21; negotiations with Tripoli (1804), 141, 143; life after Algiers, 181
Observations on the Commerce of the American States, 35
Ocak. *See* Ojak
Occident (Maghrib), 1
Ojak, 5, 16, 22, 183–96
Oran, 5, 20, 27, 89
Orient (Mashriq), 1
Ottoman Empire, 1, 3, 5, 14–16

Panzac, Daniel, 3, 9, 26, 243n2
Pasha. *See* Deys
Passports in privateering, 7
Pataqa, 198–99
Paullin, Charles Oscar, 137, 154, 168, 243n1
Peace: booty and ransom *vs.*, xiv, 5–8, 20, 80, 101–2, 133, 161; tributes required to maintain, xiv, 7–8, 93, 113. *See also* Barbary experience, relevance today; Diplomacy; Treaties; Tributes
Petition from captives to King George III (1785), 220–22
Philadelphia: captures Moroccan vessel (1803), 157; crew held prisoner in Tripoli, 62; destruction of, 138; sent to the Mediterranean to protect shipping, 135; surrender at Tripoli, 138
Philadelphia Gazette, 123, 147, 234–35
Pickering, Timothy, 132

Pinckney, Charles, 54, 68, 79, 158, 249n16, 260n1
Pinto de Souza Coutinho, Luis, 76–77, 226, 228–29
Piracy, 5, 6. *See also* Corsairs, Barbary; Privateering
Piracy and the English Government, 1616–1642 (Hebb), 9
Pirate republics and principalities, 1, 133
The plague: and death of prisoners, 11, 66, 68, 90, 116, 119, 121; reason for avoiding Algiers, 66, 76; in Tunis, 149
Playfair, Sir Robert Lambert, 60, 106
Polacca, defined, 248n10
Polly (brig), 20, 79–80, 208
Portugal: commitment from Queen Maria I to Congress (1787), 75; convoys escort American ships (1793), 79, 84, 249n16; cooperation with British, 22–28; guardians of the Strait of Gibraltar (beg. 1786), 75; truce with Algiers (1793), 75–79, 84, 100, 225–30, 249n16
Preble, Edward: admiration for, 145; Americans in crew, 62; attitude regarding ransom, 145; Beaussier on, 169; failure as diplomat, 169; negotiations with Tripoli, 138–45; performance at Tripoli, 169; replacement for Morris, 138–40; return to the U.S., 145; review of his accomplishments, 169; death of, 145
President, 131, 135, 145
Prisoner of war status for captives, 128–29, 146, 168
Prisoners, American. *See* American prisoners; Americans' return to the U.S.
The Prisoners of Algiers (Barnby), xvii
Privateering, xiv, 5–10, 16, 20, 161. *See also* Captives, treatment of; Corsairs, Barbary; Slaves/slavery
Proceedings (of the Naval Institute at Annapolis), 169–70
Procession of the Tribute, 183–96

Qabtan, Al-Haj Muhammad, 26, 205–6
Qadis, 17
Qaramanli, Ahmad (brother of Yusuf), 133, 146–47
Qaramanli, Yusuf: and Ahmad (elder brother), 134–35, 140, 258n17; and Ahmad (great-grandfather), 133; compared to other Ottoman rulers, 132; ruthlessness of, 134. *See also* Tripoli
Qaramanli, Yusuf (chronology): appointed bey (1795), 134; and O'Brien's shipment of gold (1796), 121; demands to the U.S., 135; declaration of war on the U.S. (1801), 135; negotiations through Beaussier, 139–44; reaction to American bombardment (1804), 139, 142, 145, 160; attempt by the U.S. to unseat, 135, 146–47; and the capture of Derna (1805), 147
Al-Qa'ida, xiv, 158
Quasi-War with France (1798–1801), 91, 127, 131

Randall, Paul R., 47, 50, 51
Randolph, Edmund, 86, 92
Ransom for American hostages (20th century), 158–60, 260n2
Ransom for Americans in Algiers: best course of action in retrospect, 164; estimates according to Cathcart and O'Brien, 94, 101; estimates according to Lamb, 50–56; estimates according to the Mathurins, 57, 66–68; estimates according to the prisoners, 52–53, 63–64; final agreement, 103; flaw in American approach, 64–65; funds authorized (1785), 36–37; funds authorized (1792), 69; funds authorized (1794), 92, 104, 247n10; funds authorized (1798/1799), 150–51; instructions to Jones (1792), 69; Jefferson's fear of overpaying, 65, 67, 70–71, 85–86, 93, 164, 249n2; lack of Congressional authorization, 57, 247n10; military equipment, 70, 104; princely sum paid, 159; results of delays, 67, 69, 74, 86, 93; Skjöldebrand's recommendations, 82, 101; Washington's instructions, 92–93. *See also* Naval stores; Treaty payments to Algiers
Ransom for Americans in Tripoli, 145–46, 149–50
Reagan administration and Irangate, 159, 160

Regencies, Barbary: and America's need for a navy, 160; European attitudes toward, 2–3, 243n1; extraction of payments, 3; government of, 1–3; location, xiv, *xix*, 243n1; origin of term, 243n1; privateering procedures, 7; relationship to Ottoman domain, 1, 3; and vulnerability of the U.S., 160. *See also* Algiers, government of; Morocco; Ottoman Empire; Tripoli; Tunis
Registre des prises maritimes (Devoulx), 20, 215
Relevance of the Barbary experience. *See* Barbary experience, relevance today
Ridgely, John, 155
Robinson, Betsy, 132
Rodgers, John: as Barron's replacement, 145; bellicosity of, 169, 239; criticism of, 147, 169; gunboat diplomacy with Tunis, 152; in Jefferson's letter to Hamuda Bey (1806), 239; as Morris's temporary replacement, 138; reputation, 153; review of his accomplishments, 165, 169, 171; Tripoli peace negotiations (1805), 145, 146
Rogers, Joseph, 119
Roguishness in international relations, 161

Salé (Sla), Morocco, 8
Salih Bey, 201
Sally, 107
Sandal, defined, 253n4
Sardinia, 9
Schembri, Gaetano, 138
Schiavi musulmani nell'Italia moderna (Bono), 10
Schmemann, Serge, xiv
Schooner, defined, 215
Scourge, 141
The Scourge of Christendom (Playfair), 106
September 11, 2001, xiii, 158, 172
Sequin, defined, 199
Shaler, William: American consul to Algiers (1815–28), xvii; on commerce in Algiers, 21; description of Algiers, 11; on Jews in Algiers, 17–18; on methods of declaring war, 7; as peace commissioner to Algiers, 128; *Sketches of Algiers*, 129; and the Treaty of Ghent, 129

Shari'a, 24
Sheffield, Ichabod, 127
Sheffield, John Baker-Holroyd, First Earl of, 35
Ship, defined, 215
Ships and their captives, 208–16
Short, William, 68
Shuval, Tal, 21, 244n11
Sidi Haji Abdul Rahman Adja, 41–42
Sidi Muhammad bin Abdallah, 9, 156
Simpson, James, 131, 156
Siren, 141
Sitgreaves, John, 37
Sixth Fleet, xv
Sketches of Algiers (Shaler), xvii, 129
Skjöldebrand, Mattias, 80–81, *81*, 84, 91, 250n19
Skjöldebrand, Per Erik: efforts on behalf of the Americans, 81, 91, 93, 96–97, 99, 101, 250n22; family background, 250n19; portrait, *83*
Skjoldebrand, 124–25, *125*
Slave markets, 10, 45
Slaves/slavery, xiv, 2, 8–11, 17, 43, 58, 130
Slimane, Moulay, 156–57
Sloan, Philip, 77, 94, 98, 100–101, 106
Smith, Michael, 123
Smith, Robert, 138
Smith, William, Colonel, 41
Sophia, 134, 213, 248n11
Spain: expulsion of Moors and Jews, 4; financial aid to American captives, 67; Muslim invasion of, xiv, 171; occupation of Algiers harbor, 4–5; treaty with Algiers (1791), 248n15; truce with Algiers (1785), 8, 27, 43, 74, 225; war with Algiers, 8, 23, 25, 27, 43
Spencer, William, 11, 26
Statistics on privateering, 6, 9
Stephens, Captain, 46, 52
Stereotypes of Muslims and Arabs, 151, 158, 164, 171–72, 261n9. *See also* Attitudes
Sterett, Andrew, 135
Sudan, slaves from, 17
Sumner, Charles, xvi

Ta'ifa, 16
Tangier, British consul in, 131

Terrorism, special task force on (1986), 159
Terrorists, different from Barbary corsairs, xiv, 6, 7, 23, 158
Terrorists, negotiating with, 159
Tessanier, Jacob, 52, 62
Tilley, George, 123
Timber, American, 132
Tlemcen, 3, 20
Treaties: and chronology of events, xxi–xxviii; costs to other countries, 8–10; dangers to American shipping from, 75–76; European disappointment at American success, 122; funds authorized for negotiations, 36–40, 42, 69, 92, 104, 150, 247n10; North Africans' reluctance to conclude, xiv, 7–8, 20, 80, 133, 161; privateering conduct in absence of, 7. *See also* Britain; Portugal; Spain
Treaties, terms of: with Algiers (1795), 103–4, 112–13, 234, 255n16; with Algiers (1815), 102, 104, 128–29, 234; with Morocco, xiv, 48, 156, 157; with Tripoli, xiv–xv, 41–42, 134, 137, 145–46; with Tunis, xiv, 150–51
Treaty of Amity and Commerce (1778), 34
Treaty of Ghent, 128–29
Treaty of Paris (1783), 34, 35
Treaty payments to Algiers: annual payments, 104; Bakris' involvement, 103, 105, 109, 111–15, 117–18, 120, 122–24; Barlow's involvement, 107–16, 119–24; Cathcart's involvement, 105–15, 120, 125–26; Donaldson's involvement, 105–14, 117, 120, 122–23; Humphreys's involvement, 105, 107–8, 110–11, 113, 117; O'Brien's involvement, 105, 107, 109–10, 116, 121, 124; the Skjöldebrands' involvement, 105, 110, 114
Tributes: abolition of, with Algiers, 104, 128–29; Adams on, 40; Barbary powers' preference for, xiv, 5–8, 20, 80, 133, 161; current misunderstandings of, 158; end of all tributes, 168; exacted by North Africans, 7–9, 104; humiliation of paying, 161; Jefferson on, 40, 159, 260n1; as necessary commercial expenses, 161; "not one cent for tribute," xiv, 158, 260n1;

payments to Algiers, 158. *See also* Naval stores; Treaties
Triennial tribute ceremony: al-Zahhar's description (1785), 183–94; Cathcart's version (1788), 194–96
Tripoli: ambassador's meeting with John Adams, 41–42; blockade of, xv, 141–45, 159; explosion of the *Intrepid*, 144–45; focus on naval campaigns, 133; force not a substitute for diplomacy, 131; government of, 133; lack of water, 133; in Marine hymn, xiii, 146; misunderstandings of U.S. war with, 133, 158, 172; naval campaign against, 142–44; population in late 18th century, 133; Preble's squadron engages gunboats, 142; privateering as source of income, 133; Protestant cemetery, 144–45; role of naval commanders, 168–71; treaties with, xiv–xv, 41–42, 133–34, 145–46. *See also* Treaties, terms of
Tunis: Algiers and, 147; costs of treaty with (1798), 150–51; history of, 147; noncontentious relations after 1807, 155; revisions to treaty with (1799), 151; role of naval commanders in negotiations, 168–71; U.S. negotiations with, 148–55. *See also* Treaties, terms of
Tunis et Alger au XVIIIe siècle (Venture de Paradis, Jean-Michel), xvii, 8, 21
Turks, 5, 14–15, 25. *See also* Deys; Ottoman Empire; Ojak
Tuscan Knights of San Stefano, xiv

United States, 131

Vallière, Césaire-Philippe, 96, 100–101
Venetians, Hasan's declaration of war against, 30
Venture de Paradis, Jean Michel: on annual tributes to Algiers, 8; on fees and levies in Algiers, 21; as French consular official, xvii; on janissaries in Algiers, 15; on Muhammad Pasha bin Uthman, 27–29
Vergennes, count of, 34–35, 47, 49–50, 58–59
Vixen, 141

Wakil al-kharj, and Lamb's mission to Algiers, 50, 52, 54, 55–56, 59
Walpole, Robert, 76, 225–29
War of 1812, 128
Wars, formalities of declaring, 7
Washington, George: Barclay's instructions from, 72–73; election to presidency, 68; Humphreys's instructions from, 92–93; Lear's association with, 256n19; North African involvement, xiii; role in foreign affairs, 93; view of diplomacy, 165
Werner, Dr. Philip, 91
Wilburforce, William, 91
Wolfe, John, 53
Woodside, Jane, 132

Yazid, Moulay, 156

Al-Zahhar, Al-Haj Ahmad Sharif: description of tribute ceremonies (1785), 22, 183–94; on the deys, 18; on Hasan Pasha, 29, 32; on ministers and government operations, 22; on Muhammad Pasha bin Uthman, 24–26; on murder of Jews in Algiers, 18; on Mustafa (dey), 125–26; naqib al-ashraf of Algiers, xvii
Zitouna University (Tunis), 147

Richard B. Parker is a former career Foreign Service Officer who served as ambassador to Algeria, Lebanon, and Morocco in the Ford and Carter administrations. Since his retirement from that service in 1980, he has been teaching, writing, and speaking on the diplomatic history of the Middle East. His other published works include *The Politics of Miscalculation* (1993), *The Six-Day War: A Retrospective* (UPF, 1996), and *The October War: A Retrospective* (UPF, 2001).

www.ingramcontent.com/pod-product-compliance
Lightning Source LLC
Chambersburg PA
CBHW020942230426
43666CB00005B/130